WOM...
BO...

WOMAN'S BODY
—
AN OWNER'S MANUAL

Compiled by
The Diagram Group

Wordsworth Editions

Information and statistics for chapter 9 were provided by
Women Against Rape (London), with invaluable assistance from
Women in Dialogue and the Revoke License to Rape Campaign
in Philadelphia. The views expressed in this chapter are not
necessarily those of Woman Against Rape.

WOMAN'S BODY

Editorial director:	Margaret Doyle
Editors:	Nancy Bailey, Ben Barkow, Louise Clairmonte, Carole Dease, Bridget Giles, David Heidenstam, Ann Kramer, Susan Pinkus, Barbara Schofield, Helen Varley, Robert Whittle
Contributors:	Rosie Boycott, Minakshi Compton, David Lambert , Ruth Midgley, Irene Staunton, Susan Sturrock
Medical consultants and contributors	Dr. Katherine Anderson MB, BS, DRCOG, MRCP Paul D. Blumenthal, MD, MPH Francis Scott Key Medical Center, Baltimore, MD Robert Youngson, MD
Research:	Ruth Berenbaum, Cornelius Cardew, Laura Midgley, Ray Saffney, Matthew Smout
Design Director:	Richard Hummerstone
Designers:	Darren Bennett, Robin Crane, Roger Kohn, Philip Patenall
Illustrators:	Jeff Alger, Eileen Batterberry, James Dallas, Robert Galvin, Brian Hewson, Susan Kinsey, Pavel Kostal, Kathleen McDougall, Graham Rosewarne, Diana Taylor
DTP operators:	Mark Carry, Lee Lawrence, Raul Lopez, Garreth Plumb

Foreword

This new edition of the best-selling WOMAN'S BODY gives every woman up-to-the-minute information about her body, answering many of the questions a woman has about the physical and emotional changes experienced throughout life. Over recent years, new understanding about the female physique, causes of disease, the role of counseling, and alternative medicine have all revolutionized women's attitude to health and fitness. Self-help is now more important than ever – from breast examination and nutrition to psychological well-being. Armed with increasing knowledge of their bodies and physical changes, women are able to request information about conditions and even specific treatments, or to explore therapies outside the medical orthodoxy. Packed with facts and illustrated with hundreds of explanatory charts and diagrams, WOMAN'S BODY takes the reader from the moment of conception through to retirement and beyond, providing an up-to-date view of women's health at every stage, including new infertility treatments and approaches to the problems of aging. Heading panels, numbered for cross-reference, and a comprehensive index enable the reader to find the answers to particular questions both quickly and easily.

The editors of WOMAN'S BODY have synthesized medical research and statistical data and presented it in clear and concise terms. All the material contained in WOMAN'S BODY has been presented to physicians for their review and commentary. Because medical opinions vary and often contradict each other, the editors have attempted to remain free of bias and to present as many points of view as possible.

The words "average" and "typical" appear in WOMAN'S BODY. They are reference points only and should not be made the basis of any judgment or personal assessment. The terms refer generally to what is true in a large number of cases, not to what is necessarily best or what should be.

WOMAN'S BODY has been created especially for the individual woman with the belief that a clearer understanding of her body will increase her confidence and lead her to a fuller appreciation of herself.

Contents

GROWTH AND DEVELOPMENT

The Moment of Fertilization

On the right below is shown the edge of a female ovum –
magnified about 25,000 times. The ovum is always by far the
largest cell that the body produces (despite its minuteness and
its great variations in actual size).

On the left are shown three spermatozoa, magnified in the
same way. The ovum has just been fertilized by the topmost
sperm. Immediately after fertilization the ovum's outer wall
hardens to prevent any more sperm from entering.

For a description of the process of conception,
see pp.104-5.

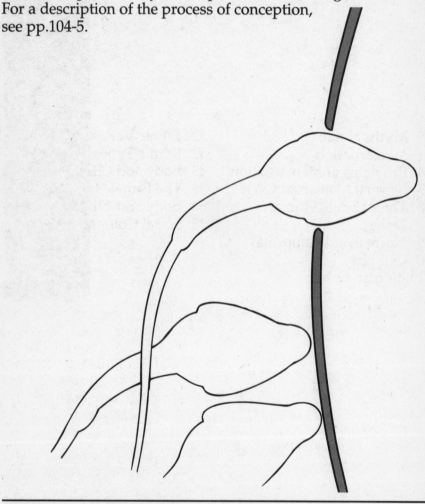

Male or Female?

In the top half of the diagram opposite, successful female cell
division results in a single ovum (**a**), containing an X
chromosome. (White arrows show other cells produced, which
degenerate.)

Male cell division (lower section of diagram) results in four viable spermatozoa, two with a Y chromosome (**b**), and two with an X chromosome (**c**).

The ovum is fertilized (**d**) by one of the sperms with an X chromosome. So the resulting embryo (**e**) contains two X chromosomes, making it female.

Every body cell contains a "blueprint" of information, which decides how it functions. The information is carried on 23 pairs of chromosomes, which lie in the nucleus of the cell.

But because of special cell division, an ovum or a sperm only contains 23 single chromosomes. So when they unite, the new fertilized cell, from which the offspring grows, again contains 23 pairs of chromosomes – each parent having contributed half.

One pair of chromosomes decides the offspring's sex. In a woman each of the pair is identical: they are both called X chromosomes. But a man has two chromosomes that do not match: one an X again, the other called a Y chromosome. Thus a sperm has either one X or one Y chromosome.

So if the ovum is fertilized by an X sperm, the resulting XX combination produces a girl.

If it is fertilized by a Y sperm, the XY combination produces a boy.

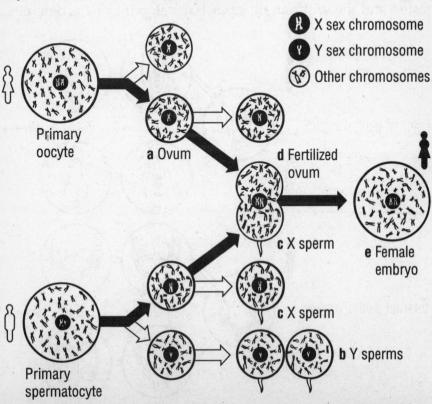

- **X** sex chromosome
- **Y** sex chromosome
- **Other chromosomes**

Primary oocyte

a Ovum

d Fertilized ovum

c X sperm

e Female embryo

c X sperm

b Y sperms

Primary spermatocyte

Sex Differentiation

External

Until the 8th week after conception, male and female fetuses still appear exactly the same. One week later – when the fetus is still only 1¹/4in (3cm) long and weighs 0.07oz (2g) – the external membrane has vanished from the genitals of the female fetus, giving entrance to a primitive vagina. Meanwhile, in the male, one end of the genital folds has begun to lengthen into a rudimentary penis. By the 11th week, the contrasting shapes of the external genitals are established.

Internal

Inside the fetus the process is more complex and drawn out. In the undifferentiated fetus there are two tube systems: the Müllerian and the Wolffian ducts. But in the female, between the 7th and 9th weeks, the Wolffian tubes almost disappear, while the lower Müllerian tubes combine to form the vagina. Then, more slowly, through to the 34th week, the undifferentiated sex glands (gonads) turn into primitive ovaries, and the upper Müllerian tubes become the Fallopian tubes. In the male, in contrast, it is the Müllerian tubes that disappear. The gonads migrate to the scrotum to become testes, and the Wolffian tubes each develop into a vas deferens.

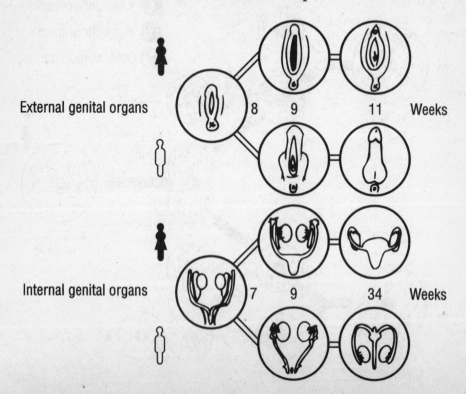

External genital organs   8   9   11   Weeks

Internal genital organs   7   9   34   Weeks

The Growing Fetus

Human development in the nine months before birth is faster
than at any time after. The drawings show the actual change in
proportion of an average fetus in 4-week stages, beginning
with the 8th week. As the fetus grows, it also shifts its position
within the womb.

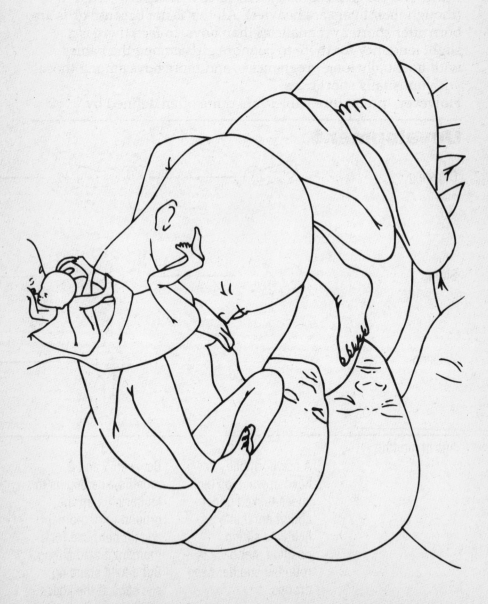

Birthweight

The 6ft (1.8m) kangaroo gives birth to a less than 0.05oz (1g) baby; the blue whale a 10-ton one. Human babies that have survived ranged from under 2lb (0.9kg) to over 29lb (13.15kg) – but it is far healthier for the baby to be just an average 7^1/2lb (3.4kg).

In fact, the girls' average is slightly lower (just over 7lb-3.17kg) and the boys' correspondingly higher (7^1/2lb-3.4kg). Girls' hearts and lungs are already marginally smaller at birth too (though their livers are heavier). All this is not because girls are born after shorter pregnancies than boys. In fact, there is a slight tendency for there to be more girls among the babies with unusually long pregnancies, and more boys among those with unusually short ones.

However, 'premature babies' are quite often defined by

Development

Crawling —————— 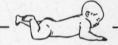 ——

Sitting —————— ——

Walking  ——————

Age in months		3
	A newborn baby lies head down, hips high, knees tucked under abdomen. If she is held in a sitting position, her back is rounded and her head droops.	Between 1 and 3 months, she begins to lift her chin off the ground for a moment, and lift her head for a moment if held sitting. But if held standing, she sags at the knees and hips.

birthweight, rather than length of pregnancy. On this basis, slightly more female babies are termed 'premature', as slightly more are under 5^1/2lb (2.5kg) in weight. But really they are of 'full-term low birthweight'. Underweight or overweight, babies that are far from the average have less likelihood of survival. Average-weight babies have under a 2% death rate; 6- or 9lb (2.72 or 4.08kg) babies a 3% rate; 4^1/2- or 10^1/2-pounders (2.04 or 4.76kg) a 10% rate. Those babies which are far below average that do survive are more likely to be handicapped. Perfectly normal babies vary greatly in their rate of development. Sitting up for a few moments without support can start anytime between 5 months and 1 year – walking without help anytime between 8 months and 4 years. Parents should not think that delay is always very serious, or that it is likely to have a lasting effect.

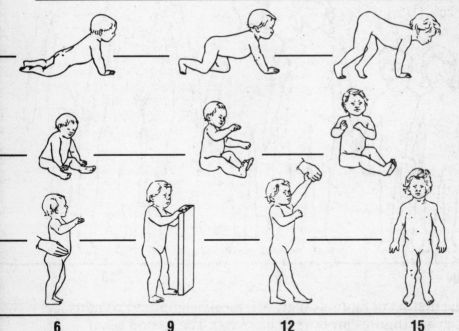

6

At about 6 months, she can support herself on her arms, lying or sitting, and can bear her own weight if held standing.

9

Between 8 and 10 months, she begins to be able to crawl on hands and knees, to sit and lean forward without support, and to hold herself upright.

12

15

At a year she can creep like a bear, on hands and feet, turn around as she sits, and walk with one hand held.
At 13 months, she can walk alone.

Growth, Height, and Weight

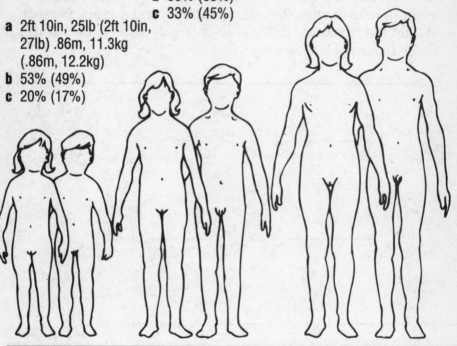

a 4ft 5in, 68lb (4ft 6in,
70lb) 1.35m, 30.8kg
(1.37m, 31.7kg)
b 83% (78%)
c 53% (45%)

a 3ft 8in, 42lb (3ft 9in,
46lb) 1.12m, 19.05kg
(1.14m, 20.9kg)
b 69% (65%)
c 33% (45%)

a 2ft 10in, 25lb (2ft 10in,
27lb) .86m, 11.3kg
(.86m, 12.2kg)
b 53% (49%)
c 20% (17%)

Age   2   6   10

The first set of figures (a) gives typical heights and weights for each age (figures for boys in brackets). The second set of figures (b) indicates how much of her eventual height a girl is likely to have achieved at each age, eg 83% at age 10 (boys' figures in brackets). The third set of figures (c) indicates how much of her eventual weight a girl is likely to have achieved at each age, eg 53% at age 10 (boys' figures in brackets). Of course, such predictions are only averages. There are two reasons why a girl may be taller (shorter) than average for her age. She may be going to be a tall (short) adult. Or she may be advancing faster (slower) than usual to an eventual average

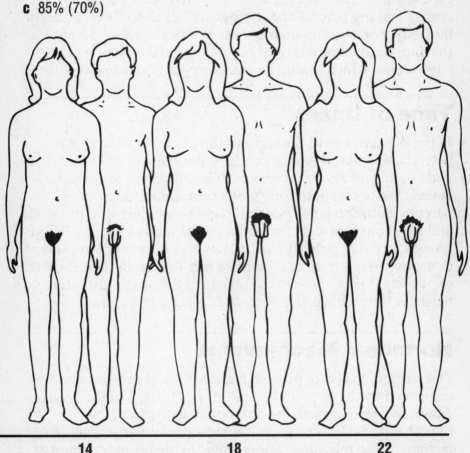

a 5ft 2in, 109lb (5ft 3in, 108lb) 1.57m, 49.4kg (1.60m, 49kg)
b 97% (91%)
c 85% (70%)

a 5ft 4in, 125lb (5ft 8in, 143lb) 1.63m, 56.7kg (1.75m, 64.9kg)
b 100% (99%)
c 98% (92%)

a 5ft 4in, 128lb (5ft 9in, 155lb) 1.63m, 58.1kg (1.75m, 70.3kg)
b 100% (100%)
c 100% (100%)

14   18   22

height: that is, she may be advanced (or behind) in her general development for her age. The development of a child's permanent teeth gives a rough guide to this general rate of development. Compare the ages at which the teeth appear with the ages on p.269. If they appear at the earlier age, the development is advanced; if at the later age, slow; if between, average.

It is interesting to note how much more slowly a child moves toward its eventual weight than its eventual height. At the age of 2, for instance, a child is already about one-half its adult height, but only about one-fifth its adult weight.

Puberty

Puberty is the time when a young person starts to be able to have children. In a girl, eggs in the ovaries begin to mature, and menstruation – probably the most important physical development of puberty – begins. (In a boy, the testes start producing sperm.) But these are only two of the physical changes taking place. Other changes affect almost every part of the body; and accompanying these physical developments are the important emotional and psychological developments of adolescence which gradually transform a child into an adult.

Time of Onset

In the Western world throughout this century, puberty has been starting younger and younger. But there is still a very wide variety of age of onset, which is difficult to explain. Several factors seem to contribute: traits inherited from parents; nutrition level; general living conditions; and physical and psychological state (mental disturbance or long childhood illness can delay puberty). All these seem to be more important than any effect – if there is one – of race or climate. But the rate of puberty does vary with the season of the year – growth in height is fastest in spring, growth in weight in autumn.

Hormonal Mechanisms

The changes that take place in a girl's body at puberty are controlled by the hypothalamus – a specific part of the brain. About two years before the onset of menstruation, the hypothalamus starts to secrete substances known as 'releasing factors'. These releasing factors travel to the pituitary gland at the base of the brain, and cause chemical substances, or 'hormones', to be released. The first hormone produced is called the follicle-stimulating hormone (FSH) because it stimulates the growth of the follicles containing eggs in the ovaries. Stimulated by FSH, the follicles produce estrogen, which helps the growth of breasts and genitals. The rising level of estrogen in the bloodstream has an effect on the hypothalamus called 'negative feedback'. It causes a reduction in FSH-releasing factor, but also makes the hypothalamus release a second substance – luteinizing hormone-releasing factor. This in turn causes the pituitary to release luteinizing hormone (LH). Luteinizing hormone causes one of the follicles to burst and release its egg for possible fertilization. The remaining collapsed follicle, known as the 'corpus luteum', continues to secrete estrogen, and starts to secrete a new substance, progesterone, which prepares the lining of the uterus to receive and nourish a fertilized egg. If the egg is not fertilized, the levels of both estrogen and progesterone in the bloodstream fall and cause the lining of the uterus to break down. The resulting bleeding constitutes the first menstrual period. This cycle repeats itself about once every 28 days, from puberty to menopause.

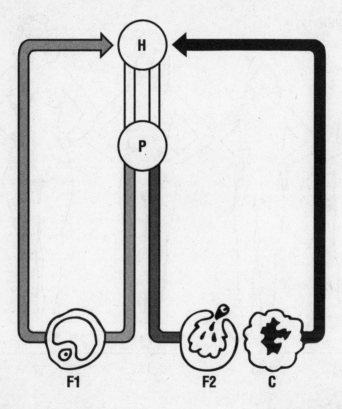

☐ Releasing factors	**H** Hypothalamus
▨ Follicle-stimulating hormone	**P** Pituitary gland
▨ Estrogen	**F1** Follicle 1st stage
▨ Luteinizing hormone	**F2** Follicle 2nd stage
■ Progesterone and estrogen	**C** Corpus luteum

Physical Development

In girls, puberty begins at any time between the ages of nine and 14, and ends between 14 and 18. (Boys generally mature later and more slowly than girls.) So some normal girls have completed puberty as others are just starting (especially as those who start early tend also to take less time over puberty). But on average, the changes start at about 11 and reach a peak at about 14. The order of events is also very variable, but changes in an average girl can be summarized.

Stages in puberty

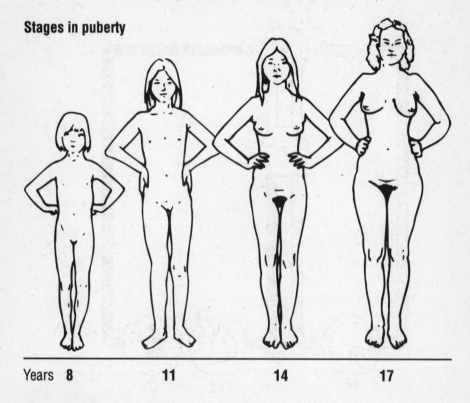

| Years | **8** | **11** | **14** | **17** |

Prepuberty

Breasts are undeveloped; there is no pubic or underarm hair; body shape is boyish.

1

Early puberty (11-13)
Face becomes fuller; pelvis starts to grow to allow future
childbearing; fat begins to be deposited on hips; breasts start to
develop and nipples stand out; pubic hair begins to grow in
the genital area; internal and external genitals begin to grow;
vaginal walls thicken and menstruation may begin.

Late puberty (14-16)
Breasts continue to grow; pubic hair thickens; underarm hair
appears; menstruation occurs.

Maturity (17-18)
Body shape more full and rounded; growth of skeleton ceases;
genitals mature; menstrual periods regular. At the same time,
more generally, many other tissues of the body increase in size.
The voice deepens slightly (though not as much as in boys)
due to the growth of the larynx. Blood pressure, blood volume,
and the number of red corpuscles all rise. The heart slows
down; body temperature falls; breathing slows down but the
lungs' capabilities increase. Bones grow harder and change in
proportion. By about 18, the bulk of growth is over – a typical
girl has usually reached her full height and almost her full
weight.

Problems

In some rare cases, puberty can fail to occur at all, because of
hormone imbalance. For most girls, however, the problems of
puberty are usually psychological. Even such physical
conditions as pimples and blackheads, excessive weight gain,
and heavy perspiration are more embarrassments than
anything else. (See pp. 226, 230 and 383-5.)
As a result of psychological changes, the adolescent girl may
appear aggressive and rebellious, and may challenge the
authority of parents and teachers (and perhaps even the
police). A common but temporary problem is lethargy. Its
causes may be psychological, but the physical effects of
hormones, the 'growth spurt', or just too many late nights, may
be responsible.

Menstruation

Around every 28th day, from about the age of 12 to about the age of 47, a woman has a discharge of blood and mucus from the vagina. The discharge lasts from 2 to 8 days (4 to 6 is most usual) and may be preceded or accompanied by various unpleasant symptoms such as headaches and nausea (see pp.26-7.) This, of course, is menstruation, or 'the period' – the outward sign of the routine cycle of egg production and hormone change in a woman's body. It is a process that requires the wearing of pads or tampons (absorbent tubes placed in the vagina), if the menstruating woman is to avoid soiling her clothes.

Egg Production

Each ovary contains groups of cells called follicles, which themselves contain immature eggs (ova). When the girl is about 12, these eggs begin to mature at the rate of one every 28 days or so – usually in alternate ovaries. (At birth, a female child's ovaries contain perhaps 350,000 immature eggs. Between puberty and menopause, only about 375 ever mature.) As each egg matures, it bursts from the ovary – a process called ovulation – and passes into the Fallopian tube leading down from that ovary to the uterus.

Process of Menstruation

If the egg is not fertilized by a sperm, it begins to degenerate 24 to 48 hours after leaving the ovary, and eventually passes unnoticed out of the body in the normal flow of fluid from the vagina. But meanwhile the uterus has been preparing to receive a fertilized egg. Hormones have caused the lining of the uterus to thicken, and to excrete a fluid so that the fertilized egg could be nourished while implanting itself. When no fertilization occurs, further hormone stimulation causes the thickened lining to crumble, and to be discharged along with a little blood through the vagina. This process is called menstruation.

Journey of the Egg

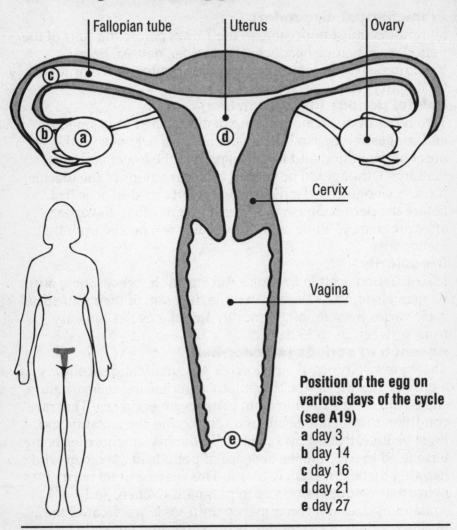

Fallopian tube | Uterus | Ovary

Cervix

Vagina

Position of the egg on various days of the cycle (see A19)
a day 3
b day 14
c day 16
d day 21
e day 27

Myths about Menstruation

Throughout history almost all societies have surrounded the menstrual process with myth and ritual. Even today, in some cultures, the menstruating woman is thought to turn milk sour, turn food bad, damage crops, and even cause animals to abort! Elsewhere she may be completely isolated from the rest of the community in a special building. Modern Western society still preserves some old myths about menstruation – all of which can be ignored. It is perfectly safe for the menstruating woman to bathe, shower, swim, wash her hair, have intercourse, and take part in any other activity she wishes.

Problems of Menstruation

Premenstrual discomfort

Symptoms (most noticeable in the 7 days before the start of the period) can include headaches, backache, nausea, breast tenderness, psychological tension, and depression. Hormone treatment is used in some extreme cases.

Painful periods (dysmenorrhea)

Two types of dysmenorrhea are distinguished – spasmodic and congestive. Spasmodic dysmenorrhea begins with the onset of the period and involves pain in the lower abdomen ('cramps'), thought to be caused by contractions of the uterine muscle. Congestive dysmenorrhea is felt as a dull ache just before the period. Spasmodic period pains often disappear after pregnancy, while congestive pains can persist until the menopause.

Irregularity

Menstruation is often irregular during adolescence. Some adult women also find, however, that the duration of their menstrual cycle varies from month to month. Regular cycles can vary from between 21 to 35 days.

Absence of periods (amenorrhea)

There are two types of amenorrhea – primary and secondary. If a girl reaches the age of 18 without experiencing menstruation she is said to be suffering from primary amenorrhea. This rare condition may be the result of an endocrine abnormality and must be investigated by a doctor. Secondary amenorrhea is the term used to describe the absence of periods in a woman who has already begun to menstruate. This may be quite normal: menstruation does not occur in pregnant women, and sometimes does not recommence until some weeks after the birth, especially if the mother is breastfeeding her child. Secondary amenorrhea, however, can also be caused by emotional stress such as shock, fear, tension or depression, and also by endocrine disorders, illness, drug-taking, traveling and poor general health.

Heavy periods

During a menstrual period, a woman usually sheds between 2 and 4 tablespoons of blood. Some women, however, discharge considerably more.

If menstrual bleeding is heavy or prolonged (and this often happens to women fitted with IUDs), iron-deficiency anemia can result (see p.317). This can often be remedied by an iron-rich diet or a course of medicinal iron.

Heavy bleeding (and bleeding between periods) can sometimes be symptomatic of problems such as hormone disorders, fibroid tumors, or cancer of the uterus. Also, occasionally heavy periods can be caused by psychological factors. Metropathia hemorrhagica is one of the conditions caused by hormonal imbalance which can result in very heavy bleeding. If the condition does not respond to curettage (see p.398), a hysterectomy may be needed. In all cases of excessive bleeding a doctor should be consulted.

Normal Menstruation Cycle

Day 1 onward: pituitary is already producing the follicle-stimulating hormone (FSH) – a new egg begins to mature in one of the follicles (**a**).

Day 4 onward: the follicle produces estrogen (E). As this builds up, it stimulates growth of uterine wall and breasts, halts FSH production, and stimulates the pituitary to release luteinizing hormone (LH).

Day 12 onward: LH causes the follicle to burst (**b**), releasing the egg, and makes the follicle develop into a 'corpus luteum', producing progesterone (P) as well as estrogen.

Day 14 onward: P makes the uterine wall prepare for a fertilized egg and halts LH production. Without LH support, the corpus luteum degenerates (**c**), E and P levels fall, and eventually the uterine lining breaks up – menstruation (day 28). E no longer inhibits FSH, and the cycle begins again.

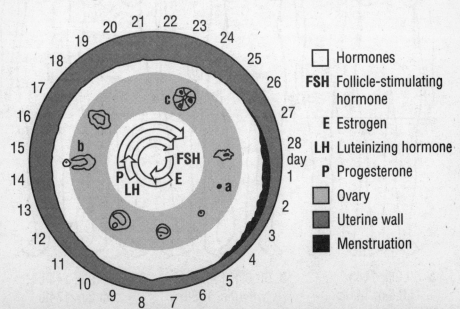

	Hormones
FSH	Follicle-stimulating hormone
E	Estrogen
LH	Luteinizing hormone
P	Progesterone
	Ovary
	Uterine wall
	Menstruation

The Average Human Being

The heights and weights for average women (age 20–25), of small, medium, and large builds, are 5ft 2in (1.6m), 114lb (52kg); 5ft 6in (1.7m), 130lb (59kg); and 5ft 10in (1.8m), 144lb (65kg). The maximum average weight reached (age over 60) in the three groups are 136lb (62kg), 154lb (70kg), and 172lb (78kg).

The heights and weights for average men (age 20-25), of small, medium, and large builds, are 5ft 6in (1.7m), 141lb (64kg); 5ft 10in (1.8m), 156lb (71kg); and 6ft 2in (1.9m), 174lb (79kg). Maximum average weight (age over 60) in the three groups are 154lb (70kg), 174lb (79kg), and 194lb (88kg).

Heights and weights
(*statistics for males)

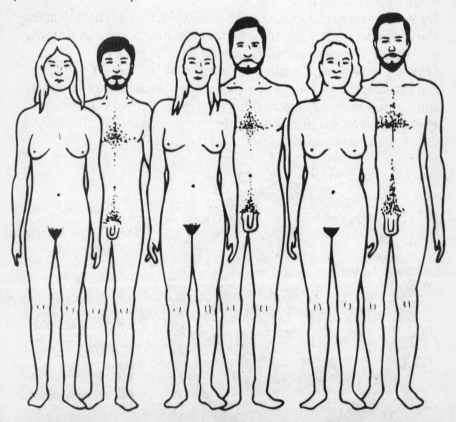

a 5ft 2in, 114lb
*5ft 6in, 141lb

b 5ft 6in, 130lb
*5ft 10in, 156lb

c 5ft 10in, 144lb
*6ft 2in, 174lb

Normal and Abnormal

Population

a   Characteristic (eg height)   z

The range of the normal is fairly small; the range of the possible is fairly wide. A convenient example is height. The average heights on the opposite page cover most of the population. But the tallest woman who has ever lived (whose height has been verified) was 8ft 1³/₄in (2.47m) at death (age 18), and the shortest was 24in (61cm) at death (age 19).

In fact, the distribution of many physical characteristics in a population can be summed up in a 'normal distribution' curve, as shown above. The range of the characteristic goes all the way from a to z, and there are people at every point between. But there are very few people at either of the extremes – and very many in the central area.

Cell Life

The full-grown body is still changing constantly: each day, millions of body cells die and must be replaced. Below, we show some of their maximum life expectancies.

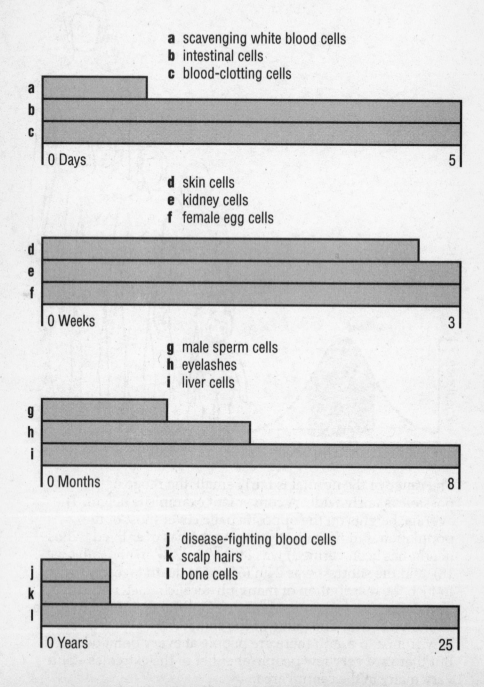

a scavenging white blood cells
b intestinal cells
c blood-clotting cells

a
b
c
0 Days   5

d skin cells
e kidney cells
f female egg cells

d
e
f
0 Weeks   3

g male sperm cells
h eyelashes
i liver cells

g
h
i
0 Months   8

j disease-fighting blood cells
k scalp hairs
l bone cells

j
k
l
0 Years   25

Woman and Man

This shows how some characteristics of the typical woman and man compare.

Average brain weight

Heart weight

Quantity of blood

Skin surface area

Lung capacity (age 25)

Ethnic Variations

No one now is very happy with the word 'race': it has been too much a part of humans' inhumane treatment of one another. But patterns of ethnic variation – that is, fairly consistent differences in the physical characteristics of different peoples – do, of course, exist. We are all aware of how people vary in stature, skin color, hair type, and facial features. But the ethnologist also notices such things as blood type, the ability to taste certain substances, and even the type of wax that forms in the ear. All these are part of the variety of human inheritance. Three great ethnic groups – Caucasoid, Mongoloid, and Negroid – account between them for almost all of the world's population. We have tried to illustrate their typical characteristics. But sometimes the differences within each group are as large as those between them. Taking, for example, the old preoccupation skin color, Negroids range from near black to sallow; Mongoloids from yellowish to flat white to deep bronze; and Caucasoids from fair pinkish in northern Europe to the dark-brown people of southern India. Another extreme variable is height. It is less totally inherited, and more immediately determined by environment, than other ethnic criteria, and it varies widely among individuals of a given people.

Ethnic Types

Basic facial characteristics

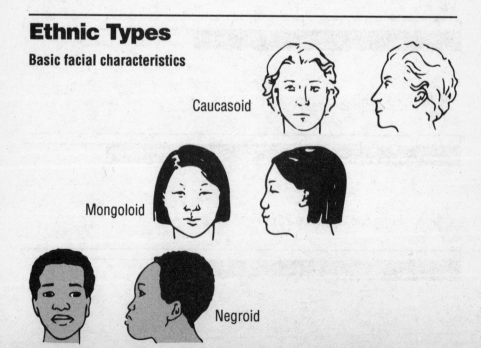

Caucasoid

Mongoloid

Negroid

1

Body and Climate

Animals of a species differ in coat color, size, limb length, and location of fat deposits, according to climatic conditions where they live. Some human variations are also related to climate.

Ethnic features

The environment did not make people acquire inheritable characteristics – but it did decide which characteristics flourished. Those people who flourished bred among themselves, and passed on these features (which are not, of course, lost if the inheritor moves to a new environment). Skin color is a well-known example. The extra melanin in dark skins gives added protection against the sun. Where the sun is no problem, pale skin allows better vitamin D formation (see p.298). Yellow skin contains a dense keratin layer that reflects light well in deserts or snow. Dark eye color also protects against sunlight; and so do the thick, folded eyelids of Mongoloids. Negroid hair protects against heat on the scalp, but allows sweat loss from the neck. Straight hair, grown long, protects against the cold. Noses typically vary with air humidity. In dry conditions they are longer and narrower, so inhaled air is moistened. But the flat Mongoloid face developed as protection against the cold, and here the nose is not prominent and exposed. The Eskimos have taken this further, by developing facial fat.

Other variables

Other features, not entirely inherited, also vary with climate. Average weight is greater the colder it is. For instance, the average Eskimo woman is considerably heavier than the average Spanish woman. Body shape also varies: two bodies that weigh the same can have very different surface areas. Body area is larger the hotter it is, for a large area gives more skin from which to sweat and to radiate heat. Metabolic rate varies in the same way. A typical European has a 'thermal equilibrium' of 77°F (25°C), ie with that temperature around her, naked, standing still, she shows no tendency to get hotter or colder. The Eskimo's metabolic rate is 15 to 30% higher than the European's, giving her a lower thermal equilibrium, while an Indian's, Brazilian's, or Australian's metabolic rate is 10% lower than the European's.

The Female Population

Worldwide, there are just over 100 women for every 100 men. But this ratio varies greatly from country to country. In most of Asia and the Middle East, and large parts of Africa, men predominate; in the United States and western Europe, women make up the majority. In some parts of the world, the lower status given to women may mean that more effort is made to save a male child than a female child. Also, as living standards rise so does the female population. However, some developing countries show a distinct female predominance. A male predominance can also arise because of immigration. Men are usually the first to go to new countries in search of better work opportunities.

Body and Climate

In most societies, fewer women than men are born. The ratio is generally about 100 female babies for every 105 male ones. But female life expectancy is longer in the United States and western Europe. Between the ages of 3 and 40, the numbers of males and females are roughly equal. After this, female numerical predominance grows steadily; for example, if a man were to reach the age of 95, he would be outnumbered by women of the same age by 4 to 1.

Female–male ratios

■ Parts of the world where women outnumber men

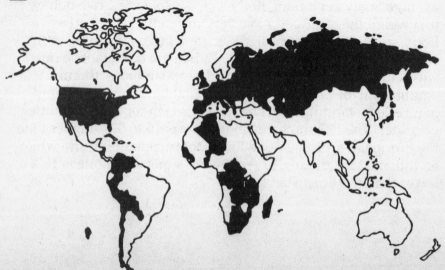

1

Cultural and Social Comparisons

Women today represent more than half the world's population, yet nowhere in the world do they share the same status as men. The well-known United Nations quote (1980) describing the economic status of women is still relevant: 'Women constitute half the world's population, perform nearly two-thirds of its work hours, receive one-tenth of the world's income, and own less than one-hundredth of the world's property.'

Women tend to work longer hours than men, have less economic and social power, and still have the primary responsibility for having and rearing children. They also continue to have primary responsibility for the sick and elderly and all aspects of domestic work, even where they also work outside the home – a common situation for the majority of women. Even in countries that have experienced considerable changes (such as the United States and Great Britain), women still earn, on average, 63% of men's income and are more likely than men to be in unskilled, poorly paid employment, with much less political power.

In the United States, for instance, although women have had the vote since 1920, there are still many fewer female than male senators. The same imbalance can be found within professional work and positions of authority. Women are also, throughout the world, still subject to sexual abuse and harassment, rape, domestic violence, and the humiliation of pornography.

But the situation for today's women still varies enormously from country to country. In Afghanistan, only 14% of women are literate; in France, it is 98%. In Belgium, 100% of adult women have access to contraceptives; in Angola, it is fewer than 1%. Women in the former West Germany bear on average two children; in Ghana, the average is six. In Jamaica, maternal mortality is 110 per 100,000 live births; in Norway, the rate of maternal mortality is 2 per 100,000.

The work of the 19th-century feminists and the great efforts of the international women's movement since the 1970s have made great changes. The right to vote has been won by the majority of the world's women, although some countries deny them full citizenship. A growing number of governments are recognizing the need to legislate for women's rights and opportunities. Much remains to be done, although there have been educational improvements. No doubt future improvements will be initiated and fought for by women.

SEXUALITY

2

External Sex Organs

Collectively, the female external sex organs or genitals are known as the vulva. Generally this refers to the clitoris and labia, but the area includes several features, as illustrated on the opposite page and described below. They include:

a) the mons veneris (mount of Venus) or mons pubis, a pad of fatty tissue over the pubic bone. From puberty (pp.22-3) this is covered with pubic hair. Extending downward and backward from the mons veneris are the

b) labia majora (outer lips), two folds of fatty tissue which protect the reproductive and urinary openings lying between them. These outer lips change size during a woman's life and from puberty their outer surfaces are also covered with hair. Between them lie the

c) labia minora (inner lips). These are delicate, hairless folds of skin quite sensitive to touch. During sexual arousal, they swell and darken in color (see pp.41-3). Below the mons area the labia minora splits into two folds to form

d) a hood under which lies the

e) clitoris. This is a small, bud-shaped organ and the most sensitive of the female genitals. The clitoris corresponds exactly as the male penis and like it is made up of erectile tissue. During sexual excitement, the clitoris swells with blood and for most women is the center of orgasm. Just below the clitoris are the

f) urethra – the external opening of the urinary passage which leads directly to the bladder – and the

g) vaginal opening, the outside entrance to the vagina (see pp.39-40).

h) The hymen, or maidenhead, is a thin membrane just inside the vaginal opening. It varies greatly in shape and size, and, in a virgin, it may be stretched or torn during the first experience of sexual intercourse, but quite often has already been stretched either by the use of tampons or during petting. If torn during intercourse there is usually some bleeding and possibly pain.

i) The Bartholin's or vestibular glands lie on either side of the vaginal opening. Contrary to previous belief, these glands play little part in vaginal lubrication. They may occasionally become infected (eg by gonorrhea: see pp.418-19).

j) The perineum is the triangular area of skin lying between the end of the labia minora and the anus. Below its surface are muscles and fibrous tissue that are stretched during childbirth.
k) The anus lies below the perineum and is the external opening through which feces pass from the rectum.

2

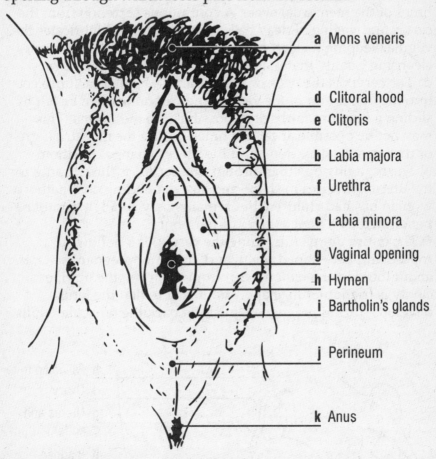

a Mons veneris

d Clitoral hood
e Clitoris

b Labia majora

f Urethra

c Labia minora

g Vaginal opening

h Hymen

i Bartholin's glands

j Perineum

k Anus

Internal Sex Organs

These are a woman's reproductive organs and consist of the vagina, uterus, Fallopian tubes, and ovaries, shown overleaf.
a) The vagina is a muscular passage, lying between
b) the bladder and
c) the rectum. It leads from the vulva upward, and at an angle, to the uterus. It is about 4-5in (10-12.5cm) long and capable of great distension. Normally the vaginal walls, which are lined

with folds or ridges of skin, lie close together. During sexual intercourse, they stretch easily to take the male penis and extend even more considerably during labor to allow a child to be born. The vagina is usually moist, though moistness increases with sexual excitement and may also vary at different times of the menstrual cycle. A continuous secretion from the cervix and vagina of dead cells mixed with fluid lubricates the vagina, keeping it clean and free from infection. It is this self-cleansing quality that makes vaginal douching unnecessary.

d) The cervix is the neck or lower part of the uterus. It projects into the upper end of the vagina and can quite often be felt by sliding a finger as far back as possible into the vagina. This may not be possible at certain times during the menstrual cycle or during sexual excitement if the uterus changes position.

e) The os, a tiny opening through the cervix, is the entrance to the uterus. It varies in shape and size depending on whether a woman has had children, but remains very small. It cannot be penetrated by a penis, finger or tampon.

f) The entire uterus (including the cervix) is a hollow, muscular, pear-shaped organ and, in its nonpregnant state, is about the size of a lemon. Seen from the front, the uterine cavity is triangular in shape, and it is here that the fetus develops during pregnancy, pushing back the muscular walls

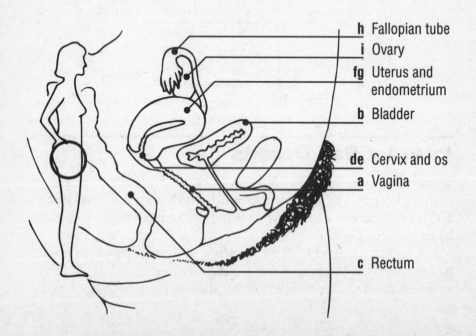

h Fallopian tube
i Ovary
fg Uterus and endometrium
b Bladder
de Cervix and os
a Vagina
c Rectum

in a surprising manner. During labor the fetus moves from the uterine cavity through the cervix and vagina to be delivered through the vaginal opening. (For a full description of pregnancy and birth, see p.100 on.)

g) The endometrium is the mucous membrane lining the body of the uterus. Once a month it undergoes various changes as part of the menstrual cycle (see p.27).

h) The Fallopian tubes extend outward and back from either side of the upper end of the uterus. They are about 4in (10cm) in length and reach outward toward the ovaries.

i) The ovaries are the female egg cells, equivalent to the male testes. They produce ova and also the female sex hormones, estrogen and progesterone. Once a month an ovum (egg) is released, which floats freely into the end of one of the Fallopian tubes. (For ovulation, see p.24.)

2

The Sexual Process

Important changes take place in the body during lovemaking, as a result of muscular tension and the swelling of certain tissues with blood. These processes were first described in detail by William Masters and Virginia Johnson in their book, *Human Sexual Response* (1966).

Stages
The act of lovemaking can be divided into four stages: the excitement phase, the plateau phase, the orgasm and the resolution phase.

Excitement phase The duration of this phase varies according to the amount and effectiveness of the stimulation. General muscular tension begins, and heart rate and blood pressure start to increase.

Plateau phase This is an extension of the excitement phase. If effective stimulation continues, sexual tensions increase and the desire for release of the tensions in orgasm is intensified.

Orgasm The orgasmic phase usually lasts only a matter of seconds. Orgasms do, however, vary in intensity and duration from woman to woman and occasion to occasion.

Resolution phase When orgasm is over, the resolution phase begins. There is gradual muscular and physiological relaxation, and within 30 minutes the body returns to its unstimulated state.

Changes in the breast

Early in the excitement phase the nipples become erect. Later, increased definition of the vein pattern in the breasts becomes obvious, and there may be an increase in the size of the breasts themselves. In the plateau phase, the breasts continue to enlarge, and the areolae become prominent, so engulfing the nipples. Also, a pink mottling known as the sex flush may appear on the breasts. In the resolution phase, the areolae subside leaving the nipples prominent, and the breasts gradually resume their normal size.

a Areola
b Nipple

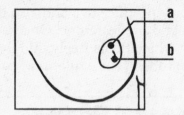

External genital changes

In the excitement phase, the clitoris increases in length and diameter. The labia majora open and spread flat while the labia minora swell and extend outward. In the plateau phase, the clitoris shortens and may disappear under its hood. The labia majora swell further, and the labia minora change color from pink to red, or from red to deep red in a woman who has had children. At orgasm, no particular changes are discernible, but during the resolution phase, the labia resume their usual color and size, and the clitoris returns to normal.

a Clitoris
b Urethra
c Vagina
d Labia minora
e Labia majora

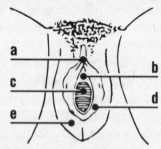

Internal genital changes

During the excitement phase, the vagina becomes moistened with a lubricant 'sweated' through its walls. The uterus and cervix pull away from the vagina, and the inner 2/3 of the vagina expands. During the plateau phase, the expansion of the inner vagina continues while the outer 1/3 contracts, gripping the penis.

The uterus continues to move away from the vagina. At orgasm, the uterus and the lower $1/3$ of the vagina experience a wave of contractions. During the resolution phase, the uterus, cervix, and vagina return to normal.

a Clitoris
b Uterus
c Cervix
d Vagina

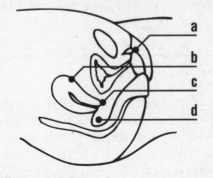

Erogenous Zones

These are the most erotically sensitive areas of the body, although, of course, they vary considerably from individual to individual. Stimulation by hand or mouth (or other light object) of any of these sensitive areas is not only an important part of intercourse, but can also be sexually satisfying in itself. It can lead to mutual masturbation or oral-genital sex, even though, traditionally, Western-style lovemaking follows a pattern of foreplay, intercourse, and orgasm. Many people – women and men alike – prefer sexual activity to end with the

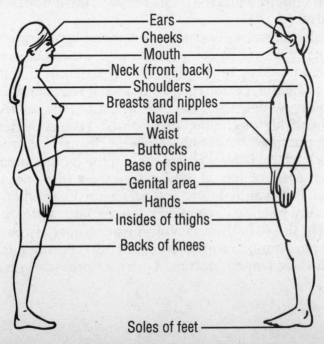

Ears
Cheeks
Mouth
Neck (front, back)
Shoulders
Breasts and nipples
Naval
Waist
Buttocks
Base of spine
Genital area
Hands
Insides of thighs
Backs of knees
Soles of feet

particular closeness of intercourse, and indeed many believe that lovemaking must always finish with vaginal intercourse; but to consider that stimulation of the erogenous zones of the body is only a prelude to, or substitute for, orgasm through vaginal intercourse, or even oral-genital sex play, is to limit the pleasures that it can bring.

Oral Sex

The mouth and genitals are potentially the two most erotic areas of the body. This role of the mouth is clear from the practice of deep kissing. But though oral sex includes lip and deep kissing, and any oral contact with the body, it most often refers to oral-genital contact, ie cunnilingus and fellatio.

Cunnilingus

This is the stimulation by the mouth of a woman's genitals. The whole area from the tip and shaft of the clitoris to the anus, including the vaginal entrance, is highly sensitive and in most women responds even more intensely to oral contact than to stimulation by the fingers. The types of oral techniques used include kissing, licking, and sucking, and if these are used, most women attain orgasm very easily.

Fellatio

This refers to oral stimulation of the male genitals. Techniques again include licking, kissing, and sucking, but also friction of the shaft and tip while the penis is inside the mouth.

Attitudes

Although oral sex is a source of considerable pleasure for both sexes, many people object to it strongly. Various objections have been raised against oral-genital sex, mainly that it is unnatural, sinful, or unhygienic. In fact, it is a common aspect of sexuality, widely used since ancient times. Its use today is as widespread, although often unadmitted. From a hygienic point of view, provided the genitals are kept clean, there are fewer and less harmful bacteria there than in the mouth, though there is the risk of spread of herpes simplex from mouth to genitalia. Both vaginal fluid and semen are just body fluids and usually tasteless. In female homosexual practice, in particular, use of oral sex is widespread – not only because vaginal penetration rarely occurs, but also because it is the most effective way for a woman to attain orgasm with a partner.

Orgasm

The female orgasm has probably been the subject of more debate and literature than any other area of sexuality. Much has been written on whether there is more than one type of orgasm and on ways to achieve orgasm. Even though the experience and intensity of orgasm vary considerably, the physical process is the same.

Foreplay and reaching orgasm

Women vary greatly in what they respond to sexually. Tell your partner your preferences to add to greater mutual enjoyment. The mons pubis, labia minora, clitoris and vaginal entrance are the most important areas for reaching orgasm. The clitoris is the most sexually responsive part of a woman's body, and usually fairly continuous clitoral stimulation is needed for orgasm. During intercourse, movement of the penis in and out of the vagina provides continual clitoral stimulation by moving the labia minora backward and forward over the clitoral tip. The tip of the clitoris is extremely sensitive, and constant manual contact can be painful. So, for the majority of women, manipulation of the whole genital area – by hand, tongue, or vibrator – is more pleasurable.

The anus is another potentially erotic area, but not as easily penetrated; lubrication, eg KY jelly, may be needed.

The feeling of orgasm

The G-spot (Grafenberg spot), a matter of debate, is said to be a sensitive area on the vagina's front wall. Some research has shown that if this is stimulated, some women lose fluid at orgasm, a form of ejaculation intensifying the sensation.

The time needed to reach orgasm varies from woman to woman, and from occasion to occasion. Just before, there is a feeling of tension lasting possibly 2-4 seconds, when all the small muscles in the pelvis surrounding the vagina and uterus contract.

The orgasm itself follows, which may last 10-15 seconds – a series of rhythmic muscular contractions, every 0.8 second, first around the outer third of the vagina and then spreading upward through the vagina. The uterus and rectum also contract. In a mild orgasm, there may be 3-5 contractions; in an intense one, 8-12. Muscles of the abdomen, buttocks, arms, face, legs, and neck may contract. Breathing is more rapid; blood pressure climbs. All return to normal, usually followed by feelings of relaxation and peace.

Multiple orgasm

Women, unlike men, are capable of multiple orgasm. That is, immediately or shortly after a first orgasm, if a woman maintains her sexual excitement at the plateau level, she can move directly into a second orgasm. Some women can experience 3-5 orgasms within a few minutes, and up to 12 in one hour have been recorded.

Experience of orgasm

Virtually all women are physically able to attain orgasm. But some never do. The Hite Report suggests that as few as 30% regularly achieve orgasm through intercourse. Kinsey's data, shown in the diagram below, indicate that such orgasm does gradually become more frequent in long-term relationships – but that even in 20-year relationships, 11% of women never reach orgasm. Women also generally take longer to reach orgasm than men (15 minutes compared to an average of 3 minutes). Nevertheless, it seems that the vast majority of women prefer intercourse to any other sexual activity, perhaps because of the closeness and affection associated with it.

As a result of the sexual revolution, women have made great strides in expressing their sexual needs to their partners, although many women still feel guilty about their sexuality and are reluctant to initiate sex.

The diagram shows what % of women experience orgasm in marital intercourse, and how often they do so

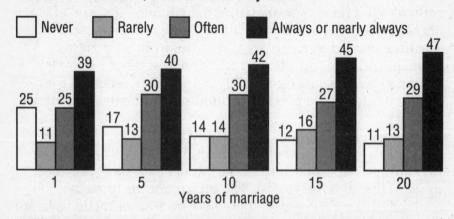

Never | Rarely | Often | Always or nearly always

Years of marriage

Entrance

The couple take up one of the positions that allow sexual intercourse to take place. The penis tip points at the entrance to the vagina. Then the man may only need to push forward from his hips: his penis slides immediately into the woman's vagina. Alternatively, in other positions, the woman lowers her vagina onto the man's penis.

But very often the following techniques are used:

a) either partner holds the penis, to help direct it into the vaginal entrance;

b) either partner holds the woman's labia apart to help the penis slide between them;

c) the penis is inserted only very gradually, beginning with the tip and progressing at first with several small forward movements and half retreats. This spreads the vaginal lubrication over the penis surface, and helps the vagina to accommodate itself gradually to the penis's size. (Also it is used as a tantalizing technique, to heighten the sensation of entrance.)

Delaying entrance

Once physiological readiness has been reached, the penis can be inserted into the vagina. But a couple may choose to delay this for many minutes. During this time, they continue lovemaking without intercourse. In fact, during lovemaking, the highest levels of sexual excitement before intercourse are usually not reached until the body has been physiologically ready for some time. This is especially true of women, but also of men.

Face-to-Face Positions

The number of positions for intercourse is almost endless. The choice of position depends on the mutual tastes and preferences of the couple. Among the most common, however, are front-entry positions with either the male or the female on top. Some typical examples are shown on the following page.

1) The so-called 'missionary position' involves the couple lying face to face with the man on top. Penetration is easy and the close proximity of the bodies allows the exchange of caresses.

2) A variation of this position can be achieved when the woman's body is supported on a bed while the man kneels on the floor.

3) A further variation of the 'missionary position' involves the man supporting the woman's body with his hands.

4) The female can take a more active part in lovemaking when she is above the man. This can be a satisfactory position for couples when the woman cannot bear the weight of her partner's body on top of her. The woman has considerable

freedom of movement and her partner can caress her clitoris during intercourse.

5) The position in which the couple kneel facing each other with the woman on top again allows the woman to take an active part in lovemaking. It has the disadvantage that the man needs to support his weight on his hands so that he cannot easily caress his partner.

6) The partners face each other, both in a half-lying position with the weight supported on their hands. This has the disadvantage that neither partner can easily caress the other.

Standing Positions

For successful intercourse in a standing position, both partners must be about the same height. If the woman is rather short, she can stand on a low stool, a pile of books, or even one step up some stairs, until she is at the correct height for easy penetration. Alternatively, her partner can pick her up and she can clasp her hands around his neck, and her legs around his waist.

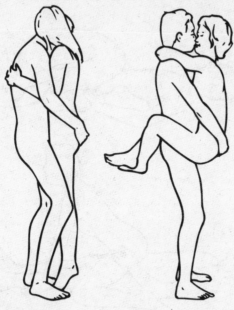

Side Positions

If the couple lie side by side, they can caress freely as neither has to support the weight of the other.

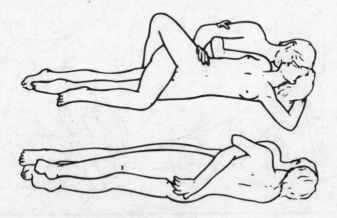

Rear-Entry Positions

The advantage of all rear-entry positions is that they allow deep and satisfying vaginal penetration, and often increased pressure against the clitoris. Entry from the rear is the natural copulation position for most mammals, though many women have found the association offensive. But the extra stimulation of the woman that these positions allow makes them worthwhile and enjoyable for many couples.

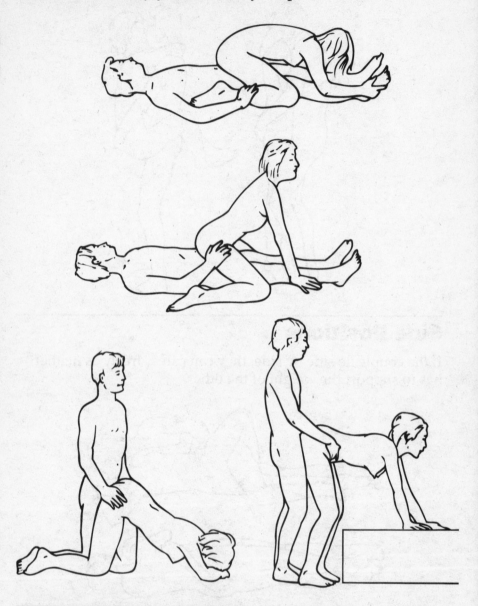

Female Stimulation

Many intercourse positions rely on the movement of the man's penis and lower abdomen for the stimulation of the woman's clitoris. For many women, this kind of stimulation is insufficiently intense to produce orgasm.

Several positions can be adapted to allow for stimulation of the labia and clitoris by either partner's hand while intercourse is taking place. Among the most useful are those involving rear entry, or those in which the woman is the active partner.

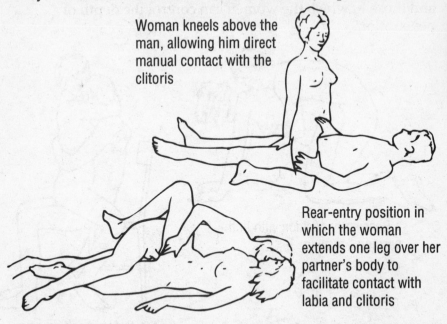

Woman kneels above the man, allowing him direct manual contact with the clitoris

Rear-entry position in which the woman extends one leg over her partner's body to facilitate contact with labia and clitoris

To increase the chance of fertilizing an egg, the woman's body should be tilted so that the vagina is in a vertical position.

This position ensures that the ejaculated semen lies in a pool at the upper end of the vagina, near the cervix

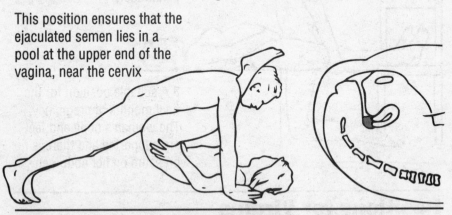

Intercourse in Pregnancy

For women who have had a previous miscarriage, intercourse in the first 3 months of a pregnancy can sometimes be unwise. The doctor will advise on this when the pregnancy is first confirmed. Later in pregnancy, the woman's thickening waistline may make intercourse in more conventional positions uncomfortable if not impossible.

A variety of positions can be adapted for use during pregnancy. Among the most suitable are rear-entry positions and those in which the women can control the depth of penetration.

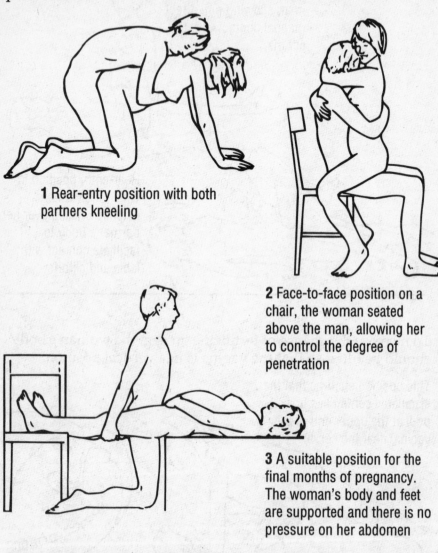

1 Rear-entry position with both partners kneeling

2 Face-to-face position on a chair, the woman seated above the man, allowing her to control the degree of penetration

3 A suitable position for the final months of pregnancy. The woman's body and feet are supported and there is no pressure on her abdomen

Positions for Virgins

Many first-timers adopt the well-known missionary position (p.48, diagram 1). But for both male and female virgins, the position matters less than the approach. This should be slow and considerate. The caressing, stroking, and fondling of foreplay will also stimulate lubrication of the vagina so that a woman should feel little discomfort, especially if past petting has stretched or torn her hymen.

Positions for People with Special Needs

A squatting position (**1**) helps full penetration of women with tight vaginas. Side-by-side facing (p.45, bottom diagram) helps the ill, old, tired, tall, and short. A side-by-side rear-entry position (**2**) is recommended for men with a weak erection. A woman-on-top position (**3**) is used in the treatment of male impotence and premature ejaculation. It is also used as a preliminary position in therapy for nonorgasmic women. Position (**4**) makes uncontrolled hip movements easier for the woman and helps her to reach orgasm.

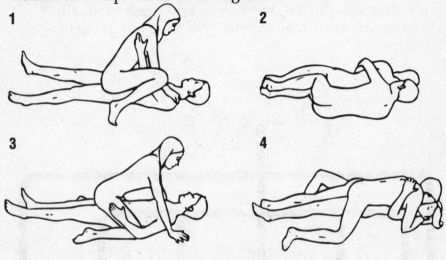

Sex and the Disabled

Certain medications can diminish sex drive and response. Also, several physical conditions can adversely affect continuing sexual activity: eg back pain, pain because of joint stiffness, or reduced or altered sensation if nerves are involved. Pain and spasm are best dealt with by finding different positions and support, and a physical therapist will usually be able to offer guidance. Women suffering from nerve injuries or disorders affecting the nervous system may need greater stimulation, perhaps with a vibrator, yet areas of the body with unaffected sensation may still be very sensitive.

Mentally handicapped women are vulnerable to sexual exploitation, but sex is equally vital as an expression of a loving relationship. Advice on contraception and the implications of fertility should be given by a person who has understanding and experience of the individual's capabilities.

Sex and the Older Woman

Although sexual topics are now much more openly discussed, the sexual needs and behavior of older people are often subject to considerable misunderstanding, even embarrassment. In society's eyes, and particularly among the young, it is still not considered 'correct' for older people, who are probably parents and grandparents, to have the same sexual yearnings and desires as younger people. Such an attitude is ill-founded and stems largely from society's current emphasis on youth and youthful attractiveness. There is no doubt that the sex drive does decline with age. In men, this starts in the twenties and proceeds gradually through life until about age 60, when the rate of decline decreases.

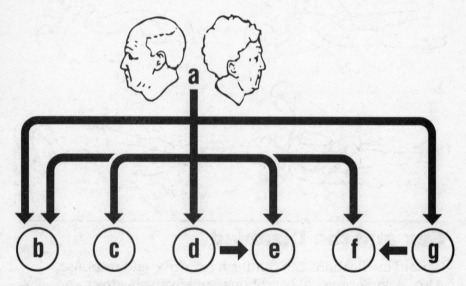

Psychological problems
An older couple with a previously enjoyable sex life may find this threatened by problems.
a Disharmony about nonsexual matters
b A too-old-for-sex attitude
c Enjoying sex, but embarrassed by what others may think
d Boredom from unimaginative lovemaking
e One seeks younger partner to reaffirm sexual prowess
f Fear of sexual decline leads to rejection of sex
g Worries about money or retirement may interfere

In women there is usually no appreciable decline at all until about age 60, after which the rate of decline is very gradual. Clearly, this is in no way consistent with the erroneous idea that old people should have no sex lives. People who enjoy sex earlier in life generally continue to do so as they get older; and, although the aging process may make it necessary to adapt their lovemaking to some extent, most older people remain capable of intercourse for as long as their health will permit.

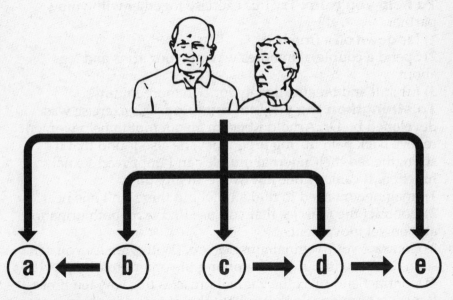

Practical problems

There are practical problems that older people may have to overcome if enjoyment of sex is not to come to an end.

a One partner is interested in sex, one isn't

b Physical problems associated with the aging of the reproductive system may make intercourse uncomfortable unless treated

c Illness or infirmity may make intercourse difficult: trying special positions may help

d Death of one partner often ends the sex life of the other: many older people are not interested in finding a new mate

e People who would like a new partner cannot always find one: women outnumber men, and some people are naturally shy

Exercises to Improve Your Love Life

Sexual intercourse is itself an excellent form of exercise. Also, if you are physically fit, you are likely to enjoy lovemaking all the more. Research has shown that the heart rate can increase to 180 beats per minute just prior to climax, and this equates with the rate experienced by professional runners during a race. Making love is known to be a relaxing activity, too, as shown by the fact that people usually sleep for longer and far more soundly afterwards. You do not need to be a top-class athlete in order to give pleasure and also to achieve orgasm yourself. But there are a number of simple exercises that a woman can practice in order to increase sensation for both partners.

To help you relax Try this exercise together with your partner.

1) Lie down on a firm bed.

2) Spend a couple of minutes waving your arms and legs about.

3) Lie still and breathe deeply for two more minutes.

To strengthen the vaginal muscles This exercise was developed by Dr. Arnold Kegel in an attempt to help women relieve back pain during pregnancy; he also found that it strengthened their internal muscles and improved sexual function. It can be done anywhere, at any time.

1) Imagine you need to find a toilet but there isn't one near.

2) Contract the muscles that you use to control both urination and bowel movement.

3) Contract your vaginal muscles too. (With practice you can soon do this without first involving the other muscles.)

4) Contract and relax the vaginal muscles this way ten times. Repeat intermittently throughout the day, and use this technique during intercourse.

To exercise the pelvic area

1) Lie on your back, bend knees, legs apart. Keep feet flat.

2) Breathing in, try to move the pelvic area upward a little. Remember, only a small amount of movement is possible.

3) Breathe out as you lower your pelvis.

4) Relax and repeat.

5) Standing with your feet apart and facing forward, relax your knees.

6) Swing your hips in a clockwise circular movement, but keeping your upper body still.

7) Repeat in a counterclockwise direction.

Improving Sexual Response

Sexual inadequacy among women chiefly takes the form of failure to reach orgasm. Some societies do not recognize that women need this sexual climax. Repeated congestion of genital organs without relief via orgasm can bring discomfort and frustration.

The cause may be the man's impotence or ineptitude. If the trouble lies in the woman, it may be organic: defects of the sexual system, imbalance of hormones, or inflammation or injury to the genitals. Certain nervous disorders, excessive drinking or drug-taking, stress or aging may also be to blame. Psychological causes are by far the most common. The woman may find the man sexually unattractive or selfish. Mentally, she rejects him as a mate; the result is a lack of sexual response. Some sexually inhibited women were taught that sex is bad, wrong and dirty. This can warp a woman's attitudes to sex so that she views with guilt, fear and shame her own sexual feelings, and tries to suppress them, remaining unresponsive. Other (often related) psychological blocks are emotional ties to the father; subconscious hatred of men; fear of pregnancy; and fear of pain or intercourse. But some women fail because they are overeager to succeed, and so too tense to reach orgasm. Treating the nonorgasmic woman involves considerate, stimulating sex play, when she is relaxed and both partners are in harmony. Techniques, such as those shown overleaf, have brought orgasm to many women who had never had it and to a very large number who had previously lost orgasmic ability.

Stimulation techniques

1a) Considerate caressing by the man when the woman is feeling relaxed may help to arouse her. He should find which areas she most likes to have stroked; rest should punctuate attempts at arousal. Tenderly telling the woman he loves her will make her far more responsive than if he roughly seizes and manipulates her.

b) Sometimes a woman finds it helpful to concentrate her mind on sexual fantasy. Reading erotic books and looking at erotic pictures may help. The man can encourage her with words of endearment to show that she gives him pleasure.

c) Masturbation by vibrator or by hand may help to stimulate some women who can be aroused, yet are sexually less sensitive than most. Other physical aids include deep penetration by the penis, and oral-genital contact. Once orgasm is achieved, it is easier the next time.

Sensate focus therapy (below)

2a) The couple sit nude on the bed: the man legs apart, propped up against the headboard; the woman seated with her back to his chest and her legs on his. She guides his hands briefly over her inner thighs, vaginal lips and clitoral region, so she can control her sexual sensations and stop them becoming too intense for her.

b) In subsequent sessions, the couple eventually work up to the point where the woman kneels astride the man and finds pleasure in keeping still with his penis inside her. She can then try moving her hips to and fro, thrusting faster and harder when she wants to. Next, she has him join in with his own hip movements.

c) Both partners lie sideways, so she rests largely on his chest, stomach, one leg and the knee of the other leg. Uncontrolled hip movements are made easier, and orgasm is made more likely for women, than positions in which they can consciously control the movements made by their bodies.

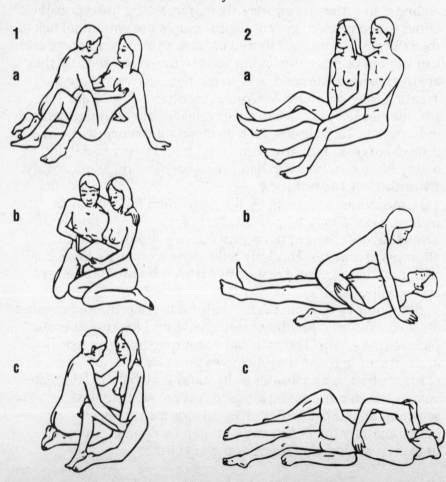

Sexual Aids

The use of stimulators for lovemaking is centuries old; some early Eastern devices are still popular today. Many women find them an exciting and often beneficial part of their sex lives.

Widely used are forms of erotica, from visually stimulating clothing and underwear to explicit magazines and videos. Another very popular aid is the dildo or vibrator, penis-shaped with an optional vibrating mechanism. Battery-powered, it may have speed variations and attachments to stimulate clitoris and vagina. Some reach a climax with a vibrator where other methods have proved ineffectual. It can also be used as a masturbation aid. Often lubrication is needed.

Many couples enjoy using brightly colored and textured sheaths, for penis or vibrator. Condom-like attachments can be put over the penis to enlarge it, stimulating for women who enjoy deeper penetration. If a man has difficulty maintaining an erection, a ring around the base of the penis traps the blood. It has been claimed that certain sprays and creams – local anesthetics – may delay a man's ejaculation; there is, however, no evidence to show that they work. Chinese balls stimulate the vagina over a period of time, vibrating as the woman moves.

Most sex aids are perfectly safe if used correctly. They can enhance pleasure and can be helpful in treating sexual problems.

Emotional Needs

Close, caring relationships are not just about sex – they are also about emotional needs. *Women and Love* (1987), by American feminist Shere Hite, presents a detailed survey of the emotional needs and experiences of 4500 women of all ages and backgrounds. It clearly shows that, despite other changes, most women today feel that their emotional needs are not being met by men.

Only 17% of the women interviewed said that communications within their relationships with men are good or made them happier. By far the majority feel that they receive much greater emotional support and understanding from other women, and that they are emotionally deprived in relationships with men. In particular, many women feel that their male partners do not listen to them, and that their opinions are undermined or trivialized; and, perhaps most importantly of all, that their male partners are either unwilling or unable to discuss deep emotions – to find a means of expressing love, intimacy, and sensitivity. For most women, if some means of meeting emotional needs is not there, a satisfactory sexual relationship cannot be sustained.

Statistics show that the majority of heterosexual women today still want to marry or to share loving relationships with men. In practice, many women find that, although there have been social changes and greater moves toward equality outside marriage, within marriage, a woman's role has remained the traditional nurturing one of providing emotional support for men – not the other way around. Their attempts to ask for a greater degree of shared emotional intimacy often lead to misunderstandings, a reluctance on the part of men to talk which, in turn, can lead to sexual problems, a feeling of being threatened, and arguments. It is thought that men's negative reactions to intimacy come from emotional impoverishment caused by social conditioning. As a result, many women separate themselves emotionally from their men, find satisfaction in work, children and friends, have extramarital affairs, or leave.

Many women are turning to counseling and couple or group therapy to find a solution; this can be successful. Again, women take the responsibility.

Increasingly, many women say that for their emotional needs to be met, men themselves have to make changes and break away from the traditional conditioning that makes it difficult for them to express feelings in a nonsexual way. For relationships to improve, men have to learn the so-called 'feminine' skills of sensitivity, warmth, and sharing, without being asked. Women are asking men to learn to love, emotionally as well as sexually.

Masturbation

Masturbation refers to stimulation of the genitals by hand or with some other object, usually to gain orgasm. It generally refers to self-stimulation, although mutual masturbation is common in both heterosexual and homosexual activity. In 1985, a study showed that 66% of unmarried women and 56% of married women reported masturbation. For many it is the most direct and successful means of achieving orgasm.

In our society, masturbation has long been a taboo subject; and, traditionally, the attitude has been one of disapproval. To some extent, attitudes toward masturbation have reflected those of society toward sexuality in general, but with an additional dimension: whereas interpersonal sex could be 'justified' on the grounds of love and marriage, masturbation by its very nature was too blatantly an expression of an individual's inherent sexuality.

In recent years, however, masturbation has become recognized as part of normal sexual experience which causes no particular physical or mental harm. In fact, the reverse may be seen as true. Not only does masturbation release acute tension due to an unsatisfactory sexual life or an absence of a partner, but it can also be used by a woman as a learning process to gain a better understanding of her sexual responses, leading to greater fulfillment with a partner. Despite more enlightened social attitudes, recent studies show that most women still suffer guilt and anxiety about masturbation.

Techniques

Women have various ways of masturbating, although the most commonly used methods are for stimulating the clitoris. More than 80% of women who masturbate regularly concentrate on direct stimulation of clitoris or labia. One or more fingers can either be rubbed over or around the clitoris, or the whole hand may be used to apply steady and rhythmical pressure. (Few women masturbate by actually rubbing the clitoral glands; more commonly they massage the shaft or general clitoral area.) A pillow, vibrator, or continuous stream of water from a faucet may be used instead of the hands. Alternatively, some women masturbate by crossing their legs and applying steady pressure from their thighs onto the genital area. In addition, while using any of these techniques, a finger or similar object may be inserted into the vagina, although few women (around 1-3%) rely on vaginal insertion alone.

Slightly different from these methods is a technique used by about 5% of women. In this, a woman assumes a position similar to that of the woman-on-top position in intercourse. Although there may be some direct stimulation of the genitals, possibly with a pillow, it is usually very slight, and climax is achieved by rhythmical pelvic thrusting combined with a build-up of muscular tension similar to that felt during intercourse.

The breasts and nipples are usually highly sensitive and, in a few cases, their stimulation alone is sufficient for orgasm. A very few women can achieve orgasm through fantasy alone.

Fantasies

It has been estimated that the majority of women fantasize during masturbation, and probably well over half of all women also fantasize when making love with a partner. Many women feel guilty or worried about fantasies, fearing that an indulgence in them somehow represents an inadequacy or an inability to gain complete pleasure with a partner. Others are concerned that the very fact of fantasizing might threaten the partner or that the fantasy, particularly if woven around a situation they might never act out in the "real" world, represents serious emotional disturbance.

But sexual or erotic fantasies are a natural part of a woman's sexual and emotional life. All women fantasize at some time or another, at any age, with any partner. It may be a fleeting image or an elaborately worked out story, returned to again and again. Until recently, this fantasy life remained unexplored. The work of researcher Shere Hite and author Nancy Friday in *My Secret Garden* and *Women on Top* broke the silence. Women themselves have been speaking out.

We now know that women's sexual fantasies are wide-ranging: sex with a stranger, fantasies of pain and torture, voyeurism, exhibitionism, a whole range of unlikely encounters with men and women, and much more. They can be used to compensate for an unsatisfactory sexual relationship, or to enhance a good sexual experience. Whether held as closely guarded secrets or shared with an understanding partner, fantasies can be a rich and healthy addition to a woman's sexual and emotional life.

Percentage of women experiencing different types of fantasy during masturbation

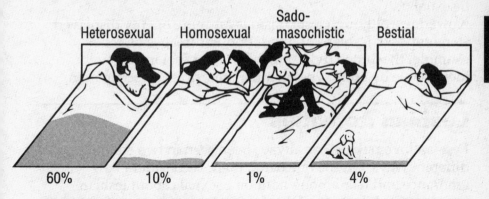

Heterosexual	Homosexual	Sado-masochistic	Bestial
60%	10%	1%	4%

Homosexuality

The word 'homosexual' is used, as with a man, to refer to women who are attracted, emotionally and physically, to members of their own sex. But, more frequently, female homosexuals are known as lesbians, a name derived from the Greek island of Lesbos, which, some 2600 years ago, was the home of the poet Sappho. Many of her poems were beautifully and movingly addressed to women, and from them comes the term 'Sapphic love' to describe love between women. It has been suggested that the term 'homoemotional' more accurately describes lesbianism, as such love between women is thought by many to be more frequently characterized by its intense emotionalism than by its sexual aspect. But, in our society, no matter which term is used, the conventional interpretation of lesbianism has been one of perversion.

With women, some degree of 'homosexual' activity is common, either in preadolescent sex play or in the schoolgirl crushes of adolescence.

Statistics of the actual number of lesbians in a population are difficult to obtain. The problem lies in whether to define homosexuality in terms of fantasy, attraction, or behavior. For instance, in 1979 Masters and Johnson found that, for heterosexual women, the fifth most common types of sexual fantasy were lesbian ones. Also, they found that heterosexual fantasies were the third most common type for self-identified lesbians. Another study found, in 1978, that only 50% of lesbian women considered themselves to be exclusively gay. In 1982, another researcher revised data from earlier surveys and estimated that 15% of women were bisexual, whereas fewer than 1% were exclusively homosexual. Yet another study found that over 33% of lesbians are 'partially bisexual', and that roughly 10% of heterosexual women are behaviorally bisexual.

Nowadays, although lesbianism is far more openly displayed, stereotypes of lesbians abound. Popular images of, for example, the 'butch dyke' are incorrect. Lesbians are not identifiable by body type, mannerisms, dress or occupation.

Lesbian Activities

Lesbian lovemaking has always been seen in two completely different ways. On the one hand, there is considerable ignorance and fear among nonhomosexuals about lesbian procedure; while on the other hand, distorted presentations of lesbian activity have long been accepted as a source of erotic arousal in classical art, and today in hard-core pornography. Both views incorrectly assume that lovemaking between women is a preliminary to, or a substitute for, heterosexual intercourse. In fact, the reverse is true. What is notable is that lesbians can achieve a far greater sexual satisfaction with each other than many other women achieve in their heterosexual relations. Nearly all lesbian lovemaking results in orgasm for both women, a fact which may explain why men have tended to feel threatened by lesbianism. Many sexual activities are common to both lesbians and heterosexuals. In both there is mutual kissing and caressing, particularly of the breasts and genitals, and the general procedures of getting used to one another and of giving affection. By its very nature there is no pre-intercourse foreplay in lesbian lovemaking, and most activity centers around clitoral stimulation. The main techniques used are mutual masturbation and cunnilingus (kissing, sucking and licking of the clitoris). Vibrators are commonly used for clitoral stimulation; the dildo, or artificial penis, is not often used; in fact, its use has been a particularly pernicious and long-lasting myth. By definition, lesbians are attracted to other women and their lovemaking does not center on penis substitutes. One additional practice which is sometimes used is that of tribadism, where one woman lies on top of another and moves in such a way as to stimulate the clitoris of each.

A common myth is that each partner takes an exclusively 'butch' (active male) or 'femme' (active female) role. In practice, if such roles are assumed, they usually alternate. This stereotyped view has confused both nonhomosexuals and lesbians themselves, not only sexually but in a social context. And this confusion has, to some degree, resulted in the ideological rejection of such roles as advocated by radical lesbians.

A further overriding myth is, perhaps, that all lesbians are first and foremost sexual beings, whereas they are no more sexually active or sexually obsessed than are most people. In fact, by comparison with male homosexuals, sexual promiscuity is rare among lesbians, as is prostitution. At the same time, particularly with the continuing emergence of 'gayness' and with the more open expression of female sexuality, promiscuity is neither more nor less frequent among lesbians than among heterosexual women.

Theories

There have been few studies investigating the nature of lesbianism. Physical explanations, such as hormone imbalance or congenital defects, have been put forward, but findings are ambiguous and not generally accepted. In the past lesbianism has been defined in terms of neurosis or of immature development, but these are generalizations based on lesbians who have sought psychiatric help. One of the most sympathetic theories is that of psychiatrist Dr. Charlotte Wolff. She has emphasized the bisexual nature of lesbianism, seeing an essentially bisexual element in the female's clitoris. This theory has been supported by subsequent studies, two of which (in 1978 and in 1979) found that two in five lesbians have been married to men, whereas only one in five homosexual men have been married to women. This may reflect one of two things: either that a greater number of women than men conform to society's expectations of them; or that there is a greater fluidity of sexual orientation among women. Although lesbianism may be an active political choice made by some members of the feminist movement, its roots are thought to lie mainly in social and cultural causes.

Bisexuality

Most of the confusion and disgust surrounding homosexuality exists because it is too frequently assumed that homosexuals deviate markedly from normality. There is very little evidence to support this. Instead it is believed by many, including Freud, Kinsey and, more recently, psychiatrist Dr. Charlotte Wolff, that each person is inherently bisexual and, depending on conditioning, may choose a partner from the opposite sex (heterosexuality), the same sex (homosexuality), or both (bisexuality).

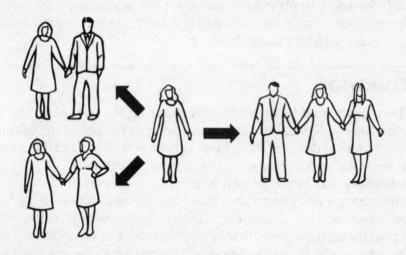

Attitudes to Lesbianism

Female homosexuality has been regarded as a deviation by some, while it has often been ignored or just ridiculed by others. These last attitudes, which reflect the approach of male-oriented societies toward women, have meant that female homosexuals have significantly escaped the same degree of legal persecution suffered by males. Lesbianism was generally accepted in ancient Greece and Rome. It is also known that the Mohave Indians openly recognized and accepted a class of homosexual women.

But references to lesbians have been scanty throughout history, even during the Middle Ages when persecution of homosexuals reached fanatical proportions. In most European countries, homosexuality was once a capital offense; but significantly more sentences were carried out on males. During the 20th century, lesbians have therefore had to fight two battles: one for basic recognition and one for acceptance. Today, lesbianism is out in the open for the first time. Despite its relative legal freedom, lack of understanding about lesbians and discrimination against them – socially and economically – are still widespread.

As a result, a woman who feels attracted to other women may fear the opinion of others, both within the family and society, and may even have difficulty in admitting her sexual preference to herself. There has been extensive liberalizing of attitudes in society in recent years; with the development of the women's movement, some have felt a commitment to lesbianism as part of a rejection of a prime need for the male. Others still feel the need to repress ordinary expression of their sexuality, and perhaps play a token part in heterosexual relations. (Sometimes this may be a part of a genuine bisexuality.)

Sexual Problems

A wide range of problems can affect a woman's enjoyment of her sexuality. They may be physical or psychological in origin, but the result is the same – distress for both partners. A very few women are truly frigid – that is, incapable of responding to any kind of sexual stimulation. But there are many who are temporarily unable to achieve orgasm. Some women find penile penetration or intercourse painful or even impossible; others have a partner with some kind of sexual difficulty. The purely physical problems are usually easy to identify; psychological problems can also be treated, but the origin of the problem must be traced first. Common underlying causes of psychological problems are feelings of fear, shame or guilt about sexual response, or anxieties connected with pregnancy. Important in the treatment of such problems are the revolutionary sexual therapy techniques developed by Masters and Johnson (see pp.68-9).

Sexual Dysfunction

This is a complex female complaint in which a woman derives little or no erotic pleasure from sexual stimulation. It has been found that women with a history of depression and/or sexual abuse (see pp.70-1) tend to have a variety of psychosexual problems. Treatment often takes the form of Masters and Johnson's techniques of sensate-focus therapy, in which the couple refrain from intercourse and orgasm for a period. During this time, they learn to caress each other's bodies until the woman is sufficiently aroused to initiate intercourse.

Problems with Orgasm

For women, the most common sexual complaints are those to do with difficulty of reaching, or inability to achieve, orgasm.

Reasons

There are many complex reasons why women may experience difficulty in achieving orgasm, not only with a partner but also by themselves in masturbation. Shame about their sexuality, fear of actually examining their genitals, and therefore ignorance about their function, are among the main reasons for some women's avoidance of masturbation. Ignorance about the physiology of sex can equally prevent women from achieving orgasm with their partner. But in a female/male situation, other problems arise. Some of the most important are probably the refusal or inability of women to express clearly what they want from sex, and a deference to, or overprotectiveness toward, the male orgasm, at the loss of their own. This often leads to the practice by some women of faking orgasm within their relationship – a practice that ultimately can cause great strain on both people.

Masters-Johnson therapy

Masters-Johnson sex therapy divides the female problems with orgasm into two main categories:

a) primary orgasmic dysfunction – women who have never experienced orgasm; and

b) secondary orgasmic dysfunction – women who have previously experienced orgasm but whose ability to achieve it has since stopped.

Such women who have problems with orgasm are often very sexually responsive, enjoy intercourse but are still unable to continue their response beyond the plateau phase (pp.41-3). Therapy consists essentially of encouraging an inorgasmic woman to bring herself to orgasm by masturbation (p.59) either by hand or with an electric vibrator – a phallic-shaped sexual aid which, when held against the clitoral area, can bring a woman to orgasm. Once a woman can achieve orgasm easily by herself, her partner is brought into the therapy. Normal intercourse takes place during which the woman makes no attempt to achieve orgasm. Instead her partner brings her to climax either manually or with the vibrator. In general, after only a few sessions, the woman will be achieving orgasm during intercourse.

2

Feminist therapy
Feminists have started preorgasmic groups to tackle the same problem of female orgasmic dysfunction. They also concentrate on encouraging women to discover their own physical sexuality, but at the same time are examining some of the male-dependence roles mentioned above.

Painful Intercourse

Discomfort during intercourse can make lovemaking an unpleasant experience for some women. There are several possible explanations for the discomfort.

Virginity
In a woman who has not had intercourse, the hymen may be intact and unstretched (**a**). The first few times intercourse takes place there may be a little pain or even slight bleeding as the hymen is stretched or torn (**b**) to accommodate the penis. A very few women have tough hymens which need minor surgery.

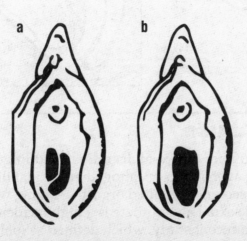

Vaginismus

This is a comparatively rare disorder in which the muscles surrounding the vaginal entrance go into spasm when penetration is attempted. Treatment involves the woman learning, over a period of time, to insert first one, then two fingers into her vagina without experiencing muscular spasm. Her partner takes part in this and, when the woman's confidence is established, intercourse can take place.

Dispareunia

This is a general term for painful intercourse. The pain may be caused by several factors. Vaginal infections and irritations can be exacerbated by the friction of the penis moving in the vagina. Insufficient vaginal lubrication can cause pain. During normal stimulation, the vaginal walls secrete a lubricating fluid which facilitates entry by the penis. Pain results if the man attempts entry before the woman is sufficiently aroused or if he is wearing a condom. In the first case, entry must be delayed until the woman is fully aroused, and in the second, a lubricating jelly, or even saliva, will help solve the problem. A common cause of pain in the pelvis is the penis hitting the cervix during particularly deep thrusts (c). Pelvic pain can also be caused by infections of the uterus, cervix, or Fallopian tubes, cysts or tumors on the ovaries, or tears in the ligaments supporting the uterus (following childbirth).

c

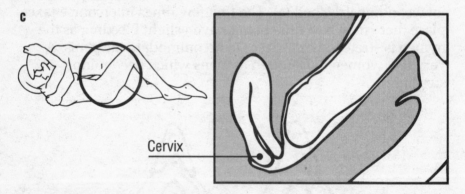

Cervix

Sexual Abuse

There are a number of sexual disorders including decreased sexual desire, aversion to sex altogether, an inability to be sexually aroused and inhibited orgasm. Among women who have suffered sexual abuse, there is a high incidence of these problems. In a recent study, which defined sexual abuse as unwanted sexual contact, it was found that 25% of women had been abused before the age of 21, 16% before the age of 16, and 12% before they were 14 years of age.

Before a couple embarks on therapy for sexual dysfunction (see p.64), the woman will need to have her psychiatric history thoroughly investigated so that the treatment may be streamlined for her needs.

2

Male Sexual Problems

Impotence

Many men experience a period of impotence at some stage in their lives. It can take two forms: inability to achieve erection, or inability to achieve orgasm despite erection. Most cases are caused by psychological factors such as fear of sexual failure, neurosis or guilt. Treatment may include psychotherapy or a series of Masters and Johnson sensate-focus exercises similar to the therapy described on p.58 for female sexual dysfunction.

Premature ejaculation

This is when the man reaches ejaculation too quickly for the woman to be sexually satisfied. Occasional occurrence is normal, but consistent premature ejaculation can lead to self consciousness, partner dissatisfaction and impotence. The major cause of premature ejaculation is simply anxiety that premature ejaculation will occur. Unsatisfactory approaches to the problem include distracting the mind, use of anesthetic creams, drugs and alcohol, and avoidance of touching the male genitals. Masters and Johnson evolved a successful therapy in which the woman manually controls and delays her partner's ejaculation.

Ejaculatory incompetence

In this condition, which is less common than premature ejaculation, the man has no difficulty in achieving an erection but cannot reach orgasm inside the vagina. The cause sometimes lies in traumatic incidents in the past, often in the context of a sexually restrictive upbringing. The Masters and Johnson therapy begins with the masturbation of the man's penis to orgasm by the woman. Later the woman takes the penis into her vagina just before the male orgasm. When the man is confident about ejaculating into the vagina he will then attempt penetration at a low level of sexual excitement.

CONTRACEPTION

Conception

For pregnancy to occur, several conditions must be fulfilled:
a) semen from the man must enter the woman's vagina;
b) the semen must contain healthy male sperm;
c) the sperm must find conditions in the vagina in which they can live;
d) the living sperm must make their way into the woman's uterus and (possibly) the Fallopian tubes;
e) they must find an egg there ready for fertilization;
f) and the egg, once fertilized, must be able to implant itself in the uterus.

By preventing any one of these, contraception is achieved. But it is important to note three things. First, sperm may reach the vagina even if the penis does not enter it. Sperm ejaculated onto the vulva or surrounding skin can still swim into the vagina.

Second, although conditions in the vagina are hostile to sperm,

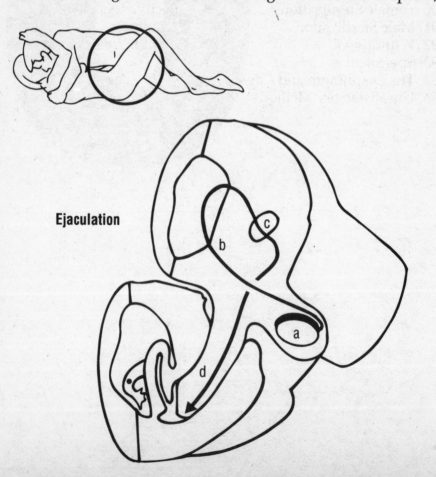

Ejaculation

they can live there for 6 hours or more. So any barrier to
prevent sperm moving up into the uterus must last at least this
long after intercourse.

Third, once sperm have reached the uterus they can live 4 to 5
days or more. So, to avoid conception, there must be at least
this time gap between the arrival of sperm in the uterus and
the arrival of the egg.

A normally fertile woman experiencing regular intercourse
with a normally fertile man stands about a 60% chance of
becoming pregnant in any one month. Therefore, for the
woman who intends to have heterosexual intercourse but not
to get pregnant, some form of safe, effective contraception is
essential.

The diagrams show the genital coupling and route of the
semen. Ejaculation occurs in two stages. Rhythmic muscular
contractions begin in the testes and epididymides (**a**) and
continue along the vas deferens (**b**), also involving the seminal
vesicles and prostate (**c**). Sperm and seminal fluid collect in the
urethra inside the prostate. Then a sphincter relaxes, letting
this semen pass down toward the penis. Contractions along the
length of the urethra (**d**) cause ejaculation. Inside the woman's
body, semen passes from the vagina into the uterus (**e**) and
Fallopian tubes (**f**).

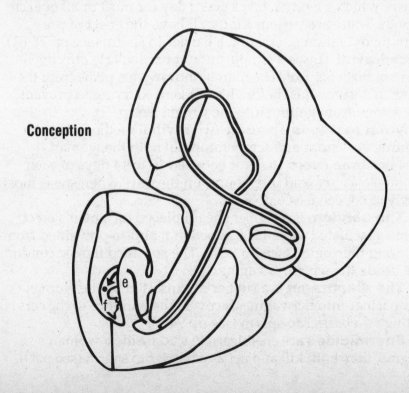

Conception

The Main Types of Contraceptive

There is a wide variety of contraceptive techniques in use today – none of which is ideal. Many concentrate on keeping sperm out of the uterus. Diaphragms and condoms aim to provide a physical barrier; spermicides a chemical barrier. Withdrawal modifies the sex act, to try to keep sperm out of the female tract completely. Other techniques – generally more effective – concentrate on interfering with the ovum. Oral contraceptive pills affect the process of ovulation. Intrauterine devices (IUDs) may prevent implantation, and there is increasing evidence that they may also inhibit fertilization. Finally, there are two other types of technique. 'Rhythm' methods simply aim (not necessarily successfully) to avoid intercourse at those times of the month when sperm might find an ovum ready for fertilization. Sterilization methods are surgical operations to make one partner incapable of having children. Techniques can be combined to give more effective contraception.

Contraceptive techniques
The various forms of contraception described below are located on the diagram opposite.

Contraceptive pill Oral contraceptives consist of small pills, one of which a woman takes every day for most or all of each month. There are various kinds; all have the effect of preventing ovulation or creating a barrier to sperm (see pp.78-81).

Withdrawal This is a simple but not particularly effective form of birth control. The man withdraws his penis from the woman's vagina just before his orgasm, so trying to prevent the semen from getting into the vagina (see p.92).

Rhythm methods There are two rhythm methods of birth control – calendar and temperature. In both the woman abstains from intercourse for between 10 to 14 days of each month so as to avoid intercourse on the days when she is most likely to conceive (see pp.86-9).

1) The condom is a rubber sheath placed on a man's erect penis. Ejaculated semen is trapped in it and so prevented from entering the vagina (see pp.84-5). The so-called female condom fits inside the woman's vagina.

2) The diaphragm is a rubber cap inserted by the woman or her partner into her vagina. It covers the entrance to the cervix, acting as a barrier to sperm (see pp.94-5).

3) Spermicides are chemicals. Placed inside a woman's vagina, they both kill and act as a barrier to sperm (see p.89).

4) The intrauterine device (IUD) is a small device inserted into the woman's womb on a long-term basis. While in place, its effect on the uterus prevents implantation (see pp.81-2).

5a) Female sterilization This consists of an operation on the Fallopian tubes, to prevent eggs passing from the ovaries to the womb (see pp.90-1).

5b) Male sterilization (or 'vasectomy') is a minor operation on the man's vas deferens which prevents sperm being ejaculated in the semen (see pp.91-2).

3

Location of contraceptive devices

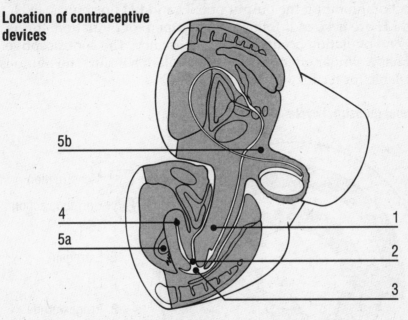

5b

4

5a

1

2

3

Most women change the type of contraceptive they use at least once or twice during their lives.

Before children If a woman is having only intermittent heterosexual activity, she will probably rely on condoms, or the diaphragm with spermicide. Condoms are the best protection against the spread of sexually transmitted diseases, so women in new relationships or who have multiple partners should use them. Once regular relations are established, many women prefer to use more continuous methods like the Pill.

Family planning Many women take the Pill between having children. Others use an IUD, or (less effectively) diaphragm, or condoms with spermicides. (An IUD can be removed by a doctor when conception is desired.) Some rely on the rhythm method, despite its failure rate.

After having children Once a woman's family is complete, she may either return to a contraceptive that she has tried and liked, or she may at this point decide to be sterilized.

Contraceptive Pill

No other form of contraception has been as revolutionary as 'the Pill'. It is easy to use, reversible, and nearly 100% effective, provided a woman remembers to use it.

The contraceptive pill uses synthetic forms of the hormones estrogen and progesterone, which are produced naturally in the body for a few days in each menstrual cycle, and continuously during pregnancy. In each case, they have the effect of inhibiting the output of FSH and LH hormones. FSH and LH are needed if follicles are to ripen for ovulation: this is why no ovulation occurs during pregnancy. The contraceptive pill has a similar effect; and, as no ovulation occurs, no ovum is available for fertilization by sperm.

Normal menstrual cycle

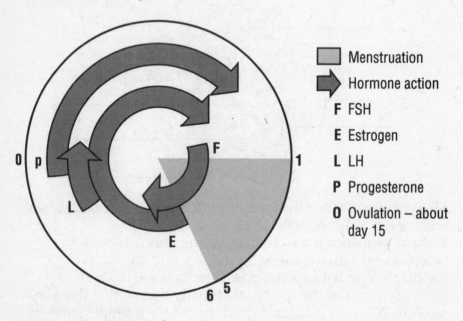

- ▨ Menstruation
- ⇨ Hormone action
- **F** FSH
- **E** Estrogen
- **L** LH
- **P** Progesterone
- **O** Ovulation – about day 15

Types of Pill

The combined pill is the most widely used and effective type. It contains both estrogen and progesterone. The woman takes the standard pill each day for 21 days, starting on the first or fifth day after menstruation, and ending on the 21st or 25th. There is a gap of 7 days, during which withdrawal bleeding occurs; some brands include seven inactive pills to be taken during this period. As well as preventing ovulation, the combined pill affects the uterus lining, so implantation cannot occur; it also causes the cervical mucus to thicken, forming a barrier to sperm.

The continuous mini-pill pack contains 28 pills, all active and all containing synthetic progesterone only. One is taken every day, even during menstruation. They work mainly by their effect on the uterus lining and cervical mucus, rather than by preventing ovulation.

Combined pill cycle

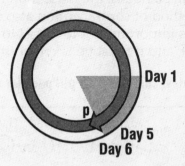

Continuous pill cycle

Day 5	First pill	p Progesterone only
Day 25	Last pill	
e	Estrogen	Menstruation
p	Progesterone	Hormone action

Taking the Pill

The contraceptive pill can be obtained by prescription from your doctor or from a family planning clinic; since there are contra-indications, seek guidance as to whether your medical history shows that it will be suitable for you.

Taking the pill is quite easy; the problem is to remember to do so. Combined pills come in packages of 21 that are labeled with the days of the week to aid memory. The first day of a period counts as day 1. Pill-taking begins on day 1 or day 5, whether bleeding has stopped or not. 'First day start', however, is currently recommended in the United States because the woman is then protected for her entire cycle. It continues until day 21 when the last pill is taken. A gap of 7 pill-free days follows before the next course, during which withdrawal bleeding occurs. For women who have difficulty remembering this sequence, combined pills are available in packs of 28 – the extra pills are dummies.

The progesterone-only mini-pill (also called the continuous mini-pill) comes in packages of 28, all of which are active.

The first package of pills may not give complete protection, and for the first two weeks additional methods of contraception should be used.

If a combined pill is forgotten, it should be taken within 12 hours of the usual time even if it means taking two in one day. If more than two are missed, and the gap between pills is more than 36 hours, the pack should be finished and a second method of contraception also used.

It is important not to forget to take the progesterone-only mini-pill, and it must be taken at the same time every day.

Typical contraceptive pill pack for combined pill

Side Effects

Most women experience some side effects on the contraceptive pill. There may be headaches, nausea, swollen or tender breasts, heavier periods (although menstruation is generally lighter) and vaginal discharge. But not all women experience these, and most symptoms disappear within the first few months. If they do not, a change of brand may alleviate any unpleasant side effects.

No woman should take the contraceptive pill without consulting a doctor. All high-estrogen pills especially carry a risk of blood-clotting. The resulting thrombosis, more likely in women over 35, may be fatal. Other disorders a doctor might consider before prescribing the Pill include heart and circulatory problems, hepatitis, diabetes, migraine and epilepsy. Opinions vary over whether the contraceptive pill increases the risk of breast and cervical cancer, but it appears to protect against cancer of the ovary and the endometrium (uterine lining). Estrogen can aggravate some types of existing cancer. Cervical smears are an important part of the medical examinations that accompany advice about taking the Pill. The length of time a woman should stay on the Pill is a matter of dispute. The average tends to be 3-4 years.

NOTE: Both types of pill can become ineffective if medication is being taken, particularly antibiotics. Also, note that after the age of 35, a woman who smokes is well advised to switch from the pill to another form of contraception.

3

Injectables and implants

Injectable contraceptives and implants are based on similar hormonal principles to those of the Pill. Injectables are used in more than 80 countries, but have not been approved in the United States for use as contraceptives. Implants, such as Norplant, are available for use in the United States; they are inserted under the skin and release progestogen into the bloodstream. They remain effective for 5 years.

Both methods are very effective but they have possible side effects and links with disease. Symptoms may include disruption of menstrual bleeding – perhaps prolonged, heavy, unpredictable, or absent – vomiting, dizziness, moodiness, headaches and weight gain. There are established links with blood-clotting disorders, and unproven ones with breast and cervical cancer (similar to the Pill).

Tests have shown that for every 100 women using implants, fewer than two will get pregnant in a year. This method is most suitable for women who cannot take the contraceptive pill or other methods. Fertility returns once the implants are removed.

Intrauterine Device (IUD)

The IUD, also known as the 'coil' or 'loop', is a small plastic device inserted into the uterus by a doctor. It may be left there for several years, and while in place works as a contraceptive requiring little attention. Intercourse can occur without restriction. Once the IUD is removed, fertility returns in 1-12 months. Comparable practices date back to biblical times, when camel drivers inserted pebbles into the uteruses of

female camels to keep them from becoming pregnant.
How an IUD works is uncertain. Theories are that an IUD
makes the ovum pass down the Fallopian tube too rapidly for
either fertilization or implantation; that it interferes with the
lining of the uterus, so that implantation cannot take place; and
that it interferes directly with the implantation process.
The IUD is very effective while in place, though some doctors
advise the use of a spermicide as well around the time of
ovulation. But it may fall out, especially during the first few
months or at menstruation, in which case it will need to be
reinserted by a professional. Tampons can be used with the
device in place; there is no effect on lovemaking.

Types of IUD

IUDs come in a number of shapes and sizes. The International
Planned Parenthood Federation now recommends the more
effective copper-bearing IUDs, eg Copper T 380A, Multilock
375, and Copper T 220C. Renewal is advised every 2-3 years.
The dominant IUD in the United States is Copper T 380A and
it is a highly effective method of contraception. It is approved
for use for up to 8 years.

Types of IUD

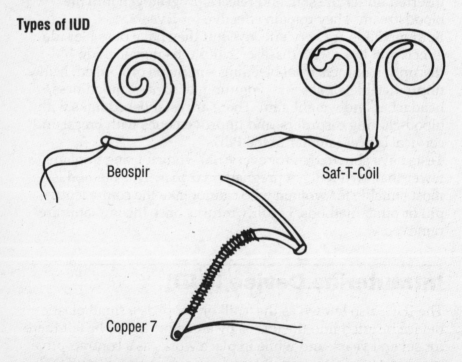

Beospir

Saf-T-Coil

Copper 7

Inserting an IUD

An IUD must only be fitted by a trained person. It is packed in
a thin plastic inserter, which may be passed without difficulty

through the cervix into the uterus (1). This is easiest during or just after menstruation. The IUD is pushed though the inserter and takes up its normal shape inside the uterus (2). This takes only a few minutes. Some women experience discomfort similar to heavy period pain, which can last for 24 hours with some slight bleeding.

The IUD has nylon threads (or a stem projection) left hanging through the cervix into the vagina (3). As a result, a woman can – and should – regularly check to ensure it is still in place.

3

Inserting an IUD

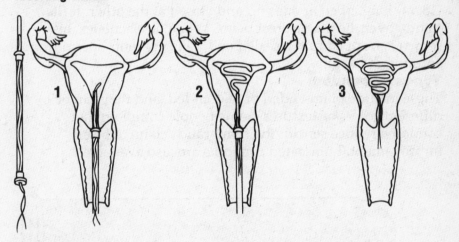

1   2   3

Side effects

Many women experience side effects of heavy periods and/or pain. IUDs may aggravate infection, or (rarely) cause it. There is also a slight risk of perforation of the uterine wall. If pregnancy does occur, the IUD should be removed; it increases the risk of miscarriage. It is generally recommended that only women who are known to be fertile (who have children), a monogamous relationship, and no history of pelvic infection use the IUD.

In the past twenty years, the use of IUDs has come under fire. The incidence of pelvic inflammatory disease (PID) is twice as high among IUD-users as among nonusers, and is highest of all in women who have had no children. In its mild form, PID can be treated with antibiotics and the removal of the IUD. Severe cases may result in sterility; surgery may be required. As a result, IUDs have fallen out of favor in the United States and manufacturers have withdrawn some products from the market.

Condoms

The condom (also known as a 'sheath', 'rubber', and 'French letter') is still probably the most widely used contraceptive. It has a long history dating back hundreds of years, popular mainly as a protection against sexually transmitted disease and now widely recommended as a protection against AIDS. Therefore, use it along with any other forms of contraception, particularly in new relationships. When used carefully, preferably with a spermicide, it is an effective method of birth control. The condom consists of a thin rubber sheath, about 7in (18cm) long, open at one end and closed at the other. It fits tightly over the man's erect penis. When he ejaculates, his semen is trapped in the sealed end. This prevents sperm from entering the vagina.

Types of condom

These include plain-ended or teat-ended, and they can be of different colors or textures. Some people complain that condoms reduce sensitivity; thin brands claim to be an improvement. Lubricated condoms are also available.

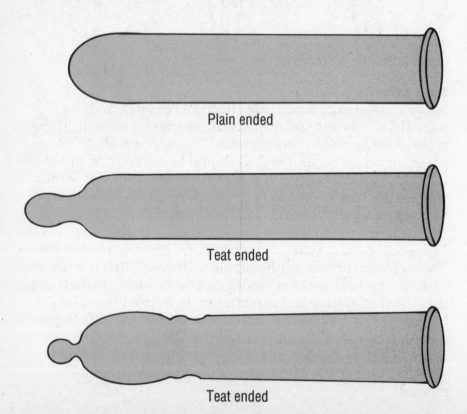

Plain ended

Teat ended

Teat ended

Using a condom

The condom is taken out of the packet rolled up, and is unrolled onto the erect penis just before intercourse. (This can be incorporated into lovemaking.)

At least 1in (2.5cm) at the tip should be left empty of air to help prevent bursting or leakage. After ejaculation, the man withdraws his penis before erection subsides. While withdrawing, he should hold the condom so that it does not come off.

3

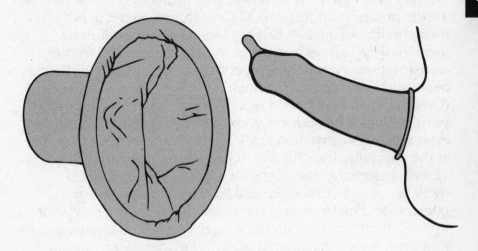

For easier insertion when a condom is used, a woman should use spermicidal cream or jelly, which also gives extra contraceptive effectiveness. Condoms are popular because they do not need medical supervision, and can be obtained and carried around easily. They are sold in sealed packets with a maximum shelf-life of 2 years, away from heat. Disadvantages of the method are that condoms must be readily available and they require the couple to interrupt lovemaking.

The female condom

This bag is inserted into the vagina before intercourse to prevent semen from touching the cervix or vaginal walls. It is held in place using rings. Used correctly it should give protection against pregnancy and sexually transmitted diseases.

Several new female condoms have been developed; one is a latex panty with a built-in 'condom'.

The Rhythm Method

With this method, a couple do not have intercourse during the part of the woman's menstrual cycle during which she can conceive, ie when a fertilizable egg is available. The menstrual cycle lasts (in principle) 28 days. During this, the egg is available for fertilization for only about 1 day – the 24 hours that follow ovulation. However, there is no direct sign of ovulation, only of menstruation. Ovulation typically occurs halfway between the menstruations – on about the 15th day. So a woman can count forward 14 days from the start of her last menstruation to guess when ovulation will occur. But the menstrual cycle is seldom perfectly regular. In most women, menstruation is erratic when periods return after the birth of a baby, and in a quarter of women it is always fairly erratic. (Other women may have a record of regular menstruation for years, followed by sudden, unexpected irregularity.) Also, even where menstruation is regular, ovulation need not occur at the midpoint, the 15th day. It can occur anywhere from 16 to 12 days before the start of the next menstruation. In fact, ovulation is sometimes induced by the stimulus of sexual intercourse. Finally, sperm can live in the woman's cervix for up to 72 hours and sometimes longer – so even if intercourse is four days before ovulation it may on rare occasions cause conception. Therefore the 'calendar rhythm method'– just based on dates – is not very effective, even if several days are kept free from intercourse around the likely date of ovulation. The 'temperature rhythm method' is better. A woman normally has a sudden rise of about 1°F (0.6°C) in body temperature during the day of ovulation, due to increased progesterone production. Use of a thermometer and a record chart should show this rise. By the time the temperature rise is actually recorded, the possible fertilization period is usually over. (Also the action of the progesterone makes the cervical mucus unfavorable to sperm penetration.) This gives a 'safe period' after ovulation, from the temperature rise up to (and including, if desired) the next menstruation. But it gives no safe period after menstruation since there is no way of telling when the next ovulation will occur. Another rhythm method involves examining the cervical mucus, the presence of which suggests an unsafe period for intercourse. Between menstruation and ovulation, only the calendar and mucus methods give any indication of safety.

Temperature Rhythm Method

The temperature should be taken first thing on waking, before any activity (even getting out of bed). A rectal thermometer is more accurate than an oral one.

The circle shows the pattern of temperature during the menstrual cycle. Low temperatures are at the outside, high at the center. There is an abrupt rise at ovulation (about day 14).

3

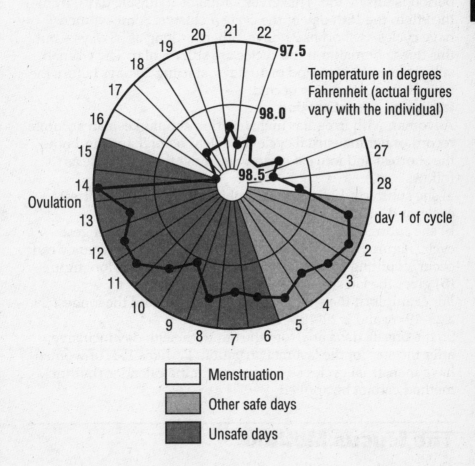

Temperature in degrees Fahrenheit (actual figures vary with the individual)

Ovulation

day 1 of cycle

☐ Menstruation

▨ Other safe days

■ Unsafe days

Calendar Rhythm Method

Regular menstruation

Suppose a woman had menstruation regularly every 28 days. Ovulation would be most likely on the 15th day of the cycle, but could happen anytime from the 13th to the 17th – a period of 5 days. Since sperm can live 72 hours and even longer, 4 days before this are also unsafe. And since the egg may still be fertilizable 24 hours after ovulation, the day after the 5-day period is unsafe too. This gives a total of 10 unsafe days, from the 9th to the 18th day of the cycle inclusive. Some women have cycles as short as 21 days, others as long as 38 days – but this does not matter if the cycles are still regular. The woman still abstains for a period of 10 days, starting 20 days before the next menstruation is expected.

Irregular menstruation

A woman with irregular menstruation should keep an accurate record of her menstrual cycle for a year beforehand, and note the shortest and longest cycles. She must then calculate as follows:

a) she subtracts 19 from the number of days in her shortest cycle; and

b) she subtracts 10 from the number of days in her longest cycle. Figure (**a**) gives the earliest day on which pregnancy can occur, counting from the start of the last menstruation; figure (**b**) gives the latest.

For example, if the shortest cycle is 25 days, and the longest 29: **a** 25–19=6; and **b** 29–10 = 19.

So the unsafe days are from the 6th to the 19th day inclusive, after the start of the last menstruation. Perhaps 15% of women have menstrual cycles so irregular that the calendar rhythm method cannot be applied.

The Mucus Method

There are changes in the nature and quantity of cervical mucus during the menstrual cycle. Take a mucus sample by inserting a finger or speculum into the vagina. For up to three days after menstruation has ceased, normally no mucus is produced – these are fairly safe days. When mucus starts to appear it is thick and cloudy, then more profuse and thin for about 2 days (peak days). Days from the first signs of mucus until 4 days after the peak days are unsafe. Consult a doctor on how to use this method.

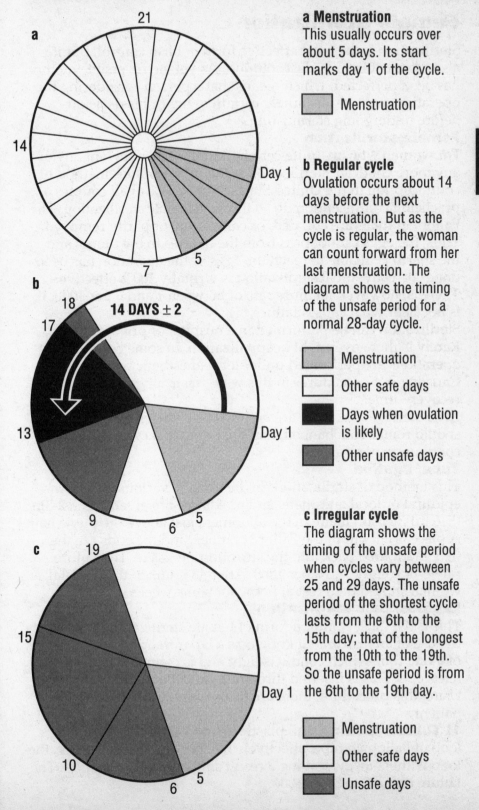

a Menstruation
This usually occurs over about 5 days. Its start marks day 1 of the cycle.

[ ] Menstruation

b Regular cycle
Ovulation occurs about 14 days before the next menstruation. But as the cycle is regular, the woman can count forward from her last menstruation. The diagram shows the timing of the unsafe period for a normal 28-day cycle.

[ ] Menstruation

[ ] Other safe days

[ ] Days when ovulation is likely

[ ] Other unsafe days

c Irregular cycle
The diagram shows the timing of the unsafe period when cycles vary between 25 and 29 days. The unsafe period of the shortest cycle lasts from the 6th to the 15th day; that of the longest from the 10th to the 19th. So the unsafe period is from the 6th to the 19th day.

[ ] Menstruation

[ ] Other safe days

[ ] Unsafe days

Female Sterilization

Sterilization is the most effective form of birth control. But it is also the most final – a last solution. As yet, no reversible method has been perfected, which means that a person considering the operation must be absolutely certain of her or his decision before undergoing sterilization.

Female sterilization

For women who are quite certain that they do not want any or any more children, sterilization is the most popular method of contraception in the United States. About 33% of all couples practicing contraception do so through female sterilization. The Fallopian tubes are cut, tied, or completely or partly removed. Thus, the eggs cannot pass from the ovaries to the uterus and the sperm is unable to reach the eggs. If the operation has been done correctly, tubal sterilization is virtually 100% effective. There is, however, a failure rate of between 1 and 6 per 1000. It is not clear what causes failure.

Sterilization can be performed in a hospital or private clinics. Rarely is there overnight hospitalization. In some centers, operations are performed under local anesthetic with sedation. Carrying out procedures in this way drastically shortens recovery time.

After sterilization, there are no obvious changes. Sexual interest should remain unchanged, and the menstrual cycle should continue as normal.

Tubal ligation

This method of sterilization can be done in various ways. An epidural or local anesthetic and a sedative are given and a 2-3in (5-7cm) incision made in the abdomen, just above the pubic hair. A piece is cut out of the Fallopian tubes, and the ends are then tied and folded back into the surrounding tissue. The failure rate is currently 1 to 2 per 1000. After 48 hours in the hospital, a woman should then rest at home for some weeks.

Laparoscopic sterilization

This is the most common form of female sterilization. It involves the use of an instrument known as a laparoscope, which consists of a fine tube which conducts light and is connected to a telescope. This is inserted through a small cut in the abdomen. Using this procedure, there are three ways to sterilize the patient:

1) Tubal banding Small plastic bands are placed around a loop of Fallopian tube, effectively blocking it off. Eventually, the loop withers away, leaving a result similar to tubal ligation. The failure rate is 2 to 3 per 1000.

2) Tubal cautery Fine forceps are inserted and an electrocurrent is passed along them to cauterize the tubes. The failure rate is 2 to 3 per 1000.

3) Tubal clipping Clips are placed across part of the tube, blocking it. Here, the failure rate is 2 to 6 per 1000; but the advantage is that sterilization is more easily reversed. Only two tiny scars will remain and the recovery time is very short.

Laparoscopic sterilization

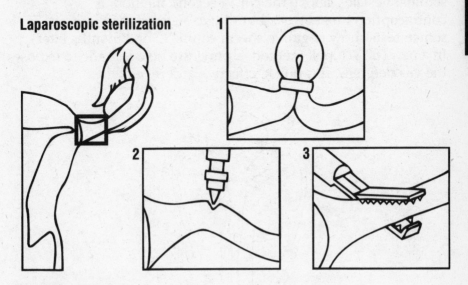

Hysterectomy

Until quite recently, a hysterectomy – which involves the complete removal of the uterus (see p.399) – was a fairly widespread means of sterilization. However, it is not now generally recommended for birth-control purposes, though it is an operation that many women have to undergo for other reasons (see pp.399-406).

Male Sterilization

Vasectomy

A vasectomy is a safe, simple surgery in which the vas deferens – the duct leading from each testis to the penis – is cut and tied off. As a result, the semen a man ejects no longer contains sperm. Unless the cut tubes have rejoined, the operation is always completely effective. It does not alter a man's ability to have an orgasm or to ejaculate. But the operation is reversible in only 50% of men, so a man and his partner must be absolutely sure before undergoing a vasectomy.

The operation lasts for under half an hour. Usually, only a local anesthetic is needed. Either one or two very small cuts are made on or near the scrotum. A piece about 1^1/$_2$in (3.8cm) long is removed from each duct; the cut ends are then folded back and tied. The man returns home, and resumes normal life in 2 or 3 days. After-effects may be soreness and bruising. It is not immediately effective; there are usually sperm stored in the seminal vesicles, above the cut. A second method of contraception must be used until two successive follow-up semen tests show negative sperm counts (2 or 3 months later). In a new 'no-scalpel' method, a puncture hole is made to expose the vas deferens; it is quick, effective and reversible.

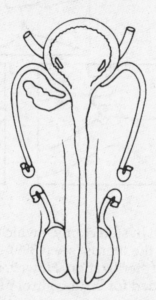

Withdrawal

Withdrawal (or *coitus interruptus*) is the oldest and simplest method of birth control. The man takes his penis out of the woman's vagina just before his orgasm. His semen is ejaculated outside her body. Used with great care, withdrawal may be effective, but only if every drop of semen is not only kept out of the vagina but also right away from the vaginal lips. It is impossible to be sure of this because:
a) some fluid containing live sperm may 'weep' from the penis before orgasm; and
b) in the pleasure of orgasm, the man may not withdraw properly. Continued use of withdrawal can also be frustrating. The woman in particular may not be able to relax through fear that the man may not withdraw.

Spermicides

These are chemical products which are inserted into the woman's vagina before sexual intercourse. They act in 2 ways: by killing the sperm and by creating a barrier of foam or fluid through which sperm cannot pass into the uterus. Spermicides come in various forms: creams, jellies, aerosol foams, foaming tablets, suppositories, and C-film, a spermicide-impregnated plastic. Used by themselves, none of these is a reliable contraceptive. Each should be combined with another method, such as the diaphragm or the condom.

Creams, jellies, and aerosols are sold with a special applicator. Using this, the woman squirts the chemical high up into her vagina. This should be done as near to intercourse as possible, and certainly no more than one hour before, as effectiveness is only temporary. Suppositories and tablets come in solid form and must be inserted by hand deep into the vagina.

Suppositories are cone shaped and melt at body temperature; tablets dissolve and foam in the vagina's moisture. Both should be inserted 15 minutes before intercourse.

The new C-film consists of a small square of soluble plastic which can either be inserted into the vagina or placed on the tip of the man's penis before it enters the vagina. It dissolves, releasing spermicide, but is no more reliable than other spermicides (and less so than some).

Some women find that spermicides irritate their genitals.

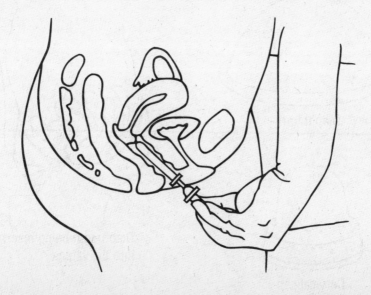

The Diaphragm and Caps

Diaphragm

The diaphragm is the best known of the female barrier methods. It is a domelike rubber device that fits across a woman's cervix. Its rim contains a coiled spring. By itself the cap is not particularly safe, but used carefully in conjunction with spermicides it is quite effective. For most women before the Pill was introduced, the diaphragm was the safest method of contraception available to them.

Putting a diaphragm in place is not very difficult, though at first it needs practice. The woman holds its edges together and pushes it by hand into the vagina so that the bottom edge rests against the vaginal wall behind the bladder. The spring causes the diaphragm to regain its circular shape so that it is held in place against the cervix. Before insertion, spermicidal cream or jelly should be squeezed onto the inside and around the rim of the diaphragm. It should be put into the vagina not more than 2-3 hours before intercourse, and it should be left in place for at least 6 hours after intercourse while the sperm die. If intercourse occurs again in that time, more spermicide should first be put into the vagina without disturbing the diaphragm; it must stay in place for 6-8 hours longer.

Diaphragms vary in size. An initial fitting by a doctor or nurse

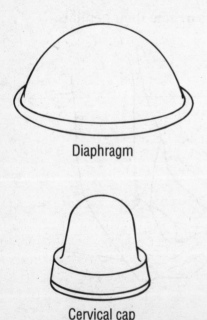

Diaphragm

Cervical cap

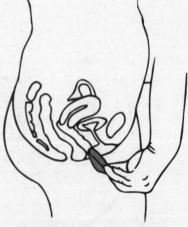

Diaphragm being inserted into the vagina

is essential, and its fit should be checked every 6 months, after a pregnancy, and if more than 10lb (4.5kg) is gained or lost in weight. It must be washed after use, according to instructions, and checked carefully for holes.

Caps

There are several types of contraceptive cap. Each fits over the cervix and is held there by suction; all are used with spermicide. The cervical cap is shaped like a thimble; the vault cap is shaped more like a bowl and is more rigid. As with the diaphragm, the cap must be professionally fitted.

Sponge

The disposable contraceptive sponge acts both as a cervical barrier and as a source of spermicide. One side of the sponge has a dimple to fit against the cervix, the other a loop of nylon to grasp for removal; it is soaked with spermicide. It is available without prescription. It is less effective than the diaphragm, and it is an expensive method because each sponge can only be used once.

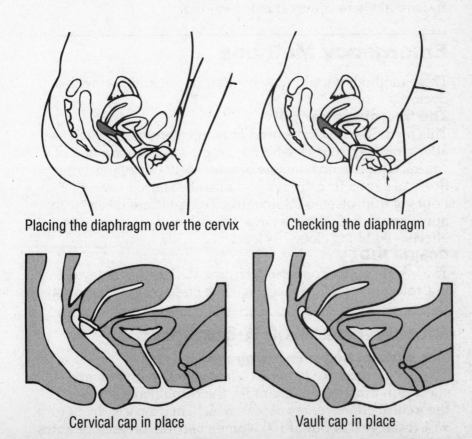

Placing the diaphragm over the cervix   Checking the diaphragm

Cervical cap in place   Vault cap in place

Unsatisfactory Methods

Breastfeeding

If a woman breastfeeds 'on demand', lactation is sometimes an effective method of contraception as long as she has not resumed menstruating, but it should not be relied on. It becomes less effective if the mother does not breastfeed on demand or regulates and lengthens the time between feedings.

Douching

Douching – washing out the vagina after intercourse – is a completely ineffective method of birth control. Not only can sperm reach the cervix within 90 seconds, but fluid squirted into the vagina could help the sperm on their way.

No orgasm

It was once believed that if a woman did not have an orgasm, she would not conceive. This is untrue; many women do not have orgasms but become pregnant.

American or Grecian tips

These short rubber condoms fit over the tip of the penis only. It is claimed that they increase sensitivity, but they fail to do so and are likely to come off in the vagina.

Emergency Methods

These methods should only be used in consultation with a doctor.

The 'morning after pill'

This method tends to be used only in emergencies, such as after a rape or in cases where a couple's normal method of contraception is unavailable or has failed. It contains large doses of synthetic estrogen and must be started within 72 hours of unprotected intercourse. Two pills are taken twelve hours apart. It is 98% effective; the risk of dangerous side effects – eg blood clots – is low.

Copper IUD

The insertion of a copper-containing IUD within 5 days of unprotected intercourse can achieve effective contraception.

Effectiveness of Techniques

The odds of becoming pregnant

There is a difference between effectiveness in theory and success in practice. For example, the combined pill has a theoretical effectiveness of 99% which, in practice, drops to 96% (each year, 4 out of 100 women become pregnant). Rates of success can be improved for less effective methods by using them with the withdrawal or rhythm methods. In this way, the diaphragm's effectiveness can be increased from 85% to over 90%. Frequency of intercourse also affects the reliability of barrier methods of contraception.

Reliability of contraceptive methods

Pregnancies per 1000 women
Vasectomy ● 1
Tubal ligation ●○○ 1-3

Pregnancies per 100 women in one year

With careful use		With less careful use, where applicable
1 ●	combined pill	●●● 3+
1 ●	progesterone-only pill	●●●● 4+
1 ●	injections	
1 ●	implant*	
1-2 ○●	IUD	
2 ●●	condoms	●●○○○○○○○○ 2-15
2 ●●	rhythm methods	●●○○○○○○○○○ 2-20
4-8 ○○○○○●●●	diaphragm and spermicide	●●●●●●○○○○ 10-18
10 ●●●●●●●●●●	sponge	●●●●●●●●●●●●●●●●●●●●●●● 25

In first year of use. Over five years, the life of the implant, the rate rises to 2 per 100 women.

Recent Developments

Research continues into alternative contraceptives. Some of these are based on concepts already in use: sex hormones to inhibit ovulation or barrier methods. The contraceptive vaginal ring (CVR) slowly releases the hormone 'levonorgestrel' (the ring is removed before menstruation). The intracervical device is mushroom shaped, blocking the entry of sperm, but a valve allows menstrual flow to exit.

The hormone inhibin may form the basis of a unisex pill. Much work remains to be done in assessing all these new methods.

PREGNANCY

4

Events in Pregnancy

At some stage in their lives most women experience the desire to have children. But it need no longer be the unplanned, haphazard process that it once was. Today a woman can decide first whether to have children, and if so, when.

But for women embarking on their first pregnancy, fear of the unknown is still a common emotion. Probably no other event causes as much apprehension and anxiety. For a woman to avoid this it is important for her to understand what is happening to her body and to her unborn child during the 9 months of pregnancy and the birth. This chapter describes the stages from fertilization to labor, including possible problems.

Fertilization and implantation

After sexual intercourse one male sperm fertilizes a female egg. A week later this attaches itself to the lining of the uterus and the embryo starts shaping into a minuscule human being.

Embryo to fetus

By the 8th week the embryo is recognizably human. Now termed a fetus, during the next 7 months its organs will increase 120 times in weight.

Pregnancy

The absence of menstruation is the first sign for most women. Other changes follow such as morning sickness, breast enlargement and swelling of the abdomen. Good prenatal care aims to prevent any complications and to ensure the good health of mother and child.

Birth

For many women this is the most alarming aspect of pregnancy. Relaxation and an understanding of the stages of labor and delivery help to make childbirth easier and allow a woman greater participation.

Complications and risks

Complications may be unavoidable, eg miscarriage. But some risk factors that may affect the unborn child, such as smoking, can be controlled by the mother.

The timetable on the following pages gives a rough guide to certain milestones and occasional problems in pregnancy. Some events relate to the mother-to-be, while others involve the development of the fetus.

Detailed developmental changes in mother and child appear on pp.114-5 and 118-19.

Most people think of pregnancy lasting 9 months. But calendar months vary in length. Our chart irons out these variations by showing a time span of 40 weeks. These can be divided into nine 31-day months (279 days) or ten 28-day (lunar) months. Traditionally, most doctors use lunar months for pregnancy calculations, dating the onset of pregnancy from the first day of the last menstrual period, despite the fact that conception occurs about 14 days later. Some dates shown are only approximate. There are large variations in the timing and even appearance or no appearance of certain signs or symptoms. One factor that especially affects some variations is whether the mother-to-be is expecting her first baby or a second or subsequent child.

The baby in the uterus (below left) showing position of surrounding organs at nine months of pregnancy as compared with the nonpregnant state (below right):

4

a Trachea	**f** Stomach	**k** Umbilical cord
b Heart	**g** Kidney	**l** Fetus
c Lung	**h** Placenta	**m** Uterus
d Liver	**i** Large intestine	**n** Cervix
e Diaphragm	**j** Small intestine	**o** Bladder
		p Pubic bone
		q Urethra
		r Anus
		s Vagina

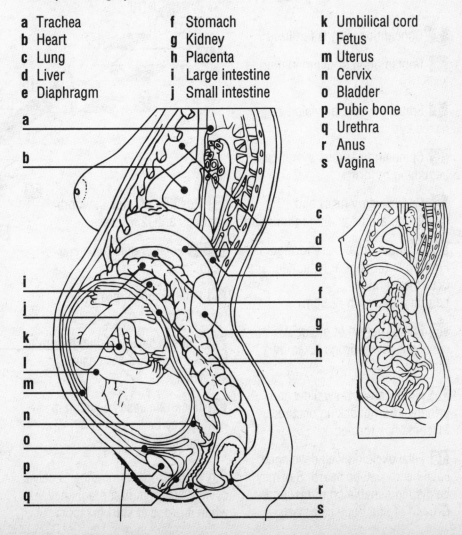

Events in pregnancy

|0| Start of last menstruation

|1-2| Intercourse

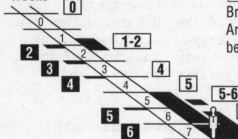

Weeks

|4| 1st missed period

|5| Urine test can reveal pregnancy (12 days after 1st missed period)

|5-6| Veins may be prominent. Breasts may be soft and enlarged. Areolae (areas around nipples) may be darker and show milk ducts

|2| Conception: egg is fertilized

|3| Implantation of ovum in uterine wall

|4| Embryo would be visible to naked eye

|5| Spine and nervous system are beginning to form

|6| Rudimentary heart and circulation are beginning to function

|8| All main organs are formed. Embryo is recognizably human, and is termed a fetus.
Length approx 1in (2.5cm)

|12| End of period of greatest susceptibility to drugs taken by mother

|14| Fetus can now swallow and urinate. Thumbsucking occurs. Placenta has formed

|16| Fetal skeleton well developed. Fetal heart may be heard. Sex may be distinguishable on ultrasound. Growth of fine body hair starts

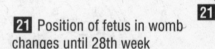

|21| Position of fetus in womb changes until 28th week

|22-24| Fetal eyelids open and hands grip

|25| Fetal length approx 13in (32cm)

|28| Fetus is legally viable. If born at this stage it has a 5% chance of survival

|34| In certain cases position in womb may be corrected by manipulation

|36| Head drops into mother's pelvic cavity (except in first pregnancy, when it drops at start of labor)

6-7 Morning sickness may begin. Gums may soften. Stretch marks may appear on breasts

8 Physical diagnosis of pregnancy possible (enlarged womb, soft cervix)

9 Fluid (colostrum) may be squeezed from breasts

10 Doctor can feel contractions of the womb

12 Morning sickness usually stops now

15 Pigmentation of breasts may occur. In dark women, a line may be seen from navel to pubic bone

16 Abdominal protrusion of womb visible. Craving for unusual foods sometimes occurs in later pregnancy

17-20 Mother may feel fetus moving (sometimes called "quickening")

24 Womb may now be felt at navel

29 Average increases
weight 19lb
breasts 14oz
heartbeat 14,000 per day

30 Navel begins to flatten

35 Ribs spread out to accommodate lungs displaced by uterus. Possible pains from trapped nerves. Traveling should be curtailed

36 Womb moves up to the ribs. The mother has to lean back to keep balance; but the level of the womb may drop ("lightening"); bladder irritability can recur. Uterine contractions increase in frequency. Gynecologist may have mother X-rayed if a contracted pelvis is suspected and likely to cause problems at birth

40 Uterus contracts rhythmically to produce labor pains; membranes in womb rupture and discharge

⚕ Visits to doctor or prenatal clinic

■ Week of pregnancy

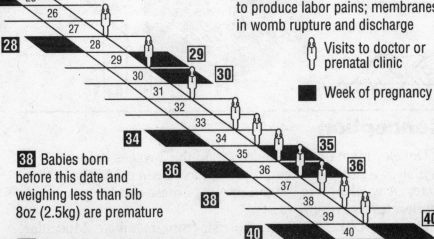

38 Babies born before this date and weighing less than 5lb 8oz (2.5kg) are premature

40 Baby is born. Approx length 20in (50cm). Weight 7½lb (3.4kg)

Ejaculation

Ejaculation

Sperm have more than 1ft (0.3m) to travel before reaching the female vagina. At ejaculation muscular contractions in the testes (**g**), epididymides (**h**), and along the vas deferens (**a**) propel the sperm toward the penis. On their way they mix with the seminal fluid secreted from the seminal vesicles (**c**) and prostate (**b**). The resulting semen is then propelled through the urethra (**e**) into the woman's vagina (**f**, **d**).

Sperm production

Sperm cells are formed inside the testes at a rate of about 200 million a day. While developing, they are stored in the epididymides. Each sperm is about 1/500th of an inch long, and takes 60 to 72 days to mature. By contrast, in a woman just one mature egg is produced a month.

The diagram shows the expulsion of semen from the male sex organs at ejaculation.

a Vas deferens
b Prostate gland
c Seminal vesicle
d Cervix
e Urethra
f Vagina
g Testes
h Epididymides

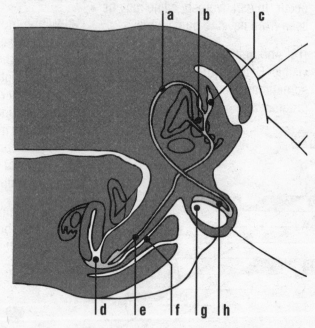

Conception

1) Development of the female egg. In the 2 weeks before ovulation a number of egg follicles have been maturing in the ovary. A week before ovulation one of these suddenly accelerates its growth.

2) Ovulation. The mature egg bursts from its follicle. Muscular contractions propel it along the Fallopian tube. If not fertilized within 24-48 hours, the egg will degenerate.

3) Intercourse takes place. About 400 million sperm are ejaculated by the man into the woman's vagina. Of these, only one sperm will fertilize the ovum. The sperm travel fast, possibly covering 1in (2.5cm) in 8 minutes; also muscular spasms may aid them.

4) The sperm arrive at the cervix. The seminal fluid has liquefied, and about half the original sperm have died in the acidic conditions of the vagina. The remainder pass through the cervical mucus. Normally a barrier to sperm, at ovulation the mucus can be easily penetrated.

5) Sperm reach the top of the uterus. There are possibly only 6000 of the original number left, but it has taken them well under an hour to arrive. About half the sperm now turn into the wrong Fallopian tube.

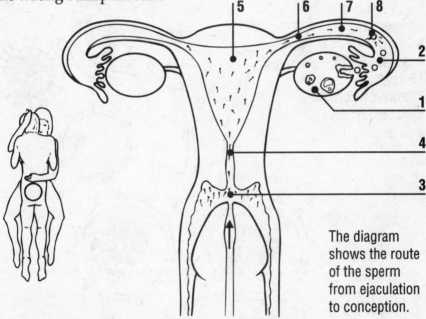

The diagram shows the route of the sperm from ejaculation to conception.

6) Remaining sperm swim into the top of the Fallopian tube that contains the matured female ovum. Conditions are favorable and sperm may survive here for up to 72 hours. Should ovulation not have taken place, sperm can therefore wait for a newly developed ovum to arrive.

7) A few hundred sperm complete their journey along the Fallopian tube to the female ovum. Enzymes released by the sperm heads now break down the ovum's outer wall.

8) Fertilization. One sperm penetrates the ovum. The cell wall immediately hardens, preventing other sperm from entering, and the nuclei of the two cells fuse together: a new human life is conceived.

The First Four Weeks

The diagrams represent the process of fertilization and
development during the first four weeks of life. The path of the
ovum, from fertilization to implantation in the uterus, is traced
with an enlarged cross-section of the various stages of
development.

1 Fertilization **2** First cell division, 1 day
3 Morula stage, 4 days **4** Blastocyst stage,
7 days. Implantation occurs at this stage
5 Internal cells differentiate, 10 days.
At this stage nourishment is drawn
by diffusion from
the uterus by the
chorionic villi (**a**)
6 Embryo (**b**)
and yolk sac (**c**),
15 days
7 Umbilical cord (**d**)
develops, 20 days
8 25 days

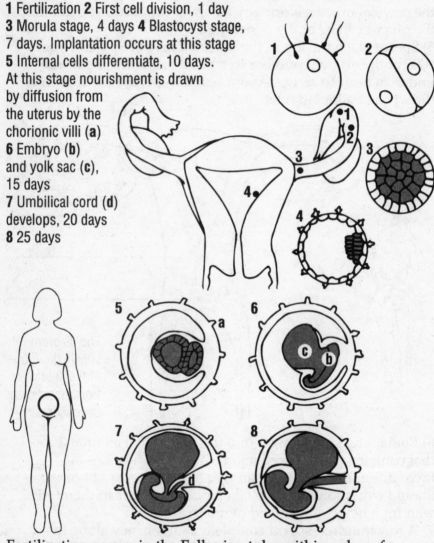

Fertilization occurs in the Fallopian tube within a day of
ovulation (see pp.25 and 104-05). There may be as many as
100,000 sperm in the Fallopian tube, or as few as 100.
But more than one sperm is needed to produce enzymes to
break down the ovum's wall. The nuclei fuse (1) and the ovum
wall hardens, preventing the entry of other sperm.

Soon after fertilization the ovum begins to divide, first into two (2), then into four, and so on. The first division takes about 24 hours. Subsequent divisions take less time. The small bundle of cells, now called a morula, looks like a mulberry (3). The ovum at this point will normally be about to enter the uterine cavity. Helped by a little uterine fluid, the cells of the morula are separated by a small space. The outer cells flatten into cellular wall, the trophoblast, and the remaining cluster of cells, the blastocyst, moves to one side (4). The amniotic sac, placenta, and fetus develop from these cells. By about the 7th day, small projections, the chorionic villi, will have formed on the trophoblast. These burrow into the uterine wall. The embryo undergoes continual cell differentiation (5-8).

Cell differentiation takes place with each cell division. Thus this is a vital stage of development. Seemingly disproportionate repercussions, ie the stunted growth of an organ of the body, can occur from the damage or loss of one cell alone. Implantation in the uterus establishes a basis of embryonic nutrition. After about 18 days, the nervous system begins to form and it continues to develop until a few weeks after birth. By the end of the first month, the embryo is about 4mm long, about the size of a tapioca grain, with millions of cells intricately organized to carry out specific functions. A primitive heart is now formed. The embryo is already 10,000 times bigger than the original ovum.

4

Implantation

The enlarged sections of the blastocyst (below) show how it burrows into the uterine wall (endometrium).

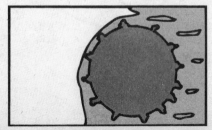

Multiple Fertilization

Since the advent of fertility drugs, multiple births have become increasingly common. The drug, which stimulates the growth of follicles, may cause the release of more than one ovum from the ovary. A single ovum may also split 3, 4 or 5 times – still utilizing a single placenta, as in the case of identical twins. Triplets, quads, and quins may develop from 3, 4, and 5 ova, with 3, 4 and 5 placentae, and 3, 4 and 5 amniotic sacs respectively. But other combinations can, and do, occur: eg triplets may be the product of one ovum plus one that has split, as in identical twins. Quads may be the result of two split ova, or of two single ova plus one split one. The sharing of the placenta is dependent upon whether or not the ovum has split. On rare occasions when the uterus is stretched to its ultimate capacity, the same amniotic sac may be shared.

Identical twins

Identical twins are the result of one ovum splitting soon after fertilization. (Siamese twins are the product of a splitting

Nonidentical twins
with separate
placenta

Identical twins,
sharing the same
placenta

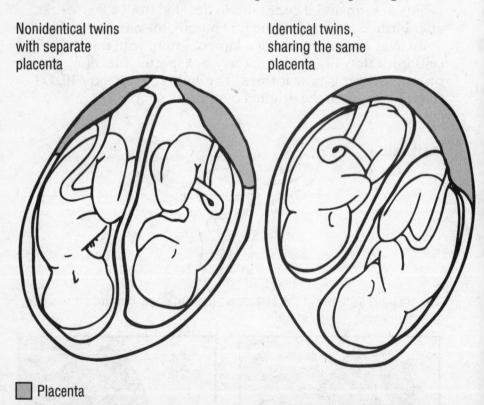

☐ Placenta

which for some reason has been arrested before completion.)
The fetuses lie within separate sacs of amniotic fluid, though
they share the same placenta. The latter means that they will be
of the same blood group. The splitting of the ovum means that
they will share the same genetic structure, ie be of the same sex
with very similar features, hair, etc.

Nonidentical twins

Nonidentical twins are the result of two ova being fertilized by
two sperm. Thus they may or may not be of the same sex,
blood group, etc. They will only share the general
resemblances of any two children born of the same parents.
Multiple births tend to be a trait inherited and carried by
women rather than men, ie the tendency to release more than
one ovum from the ovary is an exclusively female distinction.

4

Implantation Problems

If the fertilized egg does not reach the uterus within seven
days the tiny armlike protrusions (chorionic villi) which will
have formed by then will burrow into the wall of the Fallopian
tube. The latter will become sorely distended as it can only
stretch to a limited extent. The chorionic villi will continue to
burrow into the wall in search of nourishment – which is
obviously restricted. Eventually they will break through the
muscular wall or into an artery causing bleeding, pain, and the
loss of the embryo. (Surgery is always necessary.)
Occasionally, however, the embryo will escape into the cavity
of the abdomen, and the chorionic villi will burrow into the
wall where eventually a placenta will develop. Healthy babies
which have developed within the abdomen have occasionally
been delivered (by cesarian section). Ectopic pregnancies are
not uncommon, and since the same hormones are secreted as
in a normal pregnancy, causing the naturally anticipated
reactions, they are not always detected until discomfort is felt.
One in every ten women who have had an ectopic pregnancy
is liable to have another. They are often due to prior
inflammation of the Fallopian tube (see also p.128).

The Uterus

The tiny embryo has embedded itself in the wall of the uterus. Up to the 8th week, the uterus contains the growth without enlarging. Between the 4th and 8th weeks of life, the embryo develops from a small limbless object resembling a white kidney bean .15in (4mm) long into a minuscule but complete human being all of 1.5in (40mm) from head to toe.

Vertical section through the uterus 35 days after fertilization.

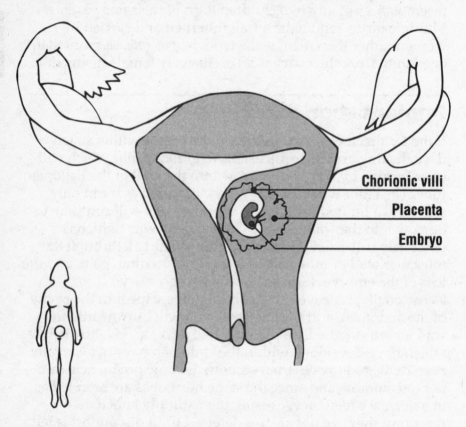

Chorionic villi

Placenta

Embryo

Development of the Embryo

By the end of the first 2 months, the initial formation of the organs is complete. The sex of the embryo is apparent by the 50th day. The embryo starts off as soft tissue. But by the 40th day, the skeleton of cartilage is growing and, by the 45th day, the first bone cells appear. We can follow the development, for example, of the arms, as an external feature, and the heart, as an internal organ.

The arms appear as buds at 30 days. By the 40th day, they differentiate into hands, and lower and upper arms. The fingers are in outline only. By the 50th day, the arms are growing and the fingers have separated. (The legs and feet develop in the same way as the arms but correspondingly later.) The heart continues to form for about 2 months, but at 30-35 days it takes over circulation of the blood, which had hitherto been circulated via the umbilical cord and the placenta.

4

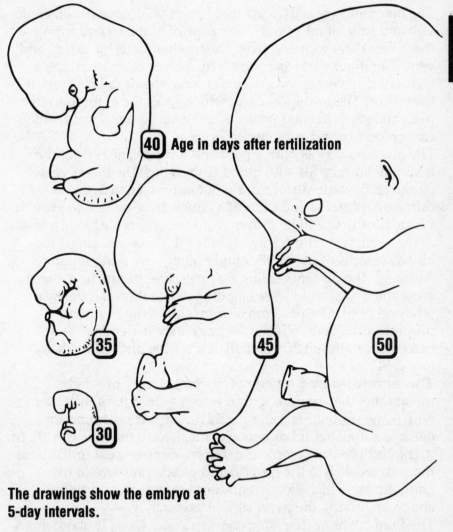

40 **Age in days after fertilization**

35

45

50

30

The drawings show the embryo at 5-day intervals.

The Support System

The placenta develops during the first 10 weeks of life from the spot where chorionic villi first burrowed into the uterine wall. The remaining chorionic villi surrounding the embryo die.

The placenta, which looks like a bath cap roughly 8in (20cm) in diameter, and about 1lb (0.45kg) in weight when fully developed, has a maternal (outer) and embryonic (inner) surface.

The outer surface is divided into roughly 20 lobes of chorionic villi and tiny blood vessels. The flow of blood to and from these vessels is supplied from the mother's uterine artery and vein. The inner surface, covered by a layer of amnion, has a series of tiny vessels radiating out from the umbilical cord at the center. The umbilical cord, which links the embryo to the placenta, supports and protects two arteries and a vein which carry blood to and from the embryo.

The placenta acts as both a pool and a filter. The cells of the maternal surface fill with blood from which the blood vessels on the embryonic surface draw not only oxygen but also, by diffusion, proteins and vitamins which are essential to growth. Waste products will be drawn from the embryo's blood vessels in the same way. But though there is this free exchange, the blood systems of the mother and embryo are quite separate. Although the placenta is largely protective in function, there are some drugs and viruses against which it has no defense (see pp.174-5). The placenta also produces the hormone progesterone, upon which the pregnancy depends. The placenta, or afterbirth, is expelled after the birth of the baby (see p.142).

The amniotic sac (or bag of waters) is a sac of tough membrane, the amnion, within which a fluid (largely water with some protein) is contained. The sac forms around the embryo soon after it has become attached to the uterus wall. In it, the embryo has complete freedom of movement until about the 30th week. It is the growth and gentle pressure of the amniotic sac which slowly enlarges the uterus, and so the abdomen, giving the overt sign of pregnancy.

The fluid cushions the embryo from knocks, etc. It maintains a constant temperature and thus insulates the embryo, providing a level of water-conditioned central heating. It absorbs the waste excreted by the embryo, and is also the medium with which the fetus first learns to swallow.

In cases of multiple birth, each fetus normally develops in its own sac. On average, at the 36th week of pregnancy, the sac contains about 1.9pt (1.1 liters). By the 40th week, however, roughly 1/3 of this will have been lost .

Cross-section through the uterus

a Placenta
b Umbilical cord
c Amniotic fluid
d Amnion

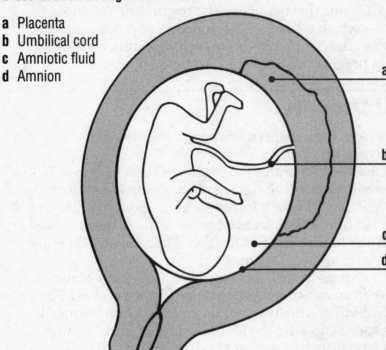

Hormones

At ovulation, the follicle which releases the ovum changes its function to become the corpus luteum, which produces estrogen and progesterone. Estrogen prevents more ova developing, while progesterone prepares the lining of the uterus for a possible implantation (see p.27). When the fertilized ovum implants, it secretes human chorionic gonadotrophin. This maintains the corpus luteum until the placenta – which takes over the function of producing hormones after 3 months – has developed sufficiently to maintain pregnancy.

Fetal Growth

After the sex of the embryo has been determined, it is referred to as a fetus.

During the next 7 months, the organs of the fetus grow. By the time the baby is born, all the organs have increased their weight 120 times. Weight increases from about 1oz (28.3g) at 8 weeks to $7^1/2$lb (3.4kg), on average, at birth. It has increased 5000 million times since fertilization. Over the next 20 years, weight increases only 20 times.

Length increases from 1.5in (40mm) at 8 weeks to 20in (50.8cm), from crown to heel, at birth. It has increased $12^1/2$ times. Growth gradually slows down just before birth, but rapidly speeds up after the first few days of birth. Besides general fetal growth, head and body hair and nails are growing by the 18th week. By the 30th week, fat is deposited under the skin, making it smoother and more rounded, and less red and wrinkled.

Eyelids, which have been growing, close over the eyes in the 9th week, to open again in the 22nd.

On the internal front, at 14 weeks the heart pumps 5pt (2.83 liters) a day. By the 18th week, it can be heard externally by placing an ear on the mother's abdomen. At around 38 weeks, the heart pumps 598pt (340 liters) per day. The total blood content is 0.5pt (0.28 liters).

Muscular reflexes develop on eyelids, palms, and feet, and swallowing reflex starts at the 14th week. Thumbsucking also takes place around this time.

Fetal movements, or 'quickening', can be felt at the 18th week. Urination into the amniotic fluid begins around the 14th week. Premature live birth is possible at 22 weeks, but survival prospects are poor. Births at 24 weeks, though, can often be kept alive in intensive care units, by open-heart surgery and use of special respirators.

4

The fetus from 8 weeks to birth

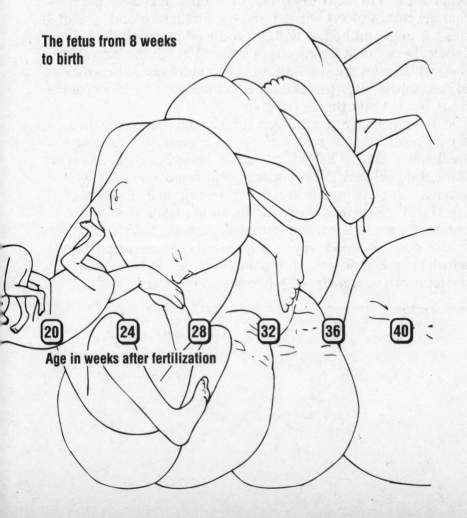

20   **24**   **28**   **32**   **36**   **40**

Age in weeks after fertilization

Rhesus Incompatibility

There are various systems of grouping blood types. Within a system the groups are usually incompatible. If an incompatible group is introduced into the body (ie in blood transfusion), antibodies will be produced to inactivate the influence of the 'foreign' blood type. In the case of blood incompatibility, the consequences can be far-reaching. One system of grouping is called the rhesus system, discovered in experiments on rhesus monkeys in 1940.

Blood is denoted rhesus positive if it contains the rhesus factor. If it does not contain the factor, it is rhesus negative. Most people (85%) are rhesus positive. Normally this is of no consequence; however, problems can arise in pregnancy when a rhesus negative woman is carrying a rhesus positive child. (If the father is rhesus positive, this is likely in three out of four pregnancies.) In the course of labor or birth, it is quite likely that the child's blood will get into the mother's blood system. If this happens, antibodies will be produced in the mother to protect her against the rhesus positive blood of the baby. But these antibodies are small enough, in a subsequent pregnancy, to pass through the placenta, and so inactivate the blood of the fetus, if it is again rhesus positive.

The dangers increase with each subsequent pregnancy. In a severe case, the fetus may suffer from anemia, jaundice, or a weak heart. One in 200 pregnancies is complicated in this way. If the child is likely to be moderately affected, it is usually given a complete transfusion of rhesus negative blood shortly after birth. As there is no rhesus factor in negative blood, no antibodies are formed, and within 40 days the baby's own rhesus positive blood will have replaced the transfused blood, which is broken down as normal in the liver. In serious cases, the fetus can be transfused while still in the uterus.

How rhesus incompatibility works:
a) small amount of fetal rhesus positive blood enters the blood system of the mother, whose own blood is rhesus negative.
b) This causes the mother to produce antibodies to inactivate the rhesus positive blood.
c) During a subsequent pregnancy, the mother's antibodies pass through the fetal rhesus positive blood.

4

+ **Rhesus positive blood of fetus**

○ **Antibodies**

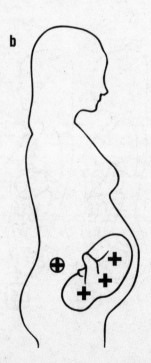

Pregnancy

Signs and symptoms

Usually the first sign of pregnancy is amenorrhea (absence of menstruation – see p.26). But if periods are normally irregular, the time of ovulation is uncertain and so amenorrhea is not a definite diagnosis of pregnancy.

The most noticeable physical manifestation of pregnancy after the 3rd month is the swelling of the abdomen as the uterus expands beyond the pelvis. (The swelling causes stretchmarks which often remain after birth.)

Between the 4th and 5th months, the mother feels the fetal movements ('quickening') for the first time. The sensations are faint at first but get stronger. From the 5th month, the fetal heart can be heard with a stethoscope and fetal movements seen from the outside.

The mother's weight gradually increases (on average by between 25 and 30lb – about $11^{1}/_{2}$ to $13^{1}/_{2}$kg). She will begin to feel tired because of her shape and size, and so become lethargic, increasingly so toward the end of pregnancy.

Pregnancy

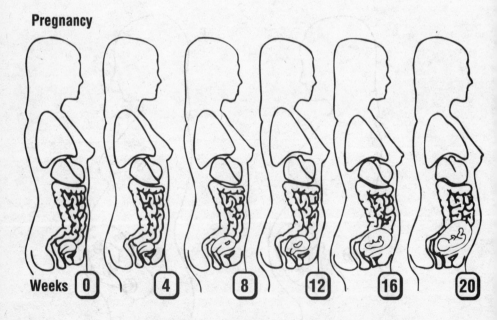

Weeks 0   4   8   12   16   20

Her posture changes, as she has to lean back to balance the
baby's weight. Because of this, backache is often experienced.
Eventually she may have to walk with a waddling movement,
with her legs slightly apart.

Most symptoms of pregnancy, some of which cause discomfort
(in turn causing insomnia), result from the changed hormone
levels and the increased pressure of the growing fetus.

Hormonal effects

a) Emotional changes. The altered hormone levels of
pregnancy cause changes in emotional states. There seems to
be a general pattern common to most women (though not all).
In the first 3 months, there are often extreme changes in mood,
with ambivalent response to pregnancy. During the 2nd
trimester the woman has accepted the fetus and prepared for
it: she has adjusted to the hormonal changes.

b) Morning sickness (see p.99). About $2/3$ of women experience
this, usually from the date of the first missed period until the
2nd or 3rd month, when it often ceases abruptly. It varies in
severity, from nausea in the morning only, to vomiting during
the day. The exact cause of morning sickness is not known,
though it is thought that the increase in estrogen is responsible.

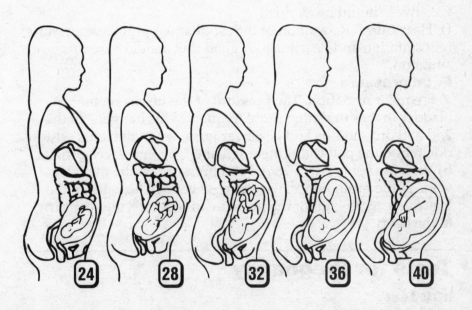

The body eventually adjusts but, while nausea continues, it is a good idea to eat small frequent meals rather than large ones. Dry toast in the morning may help, and greasy spiced foods should be avoided. For a minimum diet, see p.165.

c) The breasts start to enlarge in preparation for lactation. They may itch, tingle, or feel heavy, and are sometimes painful. Their veins become prominent. By the 16th week, they start to secrete a thin fluid from the nipples (colostrum). The areolae become mottled due to increased pigmentation. (Increased pigmentation may also appear on the face and external genitals, and a dark line may run from the navel to the genitals.)

d) Appetite. As the fetus grows, so does the mother's appetite. But pressure and reduced motility of the stomach induced by hormones reduce the capacity for large meals. There may be cravings for certain foods. With some women, this craving extends to the truly unusual – coal for example – and is then known as pica. By contrast, certain foods and substances may become repulsive for some women. Coffee, meat, alcohol and greasy foods are examples.

e) Constipation. Reduced motility of the large intestine increases the possibility of constipation, and therefore hemorrhoids. Dried fruit or bran will ease constipation. Laxatives should be avoided.

f) 'Heartburn'. Relaxation of the esophagus sphincter can cause regurgitation and heartburn. A good diet should ease this situation.

Fetal pressure

a) Frequent urination. The pressure of the uterus on the bladder makes urination more frequent. This happens in the 2nd and 3rd months and also near term, when the fetus settles down into the pelvis ('lightening,' or engagement: see p.102).

b) Varicose veins (see p.286). Fetal pressure on the main leg veins in the groin may cause varicose veins. The veins in the legs dilate as a result of the pressure of blood trying to return to the heart.

Tests for Pregnancy

hCG test

The hCG (human chorionic gonadotrophin) test for pregnancy most commonly uses a sample of urine, and takes place in a clinic or doctor's office. The test takes about 2 minutes to carry

out and is 95% accurate after the 40th day of pregnancy. It is based on the fact that the placenta secretes large quantities of hCG, a hormone, within 40 days of the last menstruation.
A drop of anti-hCG, a substance that neutralizes hCG, is combined, on a glass slide, with a drop of urine. One minute later, another substance is added (latex rubber particles with hCG). If there is no hCG in the urine, the anti-hCG will fix onto the hCG in the latex rubber particles, forming milky lumps or 'curds'. This is a negative result. If the woman is pregnant, the hCG in her urine will be fixed by the anti-hCG in the first mixture; when the rubber and hCG are added, there will be no anti-hCG left to combine with the added hCG. The particles will not form lumps but will remain smooth. A positive result needs to be confirmed by clinical diagnosis.
Alternatively, a blood test for hCG can detect pregnancy as early as 1 week after fertilization. The urine test is the more usual test, however.

Home pregnancy test
Pharmacists sell a variety of home pregnancy tests. Follow the instructions carefully. Tests can be carried out 5-7 days after a period is missed, repeated a few days later, and confirmed by hCG test and clinical diagnosis.

Clinical diagnosis (6th-10th week)
The two stages of the examination are usually painless; a speculum is inserted into the vagina in order to look at the cervix, which is a bluish color in pregnancy. After removal of the speculum the doctor gently inserts two fingers into the vagina while pressing on the abdomen with the other hand, in order to determine whether the uterus is enlarged. The test will also show up any abnormal swellings in the uterus, and a Pap smear (see pp.434-5) is often taken at the same time to check for cervical cancer.

Ultrasound
Today, ultrasound is rarely used for routine screening in pregnancy, although it might be used early on to help determine due date. If any problems are suspected, it provides a safe way to examine the fetus. A hand-held transducer placed on the skin emits high-frequency soundwaves, which pass through the tissues and are reflected by internal structures. A computer builds up a picture on a screen.

Prenatal Care

Good prenatal care – care of the mother-to-be and the unborn child – helps ensure that a pregnant woman maintains good health, follows a good diet, learns about child care, has a normal delivery, and bears a healthy child. She and her partner learn what is happening to her and what to expect.

The importance of prenatal care cannot be overemphasized. It plays a crucial part in reducing maternal and infant mortality. Some doctors now believe that good health care and diet should begin for both partners some months before conception.

Clinical visits

The woman visits her doctor to have her pregnancy confirmed. The approximate date of the birth is determined, and the doctor carries out:

a) a full consultation, including discussion of past illnesses, operations, health, physical complaints, anxieties and questions.

b) a general and then obstetrical examination, which will reveal any conditions which may affect the pregnancy, for which treatment will be given, and which enables the doctor to anticipate possible complications. Any previous pregnancies, miscarriages, or abortions will be considered. The physical examination entails a general medical checkup, a urine test, blood test, and blood pressure test, and obstetrical abdominal and pelvic examinations.

Urine is taken to see if albumin, signifying a kidney disorder, or sugar, which may suggest diabetes, are present.

A blood test determines blood type, rhesus factor (see pp.116-17), iron content, the presence of any sexually transmitted infections (see pp.166-7), hormone levels and alfafetoprotein levels.

A blood pressure test (which is taken at every prenatal visit) will show whether toxemia of pregnancy may occur. Its cause is unknown, but its effects can be severe. The arteries supplying the uterus go into spasm, reducing the blood supply to the placenta, with possible fatal results to the fetus.

An abdominal examination checks muscle tone and looks for enlargement of liver and spleen. After 12th and 28th weeks, it is used to check that growth, and later also the position, of the fetus in the uterus is correct.

The pelvic examination identifies pelvic structure and

dimensions, and an internal test is made as part of pregnancy confirmation (see p.121). Breasts and nipples will also be examined, and legs for signs of varicose veins.

The mother-to-be continues her prenatal visits every month until she is 7 months pregnant, then every 2 weeks until she is 9 months, with a weekly checkup till the birth. Visits will be more frequent if any previous illnesses (eg diabetes, heart disease, hypertension) are likely to cause complications. At each visit, the baby's position in the uterus will be checked (see p.138). When the fetal head settles down into the pelvic cavity ('lightening'), this suggests that the mother's pelvic shape and size are normal. An examination will be made to ascertain the position of the fetal head, and a cervical check made at the same time.

Illness

Report any fever, chill or illness to your doctor immediately. German measles (rubella), if contracted up to the 12th week, may interrupt fetal development, resulting in deafness and heart defects. NOTE: The rubella vaccination must be given at least three months before conception; live vaccine is used.

Weight gain

A gain of 25 to 30lb (11.3 to 13.6kg) from conception to birth is normal. Any more than this is unnecessary and even undesirable. At term the fetus weighs 7 to 8lb (3.2 to 3.6kg), and the amniotic sac and placenta $2^1/2$lb (1.1kg). The mother carries the balance as fats and fluids in her tissues.

Diet

Eating for two is definitely out! A woman's average calorie requirement is about 2,300; the fetus requires only an extra 300. So intake should only increase slightly. It is important that extra emphasis is put on proteins, vitamins, and minerals (see pp.164-5). Whole foods are preferable to refined. But vitamin and mineral supplements should only be taken on the doctor's advice.

General care

Bathing is safe and relaxing. Water in the vagina is best avoided, but is only dangerous if forced in under pressure. The genitals and breasts should be kept clean, as secretions become heavier during pregnancy. Dental care is also important, as the gums become softer and so more easily injured by food and toothbrushes. Injured gums are susceptible to infection which can cause loss of teeth (see p.271).

Drinking should be kept to a minimum during pregnancy, and it is better not to smoke at all. Some women who smoke stop wanting to during pregnancy.

Unless there is a history of miscarriage, or a possibility of complications, intercourse during pregnancy will not harm the fetus. Near term, intercourse in some positions may be uncomfortable for the woman, disturbing to the fetus, and difficult to achieve (but see pp.51-52). The vagina is self-cleansing, so douching is unnecessary and can be dangerous in pregnancy.

Prenatal Exercises

Relaxation helps relieve tension during pregnancy and labor. Before practicing, get into a comfortable position on the floor, a bed, or a chair. Near term, lying on your side may be more comfortable than on your back. You learn relaxation by concentrating on each part of the body. Afterwards, you may feel a floating sensation.

Breathing exercises should be practiced during pregnancy to gain control over the different muscles involved in breathing, which will be used in various ways in labor. In early labor, slow, deep breathing is used; relaxing during contractions. Later on, rapid, shallow panting is used, speeding up as each contraction intensifies.

The posture of a pregnant woman is altered as the abdomen enlarges. Strain on the back and abdomen can be avoided by learning a good posture, which can be obtained by pressing the whole spine length against a wall, tucking the buttocks and abdomen in, keeping the head up and shoulders back, and maintaining this posture. The small of the back should be flat, not hollowed.

Labor positions can be practiced to strengthen the inner thigh muscles and control of breathing.

It is generally advisable to exercise gently, such as by walking, stretching, and low-impact aerobics. Women who exercised regularly before pregnancy may continue, but it is unwise to push the body to the limit. When there are complications (high blood pressure, twins, etc.) rest and very gentle exercise are most beneficial. Avoid raising the blood temperature above 1 degree. One study has shown that women who exercise regularly are less likely to deliver by cesarean section, and spend less time in hospital, than those who do not.

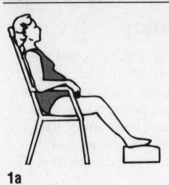

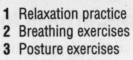

1 Relaxation practice
2 Breathing exercises
3 Posture exercises
4 Labor exercises

1a

1b

2a

2b

3a   **3b**   **3c**

4a

4b

Complications in Pregnancy

The majority of pregnancies are completely normal, but there are some (about 30%) in which complications may develop. If left unattended, these conditions can become serious, but the main purpose of prenatal care is to detect potential dangers and, where possible, to prevent them from happening. The chart shows which unusual symptoms should be reported immediately to a doctor and what the possible causes of such symptoms may be.

DANGER SIGNS	POSSIBLE CAUSES
Severe abdominal pain, possibly with slight bleeding, in first few weeks of pregnancy.	Ectopic pregnancy
Vaginal bleeding with or without abdominal pain in the first 28 weeks of pregnancy.	Threatened miscarriage
Vaginal bleeding with or without abdominal pain after the 28th week of pregnancy.	Premature separation of placenta (abruptio placenta, if pain; placenta previa, if painless)
Severe swelling of fingers and face, with blurred vision and headaches, after the 20th week of pregnancy.	Toxemia of pregnancy
Gush of water from the vagina at 28th-36th week.	Rupture of membranes (bursting of amniotic sac)

Miscarriage

About 1 in 6 women miscarry, and a threatened miscarriage is the usual cause of bleeding in the first half of pregnancy. Known more correctly as a spontaneous abortion, it occurs most often at the 6th or 10th week. The fetus detaches itself from the uterus and is expelled. Most common reasons are:
a) major abnormality in the fetus (about 50% of aborted fetuses are found to be abnormal);
b) death of fetus;
c) faulty hormone production;
d) anatomical defect or functional abnormality;
e) illness or infection;
f) defective sperm or ovum;
g) psychological conditions.

There are different kinds of miscarriage at different stages of pregnancy: threatened, inevitable, complete, incomplete, and missed are the most usual. The symptoms of a threatened miscarriage will generally appear during the first few weeks. Bleeding, red or brown, without pain, occurs (**a**). At this stage, it is uncertain whether the miscarriage will occur, and in 80% of cases the threat passes and pregnancy continues. But if the cervix opens, then the miscarriage is considered inevitable (**b**). A complete abortion means the uterus empties itself of the entire pregnancy. Incomplete abortion (**c**) leaves varying amounts of tissue in the uterus and a D & C is required (see p.394). In a missed pregnancy, the fetus has died but remains in the uterus. It is eventually aborted and a D & C is usually given. A miscarriage can be a tense and despairing time, and many women still feel expectant of the birth even though they are no longer pregnant. But miscarriage is often a sign that the fetus was defective, and so rejected; and, after a first miscarriage, the chance that the next pregnancy will be successful is high.

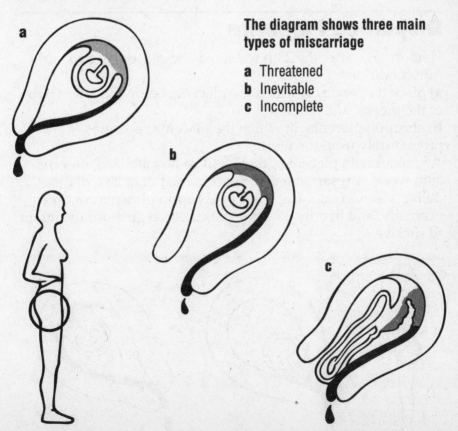

The diagram shows three main types of miscarriage

a Threatened
b Inevitable
c Incomplete

Ectopic Pregnancy

The diagram shows an ectopic pregnancy and possible areas where one might develop. Bleeding and pain in early pregnancy (6th-12th week) may be caused by an ectopic pregnancy. In this condition the fertilized egg has failed to reach the uterus and has implanted within a Fallopian tube. For a full description, see p.105.

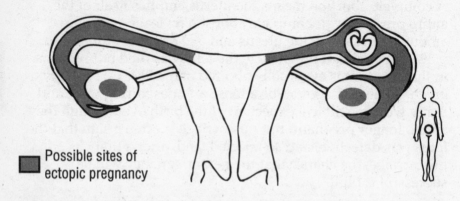

■ Possible sites of ectopic pregnancy

Displaced Placenta

Hemorrhage after the 28th week may be caused by two fairly rare conditions:
a) placenta previa, in which the placenta lies in the lower part of the uterus; and
b) abruptio placenta, in which the placenta separates prematurely from the uterus.
A woman with placenta previa will be hospitalized after the 28th week. A cesarian may be necessary, but in 20% of cases delivery is normal. Most cases of abruptio placenta continue normally, and in only 25% is separation too great for the infant to survive.

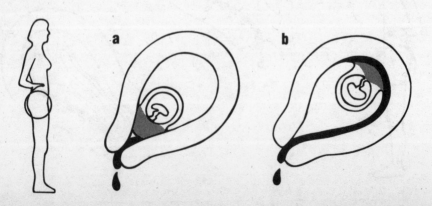

Rupture of Amniotic Sac

A gush of water from the vagina after the 28th week means that the amniotic sac in which the baby grows has burst, and amniotic fluid is escaping. If this happens before the 28th-36th week, it may precede premature labor. The woman is hospitalized, and may be given drugs, including sedatives, to discourage labor. After the 36th week, labor will not be stopped, and may be induced, as the baby is mature enough to survive.

Toxemia of Pregnancy

4

This is a serious condition that sometimes occurs in late pregnancy. It affects 7-12% of women carrying their first baby, and 3-8% of women carrying subsequent children.

Symptoms and signs

There are three main warnings:
a) edema (swelling due to water retention) of fingers, face, or legs;
b) raised blood pressure; and
c) protein in the urine.
Excessive weight gain is also associated with toxemia.

Progress

Toxemia goes through two stages.
a) Preeclampsia. This rarely occurs before the 20th week and the conditions are those mentioned above. (Some degree of edema, particularly of the legs, is, however, common in pregnancy. It becomes dangerous when associated with other symptoms.) As preeclampsia progresses, vision becomes blurred and the woman will suffer severe headaches.
b) Eclampsia is the final and most severe stage, and may be fatal. Fits, followed by unconsciousness or coma, are characteristic. It is particularly dangerous for the fetus (see p.166).

Treatment

Today toxemia rarely develops to a final stage. This is almost entirely due to prenatal care, where the symptoms can be detected early on. For this reason alone, regular attendance at the prenatal clinic is vitally important. Bed rest and a restricted diet are generally sufficient to prevent toxemia from developing. Diuretic pills may be given to get rid of excess water and salt. For more severe cases, hospitalization is necessary so that the condition can be checked.

Preparing for Childbirth

Labor and delivery are, for many women, the most alarming aspects of pregnancy. As with the physical changes of pregnancy itself, an understanding of the processes involved helps to relieve anxiety. A woman has 9 months to prepare for birth, and in order to participate fully in the experience she should become acquainted with all the available possibilities. Each woman's experience is personal and individual: whether she delivers at home or in a hospital, with or without drugs, should, in the final analysis, be for her to decide.

Natural Childbirth

Natural childbirth is the process of giving birth without the automatic use of drugs or obstetrical techniques. The idea was popularized in the 1930s by an English doctor, Grantly Dick-Read. It is based on the assumption that much of the pain of childbirth is caused by tension, itself due to the woman's anxieties and fears about labor. If these are eliminated, tension is relieved and pain will be lessened. The keynote to relaxation in labor is an understanding by the woman of all aspects of pregnancy and birth. Armed with this knowledge, Dick-Read maintained, the woman can approach labor with confidence.

Psychoprophylaxis

The psychoprophylactic method of childbirth was introduced by a French doctor, Fernand Lamaze. He felt that relaxation was not enough, and introduced prelearned muscular and breathing exercises to be used by the woman during labor. With these a woman is no longer helplessly passive, but can actively participate in the process of birth. Although the theory and exercises are the basis of childbirth preparation today, few women actually give birth without drugs – nor should a woman feel she has failed if she is not one of those few.

Home or Hospital

Seventy years ago it was not unusual for a British woman to have her child at home. Today, almost all births in Britain occur in hospitals, though there are still a few home delivery programs. The reason for the decline in home births is that placing pregnant women in suitably equipped environments greatly lowers the risks involved in childbirth.

There is, however, an increasing demand for a more homely atmosphere in labor wards. The concept of the 'labor, delivery, and recovery room' (or LDB) has been the result. These labor centers try to provide home comforts as far as is possible, while providing all the equipment needed for normal-to-difficult births, including the facilities to resuscitate a newborn child. Family members and/or friends are usually allowed to be present during labor, birth and recovery. The mother recovers in the room in which she gave birth, so that the process of bonding can begin.

Midwifery services are growing in popularity. Midwifery group practices offer patient-centered, low-impact care, and midwifery is available in many hospitals now. In such group practices, which are overseen by physicians, all prenatal and childbirth care is given by nurse-midwives; the physicians only become actively involved if any complications or emergencies occur, especially during labor. Some cities have 'birthing centers', which are independent of hospitals and which aim to provide a homely atmosphere. Although the 'natural' process of childbirth is emphasized in these centers, they are fully equipped to deal with emergencies and complications.

4

Breathing Exercises

The diagram shows four types of breathing used during labor:
a) deep chest breathing for early first stage;
b) shallow chest breathing used in the middle stage;
c) shallow rapid breathing (panting) for transition; and
d) expulsion, in which the breath is held while the woman bears down to push against the baby.

At the beginning of labor, deep abdominal breathing helps to relieve pressure. Once contractions increase so that they harden the abdominal wall, the woman switches to deep chest breathing. She continues to change as labor progresses, each time alternating her normal breathing (between contractions) with the learned form used during the contractions. Once delivery begins, expulsion breathing is used.

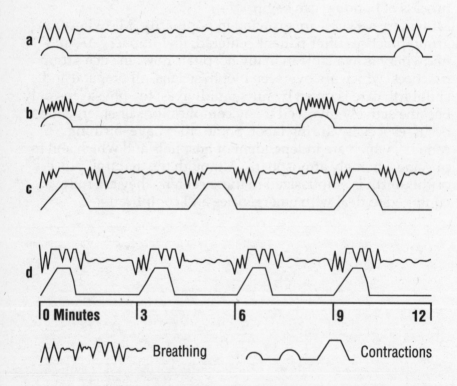

Drugs in Labor

A woman who delivers in a hospital can use a variety of pain-relieving or painkilling drugs. There are two kinds: analgesics and anesthetics.

Analgesics relieve pain. They may be inhaled or injected. During early labor, painkillers are rarely necessary, but narcotics such as Demerol (Pethidine) may be given. Sedatives are not now generally given because they can cause the baby to stop breathing.

Regional anesthetics are now widely used. They are injected into the body at a specific point, completely blocking off pain from a certain area. The epidural block is probably the most efficient of the regional anesthetics. Anesthetic is injected into the epidural cavity, which lies between the spinal cord and its covering, the dura. It numbs the entire region from the lower abdomen to the feet, and can be readministered during labor. Although it is an effective pain reliever, it can lessen a mother's ability to push, and may result in a forceps delivery (see pp.148-9).

Other regional anesthetics include the pudendal nerve block, given immediately before a forceps delivery, and the caudal block. Both anesthetize the pelvis. A paracervical block is injected into the plexus, making the cervix and upper vagina completely insensitive. A regional anesthetic is also given before an episiotomy (see p.142).

Drugs used in labor are carefully supervised, but most cross the placenta and can make the newborn infant drowsy and slow to suck. These effects, although undesirable, are temporary and should be weighed against the possible long-term effects of a painful and distressing labor.

Epidural anesthesia
a Vertebral column
b Syringe
c Spinal cord
d Epidural cavity

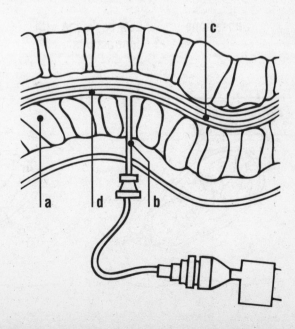

Labor

Women often find that their experiences during labor differ. However, most labors follow a similar general pattern.

Hours

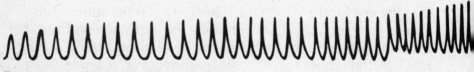

Frequency and intensity of contractions

Stage	FIRST STAGE Effacement of cervix	
Frequency of contractions	15-30 minutes	2-5 minutes
Duration of contractions	40 seconds	40-90 seconds
Drugs	Tranquilizers, narcotics, epidurals	
Sensations	Low backache with contractions	Pain becomes abdominal

Position of child

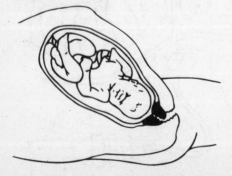 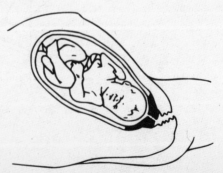

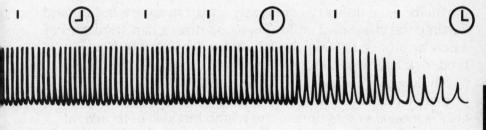

4

Dilation of cervix	SECOND STAGE Delivery	THIRD STAGE Afterbirth
2-3 minutes	2-5 minutes	5-10 minutes
40-90 seconds	60-90 seconds	
Epidural	Trilene, nitrous oxide, paracervical block	Ergometrine
The 'show' Amniotic sac ruptures (if not earlier)	Possible nausea 'Bearing down'	

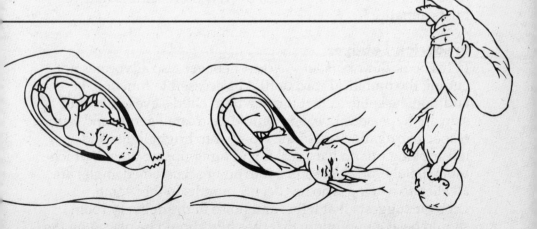

Alternative Birth Styles

The possibly damaging effects on a woman of a prolonged, painful, and distressing childbirth are now well recognized. But recently the accent has moved from the effects of birth on the mother to the effects of birth on the child. It is argued that the methods of delivery commonly used can have a lasting and detrimental effect on a child. There are three main advocates of a new approach to birth: R. D. Laing, a Scottish psychologist; Frederick Leboyer, a French obstetrician; and an American psychoanalyst, Elizabeth Fehr. All concern themselves primarily with the well-being of the child and consider that not only is it aware of its time in the womb but also of its arrival into the world. They feel that its initial impressions are critical to its future development, and that being dangled upside down and slapped on the bottom are both unnecessary and damaging.

R. D. Laing

The Scottish psychologist R. D. Laing argued in the 1960s that cutting the umbilical cord too soon is a major cause of birth trauma. The cord linking mother and baby continues providing blood, oxygen, and nutrients after birth. Laing thought that babies experience immediate severance as a shock, which could be avoided by leaving the cord uncut until it naturally ceases to function. Although it used to be common practice not to cut the cord until it stopped pulsating, as Laing proposed, doctors now tend to cut it while it is still transferring blood between mother and fetus. According to Laing's theory this is detrimental; cutting the cord after 4 or 5 minutes, when the baby's circulation has taken over, is more natural and nontraumatic.

Frederick Leboyer

In his book *Birth Without Violence*, Leboyer also advocates not cutting the umbilical cord until it has ceased to function. In addition, he believes that the newborn child's eyes, ears, and skin are hypersensitive, and should be treated gently and with respect. Struggling out of the womb into bright lights and noise, being put on hard scales and hung upside down (which immediately forces the spine into an unaccustomed angle) are all alien to a being who has been 9 months in the womb. Leboyer suggests that lights and noise in the delivery room should be at a minimum, that the child should be placed on the mother's stomach before cutting the cord and that after the cord is cut, the child should be placed in a bath of water at body temperature and allowed to move and 'open up' in a calm, unhurried way. Certainly Leboyer has noted that a baby born in this way opens its eyes and begins smiling immediately – one cry, as opposed to a torrent of tears and red-faced rage, having satisfied everyone of its ability to breathe.

Elizabeth Fehr

The late Elizabeth Fehr believed that a traumatic birth leaves a permanent impression. She introduced into psychoanalysis the process of 'rebirthing', by which a person retraces his or her life backward toward birth. As a result of her investigations, she concluded that auditory hallucinations suffered by schizophrenics might well be related to sounds heard by the child as it struggled from the womb. Her work has given added impetus to the movement for gentler birth styles.

4

Water birth – an example of an alternative birth style

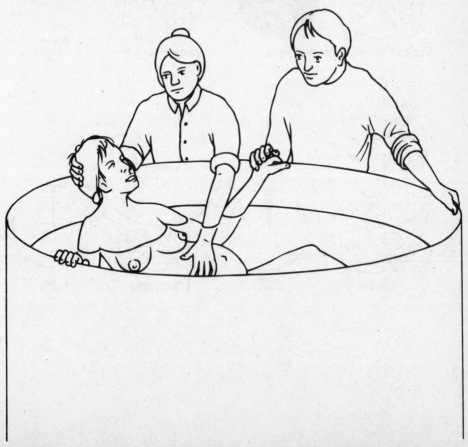

Fetal Positions

These are the positions in which the baby can lie in the mother's pelvis just before labor begins. The face-down position may cause remolding of the skull. A transverse lie can usually be manipulated into another position; uncorrected, it requires a cesarean section (see pp.147-8).

Frequency of birth positions

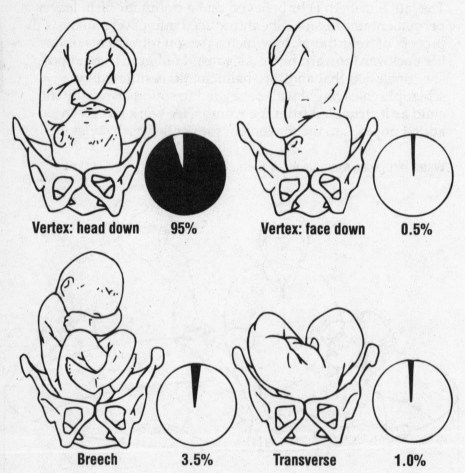

Vertex: head down   95%

Vertex: face down   0.5%

Breech   3.5%

Transverse   1.0%

Duration of Pregnancy

Pregnancy normally lasts between 36 and 42 weeks from fertilization.

Labor

Throughout pregnancy the uterus undergoes slight contractions known as Braxton Hicks' contractions. As the pregnancy nears term, these contractions become more frequent and intense. Labor itself has three distinct stages. In the first stage, the cervix is 'effaced' and 'dilated', to allow the fetus to pass without damaging it. The second stage is the actual delivery of the baby; the third, delivery of the placenta.

First stage

Before delivery can begin, the uterus must undergo a change in shape to permit the fetus to pass through the cervix. The upper uterus pulls the lower uterus and cervix up around the head of the fetus.

This process takes about 8 hours for women having their first child (primigravidae), and may take 4-5 hours for those having their subsequent children (multigravidae). By the time effacement is completed, contractions are occurring about every 3 to 5 minutes, and lasting 40-90 seconds. The mucous plug lodged in the cervix throughout pregnancy is displaced as the cervix begins to dilate to allow the baby a free passage through. The process, a continuation of effacement, reveals the amnion surrounding the baby's head. If the amnion has not been ruptured already, it is usually ruptured during dilation, either by the baby's head or by the doctor delivering. This releases a quantity of amniotic fluid (see pp.112-13). To allow the baby to pass, the cervix must dilate to accommodate its head, which is about 4in (10cm) in diameter.

As dilation proceeds, contractions become more frequent and intense; by full dilation they will be occurring every 2-3 minutes and lasting 60-90 seconds.

Dilation takes from 3-5 hours for a woman having her first child, and less for subsequent children.

4

Induced Labor

Labor may be induced artificially if the health of the mother or fetus is in danger. There has also been a tendency for births to be induced for the convenience of hospitals. Labor will normally begin within 24 hours of induction, and tends to be shorter than a spontaneous labor. But the contractions follow the same pattern as spontaneous labor, even though each stage takes much less time.

The frequency of induction varies greatly from place to place. The following are the main conditions in which induction is justified.

Preeclampsia is the major medical cause of induction, accounting for 50% of such cases. It is characterized by high blood pressure, edema, and proteinuria in the woman (see p.129). Although the danger to her is slight, danger to the fetus increases with severity. Should eclampsia (a type of epilepsy) develop, the mortality rate is very high for mother and fetus.

Postmaturity accounts for 35% of inductions. If the fetus remains in the uterus after term, it will continue to grow, making for a difficult birth. Placental function begins to fall off after the 40th week, and there is a tendency toward mental damage in postmature babies.

Hemorrhage (10% of inductions) is caused by the placenta separating from the uterus before birth. In difficult cases cesarian section is required.

First Stage of Labor

The cervix and uterus as labor begins

Contractions every 15-30 minutes

Partial effacement
Contraction and retraction of the uterus shorten the neck of the cervix

Contractions every 10 minutes

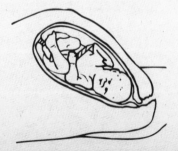
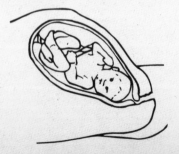

Rhesus incompatibility (see pp.116-17) necessitates induction in severe cases.

Diabetes in the mother, if untreated, results in a high mortality rate for both mother and fetus. But prenatal checks will reveal diabetes (p.122) if it has not been detected previously, so mortality is not a problem. Treatment must be carefully controlled. Even so, fetuses tend to be puffy and fat, and thus difficult to deliver. They will usually require induction by the 38th week.

Methods of induction

There are two methods: surgical and medical.

Surgical induction involves the artificial rupture of the amniotic sac, below the fetus. About a pint of fluid is drained off, and labor usually begins within 24 hours. The rupturing of the sac does not in itself make for any difficulty in delivery.

Medical induction involves intravenous infusion of oxytocin, to stimulate uterine contractions. The oxytocin is given throughout labor – though not for more than 10 hours.

Many procedures in obstetrics, including induced birth, have become controversial issues in some countries: their justification has been in question. Lack of information as to the reasons for their use exacerbates the situation, causing resentment between women and hospital staff.

Full effacement

Contractions every
5 minutes

Partial dilation
Continued contraction
and retraction dilate the
cervix

Contractions every 2-5
minutes

Full dilation
The fetus is able to pass
through the cervix
without damaging it

Contractions every 2-3
minutes

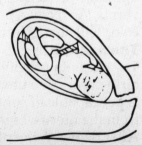

Delivery

Transition to second stage

The transition to the second stage is characterized by feelings of pressure in the low pelvis, backache, and often nausea and leg cramps. At this point, when tension rises, it is helpful and comforting for the woman's partner or friend to prompt her to do her prenatal breathing exercises.

Contractions continue, once every few minutes, and there is an increasingly uncontrollable desire to push or bear down – like trying to relieve severe constipation. However, it is not safe to bear down until full dilation has been achieved, as the cervix may tear.

Second stage

When the cervix is fully dilated, bearing down can begin. The baby is now being pushed out of the uterus and down the vagina, and will be delivered in anything from 5 to 40 minutes. If there is danger of the perineum (pp.38-9) being torn by the baby's head, an episiotomy may be performed: the doctor makes an incision from the vagina obliquely down toward the anus.

This cut is sewn up after the delivery is completed.

The fetus begins its journey on its side, head first (but see p.138). Contractions of the uterus force the fetus down into the pelvis.

The head is rotated downward beneath the pubic arch and, as the head is born, it rotates back to its original position. The shoulders and then the breech follow the same pattern of rotation as they are delivered, and the baby is born.

The second stage is now completed – in primigravidae it takes up to one hour, in multigravidae less.

Mucus is extracted from the mouth and nose of the baby, who may be suspended upside down to drain mucus from its lungs. The umbilical cord is clamped and cut, sometimes immediately and sometimes after several minutes; in a week the stump of the cord will dry out and fall off.

The baby on delivery is wet and covered in a fatty substance, vernix. As oxygen begins to circulate in the lungs, the baby's color will change gradually from bluish to pink.

Third stage

The placenta is delivered within 30 minutes of the baby. As birth occurs, the uterus retracts quite markedly. The placenta is not capable of contraction or retraction, and shears away from the uterus. Light traction on the cord aids its delivery. After delivery, the placenta is checked to ensure that no tissue has been left inside the uterus, which could cause infection and hemorrhage.

Checks

The baby is checked just after birth for congenital malformations (see pp.176-7). It will be given a vitamin K injection to help blood clotting in case of hemorrhage, and silver nitrate eye drops to help protect the eyes. Heart and lung functions are checked. A handprint or footprint is taken to check for Down's syndrome, and a mouth smear to check for PKU (see pp.162-3).

Positions for Delivery

The diagrams show delivery positions. The dorsal, in which the woman lies on her back with knees up and separated, and the left lateral, in which she lies on her left side, knees toward her chest, are most typical in many countries. The lithotomy is now used only in complicated deliveries (eg when forceps are needed or when the placenta is manually removed).

First stage

During the early stages of labor there is little active work a woman can do. She may remain up and about, waiting for the contractions to increase in frequency. Once labor is fully established she should choose the most comfortable position.

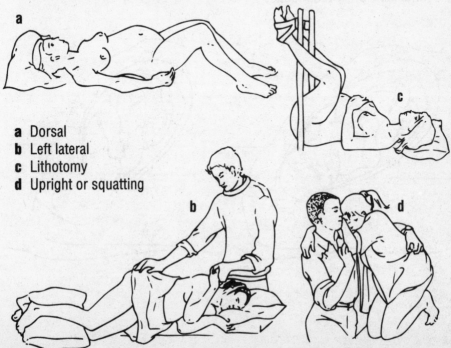

a Dorsal
b Left lateral
c Lithotomy
d Upright or squatting

During the first stage, it is not advisable for her to lie flat on her back. Sitting propped up on pillows or lying on one side improves the flow of blood through the uterus, providing more oxygen for the baby. During transition itself, a woman can squat, sit upright, or use any position which helps her the most.

Second stage

This is the time when the mother can most actively participate in labor, and she should choose the position in which she can work the best – changing at any time if she wishes. Many women find they can push best by clasping their legs, drawing them up to the abdomen.

Third stage

Once the baby is born, the dorsal position is generally used for the delivery of the placenta.

Second and Third Stages of Labor

SECOND STAGE OF LABOR
Full dilation signifies the beginning of delivery. The woman 'bears down' to help expel the baby.

The baby's head passes through the cervix and rotates to squeeze beneath the pubic arch.

Contractions every 2-5 minutes

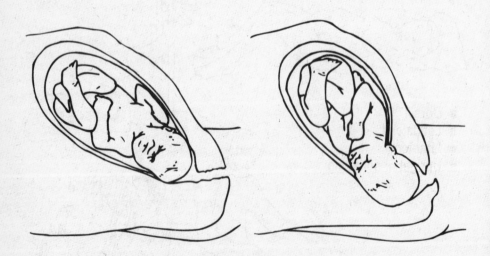

The head is born, and rotates back to its previous position. The baby's shoulders rotate to pass through the pelvis.

The right shoulder, then the left, is born.

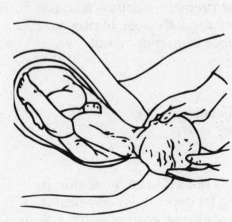 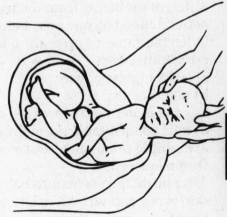

The baby breathes spontaneously. Mucus is cleaned from its face and air passages. The umbilical cord is clamped.

THIRD STAGE OF LABOR
The placenta is delivered within 30 minutes of the baby.

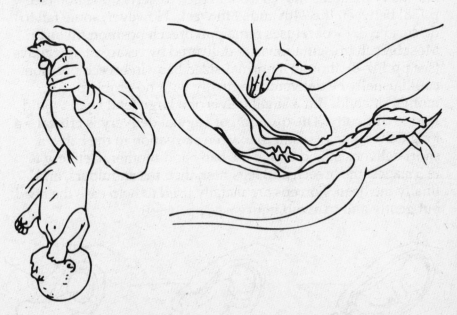

4

Premature Birth

A premature baby can be defined by weight: under 5lb 8oz (2.5kg). But low birthweight full-term babies have totally different problems from the true premature baby – who is better defined as one born before the 36th week of pregnancy. Often the cause of premature labor is unknown, but possibilities are:

a) lack of prenatal care;
b) poor health;
c) some maternal diseases (eg diabetes);
d) fetal congenital abnormalities;
e) multiple pregnancy; and
f) small placenta.

After birth, the premature baby is placed in an incubator. Its skin is red and wrinkled, lacking fat deposits – body heat is hard to maintain. Problems can also arise with breathing, as its respiratory system is underdeveloped. It cannot suck well, and has a feeble cry. But if adequately cared for, it will become as healthy as a full-term baby.

Breech Birth

Normally the fetus moves from breech to vertex position (see p.138) between the 24th and 28th week. However, some fail to do so, and 3.5% of fetuses remain in breech position till birth. Most breech presentations are delivered by cesarean nowadays (see pp.147-8), though a normal-sized baby in breech position could usually be delivered vaginally with no problems for mother or child. But a small pelvis or a large fetal head would lead to difficulty. The duration of vaginal delivery is critical – a long delivery may result in oxygen starvation to the baby; a short delivery may damage the baby and mother. Delivery is in 3 stages: the breech and legs first, then the shoulders, and finally the head. Forceps are usually used to help ease the head out gently and to avoid injury (see pp.148-9).

Multiple Births

Twins are born on average once every 85 births, triplets once every 7500 births, quadruplets once every 650,000, and quintuplets once every 57,000,000 births (see pp.108-9). Difficulties may arise in multiple births. They tend to be premature, and so must be delivered in a hospital. Labor is usually straightforward as each baby is small. The birth canal is dilated after the birth of the first baby so that subsequent ones are born easily. Toxemia of pregnancy and anemia occur more frequently in a multiple pregnancy. The maternal death rate in twin pregnancies is 2-5 times greater than in a single pregnancy. In 1 in 14 twin births, one twin dies, and with larger multiple births the likelihood of fetal death rises steeply.

4

Cesarean Birth

A cesarean section is an operation carried out to deliver a woman's baby if a vaginal delivery is not possible or not considered advisable by doctors. The procedure is necessary when there is
a) fetal distress;
b) placenta previa (the delivery of the placenta before the baby) or a very low-lying placenta (see p.128);
c) the mother's pelvis is very small, or not wide enough for the baby;
d) obstructive fibroids are present;
e) the baby is in a transverse position;
f) previous injury to the uterus;
g) a breech presentation in a woman having her first child;
h) twins, of which the second baby to be born is in the breech position;
i) severe preeclampsia; and
j) a severely premature infant in the breech position.
Epidural anesthetic is usually given, and the woman remains awake throughout the operation. A horizontal cut is made above the pubic bone, and the baby is delivered through this. Women who have had a cesarean section and a pregnancy without complications can often expect to give birth to their next baby vaginally.
It is only in the last 40 years that cesarean section has become a safe operation. It accounts for 22% of all deliveries in the United States.

There are several reasons why the numbers of cesarean births have risen so steeply over the last 20 years: the numbers of first-time mothers have risen; women are waiting longer to have their first child; cesarean section is used instead of forceps delivery; and threat of litigation encourages many doctors to carry out the procedure at the first sign of trouble.

Although physicians and other experts agree that the rate is too high, cesarean section has reduced the risk of death in late pregnancy and childbirth.

Forceps Delivery

In the United States, about 5% of all deliveries are forceps deliveries. Forceps are used in the second stage of labor to aid the progress of the fetus. They are used in the following circumstances:

a) slow or no fetal progress;

b) maternal distress, eg preeclampsia (see p.129), exacerbated by the effort required during labor;

c) fetal distress.

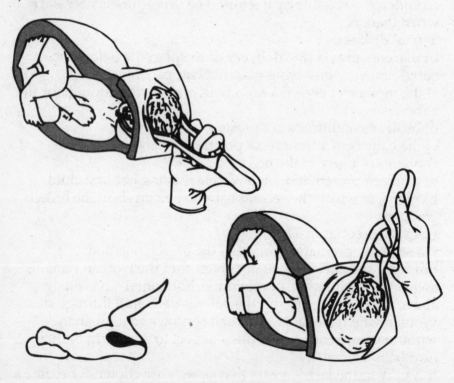

Application

Forceps consist of two curved blades that interlock and fit
closely around the fetal head. One blade is inserted into the
uterus and located in position around the head. The other
blade is then inserted and, when positioned, locked into the
first blade. Gentle traction draws the fetus down through the
vagina. Local anesthetic and episiotomy may be needed.

Conditions

a) The cervix must be fully dilated to allow insertion of the
forceps blades. Damage will be caused to the cervix and vagina
if the fetus is pulled through before dilation.
b) The amniotic membranes must be ruptured, if they are not
already, and bladder and rectum empty.
c) The forceps can only be applied to the fetal head.

4

Vacuum Extraction

Vacuum extraction is used as an alternative to simple forceps
delivery, and is used frequently in some countries. Vacuum
extraction can be started before the cervix is fully dilated. A
metal cup is inserted into the vagina and placed against the fetal
head. It is connected to suction equipment, the vacuum formed
being strong enough to allow the fetus to be gently pulled out of
the uterus. Scalp tissues are sucked into the cup, but within a
few hours of delivery any swelling subsides, unless a hematoma,
or blood swelling, forms.

Emergency Birth

In 80% of cases, a woman can deliver without any problems;
but if a birth begins unexpectedly, the help of a doctor or
hospital should always be sought. If no help is available, then
it is best simply to give encouragement to the mother, and let
nature take its course without interference. Let the mother
"bear down" (push against the baby) as soon as she wants to;
do not worry whether full dilation has occurred, for any
damage to the cervix can be repaired later by minor surgery.
Show her how to push during contractions, by holding her
breath, raising head and shoulders, and pulling the knees up.
After the birth, clean the mucus from the baby's mouth and
nose. Breathing should begin within 30 seconds. Do not cut the
cord. Keep mother and baby warm.
More than $3/_8$pt (0.2liter) of blood from the uterus (not the
placenta) signifies hemorrhage. In this case only, the abdomen
should be massaged to try to ease the bleeding.

After the Birth

For about 10 days after birth, there is a steady loss of a bloody substance, called lochia, from the vagina, as the placenta site and uterine lining break down.

The breasts produce colostrum for the first few days. This is then replaced by milk. Sometimes the breasts are overfull and painful. For a day or two after the birth, the mother may experience some constipation and difficulty in urinating; or she may urinate involuntarily, especially when coughing or laughing. This is caused by muscle slackness in the pelvic area and is best treated by early mobilization and reassurance.

Changes in hormone balance often cause the mother to be depressed and weepy for a short while after giving birth. This is called the '3rd or 4th day blues', named after the time it usually occurs.

Menstruation normally returns after about 24 weeks if the mother is breastfeeding, or 6-10 weeks if not. Ovulation starts in the first case after about the 20th week. Women who do not breastfeed can therefore become pregnant much sooner; while of those who do, the longer they breastfeed, usually the lower the likelihood of pregnancy, although this is not always the case.

Postnatal examination

This takes place after 6 weeks. The position of the uterus is checked, and the mother is asked if she has any pain or discomfort in the abdominal area, or any vaginal discharge. Often a blood test is made to check for anemia. Blood pressure is always measured.

A vaginal inspection is made to see that any stitches from an episiotomy have healed, and if there is any inflammation, or erosion, of the cervix (25% of mothers have it to some degree after giving birth). Mostly it is self-healing, but treatment is required if it persists (see p.397).

Changes in the Uterus

The puerperium is the time when the uterus and other genital organs gradually return to their normal size.

The uterus, cervix, and vagina undergo immense stretching during pregnancy and labor; but within 6 weeks of the birth evidence of the pregnancy is difficult to find. The uterus weighs, after birth, about $2^1/2$lb (1kg) and, after 2 weeks, about 11oz (350g). In rare cases the uterus retroverts following pregnancy (see pp.395-6).

4

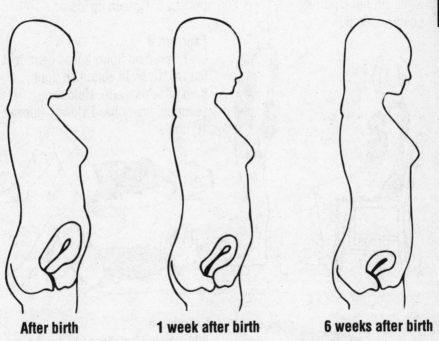

| After birth | 1 week after birth | 6 weeks after birth |

Postnatal Exercises

These are important for most women, as they retone muscles (especially those of the pelvic floor), stimulate blood circulation, and promote good posture. They should be done as many times as possible a day as soon as the mother is up and about. Some abdominal exercises can be performed while feeding the baby (see Exercise 1) or around the home (see Exercise 2).

Exercise 1
Tighten abdominal muscles while sitting in correct posture position.

Exercise 2
Stand straight, pull in abdomen and buttocks. Tighten up inside.

Exercise 3
Lie relaxed on floor, knees bent, feet flat (**a**). Draw in abdomen tightly, then raise head (**b**). Hold few seconds, lower head slowly. Repeat 10 times.

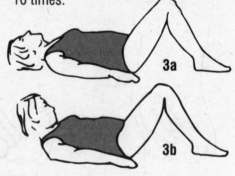

Exercise 4
Alternately straighten (**a**) and hump (**b**) back, abdominal muscles held tightly. With straight back, move head and hips first to right, then to left (**c**).

Exercise 5

Lie flat on floor, back straight (**a**). Feet must be held by another person or a heavy item of furniture. Raise body to forward position (**b**), then lie back (**c**). Arms can be stretched forward above head before lying back.

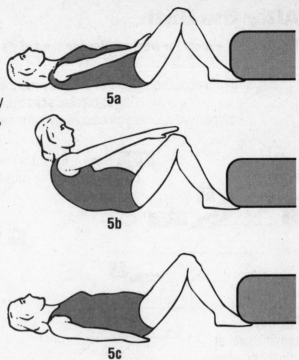

5a

5b

5c

Exercise 6

Lie on back, legs straight. Move feet up and down and round in circles (**a**).
Tighten kneecaps, tense leg muscles (**b**). Ankles crossed, press thighs together, tighten up inside (**c**).

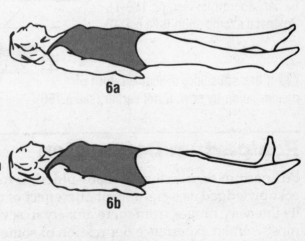

6a

6b

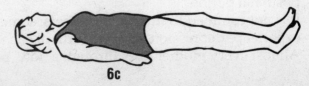

6c

After the Birth

Timetable of events for weeks following the baby's birth

1 Birth of baby. Days 1 and 2: breasts produce colostrum (see p.277)
Day 3: breasts start producing milk (see p.277)
Postpartum depression caused by hormonal changes (see below)

1-2 Days 4-8: return from hospital: depression on returning home caused by fear of inability to cope (see below)

3 Lochia discharge stops (see p.150)

7-10 Return of menstruation if not breastfeeding (see p.150)

1 Days 1 and 2: bowel or urinary problems (see p.150)

7 Uterus, cervix, and vagina should now be back to normal (see pp.150-1). Postnatal examination (see p.150)

25 If breastfeeding, probable return of menstruation by now, if not earlier (see p.150)

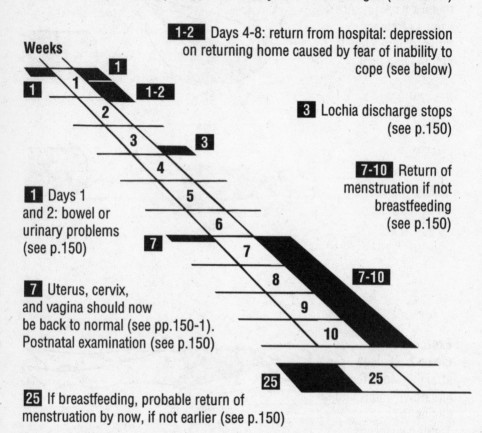

Postpartum Depression

Postpartum depression, or 'baby blues', is rapidly being acknowledged as a significant aftereffect of childbirth. Though its intensity ranges from mere anxiety to severe psychosis, most women experience depression of some kind during the postnatal period.

It is not confined to first-time mothers: some women experience depression after the birth of each of their children. Almost every mother goes through a 'low' period about 3 days after the birth, roughly coinciding with the time the breasts begin to produce milk rather than colostrum. Many more women, however, experience severe depression on return from the hospital. These feelings may last only a matter of days, but, particularly in a woman who is physically run down, may persist for a few months.

Among the feelings most commonly experienced during depression are confusion, shock, insecurity, inadequacy, fear of inability to cope with the baby, and even disappointment about its sex or appearance. Many women are frightened because they cannot rationalize their anxieties, and many fear a deterioration of their relationship with their partner. Postpartum depression is often attributed to hormonal imbalance following childbirth, but evidence is as yet inconclusive since depression has been noted in adoptive as well as natural mothers. Probably the single most important cause of postpartum depression is society's glorification of motherhood, which sets up uncertainty and guilt in women who doubt their ability to be loving, caring mothers. Treatment for the depression often involves prescribing antidepressants. If the mother receives help, support and constant reassurance from her family, friends and other mothers, the chances of a quick recovery are high.

4

Intercourse

Medical opinion generally favors delaying the resumption of intercourse until after the postnatal examination. Some people, however, argue that problems are unlikely, provided that there is no vaginal discomfort and the discharge of lochia has ceased. In any case, it is wise to wait until you feel ready. Reduced sexual interest after childbirth may be due to emotional upheaval, lowered estrogen levels, or more likely sheer exhaustion. Other problems include muscular cramps during intercourse or pain from stitches after an episiotomy.

Pregnancy is possible before menstruation resumes or during lactation. A diaphragm used before the birth will no longer fit and the Pill should not be used if breastfeeding. Condoms with spermicides are recommended.

Breastfeeding

More and more women in Western countries are choosing to breastfeed their babies. Most doctors welcome this, for they regard breastfeeding as the safest and most natural method of infant feeding, and many mothers agree that it is an enjoyable and rewarding experience (see p.277 for details of milk production in the breast).

Some women, however, are uncertain about breastfeeding. Perhaps they have commitments that would make it impossible; or they may find the whole idea distasteful. And for some women who had planned to breastfeed, problems arising after the birth force them to turn to bottlefeeding.

Current breastfeeding propaganda may make mothers who are bottlefeeding their babies feel inadequate and uncaring. This should be ignored; although breastfeeding is preferable for most babies, the vital physical contact between mother and child can be as intimate, warm and loving whether the baby is fed by breast or bottle.

Mothers who do decide to breastfeed should ensure that they take sufficient rest – tension and the inability to relax can reduce the milk supply.

Diet is another important factor. The lactating mother should ensure that she eats a high-calorie diet with particular emphasis on foods rich in protein, vitamins and calcium (see pp.164-5).

Breast or bottle?

BREASTFEEDING	BOTTLEFEEDING
Milk instantly available, at correct temperature, and sterile	Milk needs mixing and (usually) heating. Equipment must be sterilized
Antibodies protect the baby against some infections for first 6 months	No equivalent
Breast milk is cheaper than formula milk	Some expense – bottles, milk, teats must be purchased
Mother cannot tell how much milk the baby has taken without test weighings	Mother can see at a glance how much milk the baby has taken
Mother's health and well-being affect the milk supply	Milk supply independent of the mother
Milk supply usually adjusts itself to the baby's needs but cannot always meet the occasional need for extra milk	Extra feeds present no problem but can overfeed
Some drugs (such as antidepressants given for postpartum depression) can be passed to the baby via the milk	Mother's medications do not affect the baby

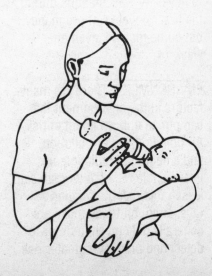

Risks in Pregnancy

Abnormalities at birth can be caused by various factors – some hereditary, some environmental – and every expectant mother worries about them. On this page we list some of the chief dangers in pregnancy. Although the fetus is well protected, its development can be seriously affected by many of the risks mentioned.

HEREDITARY FACTORS. Some genetic disorders can be inherited by an infant. Examples are hemophilia, sickle cell anemia (see pp.158-9)

AGE. Congenital abnormalities are more likely to occur in babies born to women under 16 and over 40

VACCINATION. A woman should have a German measles (rubella) vaccination at least 3 months before conception. Pregnancy should be avoided until all risks from vaccination have passed. During pregnancy, smallpox and German measles vaccinations should not be given. It is unwise to have any vaccinations during the first 14 weeks of pregnancy, but some may be given after week 14

ENVIRONMENT. There are many factors in the environment that can put an unborn infant at risk. Air pollution, water pollution, and a degree of radiation are unavoidable today. A woman can lessen this risk by avoiding X rays, although today these are generally only given in order to detect and prevent a greater risk

Factors within a woman's control: drugs (pp.174-5), alcohol (pp.172-3), smoking (pp.168-9), diet (pp.164-5), weight (pp.123 and 311)

Factors outside a woman's control: viral infection (p.167), rhesus incompatibility (pp.116-17), hypertension

Sexually transmitted infections: chlamydia (pp.166-7), gonorrhea (pp.418-21), AIDS (p.427)

ACCIDENTS AND FALLS. A fetus can only be damaged by a blow with a sharp object directly into the uterus. Falls are more likely to damage the mother than the fetus

Drugs that Cause Birth Defects

Many drugs have been shown to produce defects. Most drugs taken by the mother will cross the placenta and can therefore affect the fetus. The most serious effects are likely to occur during the first three months of pregnancy, when the fetal organs are being formed.

The most infamous drug to cause birth defects was thalidomide, which was used to ease morning sickness in pregnancy. It was widely prescribed in many countries in the late 1950s, and by 1961 it was clear that thalidomide was responsible for the birth of babies with phocomelia (in which the hands or feet are joined to the main joints like seal flippers). The drug was universally withdrawn, but not before 8000 seriously malformed children had been born.

4

This disaster tragically demonstrated the dangers of taking drugs during pregnancy, and encouraged governments to develop rigorous testing procedures for new drugs.

Many other drugs cause birth defects. Diethylstilbestrol was given to prevent miscarriages; it causes defects of the reproductive tract in daughters of women who took it. Warfarin causes fetal deformity if taken in early pregnancy. Androgens can cause masculinization of the fetus. Isoretinan A, used for acne, causes severe fetal defects; it should not be taken during the period preceding conception or during early pregnancy.

Amniocentesis

This is a method by which amniotic fluid is extracted from the uterus and analyzed for possible fetal abnormalities. Such abnormalities can now be detected early in pregnancy. Amniocentesis is best carried out between the 12th and 16th weeks of pregnancy. A local anesthetic is given and a needle inserted into the uterine cavity. About 10-20ml of amniotic fluid is withdrawn and the cells in it studied for defects. There is probably a less than 1-in-2000 risk to the fetus, though this may rise if it is carried out later. A growing number of fetal abnormalities can now be detected, including Down's syndrome and spina bifida (see pp.172-3). Those who might want the test are:

a women who have already given birth to a defective child;
b women carrying a serious disorder;
c women aged over 40, since they have approximately a 1-in-50 chance of delivering a child with congenital abnormalities.

Chorionic Villus Sampling (CVS)

CVS may be carried out either by inserting a narrow tube through the cervix or by inserting a needle through the skin of the mother's abdomen under ultrasound guidance. Cells are extracted from the developing placenta and analyzed in the laboratory for inherited or chromosomal disorders. The level of risk and efficiency depends on the experience of the operator. There is an added risk of miscarriage (above that normally associated with this stage of pregnancy). The test can be performed earlier in pregnancy than amniocentesis – between the 8th and the 11th week – and results are available in 2 to 3 weeks, enabling an early decision about termination if a disorder is found.

Ultrasound

This technique is sometimes used for routine screening in pregnancy, although many women go through pregnancy without a single scan. Others may have one scan to measure the fetus, check its age against expected date of delivery, and screen for a multiple pregnancy and obvious physical malformations. Later scans check the position and progress of twins and small babies and ensure that the placenta is functioning properly and not covering the entrance to the birth canal ('placenta previa'). It is also possible to determine the baby's sex in an ultrasound scan.

Ultrasound is also used as a guidance technique in amniocentesis, chorionic villus sampling, fetal blood sampling, and fetoscopy, and is able to give warning of poor oxygen supply to the baby. It may be used if a mother previously lost a baby because of placental insufficiency.

Ultrasound is generally considered a safe technique because it is noninvasive and no adverse effects have yet been discovered. However, its efficiency relies heavily on the skill of the operator; standards vary, and suspected abnormalities should be confirmed by another operator or by further tests. You should make sure you have a full bladder before ultrasound, so you should drink plenty of water and not go to the bathroom for at least two hours beforehand. In the examination room, you will be asked to lie comfortably on your back. Your exposed abdomen will be swabbed with oily fluid to ensure good contact with the transducer. This instrument is passed over the abdomen until the area being investigated appears cloudy on the screen.

Many mothers see their babies for the first time as they watch the viewer during a scan. The procedure takes only between 5 and 45 minutes. You should be able to go straight home afterwards. The obstetrician will discuss any findings with you, and you may be asked if you would like to know the sex of your child if this has been determined during the scan.

Fetal Blood Sampling

Direct sampling of the baby's blood can be carried out from about 18 weeks. A needle is inserted under ultrasound guidance to the point where the umbilical cord joins the placenta, and a small amount of blood is withdrawn. The blood can be tested for many conditions, and results are available in only 7 days. The risk of miscarriage is around 1%. The technique is also used to transfuse the fetal blood in cases of rhesus incompatibility (when a rhesus negative woman is carrying a rhesus positive baby).

4

Fetoscopy

This involves inserting a tiny telescope through the mother's abdominal wall into the uterus under ultrasound guidance. The operator examines the fetus under direct vision and takes samples of blood or tissue with a needle. The procedure cannot be carried out until about 18 weeks, and, because of the need for sedation and hospitalization, and increased risks of infection and miscarriage, it is only likely to be done if other tests have proved inconclusive. It will also reveal the sex of a baby and possibly visible defects, such as a cleft palate.

Use of Tests

Not all the tests described above will be used in every pregnancy. Blood and urine samples and blood pressure measurements are likely to be carried out at some stage of pregnancy; but amniocentesis, chorionic villus sampling, and fetoscopy are used only if abnormality of the fetus is suspected. The availability of a test does not mean that it will be used: a woman offered amniocentesis for the detection of Down's syndrome may decide that the risk outweighs the advantage, particularly if she would not seek the abortion of an abnormal fetus. Consultation with a specialist should be offered before invasive procedures, and the implications of possible findings discussed before a decision is made to go ahead.

Inherited Disorders

The chromosomes that the fetus inherits from its parents carry many thousands of 'genes', or units of genetic information. These decide the characteristics and activities of every cell in the body: some cells respond to some genes, some to others. Inherited defects arise in two ways. First, if any of the parents' genes are faulty, the relevant body cells may not respond in a desirable way ('gene abnormality'). Second, even if all the genes are healthy, the chromosomes may have been muddled or broken in the original pairing of ovum and sperm ('chromosome abnormality').

Gene abnormalities

There are several examples.

a) Sickle cell anemia. The red blood cells are abnormally shaped and so are destroyed by the body.

b) Phenylketonuria (PKU). Failure to produce one enzyme causes inability to process a vital amino acid contained in milk. Severe mental subnormality results unless a special diet is followed from birth.

c) 'Wilson's disease'. Defective metabolism of copper results in deposits of excess copper in the brain, liver, and eyes. Unless treated it leads to mental derangement and cirrhosis of the liver.

Some gene abnormalities show up if just one parent has the faulty gene, others only if both parents have it.

Sex-linked gene abnormalities

This special category includes hemophilia, red-green color

Patterns of inheritance of a sex-linked gene abnormality

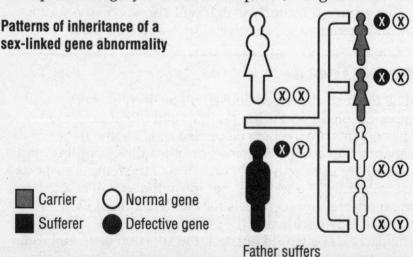

☐ Carrier ○ Normal gene
■ Sufferer ● Defective gene

Father suffers
All girls are carriers
No boys suffer or carry

blindness, and two forms of muscular dystrophy. The faulty gene responsible is carried on the X sex chromosome (see A2) – this has other functions apart from determining sex. So in a woman the disorder does not usually show up, as her other X chromosome usually supplies a healthy gene: the healthy gene is 'dominant'. But in a man, there is no other X chromosome, only a Y chromosome, with no gene responsible for the defective function; and so the disorder appears.

The diagram shows the effects of this process of inheritance: a woman who does not herself show signs of the disorder can pass it on, so her sons may suffer and daughters carry it. If a woman is found to be such a 'carrier,' there is risk not only to her own subsequent children, but also to those of her female relatives on the maternal side – because they may also have inherited the defective gene.

If no previous family history is found after a careful check, it is likely to be an isolated mutation – in either mother or child. If in the mother, she can still pass it on to subsequent children.

Chromosome abnormalities

There are two types. First are those involving the X and Y sex chromosomes – so that the fetus, instead of having XX or XY chromosomes, has XXX, XXY, XYY, or X alone. All are linked with disorders – mostly involving abnormal genitals. Second are those involving other chromosomes, eg Down's syndrome, where an extra chromosome results in physical and mental abnormalities.

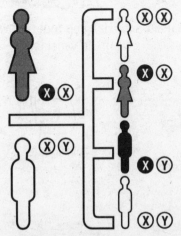

Mother is a carrier
Half girls likely to carry
Half boys likely to suffer; none carry

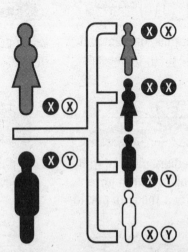

Mother is a carrier   Father suffers
Half girls likely to suffer; half to carry
Half boys likely to suffer; none carry

Diet and Vitamins

Malnutrition in the mother during pregnancy can seriously affect the fetus. It may even die from undernourishment – revealed in autopsy not only by low weight, but also by stunting of each individual organ and low cytoplasm content of the body cells. More usually, the baby is born alive but underweight – and low birthweight carries with it increased risk of cerebral palsy, epilepsy, autism, blindness, deafness, mental subnormality and neonatal death. Some sources estimate that a third of all long-term childhood handicaps are associated with low birthweight. In the US and the UK, babies weighing under $5^1/2$lb (2.5kg) at birth account for approximately 60% of stillbirths and deaths under 1 month. Low birthweight is not totally due to malnutrition, but it is a major factor. In Guatemala, a nutritional program reduced low birthweight from 20% to 5.1% of births. This is below that of many industrialized countries, so it is not just in developing countries that there is room for nutritional improvement. But careful nutrition must begin before the 20th week of pregnancy – any later improvement in diet has only limited effect; ideally, careful nutrition should begin before conception.

Minimum recommended diet

1pt milk, or ^{1}/2pt and 2oz (57g) of cheese

2-3oz portion of meat or fish, or 1 egg

Half cup root or raw green vegetable

1 medium piece of fruit, 6-8 glasses fruit juice, and/or 1 medium potato

4-5 portions wholewheat bread

1pt of water

2-3 oz portion liver or oily fish once a week

White fish once a week

1 cup bran to avoid constipation

Vitamins and minimum diet

As soon as she knows she is pregnant, a woman should talk to her doctor about vitamin supplements. Women are now advised to take folic acid supplements before conception whenever possible (see p.176).

Women should never diet while they are pregnant. Ideally, a pregnant woman should follow the normal daily food guide (pp.318-19), increasing calorie intake and weight as suggested on pp.123 and 311. But many women find that their appetite in pregnancy is small or unpredictable; and poverty may be a factor. At the least, wholewheat bread and milk are preferable to tea or coffee and cookies. But if at all possible the minimum diet shown below should be followed each day.

Women have higher daily calorie requirements during pregnancy and when breastfeeding. Estimates vary, but the increases noted here should meet the needs of most women. It is suggested that calorie intake should be increased to 2600 per day in the second half of pregnancy. This estimate has assumed some reduction in the amount of exercise taken toward the end of pregnancy.

Mothers who are breastfeeding should include an additional 500 calories per day in their diet.

Wholefoods are better than refined foods; be sure to have enough protein; and remember that for the health of you and your baby, you must have the minimum recommended diet.

4

Girls' and women's daily calorie requirements

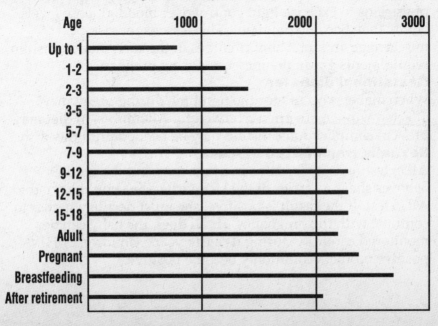

Maternal Disorders

Despite the fact that many disorders may affect a pregnant woman and her unborn child, most occur rarely. Some arise as complications of the adjustment of the body to pregnancy. Some are infections. Routine blood and urine tests will pick up most of the disorders that could be dangerous, but routine testing for some conditions, such as AIDS, is not universal.

Edema

Some swelling of the legs is normal in pregnancy and is not usually significant. However, sudden swelling, particularly of the face, should be reported to your doctor, as it may be a sign of preeclampsia (see below).

Carpal tunnel syndrome

Tingling, numbness, and pain in the wrist and hand sometimes occur for the first time in pregnancy. Diuretic (water-reducing) drugs are usually effective.

Preeclampsia (also called toxemia of pregnancy)

A serious complication of late pregnancy, affecting about 10% of women pregnant for the first time. Warning signs are high blood pressure, protein in the urine, sudden edema, headache, vomiting, and blurred vision. If there are two high-blood-pressure readings and other signs, the mother will be admitted to hospital. Fits and coma can occur at any time, endangering mother and child. Early delivery is likely.

Diabetes

Women known to have diabetes are advised by their physicians to exercise tight control over blood glucose levels before they become pregnant. This lessens the risk of miscarriage and fetal abnormalities in the early stages. Insulin requirements gradually increase during pregnancy.

Gestational diabetes

When diabetes occurs for the first time during pregnancy, affected women are often overweight. Alterations in diet may prevent complications; insulin may be needed until the birth.

Sexually transmitted diseases

AIDS testing is not routine in pregnancy, but if a mother believes she is a carrier of the HIV virus, she should have the AIDS test. If the result is positive, she must decide whether to continue with the pregnancy. If she does, the baby can be monitored carefully during its early years. Children of HIV-positive mothers commonly become positive.

Syphilis If a mother has syphilis, her baby is also likely to be infected, because the organism can cross the placenta. Antibiotic treatment early in pregnancy cures the disease, and the baby should be born healthy.

Gonorrhea and chlamydia The organisms that cause these diseases do not cross the placenta, but the baby may be infected as it passes through the birth canal. Treatment during pregnancy is therefore desirable. Both cause eye infections in the newborn which need treatment with antibiotics; chlamydia can cause a respiratory tract infection in young babies.

Genital herpes If you have herpes, you should tell your obstetrician. The virus does not cross the placenta, but if sores are present at the time of delivery, the baby may be infected and may become extremely ill. A baby will be delivered by cesarean section if the mother has an active infection.

Other infections

Any infection that occurs during pregnancy and causes a high temperature and general illness should be reported to a physician. Most viruses are unlikely to harm mother or child, but high fever may result in miscarriage.

German measles (rubella) Women who were not immunized at least three months before conception must avoid contact with anyone with the disease or a rash. In the first 4 months of pregnancy, the disease may cause the baby to be born blind, deaf or retarded. A blood sample confirms immunity.

Polio All prospective mothers should be immunized before becoming pregnant, as a developing child can be severely affect if the mother contracts the disease during pregnancy.

Cytomegalo virus This can cause brain damage and malformations in the fetus if the mother is infected with the virus for the first time during pregnancy.

Toxoplasmosis This is an infection caused by a parasite found in animal and bird feces. The mother may be unaware of it, but the virus can cause severe malformations, and even death.

Smoking in Pregnancy

As well as affecting a woman's own health, smoking will affect the health of an unborn baby. It is widely accepted that there is a connection between smoking and complications in pregnancy, and studies have shown that smoking while pregnant results in a lighter baby and an increase in perinatal mortality. Effects of smoking in pregnancy have also been found to persist into childhood. Probably the dangers are most severe if smoking continues after the first 3 months, and not all effects have been totally proven. Unlike many factors affecting her child's health, it is the mother's own decision whether or not she will smoke, and she must accept the responsibility.

Increase in smoking

In the US, as many as 25% of women smoke. The fact that lung cancer has now overtaken breast cancer as the primary killer among women is evidence of an increase in smoking.

Effect of smoking on fetal breathing

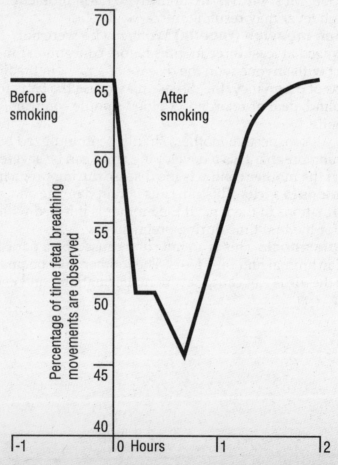

Smoking and fetal health

Fetal breathing movements are a direct measure of fetal health and well-being. Smoking has been shown to reduce the incidence of fetal breathing movements and must therefore be considered damaging to fetal health. A study of 18 normal pregnant women has shown that two cigarettes smoked consecutively produce a dramatic reduction in fetal breathing movements. The diagram on the previous page shows the percentage of time that fetal breathing movements could be observed during a test period.

Birthweight

4

Statistics suggest that women who smoke when pregnant tend to produce babies lighter in weight than those of nonsmoking mothers. One British study showed that only 4% of the live babies born to nonsmoking mothers weighed less than 5lb 8oz (2.5kg), compared with over twice that percentage born to mothers smoking at least 20 cigarettes a day when pregnant. A study in California included the smoking habits of both parents. It showed that babies weighing less than 5lb 8oz (2.5kg) at birth were most common when both parents smoked. Another study has shown that very small babies have a high incidence of neurological and mental defects and educational and social problems.

The diagram shows the difference in average birthweights of babies born (**a**) to nonsmokers – 6lb 5oz (2.87kg); and (**b**) to smokers – 5lb 15oz (2.7kg).

Percentage of babies who weigh less than 5lb 8oz (2.5kg) at birth

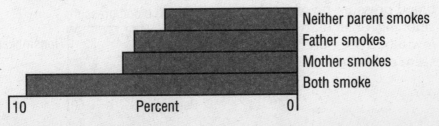

Neither parent smokes
Father smokes
Mother smokes
Both smoke

10   Percent   0

Perinatal Mortality

The relationship between smoking and unsuccessful pregnancy (miscarriage, stillbirth, neonatal death) is not yet completely clear. In findings at Cardiff in the UK (**a**), the rate of stillbirth and neonatal death with mothers smoking more than 20 cigarettes a day was 3.8%, with nonsmoking mothers only 2.5%. But in a California study (**b**), smokers' babies had a lower mortality rate than nonsmokers'. (This study, though, only considered babies born live and with birthweight under 5lb 8oz – 2.5kg.) However, a study at Sheffield in the UK clearly showed that, among women of similar blood pressure, smokers' pregnancies were much more likely to be unsuccessful (**c**). The confusing factor pinpointed was that smoking is also associated with low blood pressure (which favors successful pregnancy). But why there is this association is unknown. Does low blood pressure favor smoking, or smoking favor low blood pressure? Both seem unlikely.

Smoking and unsuccessful pregnancy

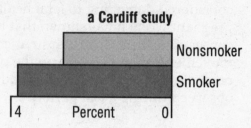

a Cardiff study

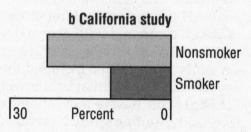

b California study

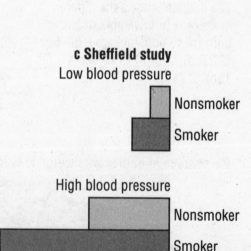

c Sheffield study

Fetal Malformation

Although there is no firm evidence that smoking is associated with fetal malformation, findings at Cardiff suggest that there may, in fact, be such a link. The incidence of congenital heart disease among babies born to women who smoked during pregnancy was 0.73% compared with 0.47% among babies born to nonsmokers. Hare lip and cleft palate were also found slightly more often among babies born to women who smoked.

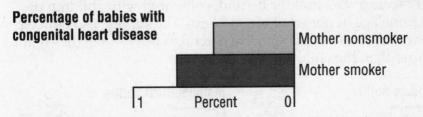

Percentage of babies with congenital heart disease

Mother nonsmoker

Mother smoker

1   Percent   0

Postnatal Development

Babies born to women who smoked while pregnant have been shown to grow more rapidly than babies born to nonsmokers. The difference in average weekly growth rates is most marked from birth to six weeks. But over a year the difference in growth between smokers' and nonsmokers' babies is negligible. So, in the end, nonsmokers' babies tend to preserve any size advantage they had at birth.

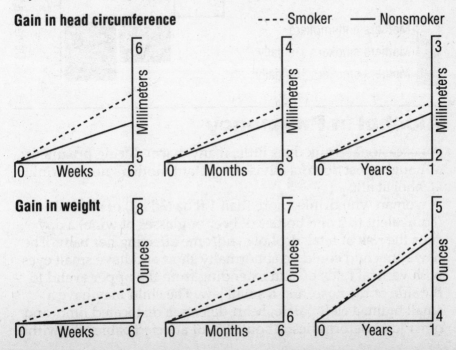

Gain in head circumference   - - - - Smoker   —— Nonsmoker

Gain in weight

Long-term Effects

The diagrams below are based on a survey taken in the UK of 17,000 children whose progress had been followed from birth. They compare the mental abilities of 11-year-old children of mothers who smoked during pregnancy with those of nonsmoking mothers. Children of mothers who smoked up to 9 cigarettes daily were some $5-5\frac{1}{2}$ months behind in school progress, and those of mothers who smoked 10+ cigarettes daily were $5\frac{1}{2}-7$ months behind, compared with children of the same age of nonsmoking mothers. The survey also noticed that children of smoking mothers tend to be $\frac{1}{5}-\frac{2}{5}$in (0.5-1cm) shorter than the children of nonsmokers.

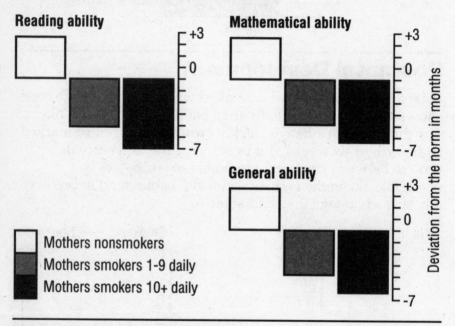

Reading ability

Mathematical ability

General ability

Deviation from the norm in months

☐ Mothers nonsmokers
▨ Mothers smokers 1-9 daily
■ Mothers smokers 10+ daily

Alcohol in Pregnancy

An occasional drink does little, if any, harm during pregnancy, although most doctors advise expectant mothers not to drink alcohol at all.

A woman who drinks more than 1 fl oz (30 ml) of alcohol (equivalent to 2 or 3 bottles of beer or glasses of wine) a day runs the risk of fetal alcohol syndrome affecting her baby. The newborn child could be abnormally short and have small eyes with vertical folds of skin extending from the upper eyelid to the side of the nose, and a small jaw. The child may have a small brain, a cleft palate, heart defects, a dislocated limb, and other joint deformities. About 20% of affected babies die within a few weeks of birth. Of those that survive, many suffer a certain amount of physical and mental retardation. The diagrams below are based on a US study of 23 children born to chronically alcoholic mothers.

They were compared with children of nonalcoholic mothers and matched for socioeconomic group, race, maternal age, etc.

a) Mortality rates. The diagram shows mortality rates among the newborn babies: 17% of those born to alcoholic mothers died within 1 week as opposed to 2% of those born to nonalcoholic mothers.

b) Growth deficiencies. The diagram compares birthweight, length, and head circumference of both sets of infants. Comparisons were based on a measurement of normality that generally only 3% of the overall baby population fails to achieve. In the survey, 13% to 32% of the children of alcoholic mothers failed to reach the measurement.

c) IQ performance. At the age of 7, 44% of the children born to alcoholic mothers had an IQ of 79 or under.

a Percentage of babies who died in the first week

2% Mother was a nonalcoholic

17% Mother was an alcoholic during pregnancy

b Percentage of babies below a given measurement of size

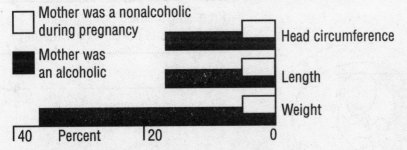

Mother was a nonalcoholic during pregnancy

Mother was an alcoholic

Head circumference

Length

Weight

40   Percent   20   0

c Percentage of 7-year-old children with an IQ below 79

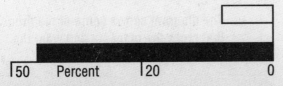

50   Percent   20   0

Drugs and Placenta Crossing

Most doctors today recommend that women avoid all drugs during pregnancy unless they are absolutely essential for the mother's well-being. The fetus maintains its hold on life through the umbilical cord and the work of the placenta (see p.108). Oxygen and nutrients pass from the mother's circulation into that of the fetus via the placenta and umbilicus, and carbon dioxide and other waste products pass back the same way.

As a result, most substances in the mother's bloodstream will reach the fetus. In the case of drugs, recent studies show that, as with thalidomide, effects on the fetus can be disastrous. This is particularly true during the first 3 months when the fetal organs are forming.

DRUGS

Caffeine (in coffee and tea)
Tannic acid (in tea)

Sleeping pills

Tranquilizers

LSD and other psychedelics

Cocaine; amphetamines

Heroin; morphine; methodone

Aspirin

Phenacetin

Antibiotics
a Streptomycin, Gentamicin
b Sulfonamides (long-term)
c Tetracycline

Antihistamines

Cortisone

Progestogens/DES (for hormone deficiency and possible miscarriage)

Antithyroid

Nicotine (in cigarettes)

The diagram shows some of the drugs that cross the placenta and what the effects on the fetus might be.

PLACENTA   **EFFECTS ON FETUS**

Stimulates fetal nervous system

Depressant

Possible malformations; but some now designed for safe use by pregnant women

Increased risk of miscarriage; possible chromosome damage

Fetal addiction acts as stimulant to fetus

Fetal addiction; can mean blood transfusion needed at birth

Large amounts can cause miscarriage or hemorrhage in newborn baby

Possible damage to fetal kidneys

a Associated with deafness in infants
b Can cause jaundice
c Possible deformities; stains teeth

Possible malformations; but some now designed for safe use by pregnant women

Fetal and placental abnormalities – possibly stillbirth; cleft lip

Genital abnormalities in female infants

Possible goiter

Low birth weight

4

Defects at Birth

These are anatomical defects present at birth. Thirty live births in every ,000 have some kind of congenital malformation. They may be so severe that life is not possible, eg anencephaly, or they may be so trivial that life is not interfered with, eg an extra finger. Many but not all defects are obvious at birth. Some, such as defects in the heart or kidneys, may be discovered within a few days, while others are only detected after many years or by chance during surgery or autopsy. Malformations are either of genetic origin or due to external factors which affect the pregnant woman, eg infection, drugs or high-energy radiation.

Most ova are never fertilized, and many of those that are fail to be implanted in the uterus. Of those that result in pregnancy, 15% are aborted spontaneously before they are diagnosed; and 20% of those that are diagnosed are aborted within the first 12 weeks. The total number of spontaneous abortions may, in fact, be as high as 40-50%. Some of these spontaneous abortions eliminate empty sacs with no embryo from the uterus; others expel defective embryos.

Congenital defects are one of the most important causes of death in the first and later weeks after birth. They mainly affect the central nervous system (brain and spinal cord).

Embryo development is a continuous process following a strict sequence. The initiation of each step in the process depends on the successful completion of the one before. Any interruption or disorganization of these processes at any time may result in a malformation. Usually, the earlier the interruption occurs, the more severe the defect.

Maternal nutrition before conception and during pregnancy – especially in the first three months – is important in preventing some birth defects. Folic acid, for example, has been shown to be crucial in preventing spina bifida, and women are now advised to take supplements of folic acid – before conceiving, if possible, but at least during early pregnancy.

The most common anatomical defects in the newborn baby

DEFECT	RATE*	DESCRIPTION *Rate per 10,000 live births
Double ureter	300	Two ureters from one kidney. Usually without symptoms or significance. Very occasionally obstructed urine flow, causing infection. Genetic. Surgery if necessary.
Male inguinal hernia	80	Hernia in the groin, between the muscles of abdomen and thigh. Developmental. Surgery needed.
Spina bifida, often with hydrocephalus	10	Spina bifida – defect leaving spinal cord exposed; hydrocephalus – obstruction in skull causing collection of cerebrospinal fluid under pressure. Genetic, or result of prenatal injury or infection. Surgery to prevent paralysis or death.
Anencephaly	6	Absence of brain and top part of skull. Replaced by fibrous tissue. Invariably fatal. More common with very young or old mothers.
Cleft lip and palate	5	Lip and palate not fused. Difficult breathing, feeding, and speaking. Partly genetic. Associated with thalidomide, rubella. Plastic surgery required.
Down's syndrome	3.5	Rate rises to 200 if mother is over 40. Caused by extra chromosome. Characterized by mental retardation, heart defects, Mongoloid features, protruding tongue.
Coeliac disease	2.5	Disorder of unknown cause, producing inability to assimilate some foods. Chronic diarrhea and malnutrition. Treatment dietary. Recovery usual, but slow.

4

Death at and after Birth

Maternal mortality

Medical advances have made childbirth safer today than ever before. A hundred years ago abnormal presentation, protracted deliveries, hemorrhage, and puerperal fever resulted in a mortality rate of up to 250 per 1000 live births in hospitals; the rate for home deliveries was, however, much lower. Developments in antiseptic and operative techniques have controlled puerperal fever and helped overcome complications of pregnancy and birth.

Today, the main causes of maternal death are: pulmonary embolism (20%); disorders due to hypertension (high blood pressure) (17%); obstetric hemorrhage (13%); ectopic pregnancy (10%); sepsis (8%); anesthesia (4%); stroke (4%). Other deaths mainly result from maternal disease (eg heart and lung complications).

Fetal mortality

Though much higher than the maternal death rate, the fetal death rate has also fallen dramatically over the last 100 years. This is due to improved techniques, and better care and diet during pregnancy. Most stillbirths are due to prematurity (see p.146), placental insufficiency and congenital defects.

Infant mortality

A century ago, 200 infants in every 1000 died in the first year of life. The rate has fallen to less than 10 per 1000, mainly because of improved prenatal and postnatal care, better delivery skills, and advanced knowledge. The main causes of infant mortality are congenital defects, rhesus incompatibility, diabetes, eclampsia, and heart disease. In addition to those deaths with known causes, about 1 in 500 apparently healthy babies dies suddenly between the ages of 8 and 20 weeks. Reasons are unclear, and there may be more than one factor: an abnormality or disease; a combination of several otherwise survivable factors, eg a mild respiratory infection; in 7%, an inherited enzyme deficiency; a tendency just to stop breathing; and unpredictable reactions to common infections. Most deaths occur in winter, in cities, in lower socioeconomic families; to boys, to bottle-fed babies, to babies of mothers who smoke, to babies sleeping on their stomachs. NOTE: Babies sleeping on their backs are less likely to die in this way. Monitoring a baby's body temperature can give an early warning.

Maternal deaths (per 100,000 live births)

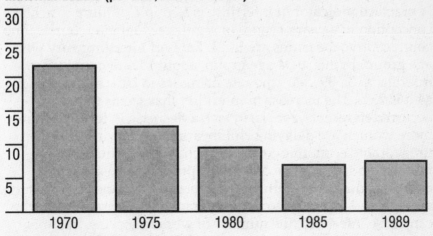

Fetal deaths (per 1,000 live births)

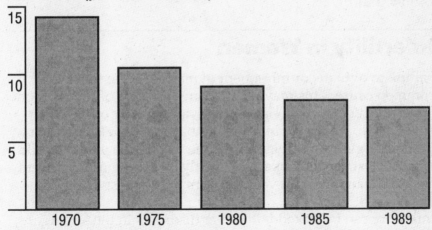

Infant deaths (per 1,000 live births)

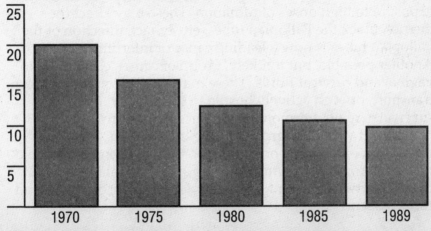

4

Infertility

A practical indicator of infertility is a couple's failure to achieve conception in a year or more of regular sexual intercourse, if no contraceptive measures are used. Rates of infertility vary with age group. In the 30-34 age group, about 14% of couples are infertile; at 35-39 years the rate increases to 20%; and at age 40-44 it is 25%. The increase in infertility that seems to have occurred in recent years is, in fact, a decrease in fertility. Many more women are delaying childbearing for varying reasons: unfavorable economic conditions, changing attitudes to motherhood, wider use of contraceptives. Because fertility decreases markedly with age, and because of other factors such as increased exposure to sexually transmitted diseases which can cause infertility, the number of women seeking treatment has grown enormously (from over 600,000 in 1988 to more than 2 million in 1992).

Infertility in Women

Failure to ovulate, or infrequent ovulation, is the most common cause. This may result from disorders of the hormone mechanism or thyroid gland, stress, anorexia or over-enthusiastic athletics. Hormonal imbalance can also prevent a fertilized egg from implanting in the wall of the uterus, while emotional stress may operate directly by setting up spasms in the Fallopian tubes, preventing them from transporting the egg.

Infertility can be linked with other disorders in the sex organs, including infection with sexually transmitted disease, cystitis, etc; growth of fibroids, polyps, cysts, or cancer; and effects of exposure to high doses of radiation. These may affect the ovaries, block the Fallopian tubes, etc. In fact, infection of the Fallopian tubes is now a leading cause of infertility.

Another possible, but unlikely, group of causes concerns the vaginal and cervical fluids. These may be inadequate for sperm transport, or even actively hostile to sperm movement or survival. (Again, hormonal imbalance may be involved.)

A final, but very rare, group is congenital causes, including possession of a hymen or vagina too tight for penetration, and malformations such as fusion of the small vulval lips; vagina divided in two or absent; uterus divided in two; or uterus and cervix absent.

Medical investigations can often reveal the cause of infertility and lead to successful treatment. About half the couples treated for infertility achieve pregnancy. Just the knowledge that something is being done may help build an atmosphere in which fertility can occur. But success varies with reason for infertility.

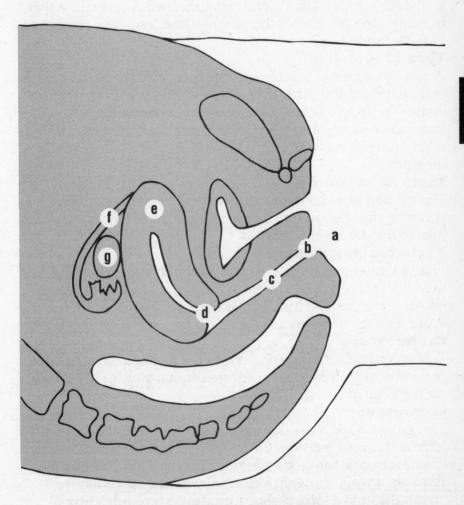

The diagram shows possible faults in the female genitals:

a Small labia fused
b Hymen too strong
c Vagina narrowed or divided
d Cervix – mucus unreceptive
e Uterus tilted backward or divided
f Fallopian tubes blocked by infection
g Ovaries fail to produce eggs

Investigations of Infertility

Diagnosis may prove simple. But if necessary a woman's doctor may refer her to a team of specialists using advanced techniques of investigation and treatment. Before any of the following investigations are done, the partner's seminal fluid is analysed. This is a simple and straightforward procedure that, in many cases, pinpoints the problem and leads to a resolution of the infertility (see pp.190-1).

Time of ovulation

A variety of tests is available to help pinpoint the time (ie day) of ovulation, if it occurs. In this type of investigation, levels of serum progesterone and hormones that indicate the imminence of ovulation – eg follicle-stimulating hormone (FSH), luteinizing hormone (LH), and estrogen – are usually measured.

Tests for ovulation

The woman is asked to record her basal temperature, bleeding patterns, changes in cervical mucus, and occurrences of sexual intercourse for several months.

Hysterosalpingography

This is X-raying of the uterus and Fallopian tubes to reveal their internal condition, by introducing into them an opaque oily or water-soluble dye. This is done before ovulation to avoid damage to the ovum.

Hysteroscopy

This procedure, often carried out in the doctor's office, uses a periscope instrument that gives an internal view of the uterus via the vagina.

Laparoscopy

This gives a good view of uterus, tubes and ovaries, without a large abdominal incision. Carbon dioxide gas is blown through a hollow needle into the abdominal cavity. This distends the abdominal wall, allowing a clear view of the reproductive organs through a laparoscope introduced through a tiny abdominal slit.

Postcoital test

This is usually made 6-18 hours after intercourse, and as near as possible to the day of ovulation. A mucus specimen is taken from the cervix. Microscopic study of this shows the quantity and quality of the sperm present, which depend on both the material originally ejaculated and the condition of the cervical mucus. The mucus should be most receptive to sperm at ovulation, but hormonal imbalance may distort this. Also, infertility sometimes results from incompatibility between mucus and sperm.

Endometrial biopsy

This can be carried out in the doctor's office. A catheter is inserted into the uterine cavity and a sample of the endometrium (the lining of the uterus) is obtained by gentle suction.

Various specialists may be involved:

a) **A gynecologist** investigates and operates on the female reproductive organs, and advises on nonsurgical treatments.

b) **A histologist** analyses tissue samples taken by a surgical gynecologist from ovaries, uterus lining, etc.

c) **A radiologist** interprets X-rays of, for example, the Fallopian tubes.

d) **An endocrinologist** looks for disturbances in the hormones of the endocrine system.

e) **A biochemist** provides the endocrinologist with precise measurements of hormone levels.

f) **A psychiatrist** helps overcome psychological barriers to pregnancy.

g) **A geneticist** assesses risks of inherited abnormality, and advises abortion if necessary.

h) **A urologist** specializes in disorders of the urinary tract.

i) **An andrologist** specializes in the male reproductive system.

The diagram shows working relationships within the medical team

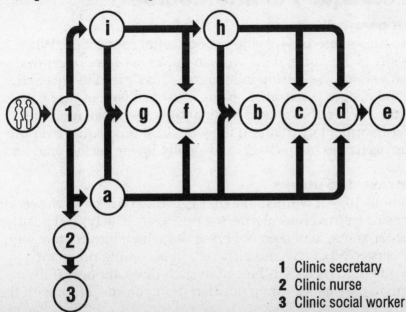

1 Clinic secretary
2 Clinic nurse
3 Clinic social worker

Timing of Intercourse

Chances of conception may be improved by concentrating intercourse on the woman's fertile phase of each month. If the charts that she keeps show that she has regular 28-day periods, her fertile phase will usually lie between days 11 and 16. With irregular cycles of between 27 and 35 days, chances of pregnancy improve if intercourse occurs on five alternate days, starting with the 13th day of the cycle. (Intercourse on all the fertile days would exhaust the man's sperm output.)

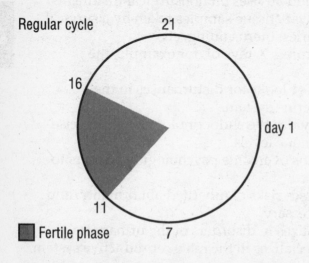

Regular cycle

21

16

day 1

11

■ Fertile phase   7

Techniques of Intercourse

Full penetration

Sometimes infertility is due to poor coital connection. When obesity is the cause, if the woman hooks her knees over the man's shoulders during intercourse, this flexes the hips and allows deeper penetration. (Care must be taken in case pain occurs.) When the cause is vaginal tightness, then (perhaps after treatment by dilation) the woman should squat over the man, as he lies on his back, and slowly lower herself onto his penis.

Retroverted uterus

In about 10% of women, the uterus is tilted back and the cervix forward (retroverted uterus, see pp.395-6). The typical position of intercourse may then not bring the semen into contact with the cervix. Most have no difficulty in becoming pregnant despite this. Fertility is helped in such cases, though, if the woman uses a face-down position (lying or kneeling), with the

man entering her from behind. The lying position should make
the pool of semen bathe the cervix – but may cause cystitis if
the penis bruises the woman's bladder. Instead, the woman
can change from a kneeling position to a lying one after
intercourse ends.

After intercourse

Fertility in any woman is usually improved if the woman
remains fairly still for at least half an hour after intercourse
ends.

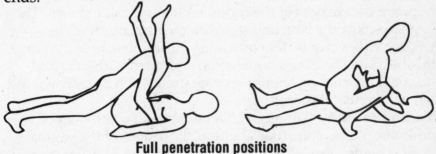

Full penetration positions

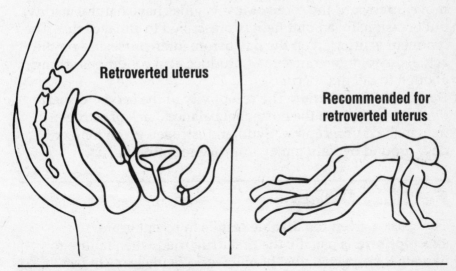

Retroverted uterus

**Recommended for
retroverted uterus**

Treating Infection

The cervix is often affected by infections involving vaginal
discharge. The cause of some of these is unknown (see pp.403-
4), but some are due to venereal disease or other diagnosable
infection, or to foreign bodies such as forgotten tampons or
contraceptive devices. Treatment usually involves a course of
pessaries, or sometimes antibiotics. (Occasionally the cervix is
cauterized under anesthetic, to burn away chronically infected
tissue.) Infection may impair fertility. Risk of spreading
infection may also prevent investigation.

Improving Receptivity

Mechanical devices and ointments may be useful for improving the sperm receptivity of various parts of the woman's genitals.

Dilation of the vagina with glass dilators or with the fingers helps in many cases where vaginal tightness prevents successful penetration.

Douching Making the cervical mucus more alkaline may improve the chances of the cervix taking up viable sperm. The woman sits in the bath and douches the upper part of the vagina with warm water containing bicarbonate of soda. For this purpose she uses a douche can equipped with tube and nozzle. This method should only be used when a postcoital test has shown that it is appropriate.

Vaginal acidity Although alkaline cervical mucus can be desirable, it also sometimes helps if the mucus of the vagina itself is made more acid: vaginal acidity seems to make sperm move up toward the cervix. Most vaginas have natural acidity, but occasionally an ointment is prescribed to enhance this. The ointment is inserted on the day before intercourse; use on the actual day of intercourse may produce acid conditions strong enough to kill the sperm.

Synthetic hormones The receptivity of the cervix to sperm depends largely on the hormonal balance. Lack of estrogen may make it unreceptive. Synthetic estrogen given for 4 or 5 days around ovulation may improve receptivity.

Fertility Drugs

These have given remarkable results in recent years.

Clomiphene is usually the first drug tried when failure to ovulate is suspected. Just how it works is unclear. (In fact, it was originally tested as a contraceptive, and found to have the reverse effect.) The woman may need no more than a single 5-tablet course taken during one menstrual cycle; with luck, ovulation follows less than two weeks after. If no pregnancy occurs after a month, a second course may be tried, and so on – with intervals – up to six courses. About 30% of those given the drug conceive. Only one ovum is released at a time, so multiple pregnancies are unlikely (twins occur in about 7% of cases). Ovarian cysts are a possible side effect; otherwise the drug seems harmless.

Pergonal is an extract of FSH and LH hormones obtained

from menopausal women. (FSH and LH stimulate the ovaries to produce estrogen and progesterone, the hormones that prepare the uterus for pregnancy; see pp.20-1.) Its use is common, especially in IVF cycles and when Clomiphene has not produced results. The drug is injected into patients under closely controlled hospital conditions. Good supervision should yield one or two ova; miscalculation may produce none, or a large number. Most unwanted multiple births due to fertility drugs stem from Pergonal. They carry increased risks to both mother and babies.

Human chorionic gonadotrophin is a hormone that is used with Clomiphene or Pergonal to promote ovulation.

Hypothalamic releasing factors are substances produced by the hypothalamus at the base of the brain. They stimulate the pituitary gland to produce FSH and LH (see pp.20-1). Hypothalamic releasing factors are now made synthetically, and have cured infertility caused by poor pituitary action. These synthetic hormones are also used with Pergonal during IVF treatment, so that ovulation can be more effectively controlled.

Bromocriptine is used when infertility is caused by the inappropriate production of milk resulting from unusually high levels of the hormone prolactin. Bromocriptine reduces prolactin levels, restoring normal ovulatory cycles.

4

Cumulative success rates claimed for the main fertility drugs

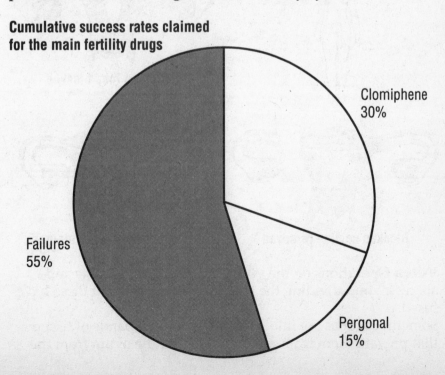

Clomiphene 30%

Pergonal 15%

Failures 55%

Operations for Fertility

A number of operations may be performed to improve fertility in appropriate cases.

Hymen Where this is too thick and rigid to be stretched, it may be cut and stitched back.

Vagina A narrow vagina may be widened and lined with a skin graft; and the longitudinal division that sometimes separates the two sides of the vagina can be removed.

Cervix A badly torn cervix can be treated by plastic surgery. Repeated abortions between the 14th and 28th weeks are sometimes prevented by stitching the cervix. Dilation may aid sperm penetration.

Uterus Fibroids and the wall that sometimes divides the uterus (uterine septum) can be removed using laser techniques, hysteroscopy or laparoscopy.

Fallopian tubes These cannot be cleared when totally blocked, as from a previous infection. But the "petals" at the ovarian ends of the tubes may need teasing out; and if the uterus end of a tube is blocked, this can be cut away and the shortened tube rejoined to the uterus.

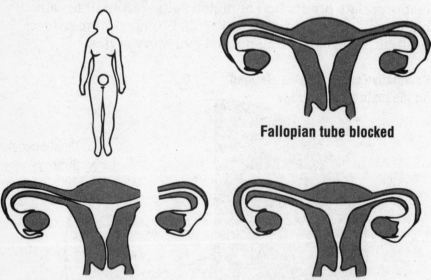

Fallopian tube blocked

Blocked section removed

Shortened tube rejoined

Vulva Operations on the vulva include opening cysts and abscesses and dividing the small lips of the vulva if these have fused.

Sometimes tubes are intact but hampered by bands of tissue that prevent them from moving to collect the ovum from the ovary. These bands can be cut away.

Ovaries Cutting a wedge from the ovaries allows egg release when this is blocked by ovarian cysts. Removal of other cysts also aids fertility. Probably one-third of gynecological operations are for the removal of ovarian cysts.

Psychiatric Help

This may be relevant. First, there are women in whom long-term failure to ovulate derives ultimately from psychological stress. These cases include those showing clear mental symptoms (eg severe depression) and those with no surface symptoms but nevertheless some underlying unhappiness or insecurity. Second, there are those men and women in whom long-term trauma interferes with the actual sexual act. Third, there are couples in whom the desire and struggle for fertility has itself given rise to mental tension, with emotional or physical consequences (eg male impotence).

Artificial Insemination

This involves the artificial transference of semen onto the cervix, usually by syringing through a tube. The procedure is precisely timed by measuring hormone levels and using sonography. Another technique that allows accurate timing of insemination combines stimulation of ovulation and insemination inside the uterus. It permits insemination to be timed accurately and bypasses a potentially hostile cervix. Success rates vary, and the technique is not wholly accepted. After insemination, the woman remains lying down for about half an hour.

The partner's sperm (AIH) may be used when physical or psychological causes prevent normal sexual relations; when the man's sperm count is low; and when the woman's cervical mucus is hostile to his sperm. The sperm of an anonymous donor (AID) is used much more frequently – generally if the partner is totally infertile or is known to be a carrier of hereditary disorders. The donor is chosen to match the partner in appearance and to be free from disease. However, because of the high number of HIV carriers in the donor population, only frozen semen is used. The success rate from artificial insemination is about 66% within the first three months. Babies conceived by this technique develop normally.

Infertility in Men

Male infertility is of two kinds:

a) cases where there is no ejaculation (ie impotence);

b) cases where the quality of the ejaculate is poor – as shown by sperm concentration, shape and mobility.

Sperm concentration This depends not only on sperm production, but also on the amount of fluid – as shown by the total amount of semen. Both very small and very large amounts are unfavorable to fertility. A small amount suggests that sperm production is also low. It also fails to buffer the sperm against the acidity of the vaginal fluids. A large amount dilutes the semen too much, and makes it more likely to spill out of the vagina.

Sperm shape The higher the number of abnormal forms, the less the likelihood of fertility. For example, fertility is probably impossible if the tapering shapes rise above 8 or 10%.

Sperm movement The length of life of the sperm (as shown by their movement) is significant not only because they may need time before encountering an egg to fertilize. For some reason not yet understood, sperm also need to survive for some time in the female reproductive tract before they are capable of fertilizing an egg.

Causes of male infertility

Causes of poor sperm production can include:

a) heat around the testicles, due, for example, to tight underclothing, obesity or working conditions;

b) factors of general vitality, such as poor health, inadequate nutrition, lack of exercise, excessive smoking and drinking, etc;

c) emotional stress; and

d) too prolonged sexual abstinence (this can increase the number of abnormal sperm).

More specialized factors (some of which can cause sterility) include:

a) some birth defects;

b) failure of the testes to descend before puberty;

c) some childhood diseases, and some other illnesses (eg mumps if it occurs in adulthood rather than childhood);

d) some hazards such as exposure to X rays, radioactivity, some chemicals and metals, gasoline fumes, and carbon monoxide; and

e) some genital disorders, such as varicocele and blocked ducts, and tuberculous infection of the prostate.

Aids to fertility

Many of these causes of infertility are treatable. But, more generally, we do not yet know of any substances that will improve male fertility. Severe lack of vitamins will impair fertility; but no special vitamin intake seems to raise the fertility level of a well-fed person. As for hormones, the pituitary hormones have only limited effect, while testosterone actually hinders sperm production – it is only useful where infertility is due to genital underdevelopment or impotence. However, there are techniques to aid fertility. One is the medical technique of artificial insemination (see p.189). Another is a practical sexual technique. It seems that the second half of a man's ejaculate – the fluid from the seminal vesicles – is actually likely to harm the sperm, while that of the prostate, in the first half, protect it. So a couple can increase their chances of parenthood if the man withdraws from the vagina halfway through his ejaculation. (They should also abstain from further intercourse for 48 hours afterward.)

4

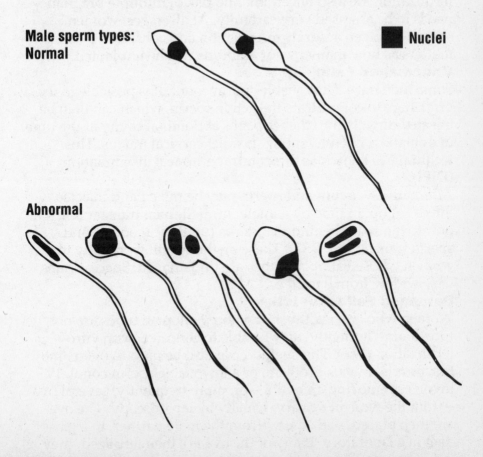

Male sperm types:
Normal

Nuclei

Abnormal

New Fertility Techniques

Several new methods of achieving pregnancy, many of them still largely experimental, have been developed in recent years. Those involving the donation and freezing of sperm, ova or embryos, bringing theoretical possibilities for genetic engineering within reach, have raised complex social and moral issues. As a result, certain research is now subject to strict legal restrictions.

Most of the new techniques rely on the use of ultrasound scanning to detect when ovulation will occur, and so allow the removal of ova. Fertility drugs may also be used to encourage the ovaries to produce several ova at a time. But the success rate of these methods is currently low, and the expense and complexity of the procedures involved may deter some couples.

Long-term effects

The long-term effects of fertility drugs, freezing, and 'test-tube' fertilization are also uncertain. The risk of multiple pregnancy needs to be assessed very carefully. At all stages, women should be given accurate information and consulted over such matters as how many ova or embryos will be implanted.

Undamaged Fallopian tubes

Some men have a low viable sperm count. It is possible to use a centrifuge to concentrate the active sperm, which can then be injected directly into the woman's abdominal cavity at the time of ovulation, circumventing 'hostile' cervical mucus. This technique is known as direct intraperitoneal insemination (DIPI).

Alternatively, ovum and sperm may be mixed and injected into a Fallopian tube by gamete intrafallopian transfer (GIFT), or into the space behind the uterus (peritoneal oocyte and sperm transfer or POST). These methods will work only for women whose Fallopian tubes are undamaged. Success rates vary widely from 0 to 30%.

Damaged Fallopian tubes

Women who are healthy, but whose Fallopian tubes are not functioning normally, may be able to conceive by in vitro fertilization (IVF). This method can also be used to overcome the 'hostile' mucus problem, or a low viable sperm count. IVF involves removing an ovum – or, more frequently, several ova – from the woman's ovary, usually by laparoscopy. The ova are then placed, with sperm from the male partner, in a glass dish in a laboratory. If any of the ova are then fertilized, they are placed in the woman's uterus. If successful, one ovum will implant itself in the uterine wall and the pregnancy will continue as normal; sometimes multiple births result, if more than one ovum implants itself. There is also a high risk of early miscarriage.

IVF is unlikely to become widely used because it is very expensive, and the success rate is low. In this procedure, ovulation is induced (usually with Pergonal). The resulting ova are collected by laparoscopy; mixed with sperm in a nutrient solution in the laboratory; then one or more multicelled embryos are transferred into the uterus. Superfluous embryos may be frozen for later transfer attempts.

There are problems with the timing of ovulation, fertilizing the ovum, and inducing the correct uterine conditions for successful implantation. All these difficulties contribute to the low success rate of IVF.

4

Surrogacy

Donor sperm, ova and embryos are also sometimes used in the procedures described above, so that in theory a woman may become a surrogate mother and bear a child for another woman who is infertile. A woman may also bear a child from an embryo that developed after her partner's sperm was used to fertilize the ovum of another woman.

ABORTION

Abortion

Termination is a controversial and emotive issue, and the decision to end a pregnancy is rarely easy. Unwanted pregnancy may result from failure to use contraception or use it correctly, or from failure of the method to work.

Confirming pregnancy

A missed period is usually the first sign of pregnancy. Others may be a feeling of sickness, revulsion against some foods, and frequent urination. Fourteen days after the first missed period, a urine test can confirm pregnancy. Home pregnancy-testing kits can be used for an initial test; as long as the instructions are followed carefully, they are reasonably accurate. The result should be confirmed by taking a sample of early-morning urine in a clean container to your doctor, clinic, or hospital for an hCG test, which is quick and 95% accurate after the 40th day of pregnancy.

Abortion and the law

In the US, according to federal law (as interpreted by the Supreme Court) abortion on demand is legal up to the point of "fetal viability" (the 24th week of pregnancy), when a fetus is considered able to survive outside the womb. The decision to have an abortion is a private matter between the woman and her doctor up to the 12th week of pregnancy. After the 12th week, certain restrictions may be imposed to protect the woman's health. After the 24th week, abortion may be severely restricted or prohibited, unless the woman's life and health are at risk. Rulings are up to individual states.

Abortion advice

The decision to have an abortion is not made lightly. Problems may arise if a woman is pressured into making a decision before she has come to terms with being pregnant. Mixed feelings such as anger, guilt, and regret are usually replaced by a feeling of relief. Pre-abortion counseling and helplines are valuable. If you find you are pregnant but are not sure you want to be, go to your doctor, a family-planning clinic, or a pregnancy advisory service for guidance and information about abortion techniques and procedures.

Nonsurgical abortion

RU-486 provides an alternative to surgical abortion. The drug has recently undergone clinical testing in the US and is now available in some parts of Europe.

Procedure

RU-486 is prescribed by a health practitioner. After pregnancy is confirmed (and ectopic pregnancy is ruled out), the first dose is taken orally. The abortion process begins slowly, with bleeding and some period-like pain over the next few days. On the third day the woman returns to the hospital or clinic, where prostaglandin is given to cause uterine cramping to expel the contents of the uterus, which happens over a period of 4 to 6 hours. Bleeding and mild pain may continue for several days. In some cases a return visit is necessary to ensure that the abortion is complete.

Advantages and disadvantages

The risks with RU-486 are lower than with surgical abortions, although the effectiveness rate is about the same (96 percent). It is a more private and more accessible form of abortion, but it can only be used in very early pregnancy (up to 9 weeks after the last menstrual period). Side effects appear to be limited to cramps and bleeding (similar to a heavy period), and occasionally vomiting and diarrhea caused by the prostaglandin. The long-term effects are as yet unknown. Women with certain medical conditions – including anemia, kidney or liver failure, asthma, severe hypertension – should not use RU-486, nor should women over age 35 who smoke.

5

Endometrial Aspiration

This technique is also called menstrual extraction and menstrual suction. It is a preemptive abortion technique – meaning that it can be carried out for up to 2 weeks after a period was due, ie before a pregnancy can be confirmed.

Equipment

This consists of a small, flexible plastic cannula (tube) about $1/5$in (4-5mm) long, attached to a suction source, usually an electrical or mechanical pump. A syringe can be used safely up to the 12th week of pregnancy.

Procedure

The cannula is passed through the cervix into the uterus. It is small enough to cause very little dilation. The endometrium, or lining of the uterus, is gently sucked out, and with it the embryo. The process takes only a few minutes and local anesthetic is rarely needed. The operation is usually carried out in a clinic or a doctor's office.

Advantages and disadvantages

Interception is fast and there are apparently few risks. The cannula is flexible, so there is little danger of damaging the uterus. Since the operation is carried out very early in pregnancy, emotional strain is minimized. However, it may be carried out unnecessarily on a woman who is not pregnant. Because the embryo is tiny, it is not always certain that it has been completely removed.

Dilation and Evacuation (D&E)

Suction curettage or vacuum aspiration is the most common method of abortion. It is safe and effective up to the 12th or 13th week of pregnancy. After this time, D&E is carried out. Some centers use this method until the 20th week of pregnancy. Essentially, the fetus is removed by suction from the uterus through a narrow tube inserted in the cervix. Surgical instruments are also used to extract the fetus.

Preparation

Very little preparation is needed. The woman's blood type is checked, and she should not eat for about 6 hours before the operation. Pubic hair need not be shaved. After an internal examination, the speculum is inserted and the patient given an anesthetic – local or general.

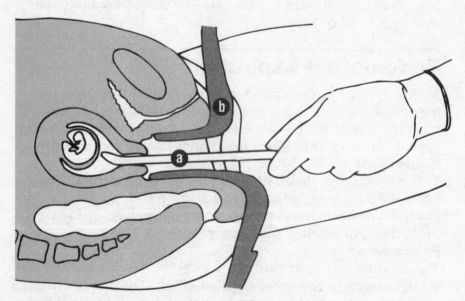

Dilation

The diagram shows the cervix being dilated. A series of polished metal dilators (**a**) are used, the largest being about the width of a finger. A speculum (**b**) holds the vaginal walls open.

Recovery

The abortion takes about 10 minutes; the rest period afterward about 2-3 hours. When D&E is performed in the hospital, patients often stay in overnight. Recovery is fast, though strenuous activity should be avoided for a couple of days. There is usually some bleeding, possibly with mild cramps, for up to 7 days. The normal period starts 4-6 weeks after the abortion. Most doctors advise that tampons and sexual intercourse should be avoided for 2-4 weeks to prevent possible infection.

Dilation and curettage (D&C)

Before the development of suction abortion, D&C was the standard method used for pre-12th week abortions. It is still a standard gynecological procedure (see p.398). After dilating the cervix, the contents of the uterus are scraped away with a curette. D&C is more complicated to perform than D&E, is more painful, requires general anesthetic, and carries more risks of perforation and infection.

5

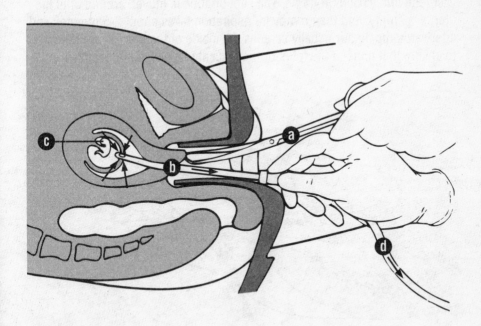

Evacuation one

Once dilation is complete the cervix is held steady with a tentaculum (**a**). A vacurette or suction curette (**b**) is inserted into the uterus until it touches the fetus (**c**). The vacurette, which is about 1/3in (8mm) wide, has 2 side openings and is attached by transparent plastic tubing (**d**) to a suction machine or aspirator.

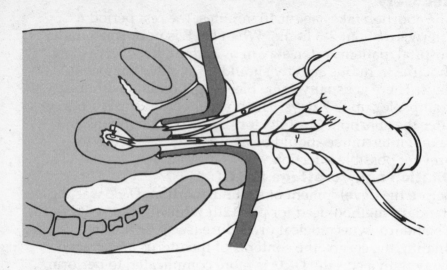

Evacuation two

With the vacurette inside the uterus the suction machine is turned on. The fetal material breaks up and is gently suctioned through the tip of the vacurette into a vacuum bottle. The suction tube is moved around until the uterus is empty, and then removed. Aspiration takes about 2-5 minutes and afterwards the doctor usually scrapes the inside of the uterus (see below) to ensure that none of the fetus or the placenta has been left behind.

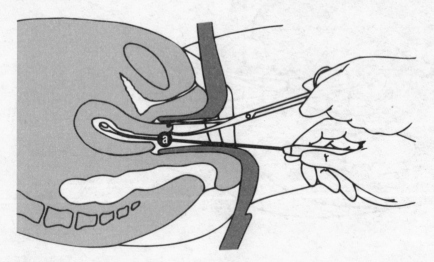

Curettage

The diagram shows the uterus being scraped with a curette (**a**). When curettage only is used as an abortion technique, the cervix is first dilated as described above. A curette – a thin metal instrument with a spoonlike tip – is then inserted into the uterus. The fetus and placenta are scraped loose and are removed with forceps.

Induced Labor Abortions

The technique currently used for late abortions is to induce miscarriage. Because it is very similar to childbirth, it can be a much more distressing experience than abortion techniques that are carried out earlier in pregnancy. There is also more potential risk, eg hemorrhage, infection, incomplete abortion and (rarely) shock. Late abortions are therefore rare and are carried out in a hospital.

Procedure

Under local anesthetic, amniocentesis (see p.159) is carried out. Amniotic fluid is withdrawn (**a**) and replaced (**b**) by a miscarriage-inducing agent using an intra-amniotic injection. The use of prostaglandin suppositories is also common; and cervical widening agents, such as small sticks of sterile, dry seaweed or magnesium-impregnated sponges, are also almost always used to help induce labor. In most cases, within 6 hours the fetus dies, the cervix dilates, and fetus and placenta are expelled.

5

a Amniotic fluid is withdrawn

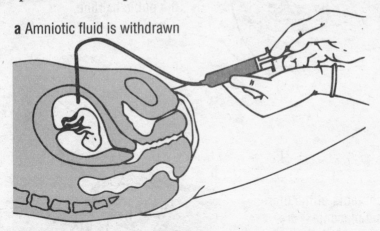

b Saline solution is injected into the uterus

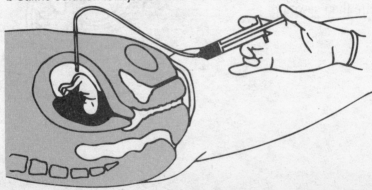

Hysterotomy

Hysterotomy (not to be confused with hysterectomy – see p.395) is a method of late abortion that is rarely used today. It is similar to a mini-cesarian section (see pp.147-8), and involves major surgery and hospitalization. Hysterotomy is the most complicated of all abortion techniques, and carries the highest risks. It is generally used only when a saline-solution abortion has failed. The resulting scar may rupture in a subsequent pregnancy.

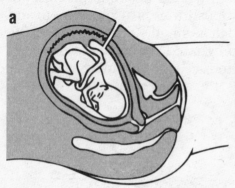

a Under general anesthetic, incisions are made in the abdominal wall, usually below the pubic hairline.

b The contents of the uterus – fetus and placenta – are removed through the incisions, which are then sewn up.

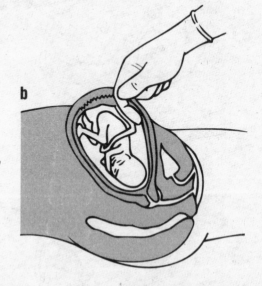

Illegal Abortions

'Back-street' and self-induced abortions are still common in parts of the world where restrictions are placed on women's access to abortion. The World Health Organization estimates that 250,000 women die every year of complications resulting from unsafe abortions. Various techniques are used, most of them either unsuccessful or highly dangerous. Inserting objects or pumping fluid and air into the uterus are among the most common methods and are often fatal. But there has always been a demand for abortion, legal or otherwise. One argument for complete legalization is that it prevents the catastrophes that result from crude, unhygienic abortions. Ironically, it was partly for this reason that abortion was outlawed in the 19th century.

5

Possible physical consequences of illegal abortion

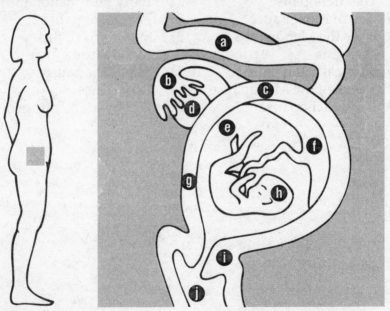

a Punctured intestine, possibly leading to peritonitis, septicemia, and intra-peritoneal hemorrhage

b Infection of Fallopian tubes

c Perforation into the peritoneal cavity

d Infection of the ovaries

e Intrauterine infection

f Perforation through placental site causing internal hemorrhage

g Blood clot (possibly infected) or air embolism (possibly lethal)

h Fetal malformation

i Laceration of cervix

j Laceration of vagina

THE MENOPAUSE

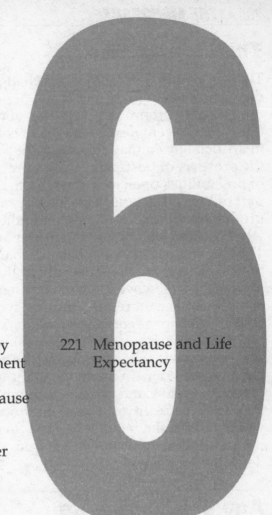

6

The Menopause

The menopause (also called the change of life) is, simply, the date of a woman's last menstrual period. This event marks the end of the reproductive phase of most women's life. (However, recent developments in controlling ovulation and in artificial insemination – see p.189 – have already brought the prospect of post-menopausal pregnancy within the range of possibilities open to women today.) The menopause is part of the climacteric, a period of gradually decreasing production of sex hormones, and other bodily changes, which begins well before the menopause.

The changes in hormonal balance may cause various noticeable symptoms, especially as the menopause approaches. However, some women experience few symptoms. The more discomfiting symptoms, such as hot flashes, disappear completely under HRT (hormone replacement therapy, see pp.216-17).

The body obviously ages during the climacteric. However, most women remain mentally and physically – including sexually – active and capable through this phase of their lives. But the reality of the aging process causes some women to see the menopause as a time of regret. For others, it represents a welcome release from unwanted biological demands on the body.

Age of Menopause

The menopause occurs at different ages in different individuals. The average age of the menopause is 51; a small proportion of women experience it in the 30s, and others in the late-50s or, rarely, the early 60s. The decrease in fertility is gradual, but by the age of 50, approximately 50% of women are unable to bear children naturally; only 5% can conceive after the age of 55.

Age of natural menopause in American women

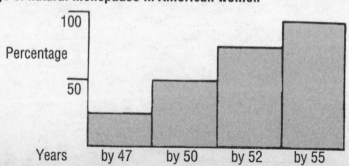

Age variations

There are many reasons for this variation in the age of the menopause. The tables below show some of the factors that influence age of the menopause, explained on the following page.

EARLY MENOPAUSE

Race		Black; southern European
Living standard		Poor
Motherhood		Non-childbearing
Weight		Fat
Puberty		Late puberty
Surgery		Ovaries removed
Heredity		Heredity may favor either early or late menopause

LATE MENOPAUSE

Race		White; northern European
Living standard		Rich
Motherhood		Childbearing
Weight		Thin
Puberty		Early puberty
Surgery		Ovaries intact
Heredity		Heredity may favor either early or late menopause

White, northern European women tend to experience a late menopause if their puberty began early. Mediterranean and black women experience a relatively early puberty and menopause. Within such groups, however, women of some families begin and cease menstruating earlier or later than is their ethnic norm.

Climate, once thought to be influential, has been proved to have no effect. But a high living standard tends to prolong a woman's reproductive life, while poor living conditions shorten it. Heavy smoking is known to bring forward the date of the menopause by as much as two years. A woman who has no children may experience an earlier menopause than normal. If a woman aged over 40 has a child, her menopause may be delayed.

How the Menopause Happens

Before the change

The top diagram opposite shows how ovaries and uterus function in a normal, 28-day menstrual cycle. The hormones FSH and LH (produced by the pituitary gland at the base of the brain) stimulate one of the ovaries to release a ripened egg into the nearest Fallopian tube, so making the egg available for fertilization by sperm. Meanwhile, as part of this process, the follicle is producing hormones too, first estrogen, then progesterone. These cause the lining of the uterus to thicken in preparation for implantation if the egg is fertilized. If fertilization does not occur, the thickened lining breaks down and the menstrual period takes place.

The cycle breaks down

In middle age, the ovaries cease to respond to FSH and LH, though secretions of these increase. As a result:

a) fewer follicles release eggs;

b) estrogen and progesterone output from the ovaries fall off;

c) the uterus lining ceases to thicken, and menstrual bleeding changes pattern and eventually stops.

Once her egg production has ceased entirely, a woman is infertile.

After the change

Large quantities of FSH and LH are still produced by the pituitary gland. Some androgenic (male) hormones are produced by the adrenal glands.

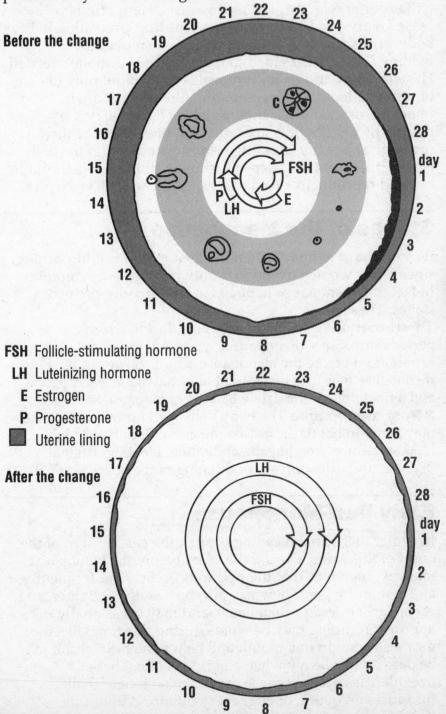

Before the change

After the change

FSH Follicle-stimulating hormone
LH Luteinizing hormone
E Estrogen
P Progesterone
Uterine lining

Surgical Menopause

If the ovaries and uterus of a premenopausal woman have to be removed in an operation called a 'total hysterectomy', she will experience a 'surgical menopause'. Her periods will cease, ovary-produced hormones will stop circulating in her body, and she will be infertile. Hormone replacement therapy (HRT) is provided to make up the hormone shortfall. Hysterectomy and ovary removal is carried out only in cases of serious illness. More commonly, the uterus only is removed, or the uterus and one ovary (see p.402). Very rarely, the ovaries only are removed. Bleeding may then continue as a result of estrogens produced within the body (see p.215) or of HRT. Reproduction is still possible through assisted reproductive technologies, AIH and AID (see p.187).

Stages of the Menopause

It can be hard to know when the menopause is approaching, since many women experience only mild or few symptoms. In fact, the menopause happens in two broadly defined stages. These are:

1 Peri-menopause This is the stage during which the periods stop. Since menopausal symptoms are often experienced before the menopause occurs, however, the peri-menopause may also be thought of as having an early phase and a final point – the date when the menopause happens.

2 Post-menopause The body's changed hormonal balance may result in hot flashes, sweating and palpitations, high blood pressure, weight gain, abdominal bloating, vaginal dryness, and osteoporosis, or thinning of the bones (see p.218).

Early Peri-Menopause

Irregular menstrual bleeding is often the earliest sign of the onset of this stage. During the years before the menopause, many women find that their periods occur more frequently and last for longer. They may also be heavier or lighter, and occur earlier or later than usual, and may occasionally not appear. Cramping may be worse during this time. Bleeding may also be light one month and heavy the next, and it may be particularly heavy when a period is late. These irregularities occur because the ovary no longer ovulates (produces an ovum, or egg) every month. Without the regular hormonal changes associated with ovulation, the irregularities associated with the peri-menopause appear. Currently, because of the increased safety of oral contraceptives physicians treat these irregular cycles with oral contraceptives or with a regimen of progestogens (such as those used as part of HRT) to better regulate menstruation. Bear in mind that irregular periods are normal, but repeated episodes of bleeding between periods or after intercourse are a warning, perhaps of cancer, and should be reported to a doctor. Mood changes may be only minor. If they become difficult to handle, discussing them with your partner or a friend may help to put them in perspective. Counseling may help you deal with any problems in your life that are making things worse. If they persist, it is sensible to discuss them with your doctor, who may be able to relieve serious symptoms by prescribing hormone treatment, or treatment with tranquilizers or antidepressants in severe cases.

Peri-Menopause

6

Your periods may diminish very gradually and cease altogether months or perhaps years later; or they may stop abruptly. Twelve months after the last period, a woman of 50 plus is estimated to be infertile. However, it is safest if she continues with contraception for 2 years after her last period, to avoid any risk of pregnancy. A woman under 50 should certainly use contraceptives. Because women on the Pill appear to continue menstruating, doctors recommend periodic switching to other contraception after the age of 42 to see if the menopause has occurred.

Symptoms of the Menopause

The physical and emotional changes associated with the menopause, such as hot flashes, may begin well before the periods finish, due to decreasing levels of estrogen. After the menopause they may intensify.

Flashes

Hot flashes, or flushes, are most common. The cause is unknown. Estrogens do, however, relieve them. Hot flashes often start as a warm feeling in the chest, moving to the neck and face, which may turn red. The hot feeling may spread to other parts of the body and be accompanied by a prickling sensation and/or sweating, then a cold feeling. Hot flashes can last up to 15 minutes and may occur several times a day, or they may be transient and infrequent. Some are experienced as night sweats, which may break up sleep. Hot flashes may continue over 2 or 3 years. They can be relieved by HRT (see p.212), which blunts the 'feedback mechanism'described above and reduces the stimulation of the temperature control center.

Genital symptoms

Hormonal changes sometimes cause itching. This can occur in any part of the body, but it often affects the genitals. Some women experience vaginal dryness (see also p.217). These conditions respond to treatment with creams and ointments.

The menopausal syndrome

Many physical discomforts have been blamed on the menopause. Doctors talk of a 'menopausal syndrome'.As well as hot flashes, this might include dizzy spells, headaches, insomnia, fatigue, lack of energy, abdominal bloatedness, digestive troubles including pain, flatulence, constipation and/or diarrhea, breathlessness and palpitations. No direct link between these symptoms and the menopause has been proved. However, many women report them (see pp.214-15). Those who do often experience them sporadically, or find they are variable. But since any of the complaints in this syndrome may be a sign of illness, they should be reported to a doctor.

Weight gain

In the months or years preceding the menopause, the appetite may become variable and may increase, while the body's energy needs fall. Diet should be controlled to prevent obesity.

Emotional factors

Moodiness, irritability, forgetfulness, anxiety, and depression are commonly reported among women around the time of the menopause. Causes may include:

a) hormonal changes. However, no direct link has been proved.

b) the mental consequences of physical symptoms, such as hot flashes, headaches, insomnia, etc.

c) psychological factors, such as fear of aging, adjustment to changes in family and career situation, regret at unrealized motherhood, and stress caused by normal problems of everyday life – such as difficulties in relationships, financial problems, or upheavals, like moving house.

Peri-menopause symptoms and treatment

a Emotional symptoms (fatigue, headaches, dizzy spells, insomnia, moodiness, irritability, forgetfulness, poor concentration, anxiety, depression). Symptoms usually disappear in time. Often relieved by HRT. Normally no other treatment. In severe cases, tranquilizers and antidepressants provided.

b Hot flashes and sweating. Relieved by HRT. Disappear naturally in time.

c Osteoporosis (thinning of bones). Prevented by HRT.

d Heart palpitations. No treatment if only a symptom of menopause. HRT protects against heart disease.

e Breathlessness. No treatment if only a symptom of menopause.

f Tendency to gain weight. Diet and exercise will improve tone and prevent obesity, but overall weight is under genetic control.

g Variable appetite, digestive troubles, abdominal bloating. No treatment if only due to menopause. May be relieved by HRT.

h Ovaries stop producing eggs and estrogen. A natural change. Estrogen can be replaced by HRT.

i Menstruation changes character. Eventually stops. A natural change. Normally no treatment needed. Monthly bleeding resumes with HRT.

j Vaginal dryness and itching. Can be relieved by lubricants, hormone creams, HRT.

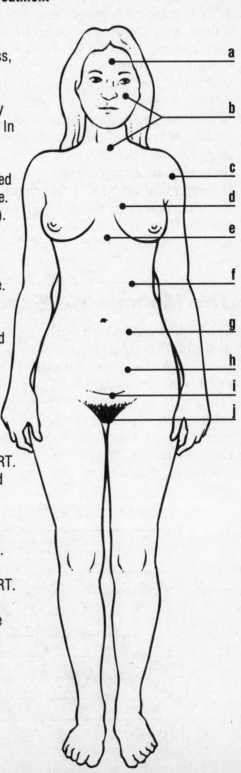

6

HRT (hormone replacement therapy, see p.216) is often valuable in controlling uncomfortable symptoms of the menopause. Women who have a positive attitude to the menopause, who continue to take an interest in other people, and who have a wide range of interests are less likely to suffer from emotional problems at the menopause. In cases of serious depression or anxiety, a doctor may prescribe a course of tranquilizers or antidepressants, and perhaps appropriate therapy.

Severity of symptoms

It seems that up to 90% of women may have one or more menopausal symptoms. Some experience great discomfort and distress. About 20% of women have symptoms severe enough to disrupt their lives.

The Menopause Experience

Symptoms associated with the menopause have been described on pp.211-13. But they are not experienced by all women. A study carried out in London covered 638 women aged between 45 and 54. They were divided into groups ranging from those who were still menstruating to those whose periods had been over for 9 or more years. The women were asked to report on 8 symptoms: hot flashes, night sweating, headaches, dizzy spells, palpitations, insomnia, depression, and weight gain. The results are

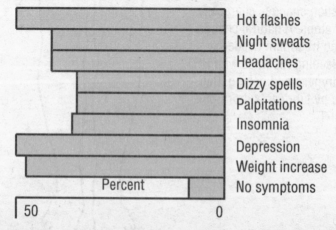

Percentage of women reporting symptoms

Hot flashes
Night sweats
Headaches
Dizzy spells
Palpitations
Insomnia
Depression
Weight increase
No symptoms

Percent

50   0

shown in the diagram opposite. Nearly half (49.8%) reported hot flashes, while 35-50% reported other symptoms. No symptoms were reported by 8.5%. Further investigation showed that, apart from hot flashes and night sweating, the occurrence of symptoms did not vary greatly from one group to another.

US statistics show that hot flashes remain the most common indicator of the occurrence of the menopause. About 60% of women have hot flashes within the first three months. Of these women, 85% experience them for over 12 months. Five years after the menopause, fewer than 30% still experience hot flashes regularly.

Nonovarian Estrogen

Some women make up for loss of ovarian estrogen by producing what is called 'low-level' estrogen in parts of the body other than the ovaries. Most of this 'low-level' estrogen is produced by the adrenal glands and the connective tissue surrounding fat cells. Overweight women may, therefore, have higher estrogen levels than their thinner counterparts. Women who produce more nonovarian estrogen may not suffer menopausal symptoms as severely as women who do not. However, while some experience fewer menopausal symptoms, the higher estrogen levels can also result in a constant low-level stimulation of the uterine lining, which is one reason why overweight women are at higher risk of uterine cancer.

6

Hormone Deficiency

Since virtually no estrogen is produced after the menopause it is clear that it is a hormone deficiency syndrome, of which hot flashes, night sweats, and vaginal dryness are symptoms. It has long been established that certain illnesses of later life, such as osteoporosis (see p.218), are part of the menopause. Estrogens are anabolic and their absence leads to loss of bone substance. It is also likely that some emotional symptoms, such as insomnia, depression and mood swings, are part of the syndrome, since they improve when estrogen is used.

Hormone Replacement Therapy (HRT)

Hormone replacement therapy (HRT) consists of supplementary estrogen and progestogens (synthetic progesterones) in the form of pills, injections, implants, skin patches or creams. It is most commonly prescribed as a once-a-day estrogen pill combined with another progestogen pill during 10 to 14 days each month. HRT for menopausal women began in the US more than 30 years ago; today, more than 10 million American women are estimated to be receiving it. Women who do not experience uncomfortable menopausal symptoms may not need it, but many have claimed that it has transformed their lives. HRT especially benefits women who have an early menopause, have their ovaries removed, take corticosteroids for asthma, and have a high risk of osteoporosis (see p.219). Many of the most uncomfortable symptoms of the menopause, especially hot flashes and genital itching and dryness, clear up with HRT. Hormone treatment may also aid irritability, depression, insomnia and other emotional problems. It has been linked to a reduction in arterial disease. Most importantly, it is proved to be effective in treating osteoporosis; it stops further deterioration of the bone mass, even restoring it in some cases.

Benefits and risks

HRT may have minor side effects, such as bloating and nausea, but these are normally temporary. If HRT is given in a 'sequential' pattern (estrogen every day and progestogen for part of the month), a short period of withdrawal bleeding occurs after the progestogen is stopped. This is normal. If, however, a woman is on 'continuous therapy' (estrogen and progestogen continuously), and has bleeding more than three months after she has started therapy, this should be brought to the attention of a doctor, although monthly spotting may continue if using combined estrogen/progestogen drugs. HRT may carry long-term risks, but these are as yet unknown. Past studies connected HRT with cancer of the uterus and breast, but this is no longer believed to be true. On the contrary, when taken properly under the care of a knowledgeable health-care provider, the combination of estrogen and progestogens virtually eliminates the risk of cancer. Raised blood pressure occurs in some women on HRT, although there is no apparent cause-and-effect link. The raised blood pressure may be due to some other factor – and there is evidence that some women with high blood pressure decrease this on HRT. There is clear evidence that HRT may reduce the risk of heart disease. HRT is currently being given to women immediately after coronary bypass operations to see if their long-term outcome is improved. The idea that HRT may increase the risk of heart disease in women who smoke has, therefore, now been discounted. Women who are smokers, have high blood pressure, are diabetic, have breast cysts, and who are obese are still eligible for HRT. Only women with conditions such as breast cancer, a history of pulmonary embolism (a blood clot in the lungs), or active liver disease should not receive HRT. Before HRT is provided, women should have an examination and a consultation in which benefits and disadvantages are explained.

Sex and the Menopause

There is no reason for lovemaking to stop at, during or after the menopause. Women occasionally experience some temporary lessening of sexual desire during the menopause, but this is normally brief. A postmenopausal woman does not necessarily lose her sexuality nor her looks; all that has changed is her ability to conceive. Sexual desire is stimulated by the male hormones, and a woman continues to produce her share of these right through her life. No woman, however old, should feel ashamed of enjoying sexual intercourse. Some women find a greater enjoyment when the risk of pregnancy is past. A menopausal woman should, however, get a doctor's advice as to when contraceptives can be abandoned safely. A doctor can also prescribe appropriate treatment for vaginal dryness (see p.212).

6

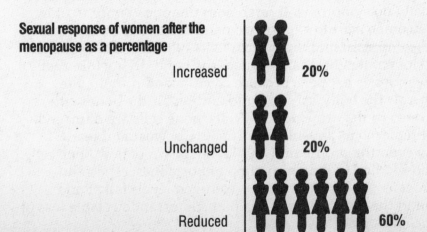

Sexual response of women after the menopause as a percentage

Increased   20%

Unchanged   20%

Reduced   60%

Post-Menopause

Estrogen influences the growth and nourishment of the breasts, uterus, vagina, smooth muscle, and skin. It also protects women against circulatory diseases and against loss of calcium from the bones. Thus the fall in estrogen accompanying the menopause heralds aging changes. Estrogen loss largely explains why muscles lose tone and skin loses elasticity and becomes wrinkled. Deprived of estrogen, the breasts gradually flatten and droop. The uterus and ovaries shrink and the vaginal wall thins. The vagina is also likely to become drier and lose some of its natural protective acidity, making it more prone to infections. In addition, sexual intercourse may become difficult and even painful. The vulva atrophies. Tissues supporting the vagina and the muscles of the pelvic floor become less elastic due to loss of tone. Prolapse of the uterus or vagina may follow (see p.395); this is often treatable without surgery. Changes in secondary sexual characteristics include the loss of some pubic hair and growth of hair on the upper lip and chin.

Osteoporosis

Osteoporosis (literally 'porous bones') is the name for thinning of the bones caused by a fall in the amount of protein and calcium they contain. In osteoporosis, the bones lose mass and, therefore, become more brittle. Loss of bone is part of aging, and so affects all old people, but women are especially susceptible to it after the menopause.

Causes

The process begins soon after the menopause, but there are usually no symptoms. It often goes unnoticed until in old age women start to experience pain, especially in the back, and compression of the vertebrae, resulting in a curved spine and loss of height. Frailty causes the bones to fracture easily. Osteoporosis happens because calcium and protein, the minerals the body uses to build and repair the bones, are excreted in the urine. Like all cells, bone cells are damaged and replaced as a result of normal daily wear and tear. However, the production and laying down of new bone cells is closely tied to the production of hormones, especially estrogen. Since most women's estrogen levels fall at and around the menopause, a gradual, almost indetectable loss of bone takes place.

Post-menopause symptoms and treatment

a Facial hair may appear. Can be removed by depilatories and electrolysis. HRT may diminish growth of new hair.

b Skin loses elasticity. Skin quality improves with good diet, exercise, massage, skin care and perhaps HRT.

c Osteoporosis results in thin, brittle bones. Bone loss prevented by HRT, high-calcium diet, regular exercise and sunshine.

d Increased risk of circulatory and heart disorders. HRT may help prevent cardiovascular problems, especially heart disease. A good diet and regular exercise are preventive measures.

e Breasts flatten and droop over time. Prevented by well-fitting bra, regular exercise, a good diet.

f Ovaries and uterus shrink. Uterine muscle becomes fibrous. Treatment usually unnecessary. Fibrous growths may need to be removed surgically.

g Vaginal wall thins and may become itchy. HRT prevents atrophy by raising body's estrogen levels. Continuing inter-course is a preventive measure. Hormone creams and lubricants facilitate intercourse.

h Vulval walls atrophy. Estrogen cream may be given by health-care providers.

i Urinary infections and incontinence. Regular exercise, especially pelvic floor exercises, and a high-fiber diet in middle age are preventive measures. HRT may improve incontinence. Infections are treated with antibiotics.

j Pubic hair thins. No treatment needed.

k Increased risk of arthritis. Regular exercise throughout life is a preventive measure. Mild pain aided by aspirin and other anti-inflammatory drugs. Persistent pain needs specialist treatment.

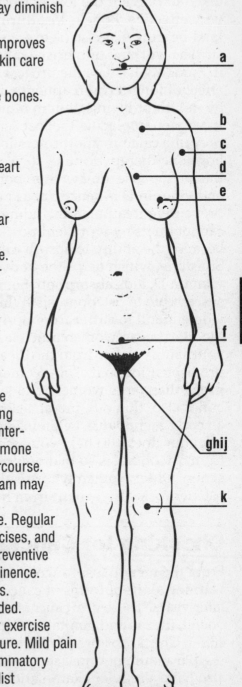

6

Prevention and treatment

Bone tissue, once lost, cannot be replaced, but action can be taken to prevent the loss of calcium and protein. Exercise is very effective. Bone is lost during inactivity, and regular load-bearing exercise (ie exercise that stresses the bones, such as working out, brisk walking and jogging) can prevent it. Smoking hastens the process, and bone thinning is a side effect of long-term treatment with corticosteroid drugs, taken by mouth or by injection in more than small doses.

In women, replacing the lost estrogen by HRT (see p.216) prevents calcium and protein loss. Research has shown that hormone therapy for 6 to 10 years, starting at or shortly after the menopause, delays osteoporosis. A diet rich in calcium and vitamin D is beneficial as part of a program of preventive treatment, including exercise and HRT. But it cannot on its own prevent post-menopausal bone loss, because the ability to absorb calcium decreases with age. Sunshine, which helps the body to manufacture its own vitamin D, aids absorption. Some women are especially susceptible to osteoporosis. White Caucasian and oriental women tend to suffer from it; African, Aboriginal, and Mediterranean women much less so. If other members of your family suffer from the disease, you may inherit a predisposition to it. Thin women with small bones are more prone than large women who tend to be overweight (whose bones also thin out, but at a slower rate). Women who have an early menopause begin losing bone early. It is sensible to ask your doctor to help you assess your risk of suffering from osteoporosis so that you can take early preventive action. Older women who are already suffering from osteoporosis also benefit from hormone treatment.

Checking for Cancer

From the menopause, a woman should be watchful for the warning signs of forms of cancer that tend to occur in the later years. These are: cancers of the breast, stomach, lower bowel, uterus and genitals. (These are described on pp.338, 432-3) Checks for breast cancer include self-examination and regular mammograms (see pp.338-9, 437-8. Women should also have a regular examination of the cervix, including a cervical smear (also called a 'Pap test', see p.434). This test, which is painless and brief, involves taking a minute piece of tissue from the cervix, usually on a wooden spatula. From it, laboratory tests can show whether cancer is likely to develop there or not. More than 80% of women operated on at an early stage of cancer of this sort have no recurrence of the disease. For menopausal women, this examination has another advantage, since it can reveal the nature and extent of any hormone lack and indicate the need for treatment.

Menopause and Life Expectancy

The menopause is a highly charged time for many women. It is the time when a woman's reproductive abilities come to an end, and it is associated with aging. Not surprisingly, therefore, some women equate the menopause with the end of a useful and productive life.

Yet in the US, almost 25% of the female population is over 55. Life expectancy of the average American woman is 79. With the average age of the menopause at 51, women at this time of life may well have one-third of their lives still to live. Their circumstances are very different from the turn of the century, when average life expectancy was 50 years and the menopause occurred in the mid- or late-40s.

6

Post-menopausal life span

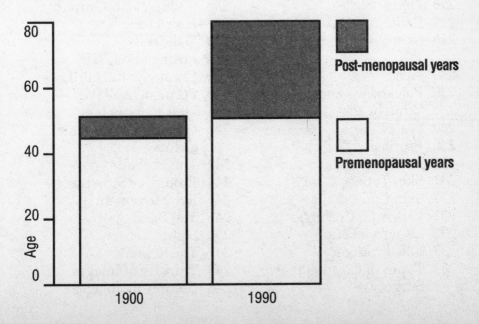

Post-menopausal years

Premenopausal years

PARTS OF THE BODY

7

The Skin

The skin is the largest organ of the body. It covers an area of about 17sq ft (1.6sq m) in the average adult woman – compared with 20sq ft (1.9sq m) in the average man. It accounts for about 16% of total body weight. Skin thickness over most of the body is about 1.2mm – compared with 0.5mm on the eyelids and 4-6mm on the palms and soles. The skin is attached to the underlying tissues by elastic fibers, which give it relative flexibility to allow for free joint movement. In old age, the body bulk shrinks and the skin loses its elasticity, causing bagginess and wrinkles.

Function of the Skin

The skin is a versatile organ with a variety of essential functions. Most important, the skin protects the more delicate internal organs, acting as a barrier against physical damage, harmful sun rays, and bacterial infection. The skin also acts as a sensory organ, being more richly supplied with nerve endings than any other part of the body. Sensations of touch, pain, heat and cold from the skin provide the brain with a continuous flow of information about the body's surroundings. Also very important is the skin's role in the regulation of body temperature: 85% of body heat loss is through the skin. During exposure to heat, blood vessels near the skin's surface dilate so that more blood flows near the surface to lose its heat. When it is cold, these blood vessels contract to reduce blood flow near the skin's surface. Body heat is also reduced by the evaporation of perspiration (see p.226) on the skin, while the chemical content of perspiration indicates the skin's function as an organ of excretion.
Finally, the skin plays a part in the manufacture of vitamin D in sunlight (see p.298), and even of some antibodies.

Structure of the Skin

The skin consists of two distinct layers – the epidermis, or outer layer, and the dermis, or inner layer. The epidermis is covered by a thin layer of keratin – the horny protein material also found in hair and nails.

Deep in the dermis, just above the subcutaneous fatty layer, lie the sweat glands which secrete sweat through ducts, or pores, to the surface of the skin. Also found in the dermis are nerves and the blood capillaries which nourish the epidermal cells. Hairs are produced by specialized epidermal cells and grow from hair follicles which extend down into the dermal layer. Each hair has its own erector muscle and a sebaceous gland which secretes grease, or sebum, to keep the skin supple.

Cross-section of the skin

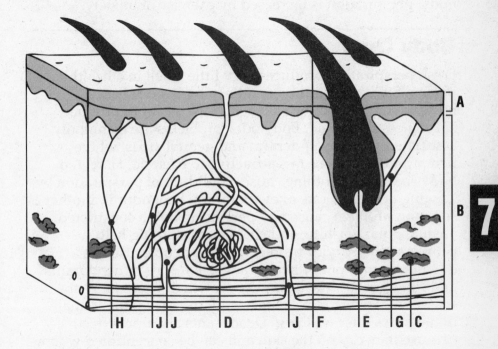

A Epidermis
B Dermis
C Subcutaneous fat
D Sweat gland
E Hair follicle
F Hair shaft
G Erector muscle
H Nerve
J Blood capillaries

Perspiration

Perspiration is a term used to describe the fluid produced by the sweat glands (sweat), and also the process during which this fluid is produced. Sweat contains over 99% water, together with small amounts of salts, urea, and other waste products. An average person produces about 8oz of sweat a day in temperate conditions. The process of perspiration helps keep body temperature down because heat is lost when sweat evaporates. Some sweating, however, occurs when the body is cool and the skin dry. In some areas of the body, perspiration is increased by exercise or anxiety.

Body Odor

Fresh perspiration produces very little smell in a healthy person. Stale perspiration results in body odor because bacteria that live on the skin act on the sweat to produce substances that smell. Body odor problems are commonly associated with the underarm and genital areas, where perspiration contains fats attractive to bacteria. Here, too, body shape and clothing cause a build-up of perspiration by slowing down the rate of evaporation. Foot odor is another common problem caused by perspiring into a constricted area. Regular washing and changes of clothing help counteract body odor problems. Most people also use a deodorant and/or antiperspirant. Chemicals in deodorants and some soaps slow down the growth of bacteria. With soaps, any lasting effect comes only from soap that remains in the pores after washing. Deodorants are more effective because they dry on the skin and can be concentrated where needed. Antiperspirants reduce perspiration in areas where they are applied, although perspiration over the body as a whole is not reduced. They work by blocking the pores, or by swelling the surrounding area to shrink the pore size. Manufactured sprays, sticks, roll-ons and creams usually contain both deodorant and antiperspirant.

Skin Color

A person's skin color is due partly to color pigments found in the skin cells and partly to the presence of tiny blood vessels near the surface of the skin. The most important of the skin-coloring pigments is melanin. It is a brown pigment in skin cells called melanocytes. The melanocytes of dark-skinned people contain more melanin granules than those of people with fairer skins. The concentration of melanin in an individual's skin is largely determined by heredity – but can be considerably modified by exposure to sunlight (see below). There are a few individuals whose bodies contain no melanin pigment at all. Known as albinos, these people have white hair, light-colored eyes, and pale skin tinted pink by blood vessels.

Skin and Sun

Exposure to the ultraviolet rays of the sun produces an increased concentration of melanin (see above) in the skin. In fair-skinned people this increase in melanin produces freckles and tanning.

Freckles are brown spots formed by patches of melanin. A suntan results from a more even increase in the skin's melanin content. Many people believe that they look more attractive when they have a suntan – and lying in the sun is a popular vacation pastime. Certainly the sun often produces an improvement in skin conditions such as acne (see p.230), and sunbathing can produce feelings of relaxation and general well-being. If you are unused to the sun or have very fair skin, it is essential to sunbathe with moderation.

Overexposure can cause painful sunburn and sunstroke. Gradually building up sunbathing time and using protective oils and creams are simple precautions that are well worth the trouble.

Overexposure to the sun

Overexposure to strong sunlight is dangerous. Short-term overexposure causes sunburn. Overexposure in intense heat can lead to heat stroke or heat exhaustion. Repeated overexposure over a long period causes premature aging of the skin and the production of flat, pigmented growths called solar keratoses. More important, the risk of skin cancer is seriously increased. Lupus erythematosus is one of a few diseases that can cause photosensitivity – abnormal sensitivity – to light that results in a skin rash.

Sunburn danger areas

Birthmarks

Birthmarks are various types of skin blemish present at birth. They include strawberry marks, port-wine stains, vitiligo, and liver spots. Strawberry marks are red, slightly raised and spongy areas of skin containing enlarged blood vessels. They are usually fairly small and often disappear without treatment. If a strawberry mark persists, it may be shrunk by injections or removed surgically.

Port-wine stains are dark red, flat areas of skin containing enlarged blood vessels. They tend to be extensive and often occur on the face and neck. They can be caused to fade by laser treatment, which is usually most effective for young people. Other treatments are used by dermatologists to make the mark less noticeable, and special cosmetics can provide satisfactory concealment.

Vitiligo can be present at birth. It is a condition in which an area of skin always remains white whatever the color of the skin around it. It can be concealed, but there is no treatment.

Liver spots are dark patches of skin resembling large freckles. They are caused by concentrations of the brown pigment, melanin.

Moles

Moles are raised brown skin blemishes comprising a mass of cells with a high concentration of melanin. They are sometimes present at birth or may develop later – pregnancy often causes an increase in their size or number. Some moles have a growth of hair which should not be plucked because of the risk of infection. If removal of a mole is considered, it is important to consult your doctor. Most moles are harmless, but occasionally a mole may become malignant. Medical advice should always be sought if a mole changes character and enlarges, ulcerates, or bleeds.

Dermatitis (Eczema)

Dermatitis is a general term for inflammation of the skin. It is usually caused by exposure to a particular substance, but may also be of nervous origin. Some substances usually have an irritative effect on the skin: others affect only those people who are hypersensitive, or 'allergic',to them. Frequent culprits include cosmetics, paints, detergents, insecticides, metals, textiles, rubber and some plants. After contact with the offending substance, the blood vessels dilate and become porous. This allows fluid from the cells to collect in the skin and form blisters, which eventually burst. Later, the fluid dries out and the area becomes encrusted. The skin thickens around the sores and flakes off in scales. There is a serious risk of infection if the affected area is scratched or left untreated. Recurrence can be prevented by identifying the cause, then avoiding the substance responsible.

Hives

Hives (nettle rash; urticaria) is a common allergic reaction with painful, irritated skin welts. It is often caused by an allergy to a type of food (eg citrus fruits, shellfish, wheat products, chocolate) or by antibiotics, dust, pollen or stress. Sensitive skin tissues react to the allergy or substance by releasing the chemical histamine, dilating the blood vessels, increasing the flow of blood to the skin, which creates welts. This is not usually serious and may be helped by soothing lotions. Seek medical attention immediately if large swellings near the mouth and throat affect breathing. This is life threatening.

7

Boils

Boils are painful, pus-filled lumps caused by bacterial infection of a hair follicle, a sebaceous or sweat gland, a cut, or some other break in the skin. They occur most commonly around sites of friction with clothing, such as the neck or wrists, and may be an indication that a person is run down. Only after the dead skin that forms the boil's core has been released will the boil disappear. Most boils require no more than a protective dressing. A doctor should be consulted if a boil is particularly painful, if several boils occur, or if the sufferer is very young or very old.

Skin Changes and the Pill

Freckles, irritation, oiliness, nodules under the skin, sensitivity to sunlight and acne are all known reactions to various types of contraceptive pill, which usually disappear after switching to another pill or method of contraception.

Acne

Acne is an infection of the sebaceous glands resulting in pimples, blackheads, whiteheads, and somtimes boils and cysts. It characteristically develops in adolescence, when the sebaceous glands become more active. Face, neck, shoulders, chest, and back may all be affected. Most cases clear up if attention is paid to diet, hygiene, and choice of cosmetics. Treatments include lotions and creams to reduce the spread of infection, make the skin peel, and unblock the pores. Antibiotics may be needed in severe cases. Exposure to sunlight or ultraviolet rays can also help make the skin peel, and through tanning, hide the spots.

Blackheads and Whiteheads

A blackhead or whitehead appears when a skin pore becomes blocked by dust, dirt, or sebum. The waxy plug that blocks the pore is called a comedo. This forms a blackhead when it is exposed to the air: oxidation turns the head of the comedo black. If it is not open to the air, a whitehead is formed. A pore may be cleaned by gently pressing out its contents, but unless this is done soon after the plug is formed the spot is probably best left to take its own course. When cleaning out pores, it is important to avoid damaging the skin or spreading infection. A preliminary wash with warm water will loosen the plugs.

Warts

Warts are small benign tumors of the skin. As well as the type common on the hands, plantar warts (see p.285) are common on the feet, and moist warts occur on the genitals (see p.425). Many vanish without treatment – otherwise they can be 'frozen' or removed chemically.

Psoriasis

Psoriasis is a chronic skin complaint characterized by red spots and patches covered with loose, silvery scales. The skin of the elbows, forearms, knees, legs, and scalp is most usually affected. The condition results from large-scale production of an abnormal type of keratin. It takes 28 days for normal skin to produce mature keratin cells, but only 4 days for a person with psoriasis. The cause is unknown, but there may be a genetic link. Psoriasis is not infectious and does not affect general health. The condition comes and goes intermittently but there is no cure. Various types of treatment bring some relief.

Bruises

Bruises develop when small blood vessels under the skin are ruptured. Blood seeps into the surrounding tissue to give the bruise its color – usually bluish or blackish at first, often changing through purple and green to yellow as the blood cells are broken down and their constituents reabsorbed. Cold, wet compresses speed healing and ease pain, but even without treatment most bruises disappear after about a week. A severe bruise that remains painful may be a sign that a bone is broken.

Skin Type

Normal skin is smooth, without any enlarged pores or flaking cells. Pimples and blemishes are rarely troublesome. **Oily skin** is coarse in texture, with open pores around the nose and on the chin. A tissue held against the face will be slightly greasy when it is removed. Oily skin is very prone to pimples and even acne. **Dry skin** is flaky and tends to become lined early. It may become sore and red in cold weather, but pimples are rare.

7

Skin Care

To maintain healthy, blemish-free skin, and to stave off wrinkles, it is a good idea to follow a 3-part skin care plan involving cleansing, toning and moisturizing. (This procedure varies with skin type.)

Choosing Cosmetics

Special hypoallergenic products made without perfume are useful for hypersensitive skins. It is unnecessary to spend a lot of money on skin care and make-up products, though it is probably wise to avoid highly perfumed preparations or heavy, sticky creams, and to concentrate on simpler preparations containing natural ingredients rather than chemicals.

Using Make-up

Make-up can accentuate the face's good points and disguise its bad ones. Always choose a basic foundation which suits your skin type and matches its natural color. By the skillful use of a darker shade of foundation or a blusher on top of the basic foundation, you can make the shape of your face look different. The illustrations suggest simple make-up tricks that can help you do this.

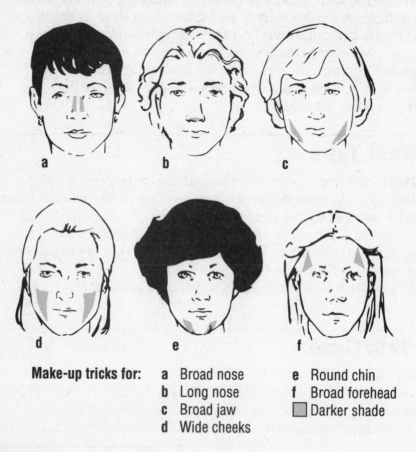

Make-up tricks for:
a Broad nose	**e** Round chin	
b Long nose	**f** Broad forehead	
c Broad jaw	▨ Darker shade	
d Wide cheeks		

Plastic Surgery

Plastic surgery is used to correct or improve minor disfigurements which are either congenital or caused by illness or injury. The branch of plastic surgery which alters facial characteristics considered aging or disfiguring is often called cosmetic surgery. Cosmetic surgery on the face can be used to remove the deep folds of skin or fat found as a double chin, sagging cheeks or bags beneath the eyes.

An incision is made, generally along the line of a fold. The flap of skin is pulled taut, fat removed if necessary, and the remainder stitched back into place. Cosmetic surgery can also be used to rid the face of wrinkles. These techniques are sometimes known as facelifts. All cosmetic surgery is very costly and it can be a long time before all evidence of surgery has finally vanished. For many women, however, cosmetic surgery is invaluable, for it can relieve extreme anxiety and restore undermined confidence.

Types of Cosmetic Surgery

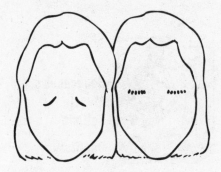

Bags under the eyes can be removed by making small tucks in the skin of the lower eyelids.

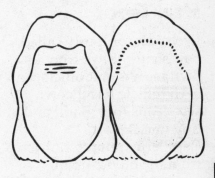

Forehead lines and wrinkles can be smoothed away by making a tuck just under the hairline.

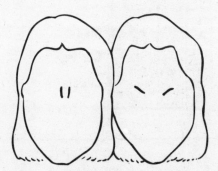

Wrinkles between the eyes can be smoothed out by tucks made beneath the eyebrows.

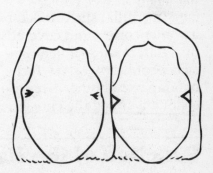

'Crow's feet' at the corners of the eyes can be removed by making tucks inside the hairline at the temples.

7

Hair

Hair is found over the whole surface of the human body except the palms of the hands, soles of the feet, and parts of the genitals. There are three types of hair: scalp hair, body hair, and sexual hair. Scalp hair resembles the body hair of other mammals. Human body hair is usually fine and light in color. Sexual hair develops around the genitals, the armpits, and (in men) the face. Its growth is dependent on the male sex hormone testosterone, produced by both sexes at puberty.

Hair Root

Each hair, properly called hair shaft, grows from its own individual follicle, and each follicle has its own sebaceous (oil) gland and tiny muscle.
Capillaries supply nutrients from the bloodstream.

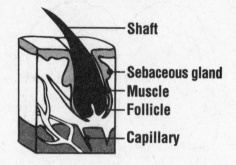

Hair Shaft

A cross-section through the hair shaft shows a hollow core (medulla) surrounded by an outer cortex, and covered by a thin coating of keratin – a sheet of horny cells which overlap one another. This coating is called the cuticle.

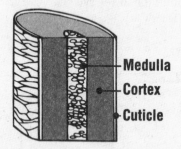

Function of the Hair

Hair has two major functions: it acts as a protective barrier and it acts to conserve heat. The eyelashes protect the eyes, and the hairs in the nose and ears prevent the entry of foreign bodies. The eyebrows prevent sweat from dripping into the eyes. Air trapped between hairs on the body insulates the skin and reduces heat loss. In the cold, or in danger, a tiny erector muscle attached to each hair follicle contracts to make the hair stand on end. The resulting "goose flesh" means that more air can be trapped, reducing even further the heat loss. Hair on the head is a particularly effective insulation. Besides fulfiling these roles, hair is often considered an attractive bodily feature, and it can play a part in sexual attraction.

Growth of the Hair

Hair on the scalp grows at the rate of about $1/2$in (1.25cm) per month. (This means that the end of a hair measuring 18in – 45cm – is about 3 years old.) The root is the only live part of the hair: it grows and pushes the dead shaft out above the skin. Hair growth is cyclical with a growth phase followed by a rest phase in which the hair is loosened. The loosened hair is then pushed out by a new hair growing in its place. In this way, up to 100 hairs are lost each day from a normal head of hair.

Thickness of growth

The thickness of the growth of the hair depends on the number of hair follicles. The follicles are established before birth and no new ones are formed later in life. The thickness of individual hairs is influenced by hereditary factors.

7

Straight or Curly

The degree of curliness of the hair depends on the shape of the follicle from which it grows.

Straight hair grows from a more or less round follicle and is round in cross-section.

Curly hair is oval in cross-section. It grows from a very curved follicle which forces the growing hair into curls.

Wavy hair is kidney shaped in cross-section. The extent of the curl depends on the curve of the follicle.

The shape of a person's hair follicles is usually determined by hereditary factors.

Hair Care

a) Wash your hair regularly. For normal hair, this means every 2-3 days, but if you have oily hair (caused by overactive sebaceous glands), you will need to wash it more often. Remember, however, that washing can actually stimulate the glands through rubbing the scalp. Also, the detergent in the shampoo can strip the hair of its natural oil and cause the glands to work overtime to replace it.

b) Always choose a mild shampoo. Lots of lather feels good, but it is caused by detergents. Use an appropriate shampoo for your hair type: lemon-based for oily hair and cream for dry hair.

c) Stick to a sensible diet (see pp.319-20).

d) Choose a good-quality brush and comb. Sharp teeth or bristles can damage the structure of the hair.

e) Unclean brushes and combs spread infection and bacteria. Keep them clean and do not lend them to anyone else.

f) Do not tug at tangles as this will break your hair. Take a small strand at a time and beginning near the end, comb downward. Continue working toward the scalp, gently easing out the tangles as you go. Take special care when the hair is wet; it is more prone to splitting in this state.

g) Rubber bands should be avoided because they break the hair. There are special fabric-covered rubber bands for holding hair.

h) Do not sleep in rollers. Again, they will cause the hair to split or break.

i) Be careful to wind your hair carefully around rollers. Hastily rolled hair causes knots when the rollers are removed.

j) Remember that the condition of your hair reflects your state of health and general well-being. A balanced diet, plenty of sleep, and regular trimming will do more to make your hair look good than anything else.

Hair Color

The color of the hair is decided by heredity.
Special pigment cells at the base of the hair follicle give a hair its color. These cells inject colored granules of black, brown, or yellow into the hair. If the cells receive no pigment, the cortex of each hair becomes transparent and the hair appears white. 'Gray' hair is the result of a mixture of dark and white hairs.

White hair:
Cortex contains
transparent cells

Normal hair:
Cortex contains
pigment cells

Diet

Protein, vitamins of the B complex, and certain minerals are
all essential for strong, healthy hair. The best sources of
protein are meat, fish, milk, cheese and eggs. Vitamin B is
obtained from liver and from brewer's yeast – easily
available in tablet form.

Iron, copper and iodine are probably the most important
minerals for healthy hair. Iron and copper are readily
available in everyday foods like meat and green vegetables,
and iodine is present in fish and shellfish. Women with oily
hair should avoid fried and fatty foods and concentrate on
meat, fresh fish, salads, fruits, vegetables, eggs and cheese.
They should also drink plenty of water. Women with dry
hair should include vegetable oils in their diet.

7

Scalp Massage

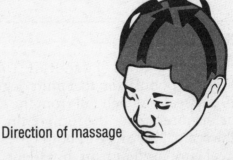

Direction of massage

Massaging the scalp with the tips of the fingers increases the
blood flow to the massaged area. This stimulates the follicles
and can aid hair growth. It also means that the scalp is kept
more healthy, with a greater supply of nutrients and
speedier removal of waste products. In scalp massage, it is
important that the fingers do not slide over the scalp. This
exerts pressure on the hair and can damage it. Massage can
go from the neck up to the crown, and then again from the
temples back to the crown, thus covering the whole scalp.

Sudden Hair Growth

This is usually due to a hormonal imbalance and can occur when the Pill is first taken or is left off, during pregnancy or during the menopause. Tufts of hair on either side of the chin or a fine down on the upper lip may appear. Very often these will disappear once hormonal balance restores itself. However, if the growth is unusually marked and distressing, other hormones can sometimes be given to help adjust the balance – although the treatment of hormonal imbalance is a very complex and delicate process.

Hair Lice

Two species of lice affect humans: *Phthirus pubis*, found in pubic hair (see p.425); and *Pediculus humanus*, found in the hair on the head. The latter can be acquired not only by contact with an infected person, but also via objects such as combs and hats. The infestation causes severe itching. It is most easily diagnosed by examining the scalp for the tiny eggs ('nits') attached to the hair shafts. The lice themselves are more difficult to find. Suitable treatment should be obtained from a doctor or pharmacist: it will include a special shampoo and often a scalp emulsion.

Dandruff

There are two kinds of dandruff. The first, affecting about 60% of the population to a mild degree, takes the form of fine, dry scales which fall from the scalp. The second kind, which is rarer, takes the form of thick, greasy scales adhering to the scalp. The cause of both types is unknown, and there is no real cure for dandruff, but there are things that can be done to control it. Washing the hair with ordinary shampoo may not help, in which case a medicated shampoo can be used instead. These shampoos are designed to remove the scales and delay the recurrence of dandruff. Some have a simple antiseptic, and others contain stronger chemicals. The most effective contain zinc pyrothionate, 'ZP11'. However, if you do have difficulty in controlling dandruff, it may be caused by a skin disorder or some other condition that a doctor should treat.

Losing Your Hair

A number of hairs are lost from the scalp every day. These are usually replaced by new head hairs, but if they are replaced by fine, downy hairs of the kind found on the face or arms, a thinning of the general growth of head hair results. Only in very exceptional cases do women lose all their hair, though many notice a general thinning, particularly as they grow older. This condition is known as diffuse alopecia and is caused by an increase of male sex hormones in the body. If this hormonal imbalance is corrected, the full head of hair is usually restored.
Stress can also cause hair loss because it interferes with the production of the hormones that stimulate hair growth. When the period of stress is over, normal hair growth is resumed. After childbirth, many women notice an acute loss of hair. This too is a hormonal problem, but the hair soon returns to normal.

Coping with Hair Loss

There are several ways of coping with hair loss.
Trichological treatments
Several clinics now offer a variety of different treatments for the scalp disorders that cause hair loss. These treatments can include: creams, lotions, massage, shampoos, and ultraviolet and infrared radiation. Courses of these treatments are expensive; but there are no good medical grounds for them. In fact, there is a risk of wrong diagnosis and inappropriate treatment being given for a condition that should be dealt with by a doctor.
Transplants
Disks containing many hair follicles are removed surgically from parts of the head where growth is abundant (often the nape of the neck) and implanted in the bald areas. This treatment is costly and takes considerable time, but there is no guarantee that the hairs will grow in their new location.
Wigs and hairpieces
The hairpiece is built from a base shaped to the bald area. Hair is attached to the base and cut to match the rest of the hair. The hairpiece is fixed to the scalp with strips of double-sided tape.

7

Hair weaving

Also known as hair linking or hair extension, hair weaving can take two different forms. In the first, a hairpiece is made in the usual way and then attached to the scalp by stitching the side of it to the normal hair. In the second, threads are strung across the bald area and pieces of hair, sewn together in clumps, woven directly into this.

Permanent Wave

A 'perm' or 'permanent' is a 2-stage chemical process which causes each hair to alter the chain of the cells in its cortex. (The process is not literally permanent as the artificially created waves grow out as the hair grows.) After washing, the first solution is applied to the wet hair. This is an alkaline-based solution designed to soften the hair by breaking the chain of the cells. The hair is then wound around small curlers and the second solution applied. This is an oxidizing lotion that halts the softening process and causes the cells to coalesce again, but this time under the stress of the roller which gives the hair its 'permanent' wave. The hair is then rinsed and wound around larger rollers for drying. Some women are allergic to the chemicals involved, so it is important to make a test curl first to check for hypersensitivity. Dyed or bleached hair is particularly sensitive to the chemicals, and it is essential to leave an interval of about 4 weeks between a 'permanent' and a change of hair color.

Hair Removal

Superfluous hair can be removed in several ways. The different methods suitable for different parts of the body are shown below.

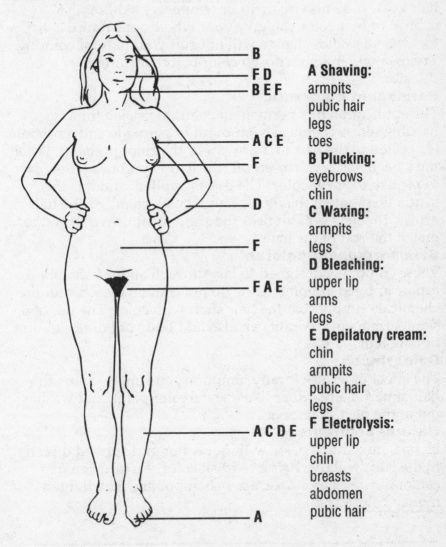

B

F D

B E F

A C E

F

D

F

F A E

A C D E

A

A Shaving:
armpits
pubic hair
legs
toes

B Plucking:
eyebrows
chin

C Waxing:
armpits
legs

D Bleaching:
upper lip
arms
legs

E Depilatory cream:
chin
armpits
pubic hair
legs

F Electrolysis:
upper lip
chin
breasts
abdomen
pubic hair

7

Changing Your Hair Color

The color of your hair can be changed by the application of chemical or natural colorants. The color change can be permanent (not literally, because the effects grow out as the hair grows), semipermanent or temporary. Although a change of hair color can give your whole appearance a 'ift', too drastic a color change will not suit your natural coloring. Try on a wig in your chosen color before making the decision.

Permanent colorants

The application of a permanent colorant is a job for a hairdresser. A chemical compound of peroxide and ammonia is applied to the hair to 'burn' away the color pigment. When the bleach has been rinsed off, the hair is porous and ready to receive the new color. The dye is applied, and it is this synthetic pigment that gives hair its new color. As the hair grows, the new growth near the scalp must be retouched to match the rest of the hair.

Semipermanent colorants

These colorants, designed to last through about 6 shampoos, can be applied at home. They do not contain bleach, and the chemicals simply coat the hair shaft with color. The use of a semipermanent colorant can also add body or bounce to thin or lank hair.

Color rinses

The effect of a rinse is only temporary. It simply colors the hair superficially rather like a watercolor paint, and washes out at the next shampoo.

Natural colorants

Henna, mixed to a paste with hot water and applied directly to the hair, will dye hair a reddish color. An infusion of camomile, used as a rinse after shampooing, may lighten mousy-colored hair.

The Eyeball

The conjunctiva is the membrane covering the front of the eyeball and the inside of the eyelids. It has a rich supply of blood vessels and is extremely sensitive.

The cornea is the clear part of the eyeball which lets in the light.

The iris controls the amount of light entering the eyeball. By contracting, it reduces the size of the pupil (the hole through which the light enters). It is the iris which gives the eye its 'color'.

The lens has a firm center, surrounded by a softer substance contained in a fibrous capsule. By being stretched or thickened, it focuses light on the back of the eyeball.

The suspensory ligaments are attached at one end to the lens and at the other to the ciliary body. They hold the lens in place.

The ciliary body. The muscles of the ciliary body control the shape of the lens. If they contract, the lens is stretched, and light rays from long distances are focused on the retina (are 'accommodated'). If they relax, the lens thickens, and close objects are accommodated. Both the lens and the iris are under the control of the autonomic nervous system and cannot be controlled at will.

The anterior chamber lies in front of the lens and is filled with a watery fluid called the aqueous humor.

The sclera or sclerotic coat is a layer of dense white tissue. It completely surrounds the eyeball, except where the optic nerve enters at the rear, and where it is modified at the front to form the transparent cornea. The sclera forms the 'whites' of the eyes.

The choroid tissue lies beneath more than two-thirds of the sclera. It is colored brown or black and contains blood vessels. The ciliary body and the retina are formed from the choroid. Its color absorbs excess light within the eyeball, making for clearer vision.

The retina is a thin layer of light-sensitive cells which lines the inside of the eyeball. It has a rich blood supply.

The fovea lies on the visual axis of the eyeball. It is a small depression in the retina, at which vision is sharpest. It contains only 'cone'cells (see p.247).

The optic nerve is a direct extension of the brain. It enters the eyeball at the rear. The head of the optic nerve is called the optic disk. It forms a blind spot in the vision, as there are no light-sensitive cells there. We are sometimes aware of this blind spot as a black dot at one corner of our vision.

7

The vitreous body occupies the space behind the lens. It is a transparent jelly-like substance that fills out the eyeball, giving it its shape. It contains small specks which are often seen when looking at white surfaces.

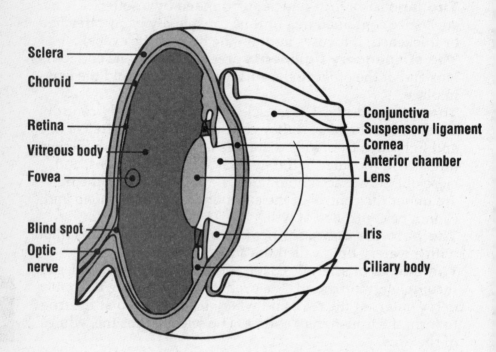

Sclera — Choroid — Retina — Vitreous body — Fovea — Blind spot — Optic nerve — Conjunctiva — Suspensory ligament — Cornea — Anterior chamber — Lens — Iris — Ciliary body

Protective Structures

The eyes – the organs of sight – lie in deep hollows in the skull, on either side of the nose, and are protected in various ways.

The eyebrows prevent moisture and solid particles from running down into the eye from above.

The eyelids are folds of skin which, when closed, cover and protect the eyes. The inner membrane of each eyelid is a continuation of the 'conjunctiva' which covers the front of the eyeball.

The eyelashes are hairs that protrude from the eyelids. They prevent foreign bodies from entering the eye, and trigger off the protective blinking mechanism when touched unexpectedly.

The lacrimal glands produce a watery, salty fluid that cleans the front of the eyeball. It also lubricates the movement of the eyelid over the eyeball. When stimulated by strong emotion or irritants, the glands produce excess fluid.

The lacrimal ducts drain the fluid from the eyeballs into the lacrimal sacs which lead into the nasal passage. When the ducts cannot clear the fluid fast enough, it overflows and runs down the face as tears.

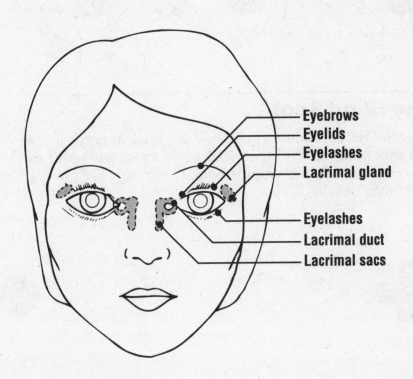

- Eyebrows
- Eyelids
- Eyelashes
- Lacrimal gland

- Eyelashes
- Lacrimal duct
- Lacrimal sacs

7

Blinking is a protective action of the eyelids which spreads the lacrimal fluid over, and cleans, the front of the eyeball. Blinking is controlled by the brain. It occurs every 2 to 10 seconds, and the rate increases under stress, in dusty surroundings or when tired, and decreases during periods of concentration.

Eye Movement

Movement of the eyeball is controlled by six muscles attached to the outside of the sclera.

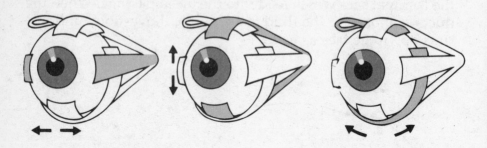

The Blind Spot

How to find your blind spot. Hold the book at arm's length, and shut your left eye. Then look at the cross with your right eye, while slowly moving the book towards you. At one point the dot will disappear.

Sight

When the light rays from an object enter the eye, they are bent ('refracted') by the cornea and the lens (and to a lesser extent by the aqueous humor and vitreous body). Because of this refraction, the rays are focused on the retina (though the image is upside down). The action of light on the cells of the retina triggers off an impulse which travels down the optic nerve to the visual centers of the brain. Here the impulses are interpreted and 'seen' as colors and shapes the right way up.

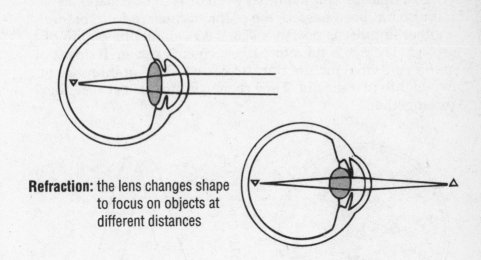

Refraction: the lens changes shape to focus on objects at different distances

---

The Retina

There are two types of light-sensitive cells in the retina. They are classified by shape: rods and cones. They are connected by nerve fibers to the optic nerve.

Rods

There are about 125 million rods in each eyeball. They are sensitive to low-intensity light and are used mainly in night vision. They are not sensitive to color and therefore give only a monochrome image (black, white and shades of gray). They are less than one four-hundredth of an inch in length and one-thousandth of an inch thick. The rods contain a purple pigment called rhodopsin. Light bleaches the rod as the pigment breaks down. This sets off electrical charges in the rods, which are transmitted down the optic nerve to the brain in the form of nervous impulses.

Cones

These are shorter and thicker, for most of their length, than the rods. They are used for high-intensity light, such as daylight, and give color vision. The actual process of color vision is not known, but it is thought that there are three different classes of cones, each containing a different pigment. Each pigment would be sensitive to a different color: blue, green or red. Other colors would be combinations of these. It is thought that the nerve messages are produced by bleaching, as in the rods.

7

Response to light

When a light-cell pigment has been broken down and an impulse has been passed, the pigment must re-form before another impulse is possible. This takes about one-eighth of a second. The eye is therefore like a cinema screen. It does not give a continual picture but successive 'stills' at intervals of one-eighth of a second. They seem continuous because they run together.

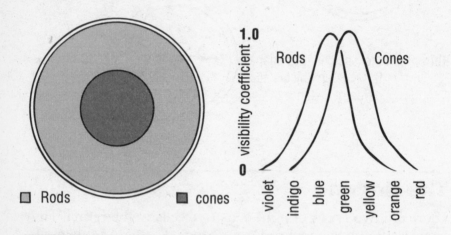

□ Rods   ▨ cones

Transfer of Images

The nerves from the left sides of the two retinas travel to one side of the brain, and those from the right sides to the other side of the brain.

a Eyeball
b Nerve
c Brain

Composite Images

Each eye sees a slightly different view of the same object. The images received in the two visual centers (at the rear of the cerebral hemispheres) are composite images from both eyes, mixed 50:50. The further away the object is, the less the discrepancy between the two views. This, plus the amount of tension needed to focus and the amount of blurring, forms the basis of judgment of distance.

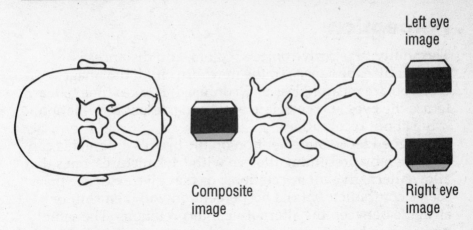

Left eye image

Composite image

Right eye image

Visual Scope

The field of vision is the area that can be seen by an eye without moving it. The size of the field varies with different colors. White has the largest, then yellow, blue, red and green.
The range of movement of the eyeball, with the head still, is also limited. The human eyeball can tilt 35° up, 50° down, 50° in (ie toward the other eye), and 45° out. The greater angle available when turning in allows an eye to focus on an object that is just within the other eye's outer range.
The area of vision is the total range through which a creature can see without moving head or body. It is determined by: the position of the eyes in the head; the shape of the head; the eyes' range of movement; and, at the edge, by the eyes' field of vision.

7

Field of vision

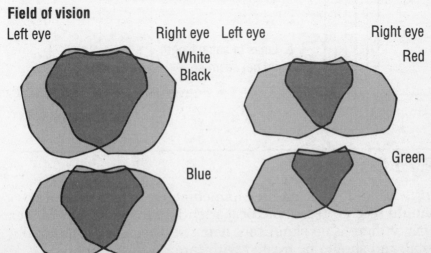

Left eye

Right eye

Left eye

Right eye

White
Black

Red

Blue

Green

Perception

The ability to perceive objects, colors, and distances is learned by experience. To the newborn child, the images received are meaningless and confused. It takes time to learn to use the eyes and correlate past with present information to bring about recognition.

This dependence of perception on the brain's judgments can be shown by presenting the eye with trick pictures: ones that allow alternative interpretations, or that give evidence that seems contradictory (**a**). Our perception will then shift or struggle between the alternative interpretations. The same process can be observed when waking up in unfamiliar surroundings – a series of alternative pictures flashes through the brain as it tries to make familiar sense of the data it is receiving. In other cases, though, the brain accepts deceptive information unquestioningly (**b**).

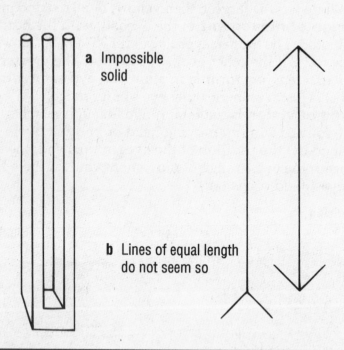

a Impossible solid

b Lines of equal length do not seem so

Eye Care

Injuries to the eye and the immediately surrounding area should receive expert medical attention. Infection is a danger even if there is no significant damage. The eyes are tough but vital, and should be treated with care.

Small foreign bodies that get stuck in the eye can usually be removed by blinking. If this fails, then pull the upper lid outward and downward over the lower lid. When the upper lid is released, the particle may be dislodged. A particle can also be removed with the corner of a clean handkerchief or by blowing it toward the edge. If none of this succeeds, get help and if necessary medical attention.

Black eyes are bruises of the eyelids and tissues around the eyes. They can be treated by applying a cold compress. If a black eye appears after a blow elsewhere on the head, see a doctor.

A stye is an inflammation of the sebaceous gland around an eyelash, and is caused by bacterial infection. It is most often found in young people. A large part of the eyelid may become affected. To treat a stye, remove the relevant eyelash and bathe the eye with hot water. Antibiotics should only be used in extreme cases.

Conjunctivitis is inflammation of the conjunctiva. It can be caused by infection or irritation. If due to bacterial or viral infection, it needs the appropriate antibiotic eyedrops; if due to irritation, the irritant (eg an ingrown eyelash) is removed. Bathing the eye with warm water and lotions is soothing and is all that is needed in mild cases. Bandages or pads encourage the growth of bacteria, but dark glasses or eyeshades protect the eye from light and wind. Conjunctivitis is not very serious in itself (except for the trachoma form found in the tropics), but can sometimes cause serious complications such as ulceration of the cornea.

7

Corrective Lenses

Eyeglasses (and contact lenses) are used because of faulty focusing in the eye. The artificial lens corrects the work of the defective part of the eye.

Nearsightedness (myopia) is due to the refractive power of the eye being too strong (eg the lens may be too thick) or to the eyeball being too long. In both cases, the light rays are focused in front of the retina, giving a blurred image. Concave corrective lenses are needed to focus on distant objects.

Farsightedness (hypermetropia) is due to the eye's refractive power being too weak or the eyeball too short. The light rays are focused behind the retina, again giving a blurred image. Convex corrective lenses are needed for close work such as reading.

Astigmatism means that the cornea does not curve correctly, and the person cannot focus on both vertical and horizontal objects at the same time. A special spectacle lens is needed that only affects the light rays on one of these planes. Alternatively, a hard contact lens can be used, as the fluid layer between eye and lens compensates for the cornea. **Presbyopia** occurs in old age .

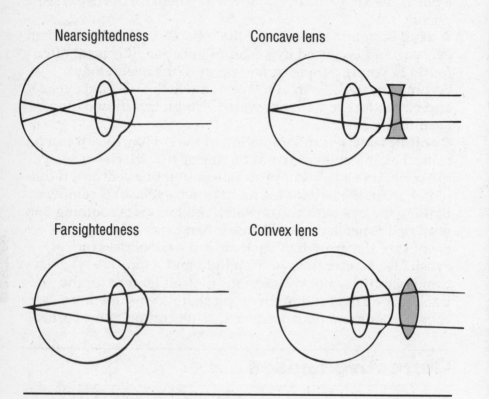

Nearsightedness   Concave lens

Farsightedness   Convex lens

Contact Lenses

Contact lenses are thin round disks of plastic that rest directly on the surface of the eye. They are increasingly used instead of glasses, as they do not affect the appearance, often give better vision, and counteract many year-to-year changes in eyesight. However, not everyone can wear contact lenses, and some people can wear them only part of the day. They also require more care because of their size and fragility and because of the effect a damaged lens can have on the eye. They must be cleaned and stored in a special fluid, and it is wise to insure them against destruction or loss.

Types of lenses

Contact lenses can be 'hard', 'hard, gas-permeable' or 'soft'.
Hard lenses are either 'scleral' lenses – covering the whole of
the visible part of the eye – or 'corneal' lenses, which rest on
the center of the eye, floating on a film of tear fluid. Soft
lenses are the most popular, but scleral lenses are useful for
very active sports. Soft lenses differ because they absorb
water from the tear fluid.

Disposable lenses have been known to lead to infections and
require careful use. The daily disposables introduced
recently are thought to pose fewer risks than extended-wear
disposables.

Tinted lenses in different eye color are also available.

Comparing hard and soft lenses

Soft lenses are immediately comfortable, easy to get used to,
can generally be worn for long periods, can be left off for
several days and then worn again without discomfort, and
can be worn with little discomfort in dirty atmospheres.

Hard lenses are comparatively cheap and difficult to
damage, last for perhaps 6-8 years (compared with 2-3 years
for soft lenses with routine wear and tear, and often under a
year if damage occurs), and are more suitable for most
prescriptions. They often give clearer vision than soft lenses,
are easier to keep free from bacteria, and are much easier for
an optician to adjust if difficulty arises.

Gas-permeable lenses have similar qualities to hard lenses,
but are more comfortable because oxygen is able to pass
through them to the eye. They do not last as long (perhaps
up to 5 years) and they are more expensive.

7

Blindness

Obstruction of light

When areas of the naturally transparent part of the eye
become opaque, light rays are prevented from reaching the
retina. Opacity of the cornea can be caused by corneal ulcers,
or by keratitis, ie inflammation of the cornea. Opacity of the
lens is commonly caused by its becoming hard – "forming a
cataract." Cataracts most often occur with aging, but can also
be caused by wounds, heat, radiation and electric shock.

Diseases affecting the retina

These are often caused by diseases elsewhere in the body,
especially those involving the blood supply.

a) Retinitis is inflammation of the retina with consequent loss of vision. It is associated with diabetes, leukemia, kidney disorders and syphilis.

b) Retinopathy covers any disease of the retina that is not inflammatory. It is usually caused by degeneration of the blood vessels, impairing the retina's structure and function. It can be due to high blood pressure, diabetes, kidney disorders and atherosclerosis.

c) Primary detachment of the retina occurs if damage to the retina allows fluid from the vitreous body to leak through and lift the retina from the choroid. Treatment is possible. Secondary detachment occurs if the retina is pushed away from the choroid and damaged by underlying tumors, bleeding or retinal disease. No treatment is possible.

d) Glaucoma can occur in old age.

e) Choroiditis is inflammation of the choroid due to infection (especially syphilis) or allergy. The effects depend on the size and position of the inflammation: the nearer the fovea, the greater the vision loss. The inflammation can be treated, but damaged vision is seldom improved.

Declining field of vision in a case of progressive blindness in both eyes

Left eye   Right eye

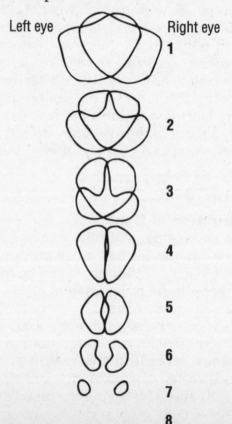

The Ear

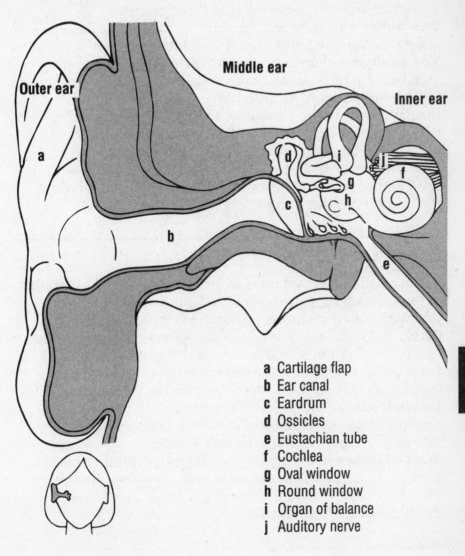

Outer ear

Middle ear

Inner ear

7

a Cartilage flap
b Ear canal
c Eardrum
d Ossicles
e Eustachian tube
f Cochlea
g Oval window
h Round window
i Organ of balance
j Auditory nerve

The Ear

The structures of the ear fall into three groups.
The outer ear includes: the external flap of cartilage (the 'pinna' or 'auricle') and the ear canal (the 'meatus').
The middle ear includes: the eardrum (the 'tympanic membrane'); three small bones called the 'ossicles' and known individually as the hammer ('malleus'), anvil ('incus'), and stirrup ('stapes'); and the eustachian tube, which opens into the back of the throat and keeps the air pressure in the middle ear equal to that outside.
The inner ear includes: the cochlea, a spiral filled with fluid and containing the 'organ of corti'; the oval window; the round window; and the organs of balance.

Sound

When a solid object vibrates in air, it passes on this vibration to the surrounding air molecules. Sound waves are the vibrations of air molecules. Sound has three qualities:
Pitch, the highness or lowness of a sound, depends on the "frequency" of the sound waves, ie the number of vibrations per second. High-pitched (piercing) sounds have a high frequency. Low-pitched (deep) sounds have a low frequency.
Intensity is the loudness of a sound and depends on the amount of energy in the sound waves, ie how widely they vibrate. Intensity is measured in 'decibels'.
Timbre is the quality of a sound. Sounds with the same pitch and intensity can be distinguished by their timbre. Timbre is created by the subordinate tones that accompany the pitch, or main sound.

Hearing

The outer ear Sound waves are collected by the pinna and funneled into the ear canal.
The middle ear The eardrum vibrates in time with the sound waves. This vibration is passed on along the three ossicles to the oval window. The lever action of the ossicles increases the strength of the vibration. This allows the vibration to be passed from the air of the outer and middle ear to the fluid of the inner ear.
The inner ear The vibration of the oval window makes

the fluid in the cochlea vibrate. The pressure changes in the fluid are picked up by specialized cells in the organ of corti. This organ converts the vibrations into nerve impulses, which pass along the auditory nerve to the brain.

Meanwhile, the vibrations pass on through the cochlea and back to the round window, where they are lost in the air of the middle ear and eustachian tube.

Sensitivity

Loudness The human ear can hear sounds ranging in loudness from 10 decibels to 140 decibels (though the loudness becomes painful after 100 decibels). On the decibel scale, a ten-unit increase means 10 times the loudness. Therefore, the quietest sound the human ear can hear is one 10 million millionth the loudness of the loudest.

Pitch Different frequencies stimulate different parts of the organ of corti. That is why we can distinguish one sound from another. The human ear can hear sounds ranging in pitch from 20 cycles per second (low) to 20,000 cycles per second (high). Frequencies above this are called ultrasounds, and can be heard by some animals but not humans.

Direction The slight distance between the ears means that there are minute differences in their perception of a given sound. The brain interprets these differences to tell from which direction the sound came. But if a sound comes from directly behind or in front of the listener, both ears receive the same message, and the listener must turn her head before she can pinpoint the location.

Decline in hearing often progresses with age.

7

Balance

The organ of balance is in the inner ear next to the cochlea. It consists of three U-shaped tubes ('semicircular canals'), at right angles to each other. They are filled with fluid, which is set in motion when the person moves. Hairs at the base of each canal sense this movement and send messages to the brain, which are interpreted and used to maintain the person's balance. The organ also contains two other structures, the saccule and the utricle. These have specialized cells which are sensitive to gravity, and so keep a check on the body's position.

Ear Care

The outer ear should be kept clean at all times, to prevent wax and bacteria from collecting in the ear canal and damaging the eardrum.

To examine the outer ear, a beam of light from a flashlight is shone down the ear canal.

The inner ear is tested by using a tuning fork. The fork should be heard clearly when it is held in front of the ear. If the tuning fork is heard more clearly when placed on the bone behind the ear then either the outer ear is blocked with wax or, if not, the middle ear is faulty, since sound vibrations are being heard better through the skull. If hearing is still poor when the fork is placed on the bone behind the ear, it is the inner ear or the auditory nerves that are at fault.

Syringing of the outer ear cleans it and washes out obstructions such as wax or foreign bodies. A large glass or metal syringe is used – one with a blunt point not more than 1in (2.5cm) long, so it cannot hurt the eardrum. The syringe is filled with warmish water, containing, if necessary, an antiseptic and/or wax-dissolving agent. The fluid is directed along the upper wall of the canal, and flows out along the lower.

Symptoms of Disorder

Deafness can be temporary or permanent, caused by obstruction or disease.

Earache is usually caused by infection and inflammation in the ear. In the outer ear this can occur through physical damage, boils or eczema (a skin disorder). Large wax deposits can also cause earaches.

Germs from throat infections may spread up the eustachian tube and cause inflammation of the middle ear (especially in children). This is common after tonsilitis, measles, flu or head colds, and can be very painful. Earache can also arise without any ear disorder, because of disturbances affecting the nerves it shares with other parts of the head. Tonsilitis, bad teeth, swollen glands and neuralgia can all cause earache in this way.

Ringing in the ears ('tinnitus') is usually associated with earache in the middle ear and/or high blood pressure. It is also caused by certain ear diseases.

Giddiness or vertigo can be caused by infections of the inner ear that affect the organs of balance.
Discharges can come from boils or other infections.

Sites of Disorder

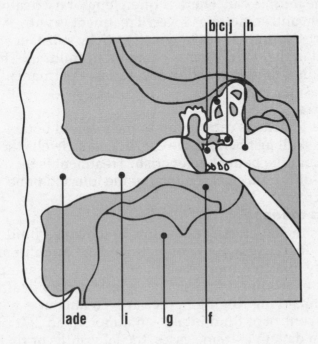

a	Blockage	f	Otitis media
b	Ringing	**g**	Mastoiditis
c	Vertigo	**h**	Ménière's disease
d	Discharge	**i**	Fungus
e	Otitis externa	**j**	Otosclerosis

Ear Disorders

Otitis externa

This is infection and inflammation of the outer ear, due to physical damage, allergy, boils or spread of inflammation from the middle ear. There is itching and often a discharge, which may cause temporary deafness if it blocks the ear canal. Treatment is by antiseptic syringing and use of soothing lotions. Hot poultices and aspirin may relieve the pain.

Otitis media

This is middle-ear infection, usually due to bacteria arriving via the eustachian tube. The eardrum becomes red and swollen, and may perforate. Pressure and pain increase as pus fills the middle ear. There is often temporary deafness and ringing, and sometimes fever. Treatment is with antibiotics. A form of otitis in which a sticky substance is discharged in the middle ear is common in children. The ossicles cannot function, and in severe cases permanent deafness results.

Mastoiditis

Middle-ear infections can spread to the mastoid bone – the part of the skull just behind the ear. Infection swells the bone painfully, and the patient is feverish. Treatment is by antibiotics or the surgical removal of the infected bone (mastoidectomy).

Ménière's disease

This affects the inner ear, and results in too much fluid in the labyrinths. Its cause is not known. It tends to occur in middle age, usually affecting more men than women. The symptoms are attacks of giddiness and sickness, followed by deafness with accompanying ringing in the ears. Treatment is with drugs and control of fluid intake – not more than $2^1/2$ pints (1.2 liters) a day. In extreme cases, the labyrinths or their nervous connections are destroyed.

Fungus infections

Fungus infections can occur in the outer ear. They are more common in tropical climates. There is persistent irritation and discharge, which is treated with antibiotics and antiseptic cleansing of the ear canal.

Deafness

Types of deafness

'Conductive deafness' refers to any failure in the parts of the ear which gather and pass on sound waves, eg blockage of the ear canal, eardrum damage, ossicle damage, etc. 'Perceptive deafness' refers to any failure in: that part of the ear which translates the sound waves into nerve impulses (the cochlea); or in the auditory nerves which transmit the impulses to the brain; or in the auditory centers of the brain which receive the message. Perceptive deafness may not mean that the person can perceive no sound. It may be that sound is received, but so scrambled as to be unintelligible.

Causes of deafness

a) Disease. Some disorders can end in deafness (see pp.259-60).
b) Noise-induced. Any exposure to extremely loud noise, or continued exposure to moderately loud noise, can damage the eardrum and middle ear, causing hearing decline and eventual deafness. The main victims are those who work in very noisy surroundings, and also the fans – and performers – of loud music.
c) Congenital deafness. Deformities at birth range from complete absence of the ears to minute mistakes in the internal structure. The latter can often be cured surgically. Congenital deafness can be due to heredity (genetic defects). It can also result from certain infections in the mother in the first few months of pregnancy, including German measles, flu, and syphilis. If there is anything in your child's response to sounds that gives rise to worry, consult your doctor.
d) Otosclerosis. This is a condition in which the stirrup becomes fixed within the oval window, due to deposits of new bone. About one person in every 250 suffers from this, and it is more common in women than men. Surgical treatment may give improvement, but there is no way of halting the process responsible (though it may stop spontaneously).

7

Hearing Aids

Hearing aids work by amplifying sound. If the amplification is loud enough, it can overcome the blockage or damage that causes conductive deafness, and allow the sound to reach the inner ear. Amplification also seems to help in many cases of perceptive deafness. However, sometimes the aid does not allow speech to be distinguished: it only makes the person more aware of unintelligible noise. The performance of a hearing aid depends on:

a) the frequency of response – normal speech usually lies between 500 and 2000 cycles per second;
b) the degree of amplification;
c) the maximum amount of sound that the aid can deliver. Too much sound can make speech unintelligible, and/or damage the ear mechanisms. One problem with hearing aids is 'acoustic feedback'. This is the reamplification of sound

vibrations that have already passed into the ear but have partly leaked out again.

Insert receivers are the most common type of aid. They are molded to fit into the ear canal and form a perfect seal. No sound escapes, there is little or no acoustic feedback, and background noise is at a minimum. They can also be very small and, if transistorized, need no wires or attachments. A high degree of amplification is possible.

Flat receivers fit against the external ear cartilage, and are kept in place by a metal band. They are usually used only if there is a continuous discharge from the ear, or if there has been a serious mastoid operation. Because of the bad contact, many sounds escape, and acoustic feedback produces much background noise.

Bone conductors amplify the sound waves and send them through the bone of the head, not the air passages of the ear. They are uncomfortable and not very efficient, and are usually only used where some ear condition rules out an insert receiver.

Other devices and developments Amplified telephone receivers, flashing lights (instead of telephones that ring and doorbells), remote receiver headphones for televisions, and teletypewriters have all been developed to improve circumstances for the deaf and hearing impaired. Promising new medical developments include cochlea implants (to help nerve conduction deafness) and temporal bone implants (for bone conduction deafness).

The Nose

The outer nose consists of tissue and cartilage supported at the top by the nasal bones. The nasal cavity beneath is

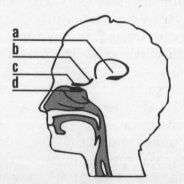

a Brain center for smell
b Olfactory tract
c Olfactory bulbs
d Olfactory hairs

divided into two (left and right) by a wall of bone and cartilage called the nasal septum. The nose has two functions: it is an opening to the respiratory system, and it houses the organs of the sense of smell (the olfactory system). The olfactory system consists of tiny hairlike nerve endings in the roof of the nasal cavity which detect odorous molecules in the air and transfer signals to the brain via olfactory bulbs and a set of nerve fibers called the olfactory tract.

Sense of Smell

The sense of smell is one of the keenest of all the human senses. (It can, for instance, distinguish more odors than the ear can distinguish sounds.) It is a vital part of the taste process – people who have lost their sense of smell cannot taste the full flavor of foods. The precise mechanism of smell remains a mystery. Similarly, attempts to classify different odors have mostly been unsuccessful. One theory proposes four categories – fragrant, burnt, acid and rancid – and suggests that every smell is a blend of these four basic odors.

Disorders

7

Common cold is an infectious disease of the respiratory system caused by viruses. It results in a running nose, reduced sense of smell and sometimes a cough.
Hay fever is an allergic reaction which causes the mucous membranes in the nose and eyes to become swollen and irritated. It may also cause a watery discharge or sneezing. Antihistamine drugs are often prescribed to give relief.
Nose bleeds are usually caused by the rupture of a blood vessel inside the nose. The bleeding may be the result of a blow, violent exercise or exposure to high altitudes, or may be a sign of high blood pressure. It can usually be relieved by pinching together the nostrils; severe or persistent bleeding needs medical attention.
Polyps are benign tumors in the nasal passages which cause a permanently stuffy nose. Often the result of frequent colds, they are easily removed by simple surgery.
Rhinitis is inflammation of the nose's mucous membranes caused by colds or hay fever.

Sinuses

Sinuses are air cavities in the skull which open into the nasal passages. Sinusitis is caused when the sinus outlets become blocked by thick mucus, or inflamed mucous membranes, resulting in infection. Symptoms include headaches and pain in the cheekbones. Sinusitis may be acute or chronic. In the acute form, areas of the face overlying the sinuses swell and are often very painful. Decongestant treatments are used to unblock them, and antibiotics prescribed for the infection. Chronic sinusitis (in which the nose is permanently blocked) is dealt with in much the same way. As a last resort, however, the sinuses may be flushed out with saline solution.

Location of the sinuses

Cosmetic Surgery

Surgery can correct the bridge line, shorten the nose, build up a depressed nose, straighten a crooked one, or alter the shape of the tip. All involve shaving back or implanting extra bone or cartilage. The incisions are made inside the nose, and the new shape takes about 6 months to settle. Though cosmetic surgery of this kind is often performed at the whim of the patient, in many cases it relieves very real distress.

The Mouth

The mouth is the entrance to the digestive system and one opening of the respiratory system. It is completely surrounded by muscle except for the hard palate and lower jaw which are rigid. Behind the hard palate is the soft palate from which hangs the uvula, a projection of muscle tissue important in speech. On either side at the back of the mouth are the tonsils – oval masses of lymphoid tissue. The cavity is lined with mucous membrane. The mucus it secretes, along with saliva from the salivary glands, cleanses the mouth and keeps it lubricated.

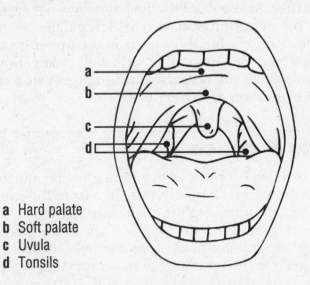

a Hard palate
b Soft palate
c Uvula
d Tonsils

Disorders

Very few serious disorders affect the mouth. A mixture of saliva, mucus, and secretions from the tonsils keep it moist and mostly germ-free. Any injuries to the mouth seem to clear up more quickly than they do elsewhere, and there is considerable resistance to infection. The most common minor disorders are ulcers, cold sores and thrush.

Ulcers are inflamed sores in the mouth's mucous membrane, usually caused by a scratch or similar injury. Most people suffer occasionally from small ulcers of this type (aphthous ulcers) which usually heal on their own, but mouth ulcers can also be signs of diseases such as diphtheria, leukemia and cancer.

Cold sores (herpes simplex) are small inflamed blisters that appear around the mouth. They are usually the result of a virus which many people carry around in their bodies all their lives. An eruption can be triggered by another infection, or by exposure to very hot or very cold weather.

Thrush (moniliasis) is an infection of the mucous membrane in the mouth, caused by a yeastlike fungus. It produces white patches inside the cheeks, but it can usually be treated by antifungicides.

7

Congenital Defects

Cleft palate In the unborn baby, the palate develops in two halves which fuse. In some babies the palate has not fused completely. This condition is known as cleft palate.
Harelip is the failure of the three parts of the upper lip to join – a congenital defect associated with cleft palate. Both defects can usually be corrected by plastic surgery in a series of operations beginning soon after birth.

The Taste Process

Before it can be tasted, a piece of dry food must be moistened and partly dissolved in the mouth by saliva from the salivary glands. The saliva, containing the particles of food, stimulates the taste buds on the tongue. Different areas of the tongue register different tastes (see below). The taste buds send signals to the brain which interprets these signals as tastes. The sense of smell is also part of the taste process. The odors of food enter the nasal cavity and stimulate the olfactory system (see pp.262-3). This greatly heightens the sensation of taste.

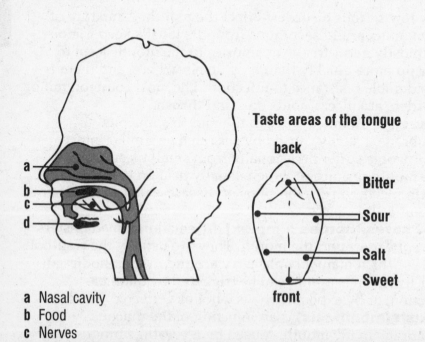

Taste areas of the tongue

back

Bitter

Sour

Salt

Sweet

front

a Nasal cavity
b Food
c Nerves
d Salivary gland

Teeth

Teeth are hard structures set in bony sockets in the upper and lower jaws. Their main function is to chew and prepare food for swallowing. They also help in the articulation of sounds in speech. In humans there are three main types of teeth.

Incisors are sharp, chisellike teeth at the front of the mouth, used for cutting into food.

Canines are round, pointed teeth at the corners of the mouth, used for tearing and gripping food.

Molars and premolars are square teeth with small cusps, which grind food at the sides of the mouth.

A tooth consists of two parts: the root, which is embedded in the jaw; and the crown, which projects out of the jaw. Where the root and crown meet is called the neck. Each tooth is made up of enamel, dentine, pulp and cementum.

Enamel is the hardest tissue in the body, and it protects the sensitive crown of the tooth.

Dentine is a slightly elastic material which forms the bulk of the tooth under the enamel. It is sensitive to heat and chemicals.

Pulp is the soft tissue inside the dentine, and contains nerves and blood vessels, which enter the root of the tooth by a small canal.

Cementum is a thin layer of material which covers the root of the tooth and protects the underlying dentine. It also helps attach fibers from the gum to the tooth.

7

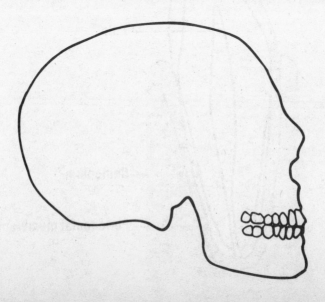

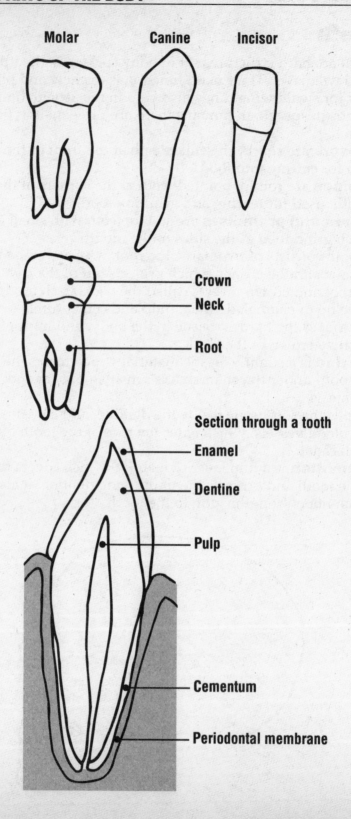

Molar   Canine   Incisor

Crown
Neck
Root

Section through a tooth
Enamel
Dentine
Pulp
Cementum
Periodontal membrane

The Teeth We're Given

In humans there are two successive sets of teeth. The primary or 'milk' set arrive 6 to 24 months after birth. Later, they gradually fall out, from the age of 6 on, as the permanent teeth appear. Most of these are out by the age of 13, but the 3rd molar or 'wisdom tooth' can erupt as late as the age of 25, or never. Human teeth do not keep growing, but reach a certain size and then stop. Also, when the permanent teeth fall out, they are not replaced by a new set. But in some animals, such as the rabbit, the incisors keep growing, as they are worn down by use, while the shark grows set after set of teeth – to its great advantage!

Age of appearance

These are average figures only: actual dates vary greatly from child to child.

Primary teeth

Central incisors	6 to 8 months	1
Lateral incisors	9 to 11 months	2
Eye teeth	18 to 20 months	4
First molars	14 to 17 months	3
Second molars	24 to 26 months	5

Adult teeth

Central incisors	7 to 8 years	2
Lateral incisors	8 to 9 years	3
Canines	12 to 14 years	6
First premolars	10 to 12 years	4
Second premolars	10 to 12 years	5
First molars	6 to 7 years	1
Second molars	12 to 16 years	7
Third molars	17 to 21 years	8

7

The end numbers list the typical order of appearance. The final number of adult teeth is between 28 and 32, depending on how many of the wisdom teeth appear.

Sequence of appearance of adult teeth (upper jaw)

Primary teeth

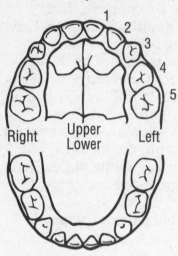

Right Upper Lower Left

5 years

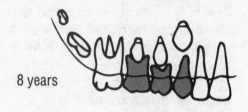

8 years

10 years

Looking into the mouth

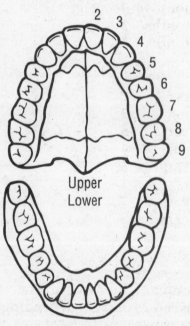

Upper Lower

Adult teeth

11 years

12 years

Adult

Dental Disorders

Tooth decay is the most universal of human diseases. It especially afflicts those who eat a highly refined diet which is overcooked, soft, sweet, and sticky. Bacteria in the mouth change carbohydrates in the food into acids strong enough to attack tooth enamel. Gradually the enamel is broken down, and bacteria invade the dentine, forming a 'cavity'. The pulp reacts by forming secondary dentine to wall off the bacteria, but without treatment it becomes inflamed and painful (toothache). The infection may then pass down the root and cause an 'abscess' – a painful collection of pus under pressure, affecting the gum and face tissues.

Periodontal disease

This is a general term for disorders in the supporting structures of teeth: the gums, cementum, and other tissues. The most common cause is overconsumption of soft food, which cannot stimulate and harden the gums. Other causes include sharp food which scratches the gums, inefficient brushing, badly contoured fillings, ill-fitting dentures, irregular teeth, and teeth deposits. General factors, such as vitamin deficiencies, blood disorders, and drug use, may also be involved. Periodontal disease can be painless but, if allowed to progress, the gum may become detached from the tooth. The socket enlarges, securing fibers are destroyed, and the tooth loosens. Many teeth can be lost in this way. Painful periodontal disorders include abscesses in the gum and 'periocoronitis'. The latter is inflammation around an erupting tooth (usually the 'wisdom tooth'), caused by irritation, food stagnation, pressure or infection. It may accompany swollen lymph glands.

7

Dental Treatment

The dentist's intricate work has to be carried out in the confined, dark, wet and sensitive environment of the mouth.

Filling cavities

Tooth decay is dealt with by drilling out the decayed matter and filling up the resulting cavity. All decayed and weakened areas must be removed; otherwise decay will continue beneath the filling. Also the cavity must be shaped so that the filling will stay in securely and withstand pressure from chewing. High-speed electric drills are now usual, and so is the use of injected local anesthetic to make the procedure painless. A lining of chemical cement is put in the prepared cavity to protect the pulp from heat and chemicals. The filling, placed on top of this, is usually an amalgam of silver, tin, copper, zinc alloy, and mercury. Translucent silicate cement may be used for a natural appearance, but since it can wear away, it cannot be used on grinding surfaces.

Other restorative work

Some other replacement work can be prepared outside the mouth, and then cemented into place.

Inlays are cast gold fillings, shaped to fit a cavity in the crown of a tooth. A wax impression of the cavity is made and the resulting mold filled with molten gold. Crowns are extensive coverings to the crown of a tooth, made of porcelain or gold. The whole of the enamel of the tooth is removed, an impression made, and the crown made from a model.

Pulp and root canal treatment

This is carried out when the pulp is dead or incurably infected. The pulp is removed and replaced with antibiotic paste, the tooth sealed, and a temporary filling left for a week. Once the cavity is sterilized, it is filled with paste and/or tapering, metal-oxide 'points', and the tooth is sealed.

Extraction

Teeth need to be removed if they are irretrievably decayed, or so broken that they cannot be repaired, or if new teeth are erupting and have no room. Forceps are used. They grip the tooth at the neck, while the blades of the forceps are inserted under the gum. The tooth is then moved repeatedly to enlarge the socket, and finally can be pulled out. Local or general anesthetic, by injection or gas, usually makes extraction painless.

Treatment of gum disorders

Acute conditions are treated by pus drainage, antiseptic mouthwashes, antibiotics and tooth extraction if necessary. Surgery may be needed to cut away the diseased gum. Long-term treatment aims at eliminating as many causative factors as possible, by improving oral hygiene, diet and general health.

Orthodontics

This is the branch of dentistry concerned with preventing and correcting irregularities of the teeth, eg variations in the number of teeth and abnormalities in their shape, size, position and spacing. All these can cause defects in eating, swallowing, speech and breathing. Malocclusion is the typical example. This means that the teeth are not in the normal position when the jaws are closed, relative to those in the opposite jaw. Teeth may stick out or in, or there may be spaces between the biting surfaces due to uneven growth of the teeth or jaws.

Irregularities may be caused by bottlefeeding, thumb-sucking, loss of teeth, nonappearance of teeth, appearance of extra teeth, birth injuries, heredity, disease, and poor general health.

Treatment

Treatment may be long term, but it is needed if the health, function, and aesthetic appearance of the mouth are to be preserved. Methods include: elimination of bad habits such as thumb-sucking; practice of exercises to strengthen certain muscles and improve mouth movements; relief of overcrowded teeth by extraction; and surgery on the soft tissues or bones to recontour the jaws.

The most common technique, however, is to attach 'braces' or similar appliances to the teeth, to apply continual pressure and so make them shift position. Fixed appliances consist of brackets, cemented to each tooth, with a steel wire threaded through them. Teeth cleaning is difficult with this type. Removable appliances consist of a removable plate that covers the roof or floor of the mouth, to which are attached springs, bows, screws, and/or rubber bands. Braces are more effective in young than in older people.

7

False Teeth

Ideally, false teeth ('dentures') should preserve normal chewing and biting, clear speech, and facial appearance.

Types of dentures

These include full sets, partial dentures, and immediate dentures. For the construction of a full set, all the teeth are removed, and the healed bony ridge acts as a base. Impressions of both jaws are made in warm wax, and these give the basic patterns from which the dentures are made up.

With partial dentures, the new teeth are attached to surviving natural ones to keep them anchored. Where the anchoring teeth are not immediately alongside, they are linked to the false teeth by a bridge. With immediate dentures, the false teeth are prepared before the teeth being lost have been removed. After extraction, the empty sockets are immediately covered with the new dentures, and healing takes place beneath. A new set is then needed after about 6 months, as the ridge where teeth have been extracted shrinks.

Using dentures

Dentures can be uncomfortable. To prevent gum soreness when dentures are new, eat only small amounts of soft foods at first. If soreness occurs, consult a dentist. Don't leave the dentures out of the mouth for more than a day or two, or the remaining natural teeth may begin to shift position.
Brush false teeth after every meal; soak detachable dentures overnight in water containing salt or denture cream.

New Teeth for Old

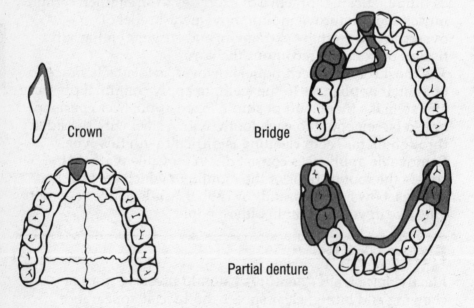

Crown

Bridge

Partial denture

Bonding

This technique can be used for cosmetic reasons or to prevent decay. A sealant is used to attach plastic or porcelain to fill gaps or level off chipped teeth. However, it may not be as strong as a crown, and may need renewal every few years.

Preventing Dental Trouble

Diet

At any age, the ideal diet for dental health should be well balanced and adequate so general health is maintained, chewable enough to stimulate the gums, and low in sugar content.

The balance and adequacy of the diet is especially important in the case of expectant mothers and growing children, so that strong teeth form.

Oral hygiene

Teeth should be cleaned at least twice a day; after every meal is best. This polishes the teeth and removes debris.

Methods of cleaning vary from culture to culture. To use the toothbrush effectively: backward and forward strokes are good for the biting surfaces of molars; for the front teeth, brush repeatedly in one direction – upward on the bottom teeth, downward on the top ones.

Toothpaste contains useful mild abrasives, soap, and sometimes valuable additives such as protein sealants – to desensitize – and flouride. Brushing stimulates the gums and cleans effectively.

Dental floss or toothpicks of soft wood help to dislodge food. Disclosure tablets show the extent to which you need to brush to remove plaque. A tablet is chewed and spread with saliva on to all tooth and gum surfaces. After rinsing with water, all areas of plaque are stained red. The plaque can then be removed by brushing.

Dental inspections

Regular visits to the dentist about every 6 months catch disease in its early stages and so avoid drastic measures in the future.

Fluoride

Fluoride is a tasteless, odorless, colorless chemical, which, if present in drinking water in small amounts, reduces tooth decay in children under 14 by 60%. (Excessive amounts can cause the enamel to become mottled.)

7

The Breasts

The adult female breast, or mammary gland, consists of 15-25 lobes that are separated by fibrous tissue, rather like the segments of an orange. Each lobe resembles a tree and is embedded in fat. After childbirth, milk produced in the alveoli of each lobe (the 'leaves' of each 'tree') travels along small ducts into the main 'trunk' or milk duct. This duct is enlarged to form a reservoir just below the areola – the dark ring visible around the nipple. A narrow continuation of the duct links this reservoir with the nipple's surface. Each of the breast's 15-25 lobes has its own opening on the nipple.

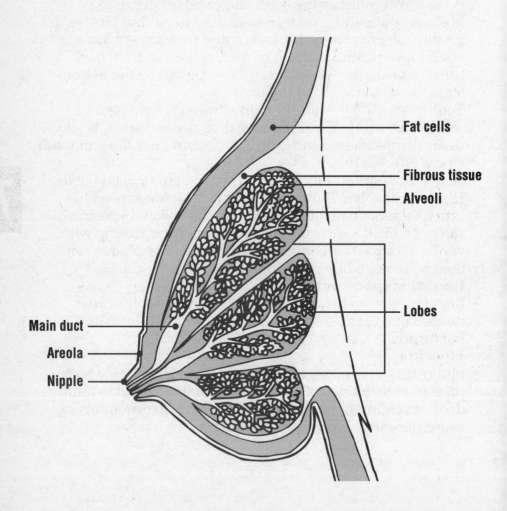

Fat cells

Fibrous tissue

Alveoli

Lobes

Main duct

Areola

Nipple

Breastfeeding

Breast milk is sterile and better suited to most human babies than cow's milk. Breastfeeding also helps to establish the important physical contact between mother and baby.

Milk secretion by the breast begins just before childbirth as estrogen and progesterone output from the ovaries decreases. The reduction of the level of these hormones in the bloodstream affects the hypothalamus, which then causes the pituitary to produce prolactin. It is this hormone that sparks off milk secretion in the breasts. The first substance secreted is not milk but colostrum – a thick, yellow liquid rich in antibodies (as the milk itself is). These antibodies give the newborn baby protection against disease and infection for up to 6 months.

Milk yield starts only about 3 days after childbirth. The flow is set off by the baby sucking the nipple (**1**). This sends nerve impulses (**2**) to the hypothalamus, which releases oxytocin that travels via nerve fibers (**3**) to the pituitary. From there, oxytocin flows through the bloodstream (**4**) to the breasts, causing the alveoli to contract and force liquid through the ducts to the nipples. Milk flow usually starts about 30 seconds after suckling begins. For discussion of breastfeeding of babies, see pp.156-57.

7

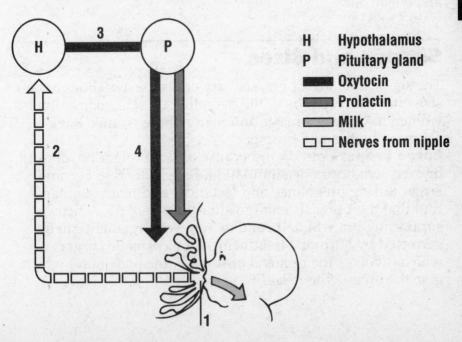

H	Hypothalamus
P	Pituitary gland
▬	Oxytocin
▨	Prolactin
▭	Milk
☐☐	Nerves from nipple

Changes in the Breast

The breasts undergo great changes during a woman's life.

Before puberty

The breast is simply a nipple projecting from a pink area –
the areola.

Puberty

By the 11th year, the areola bulges, the nipple still projecting
from it. Secretion of the hormones estrogen and progesterone
stimulates breast development. The milk ducts develop from
the nipple inward and fat accumulates around them, so that
by the age of 16 or so, the breasts are prominent.

In pregnancy

Early indicators of pregnancy often include swollen areolae,
breast tenderness, and a marbled appearance produced by
prominent veins in the breast. In the first 3 months, changes
in blood supply and growth of milk ducts and alveoli
enlarge the breast by 20-25%. Toward the end of pregnancy,
breasts are about $1/3$ larger than normal. Breastfeeding
triggers further development but the breasts resume their
former shape once breastfeeding ceases.

In later life

Around the menopause, breasts begin to droop and become
less firm, as fibrous tissue slackens and milk ducts and
alveoli shrink.

Shapes and Sizes

The shape and size of breasts vary enormously. Though their
size often corresponds to the overall body size, many slim
women have large breasts and many obese women have
comparatively small breasts.

Large breasts can occur because of fluid retention, obesity,
or excessive hormone stimulation. Breasts tend to become
larger during pregnancy and lactation, and many women
find that their breasts enlarge after the age of 35. A firm
supporting bra will help, and extreme enlargement can be
corrected by hormone treatment, or by cosmetic surgery
which involves the removal of some of the pads of fat which
give the breasts their size.

Small breasts can occur because of too little hormone stimulation or just because the woman is slim. Underdevelopment at puberty can occasionally be helped by rubbing estrogen creams into the breasts, but these creams enlarge only the ducts and not the pads of fat. Cosmetic surgery can also help. Surgeons can insert implants containing saline between the breasts and the pectoral muscles – but the breasts sometimes become infected later as a result. For most women conscious about their small breasts, a padded bra, upright posture, and perhaps exercises to strengthen the underlying pectoral muscles will help.

Is a bra necessary? It seems that a bra aids in supporting the breasts and preventing tissue strain. Women who have large breasts, who enjoy participating in sports, or who are in late pregnancy or breastfeeding are especially advised to wear one.

Abnormal nipples Naturally inverted nipples are a developmental fault that makes breastfeeding difficult. (But inversion of previously normal nipples may be a sign of breast cancer – see p.338). Extra nipples sometimes occur, usually in the armpits.

7

Sexual Response

Sexual stimulation affects the breasts in several ways. The nipples become erect and enlarged, then intermittently soft and pliable. Increased blood supply to the breasts causes their temporary enlargement by as much as 25%, especially in younger women who have not breastfed a baby. Also the areolae swell often, in younger women, sufficiently to engulf the base of the nipples. (In women over 50, this swelling is less marked, and may occur in one breast only.) Finally, in many younger women, a pink flush mottles the breast just before orgasm. After orgasm, first the flush, then the areola swelling, soon vanish. But nipple erection may persist for hours, especially in older women or in those who have not had full release of sexual tension.

Hands

The hand is remarkable for its flexibility. In particular, the thumb's ability to move in opposition to the fingers enables the hand to grasp objects and perform other delicate tasks. The hand contains 3 important sets of bones: carpals in the wrist, metacarpals in the hand itself, and phalanges in the fingers. Movements of the fingers are controlled by tendons attached to the muscles in the forearm. The hand is very strong – even a tiny baby can exert a very powerful grip.

Hand care

The following points will help to keep the hands in good condition.

a) Do not wash hands more than necessary – soap removes some of the oils that keep the skin pliable.

b) Use hand cream when necessary to prevent dryness and redness, eg if hands have constantly been in water, and in cold weather.

c) Wear rubber gloves for all heavy jobs and for washing dishes.

d) Avoid direct contact with detergents and scouring products – an allergic reaction (contact dermatitis – see pp.228-9) may result.

e) Do not expose hands to extremes of temperature.

Hand problems

Only a few serious disorders affect the hands.

Chilblains in cold weather feature purplish swelling and great discomfort. They can be prevented by keeping hands warm.

Clubbing of the fingers usually points to chronic lung disease, lung cancer, and some forms of inherited heart disease.

Rheumatoid arthritis is probably the most severe of the common diseases affecting the hands. The lining of the finger joints becomes inflamed, causing the joints themselves to swell painfully. Treatment varies, but medical advice should be sought as early as possible.

Warts often appear on the hands and are a particular problem in childhood (see p.230).

Whitlows or felons are areas of inflamed tissue surrounding the nail. Pus often develops, and a poultice may be used to draw it out, and antiseptic creams applied to prevent the spread of infection. Alternatively a whitlow may be lanced by the doctor.

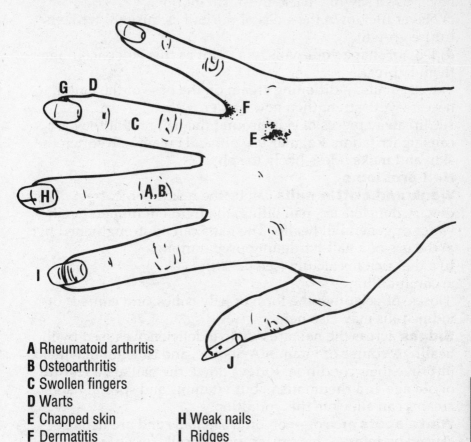

A Rheumatoid arthritis
B Osteoarthritis
C Swollen fingers
D Warts
E Chapped skin   H Weak nails
F Dermatitis   I Ridges
G Whitlows   J White spots

Nails

A nail consists of a small plate of dead cells. The horny,
visible portion is made up of keratin – the substance found in
skin and hair. The nail grows from a bed, or matrix, which is
protected by a fold of skin at the base. The white crescent at
the base of the nail is the visible part of the nail bed. The nail
rests on soft tissues which contain blood vessels to nourish
the matrix. Nails grow about $1^1/2$in (3.8cm) per year, though
the rate varies with the individual.

Nail care Nails are easily damaged, and it can be a long
time before the damage grows out. To keep the nails in good
condition, several points may be helpful.

a) Never use a steel file; it will tear the delicate keratin
layers. Instead, use an emery board.

b) Always file from each side of the nail toward the center –

never use a sawing, back-and-forth motion.

c) Never file down the sides of the nail as this will weaken future growth.

d) Do not shape your nails to a point as this will encourage them to break.

e) Use a nail-conditioning cream on the base of the nail if necessary, to strengthen new nail growth.

f) Clip away pieces of skin around the nail only if they are causing irritation. Regular use of hand cream will soften the skin and make it less likely to split.

Nail problems

Weak and brittle nails can be the result of incorrect filing, dietary deficiencies, nail biting, too frequent immersion in water or general ill health. The nails can be strengthened by:

a) the use of a nail-hardening preparation;

b) a diet rich in calcium (see p.300);

c) careful filing.

'Doses' of gelatin in the form of jelly cubes, and courses of iodine pills may also help.

Ridges across the nail are due to a deficiency caused by ill health. A course of vitamin A, iodine, and calcium may help improve their condition. Ridges down the nail are a feature of old age and rheumatism, but vitamins and special nail creams can alleviate this condition.

White spots are common on weak nails and are usually caused by injury. This causes the nail cells to separate and allows air to filter between them. Overacidity may also be a cause of white spots.

Nail biting This common problem often begins in childhood, perhaps caused by stress of some kind, whether from a nervous disposition or a specific outside cause. It then develops into a habit difficult to break. Biting off the nail leaves it weak and rough, and the irritation caused by the ragged edge will encourage further biting. Use of evil-tasting chemical preparations painted on the nails is an effective means of discouraging nail biting; but it is also a good idea to try to pinpoint and remove any causes of stress. Adults anxious to break the habit may find it helpful to concentrate on allowing one nail at a time to grow longer.

The Leg

The leg contains 3 important bones – the femur (thighbone)
in the upper leg, and the tibia (shinbone) and fibula in the
lower leg.

The upper femur meets the hip in a ball-and-socket joint
(which allows free movement). The lower femur and upper
tibia meet at the knee joint, a hinge joint (allowing movement
in one direction only). Here cartilage forms buffers between
these bones, and the front and base of the lower femur abuts
the synovial membrane – a sac filled with lubricating fluid.
The patella (kneecap) covers and protects the knee joint. The
thigh muscles are used to bend the knee, while the lower leg
muscles move the feet and toes. The sciatic nerve – the
longest and thickest in the body – provides the nervous
system for most of the leg. Blood feeds into the thigh
through the femoral artery, and back toward the heart
through two systems of veins, one deep, one superficial.

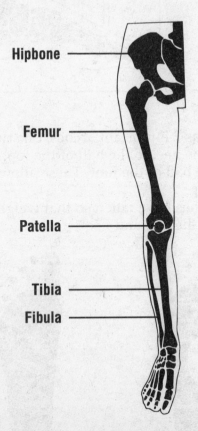

Hipbone

Femur

Patella

Tibia

Fibula

7

The Foot

Each foot is comprised of 26 bones with 33 joints, linked by more than 100 ligaments. Muscles, tendons, and ligaments keep the foot in different positions.

There are 3 sets of foot bones:

a) 14 phalangeal or toe bones, 3 for each small toe and 2 for the big toe;

b) 5 metatarsal or instep bones forming the front of the instep; and

c) 7 tarsal or ankle bones forming the ankle and the rear of the instep, and jointed for foot rotation.

Bones in the foot

a Phalanges
b Metatarsals
c Tarsals

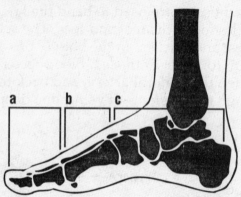

Arches

The normal foot has 2 important arches, one running lengthwise from the heel to the ball of the foot, the second running across the ball of the foot. These allow the spring needed for walking.

In flat feet, the arches have fallen so that weight is borne on the sole as well as the ball and heel.

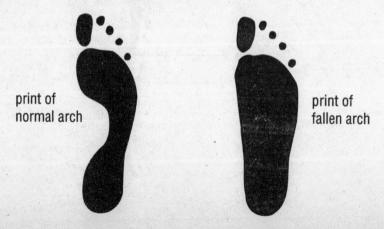

print of
normal arch

print of
fallen arch

Athlete's Foot

This is a common disorder, best avoided by keeping the foot clean, dry and cool, and avoiding contact with infected people and with changing room floors. It is caused by a fungus infection, and first appears in the toe clefts. There may be splits and flaking, or pieces of dead white skin. Treatment involves rubbing away the dead skin, applying a mixture of water and medicinal alcohol, and using a special dusting powder. A fungicidal ointment may be prescribed by the doctor. The feet should be exposed to the air as much as possible, and tights and socks should be clean every day.

Common Foot Disorders

Calluses are areas of skin hardened to form protection for parts that suffer pressure or friction. To clear them, soak the foot in warm water and remove the callus by rubbing with an emery board.

Corns are a type of callus usually caused by ill-fitting shoes. They have a cone-shaped core which causes pain when it presses on nerve endings. Corn pads may relieve pain but removal should be left to a chiropodist.

Verruca, or plantar warts, are the result of a virus infection, and are often contracted at swimming pools. The warts grow into the skin and cause pain. Verrucas should be treated by a doctor.

7

Disorders of the Legs

Dislocated hip Hip dislocation may be present at birth or occur later. It causes a lurching gait, backache in middle age, and sometimes osteoarthritis. Treatment varies with age, and may involve an operation.

Dislocated knee Slipping of the kneecap to the side may result from an injury, or the tendency may be present from birth. Doctors may recommend rest, or sometimes an operation.

'Housemaid's' knee Kneeling on hard surfaces for long periods may inflame the fluid-filled sac (bursa) that lies in front of the kneecap. Tissues at the knee joint swell, become tender, and make knee-bending painful. Poulticing or minor surgery may be needed.

Water on the knee This is a collection of fluid beneath the kneecap. It may be due to infection, rheumatoid arthritis, or to a blow or strain. Rest usually brings recovery.

Rheumatoid arthritis Hips, knees, ankles and feet can be badly affected. Painful joint swelling is sometimes followed by joint erosion and dislocation. Cortisone treatment is used, and hip and knee joints are sometimes replaced with metal or plastic devices.

Sciatica Inflammation of the sciatic nerve produces a form of neuritis called sciatica. A slipped disk in the spine may press on a nerve, producing intense pain in the leg and lower back. Bed rest, heat applied to the painful area, physiotherapy, and special exercises may bring relief.

Varicose veins are swollen veins in the legs, which stand out above the surface and can be acutely painful. Their exposed position also makes them vulnerable to bleeding and ulceration. Varicose veins develop if the valves in the leg veins fail to prevent the backflow of blood. They are more likely in occupations involving long periods of standing – and also where there is a swelling of the abdomen, as in obesity, chronic constipation, and pregnancy. This last is why 1 in 2 women over 40 suffer from varicose veins, but only 1 in 4 men of the same age. Possible treatments include: wearing pressure bandages and resting with the leg raised; courses of injections; and surgical tying or removal of the varicose veins.

Thrombophlebitis A blood clot in a deep vein produces deep pain and a swollen ankle. A blood clot in a superficial vein produces tenderness and a red, cordlike formation beneath the skin. The patient may feel ill and have a high temperature. Medical aid must be sought. Treatments include anticoagulants, supportive stockings and resting the leg.

Bunions and Hammer Toes

A bunion is a hard swelling at the base of the big toe. Ill-fitting shoes cause the big toe to bend in, forcing out the base of the toe in a bony outgrowth. A fluid-filled sac (bursa) may develop between the outgrowth and the skin.

A hammer toe is a toe bent up at the middle joint, where it presses on the shoe and causes a corn. Both these conditions can improve with exercise, manipulation or well-fitting shoes, but severe cases may need surgery.

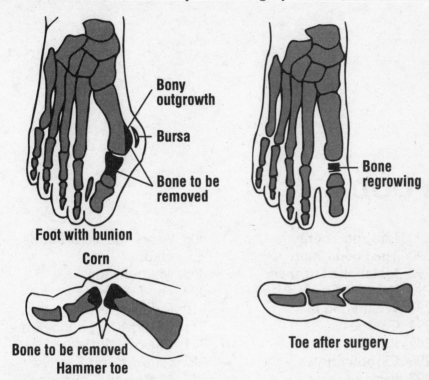

Bony outgrowth

Bursa

Bone to be removed

Foot with bunion

Bone regrowing

Corn

Bone to be removed
Hammer toe

Toe after surgery

Foot Care

a) Wash feet at least once a day. Soaking in cold salt water or diluted cider vinegar refreshes the feet in hot weather.
b) Dust the feet daily with a special foot powder to avoid friction, to help dry out the feet, and to prevent odor.
c) Cut toenails straight across and not in at the edges.
d) Wear clean tights or socks every day.
e) Keep the feet free of corns and calluses (see p.285).
f) Wear comfortable, well-fitting shoes. Very high or very flat heels on shoes can force the body into an unnatural position and cause considerable damage.

FOOD

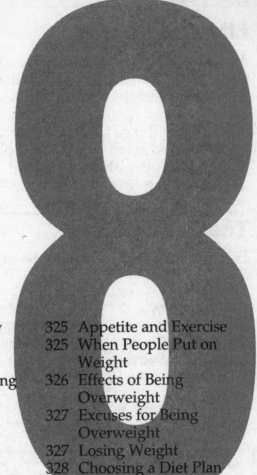

8

Life and Energy

All living things need sources of energy and material, because all life uses up energy and material: in movement, repai, and growth, and just in the internal processes of maintaining its own existence.

Where living things find these sources is what governs their primary division into animals and plants. Most plants survive on inorganic (ie nonliving) material – chemicals drawn from the soil and the air, and then processed within them in the

The Food Chain

This series of diagrams shows the energy transferred in the food chain.

The sun's energy
Energy from the sun arrives at the edge of the earth's atmosphere at the rate of 2 million billion calories per second. Of this, at least 30% is reflected and 20% absorbed by the atmosphere. The remaining 50% or less reaches the earth's surface at the average rate of 110 calories per square foot per day.

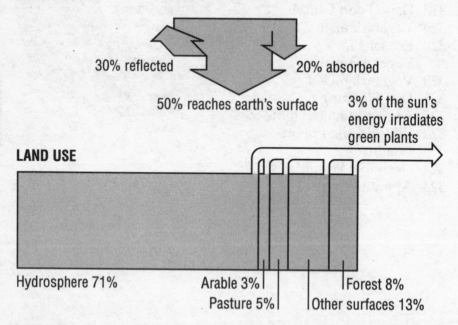

30% reflected   20% absorbed

50% reaches earth's surface   3% of the sun's energy irradiates green plants

LAND USE

Hydrosphere 71%   Arable 3%   Forest 8%
          Pasture 5%   Other surfaces 13%

Land use
Of the energy reaching the surface, 71% irradiates areas of water, and 29% land areas. The land areas include forest and uncultivated land. Only a fraction of the land surface is primarily in the food chain, involving humans, as arable land or pasture.

presence of sunlight. They can build up complex substances out of simple ones. Animals cannot make food in this fashion. They must get it ready-made by eating plants or other animals. For them, food is the source of chemical energy and material. From the already complex substances in food, they break down the chemicals that they need.

So the synthesis of food from plants begins a chain of energy transference: energy and matter are passed on, thereafter, because one life form consumes another.

Plants

In all, only about 3% of the sunlight actually irradiates green plants on the land surface or algae in the sea. The land plants include cereals, grasses, root crops, and vegetables and fruit.

Human sources of energy

The chain reaches us in the form of food grains, livestock products, root crops, vegetables and fruits, fats and oils, sugar, and fish.

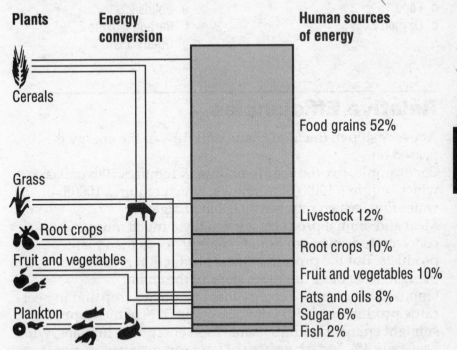

Plants   **Energy conversion**   **Human sources of energy**

Cereals

Grass

Root crops

Fruit and vegetables

Plankton

Food grains 52%

Livestock 12%

Root crops 10%

Fruit and vegetables 10%

Fats and oils 8%

Sugar 6%

Fish 2%

Energy conversion

The plants convert about 1% of the energy reaching them into chemical energy. Some of this is stored in the food chain, the plants are consumed, and about 10% of the plants' stored energy is stored by the animal that eats them. Similarly, when the animal is eaten, about 10% of its stored energy is stored by the eater.

Metabolic Turnover

The diagram shows the daily input and output of a 135lb (61kg) woman in a closed enviroment.

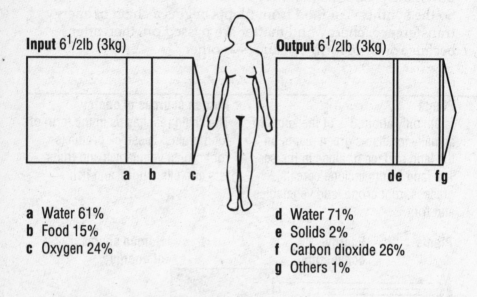

Input 6^1/2lb (3kg)   a b c

Output 6^1/2lb (3kg)   de fg

a Water 61%
b Food 15%
c Oxygen 24%

d Water 71%
e Solids 2%
f Carbon dioxide 26%
g Others 1%

Relative Efficiencies

At every step in the food chain, only 10% of the energy is passed on.

For example, to produce 1lb of human requires 10lb of bass, which requires 100lb of minnows, which requires 1000lb of water flies, which requires 10,000lb of algae.

Meat and animal products are usually a much more concentrated source of human dietary needs than plant products. But the process of their production is far more inefficient, as there are more steps in the chain.

Opposite we compare energy loss in a potato crop and in beef cattle production. With potatoes, about 30% of the trapped sunlight energy becomes usable food energy for humans; with beef, only 4%. In fact, an acre of land can produce, in a year, almost 9 times as much potato protein as beef protein.

Energy loss in the food chain

Potato
a Plant metabolic loss 37%
b Farming loss 24%
c Available for processing 39%
   Available after processing 30%

Cattle
d Plant metabolic loss 34%
e Farming and feeding loss 25%
f Animal metabolic loss 35%
g Available for processing 6%
   Available after processing 4%

 Available after
processing

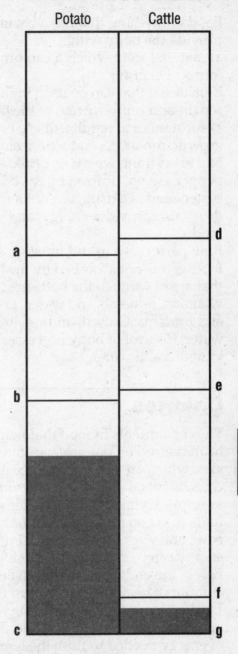

What Food Is

Food is anything that has a chemical composition which can provide the body with:

a) material from which it can produce heat, activity, and other forms of energy;

b) material that can be used in the growth, maintenance, repair, and reproduction of the body; and/or

c) substances to regulate these processes of energy production, growth, repair, reproduction, etc.

Not everything we eat or drink is food. Flavorings such as pepper are not utilized by the body. Tea affects the nervous system and is a drug, but not a food. (But alcohol, though it is a drug, also provides energy, and so falls within the definition of food.)

Bran performs a useful function as a laxative, but again is not food as it is not absorbed by the body. The constituents of food that are of value to the body are: proteins, carbohydrates, fats, vitamins, minerals and water. Energy uses carbohydrates, fats and proteins. Growth and repair use proteins, minerals and water. Control of body processes uses proteins, minerals, vitamins and water.

Calories

The constituents in food that help growth and repair cannot all be measured on one scale: different constituents do different jobs, which are not interchangeable. The same applies to the constituents that control body processes. It is no good, for example, trying to add together vitamin A units and calcium units to get so many 'control units'. That is like trying to add cows and washing machines. But the constituents that provide energy can be measured on a single scale and added together. For, in the end, all of them can be measured in terms of the amount of heat they produce in the body.

The basic unit for measuring any energy (including heat output) is the scientist's calorie. This is defined as the amount of energy needed to raise the temperature of ice or water by 1°centigrade. The measure used in talking about food and human energy needs is a thousand times larger than this: the kilocalorie, which is sometimes written as 'Calorie', ie with a capital 'C', but is now more usually expressed as 'kcal' or simply as 'calorie'.

For example, a typical number of calories for a woman to use up in a day is about 2500. So this is the amount of energy her food must supply, unless she is to run down her stored reserves. Protein, fat, and carbohydrate are all sources of energy (though protein is more vital as a source of other things). One ounce of protein produces more than 113 calories in the human body, one ounce of carbohydrate the same, and one ounce of fat 225 calories. (An ounce of alcohol – rich in the carbohydrates that we call sugars – produces 180 calories.) Actual foods range in calorific value from, for example, 105 calories to the pound (tomatoes) to 4200 calories to the pound (lard).

Proteins

Protein is the basic ingredient of the living organism. There is no substitute for protein, for it is the only constituent of food which contains nitrogen – essential for the growth and repair of the body. Proteins, in fact, provide raw materials for the body's tissues and fluids. They also have certain specialized functions. They help to maintain the chemical fluid balance in the brain, spine and intestine, and they aid the transport of food and drugs.

Proteins are very complex substances made from a number of chemicals called amino acids. About 20 different kinds of amino acid are found in protein food, and the thousands of different ways these can be linked up produce the many types of protein that exist in food. A single protein molecule can contain as many as 500 amino acid units linked together. The two main sources of protein are from animals, in the form of meat, fish, eggs and dairy produce, and from plants in the form of nuts, peas and beans, grains and grain products (such as bread, especially wholemeal) and in small quantities in many tubers and vegetables.

Most animal proteins contain all the essential amino acids that humans need, and so are called complete proteins. But vegetable proteins are all, individually, more or less incomplete. They can carry out some individual jobs in the body, but cannot fulfill the vital task of cell repair and growth unless combined together, or with animal protein. Most proteins are insoluble in water. Some are soluble – such as casein (milk) and albumen (egg white) – but become insoluble when heated or beaten.

8

Carbohydrates

Carbohydrates provide our main source of energy for immediate use. Energy is used up even during sleep, to keep body organs functioning. Carbohydrates play a vital role in the proper functioning of the internal organs and the central nervous system, and in heart and muscle contraction. Our bodies cannot manufacture carbohydrates, so we get them from plants or from animals that feed on plants. Plants synthesize carbohydrates out of the reaction of sunlight on water and carbon dioxide. This is called photosynthesis, and it occurs in the green leaves of plants.

All carbohydrates are made up from carbon, hydrogen and oxygen. The end product of these three elements is first sugar and then starch, which is stored in plants for future use. There are several different kinds of carbohydrates.

Sugar

This is one kind, of which there are various types:

Glucose is the form in which fuel is transported in the body (though when eaten it gives energy no more quickly than other sugars).

Fructose comes from most fruits and from honey. It can also be made out of sugarcane. Glucose converts to fructose during the process of the release of energy in the body.

Sucrose is a chemical combination of fructose and glucose and occurs naturally in sugar beet and sugarcane. It is also present in fruit and in carrots. Sucrose forms the common household sugar, which is available in various grades and crystal sizes due to different refinement processes.

Lactose occurs naturally in human's and cow's milk and is not as sweet as sucrose. It is a combination of glucose and galactose.

Maltose is derived from malt and is also produced naturally from starch when grain germinates.

Starch

This forms the largest part of the carbohydrate in our food. It is the stored food in plant seeds, intended for use in maintaining the growing plant until it is able to feed itself by photosynthesis. Unripe fruit contains starch which converts to sugar as the fruit ripens. Starch is composed of complex chains linked together with glucose units. Starch is indigestible unless it is cooked, when the starch granules swell and burst.

Glycogen

Glycogen is similar to starch, and it serves the same purpose in animals as starch does in plants, ie it stores fuel – in this case in the liver and muscles. It is not found in most meat as it breaks down into glucose after the animal is killed, but horse meat and oysters do retain it.

Other forms

Cellulose is the compound produced in plants to give themselves rigidity and strength. It is fibrous and indigestible to most animals except some insects (but does function as roughage). Pectin is present in apples, other fruits, and turnips. It has no direct food value but has the property of making jam set.

Sources of useful carbohydrates include bread, potatoes, pasta, rice, wheat, sugar, honey, vegetables, fruit, jam, liver, milk, eggs and cheese.

Fats

Fat is the most concentrated source of energy. Also, when stored in the body as a layer of fat beneath the skin and around organs, it provides insulation and protection for body structures. Finally, certain fats carry the fat-soluble vitamins (A, D, E and K).

Fat contains the same three elements as carbohydrates – carbon, hydrogen and oxygen, but combined in a different way. Chemically, fat is a combination of fatty acids and glycerine. At normal temperatures, fat can be solid as in animals or liquid as in vegetable and fish oil. But all fat can be made liquid by heating and made solid by cooling.

Fat is not soluble in water, though it is in alcohol, ether and chloroform. But by chemical treatment with alkalis, fat can be broken down into its separate units, and then can be mixed with water. This is the process by which fats are digested in the body. Mineral oils such as Vaseline and paraffin cannot be broken down in this way and are therefore not digestible by the body and of no value as food.

Fat in the diet falls into three categories. Sources such as butter, lard, margarine and oils are added to recipes in a recognizable and measurable form. Other sources, such as the fat found in meat, fish, eggs, etc, are not so readily measurable, and vary with the quality of the source, the time of year, and so on. In addition, when fat is added as a cooking medium, it finds its way into the outer layer of the food, increasing its fat content.

8

Vitamins

Vitamins are organic compounds that occur in minute quantities in food. They are coenzymes: chemicals that work with enzymes to effect chemical processes in the body, and thus influence growth and development and protect against illness and disease.

The role of vitamins in nutrition was only discovered in the present century, but there are now known to be about 40, of which 12 or more are essential in the diet. Because of the haphazard process of their discovery, they originally formed a jumbled list of alphabetic names (A, B1, B6, etc). But now their chemical structures have been identified, chemical names are often used for many of them. Identification has also meant that some can now be made artificially.

The vitamins are chemically very different. The body can manufacture only vitamin D (from sunlight) and pyridoxine, a B vitamin (from bacteria in the intestine); the rest come from food or are taken as supplements.

Vitamins in the diet can be divided into those soluble in fat (A, D, E and K) and those soluble in water (C and the B vitamins). All are needed by the body in only tiny amounts. For example, the body needs only 1oz of thiamine (vitamin B1) in its lifetime, although that 1oz is vital. However, whereas excessive quantities of water-soluble vitamins can be diluted and excreted in the urine, unused quantities of fat-soluble vitamins remain in the body and, if they are present in large quantities, become poisonous.

Vitamin A is found in halibut and cod liver oil, milk, butter and eggs. It is destroyed by cooking and sunlight. It is essential to the formation of bone and of the enamel and dentine in teeth, and maintains healthy skin. It also enables the eyes to adapt to dark. In excess, it can damage the liver.

Vitamin D is found in eggs, milk, butter and fish liver oils. It is also synthesized in the skin during exposure to sunlight. It plays a part in the digestive absorption of some minerals, such as calcium and phosphorus. It is also necessary for retaining calcium in bones.

Vitamin E is found in wheat germ, oil, lettuce, spinach, watercress, etc. It is an important anti-oxidant, needed for protection against damaging free radicals.

Vitamin K is found mainly in green plants such as spinach, cabbage and kale. But it is also synthesized in the gut by the action of bacteria. It is a necessary factor in the blood-clotting mechanism, as it is needed for the production of prothrombin.

Vitamin C (ascorbic acid) is found in fresh fruit and vegetables, especially citrus fruits, strawberries, canteloupe melons, tomatoes, potatoes, green leafy vegetables and green peppers. It is easily destroyed by cooking, especially if the food is chopped. Vitamin C is important in the formation of dentine, cartilage, bone, gums, ligaments, blood vessels and red blood cells. It is essential to the successful healing of wounds and broken bones. It helps produce certain neurotransmitters (chemicals that conduct electrical impulses between nerve cells). It also has a role in the immune response to infection. Serious deficiency causes weakness, nose bleeding, swollen gums, scurvy and anemia. Deficiency of vitamin C is more common than is supposed, especially in people on fruit- and vegetable-free diets. Vitamin C is an important anti-oxidant with valuable protective properties against free radicals that damage body tissues.

Vitamin B is in fact a complex of 15 different substances, but they are classed together because they occur together in the same types of food, such as yeast and wheat germ. Unlike the other vitamins, at least some vitamins of the B group are found in all living plants and animals. The following are the most important B vitamins.

Thiamin forms the part of the enzyme system essential for the breakdown of carbohydrates and the nutrition of nerve cells.

Riboflavin acts with thiamin and nicotinic acid in the oxidation of carbohydrates. It is also important for the growth of the fetus and may play a part in the mechanism of vision.

Pyridoxine (B6) helps the breakdown of protein into amino acids and is needed for blood cell formation. Sufficient pyridoxine for daily needs is produced by the action of bacteria in the intestine. Extra dosages may relieve pre-menstrual syndrome (PMS).

Pantothenic acid probably plays a part in the detoxification of drugs and the formation of chemicals that pass nerve impulses along the nerves.

Niacin is needed for healthy skin and nerves and digestion.

Folic acid is an anti-anemic factor found in green leaves and in liver and kidneys. It is especially important early in pregnancy, to prevent spinal disorders in the fetus.

Cobolamin (B12) is the only vitamin containing a metal, cobalt. It is found in a high concentration in the liver and is essential for the formation of red blood cells. Unlike the other B complex vitamins, it has no vegetable source.

8

Minerals

Minerals do not supply any heat or energy, but play a vital role in the regulation of body fluids and the balance of chemicals.

Macronutrients

These are the minerals needed by the body in comparatively large quantities.

Calcium is found in milk, cheese, fish, some green vegetables, and in "hard" drinking water. It is necessary for the proper formation of bones and teeth; also for the functioning of muscles and clotting of the blood. During growth, calcium is constantly being laid down in bones and simultaneously withdrawn into the bloodstream for use elsewhere. The body of an adult normally contains 2-3$\frac{1}{2}$lb of calcium of which at least 99% is present in the bones.

Phosphorus is found in animal organs, such as brains, kidneys, and liver, and in cheese and other dairy products. It is important for energy transfer, and its function is linked with that of calcium.

Sodium and chlorine occur together in the familiar form of common salt, and also in animal protein. Both are vital for life: they maintain water balance and distribution, osmotic pressure, acid-base balance, and muscular functioning. The amount taken in a normal diet is usually more than enough, but in hot weather much may be lost in sweat.

Potassium is related in function to sodium and chlorine. It is found in meat, fish, vegetables, chocolate, and dried fruit.

Sulfur occurs in certain amino acids, especially in animal proteins. Sulfur in the body is found especially in insulin, which regulates the level of sugar in the blood and in human hair.

Magnesium is in nuts, beans, cereals, dark-green vegetables, seafood and chocolate. Its function is similar to calcium.

Iron is found in fish, liver, eggs, blood sausage, beans, green vegetables and oatmeal. The body of a healthy adult contains about 4g of iron – roughly the amount of a 3in (7.5cm) nail. It is a component of hemoglobin in red blood cells, which enables the blood to absorb oxygen from the lungs and carry it to all the cells in the body.

Micronutrients

These are minerals needed in comparatively small quantities.

Iodine is important for the healthy functioning of the thyroid gland. It occurs in seafish, shellfish, iodized table salt, and vegetables grown in soil naturally containing iodine.

Fluorine is found naturally in seafish, some 'hard' drinking water and China tea. It is also added to the water artificially in some localities. Traces of fluorine are present in bones, teeth, skin, and thyroid gland. It can help prevent tooth decay.

Other micronutrients are zinc, selenium, manganese, copper, molybdenum, cobalt and chromium.

Cholesterol

This is a fatty substance found in the blood and in all cell membranes. Deposits of cholesterol in the walls of arteries are a feature of a serious disease – atherosclerosis. It is advisable to reduce the amount of fat in your diet and consume mainly unsaturated and polyunsaturated fats (see p.314).

Trace elements

These are found in the body in tiny amounts, but their function, if any, is not yet known. They include strontium, bromine, vanadium, gold, silver, nickel, tin, aluminum, bismuth, arsenic and boron.

Dietary fiber

This is important. Foods high in fiber make us feel full and help regulate food intake. Fiber maintains the bulk and softness of the intestinal contents, so preventing constipation and straining. It is best eaten in the form of wholemeal bread, muesli, brown rice, pulses, fruit and vegetables.

Water

8

Water is not really a food, but it is an essential part of all tissues. Our bodies are composed of about $2/3$ water. It acts as a form of transport: the blood, which is mainly water, carries food in its basic forms to the tissues and takes away waste products to be excreted. Chemically, water is a simple compound of oxygen and hydrogen, but is never found pure as it contains traces of minerals, dissolved gases, and solids. The amount of these depends on the water's source. As well as in liquid form, water is also found in most solid food. Since it is constantly being lost in sweat, urine and breathing out, it must be replaced every day or dehydration of the body will occur. However, the body's need for water at any time is very accurately registered by the degree of thirst.

The Digestive System

The digestive tract forms a tube over 30ft (9m) long, beginning in the mouth and ending in the anus. Between these it includes the esophagus (gullet), stomach, small intestine and large intestine.

In the mouth, food is chewed into smaller pieces, mixed with saliva, and formed into a rounded ball ('bolus').

On swallowing, the bolus passes down the esophagus into the stomach.

The stomach varies in shape and size according to its contents. Its maximum capacity is about $2^1/2$ pints (1 liter). Here food is churned into even smaller pieces, and mixed with gastric juices, including hydrochloric acid. Fat is melted by the heat.

From the stomach, food passes into the small intestine. In the first 12in (30.5cm) of this (the duodenum), the food is mixed with pancreatic and intestinal juices and with bile from the gall bladder. Then here, and in the remaining 21ft (6.5m) of small intestine, most of the useful elements in food are absorbed through the intestinal walls into the blood and lymph streams.

In the 6ft- (2m)-long large intestine, water is absorbed into the body, turning the waste products into a soft solid (feces): a mixture of indigestible remnants, unabsorbed water, and millions of bacteria. Finally, the feces pass out of the body via the anus.

Food takes from 15 hours upward to pass through the whole system. It usually stays in the stomach 3 to 5 hours, the small intestine $4^1/2$ hours, and the large intestine (where the sequence of meals may get jumbled) 5 to 25 hours or more.

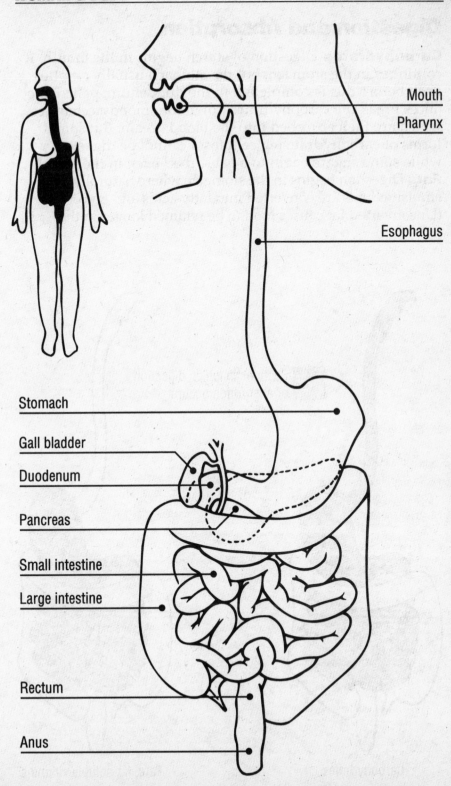

Mouth

Pharynx

Esophagus

Stomach

Gall bladder

Duodenum

Pancreas

Small intestine

Large intestine

Rectum

Anus

8

Digestion and Absorption

Carbohydrates Digestion of starch begins in the mouth. It continues in the stomach, but the stomach usually empties itself before this is completed. In the duodenum, pancreatic juices break the carbohydrates down into monosaccharides, which are then absorbed into the bloodstream. But some forms of carbohydrate (eg cellulose) cannot be digested, while some sugars begin to be absorbed even in the mouth.

Fats Digestion begins in the stomach, where naturally emulsified fats are converted into fatty acids and glycerol. (Unconverted fat causes food to be retained longer in the

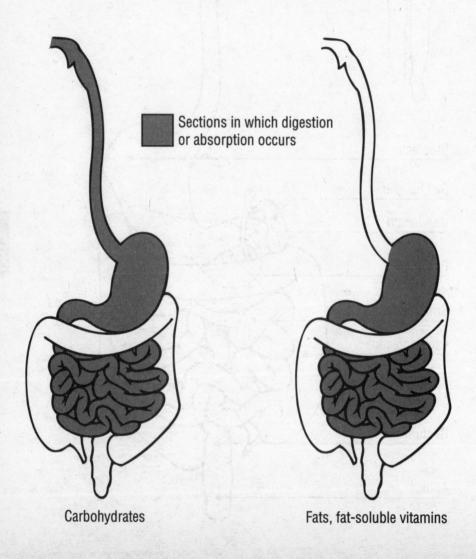

Sections in which digestion or absorption occurs

Carbohydrates   Fats, fat-soluble vitamins

stomach.) In the small intestine, bile emulsifies the
unemulsified fats, and pancreatic juice converts them into fatty
acids. These are absorbed into the lymph vessels (70%) or the
bloodstream (30%). Fat-soluble vitamins are absorbed at the
same time.

Proteins Digestion begins in the stomach, where proteins are
broken down into peptones. In the small intestine, the
pancreatic and intestinal juices break the peptones down into
amino acids. The amino acids are absorbed into the
bloodstream.

Water is absorbed in the large intestine, into the lymph vessels
and bloodstream. It is not digested before absorption.

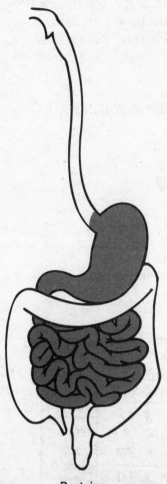

Proteins

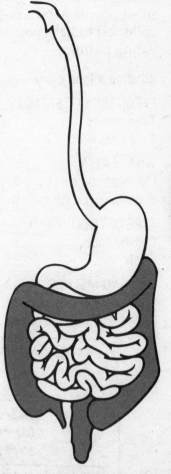

Water, water-soluble vitamins

8

Assessing Your Eating Habits

Although there are many different views on healthy eating, one point on which all experts agree is that you need to follow a varied diet that includes all the different food types. They recommend that you cut down on refined foods and animal fats, replacing them as far as possible with fibrous carbohydrates, more fresh fruit and vegetables, wholegrain cereals, and unsaturated fats.

You and food

Do you want to change to a healthier pattern of eating? In order to work out how, you will need to study your present eating habits. Make a chart using the suggestions below as guidelines. Fill in the chart honestly for two weeks, and see if a pattern emerges. Each time you eat, ask yourself why you are eating: are you hungry, or is it just because it is the time when most people have a meal? Use the information you have collected to help you break any bad habits and plan a new eating pattern.

Keeping a food diary

FREQUENCY OF EATING
Time started
Time finished

WHAT EATEN
List what you eat
every time you eat

TYPE OF FOOD
Convenience
Fresh

COOKING METHOD
List how food was cooked
(raw, fried, steamed, etc)

POSITION IN WHICH YOU EAT
Sitting
Standing
Walking
Running
Lying

EFFECTS OF EATING
Fullness
Hunger
Physical discomfort

		FREQUENCY OF EATING			
			TIME		
			STARTED	FINISHED	KING
					HOOD
Monday	BREAKFAST		8:20	8:35	
	LUNCH		12:05	12:20	AW
	SUPPER		7:10	7:30	'LED
					EAMED
Tuesday	BREAKFAST		8:15	8:30	
	LUNCH		12:10	12:25	'EO
					SAMED

Know your food

This list shows the calorific changes that take place in a potato when it is cooked by different methods or processed commercially.

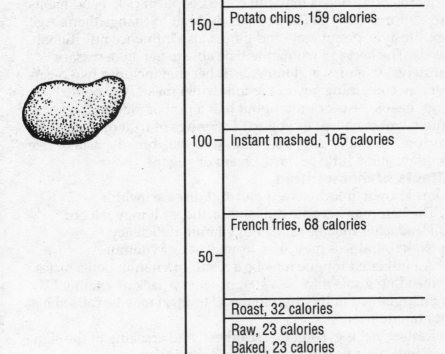

150 — Potato chips, 159 calories

100 — Instant mashed, 105 calories

French fries, 68 calories

50 —

Roast, 32 calories

Raw, 23 calories
Baked, 23 calories
Steamed, with skin on, 23 calories
Boiled, without skin, 23 calories

8

Buying and preparing food

It is best to choose ingredients that look and smell fresh. Fruit and vegetables should not be wilted or discolored. Cracked or wilted vegetable leaves indicate a mineral deficiency in the plant, so they may not provide you with the minerals you need. White meat and fish contain less saturated fat than red meat. Brown rice, wholewheat bread, wholewheat flou, and wholewheat pasta contain more fiber, minerals and vitamins than their white equivalents. The vitamin content of raw fruit and vegetables is reduced by boiling, but vitamins will pass into the cooking liquid, which may be used as stock. It is sensible to eat at least one salad a day and to cook foods without adding fat – steaming fish instead of deep frying, boiling, baking and grilling instead of frying. Replace foods high in fat with a low-fat alternative; for instance, use plain yogurt instead of cream to top a fruit salad.

Malnutrition

Malnutrition ('bad' nutrition) should not be a problem today for women in the developed world, but poverty and ignorance of what the body needs may put some people at risk. Food habits are acquired early in life and it is difficult to change them. Age, sex, lifestyle, pregnancy, and illness also influence nutritional needs. The average woman will be able to get all necessary nutrients, vitamins and minerals if her diet includes two meals per day containing any of the following: meat, fish, poultry, eggs, beans, peas or nuts; about half a pint of milk or the equivalent in cheese or yogurt; 4 servings of fruit or vegetables (include both) per day; 4 servings of cereal, bread, pasta or rice per day; and a little oil, lard, cream or sugar.

Effects of malnutrition

Some known links between diet and disease include:

a) The hair may become dull and brittle, or it may fall out.

b) Headaches may be related to vitamin deficiency.

c) Night blindness may arise from a lack of vitamin A.

d) An inflamed tongue may be a result of vitamin deficiencies.

e) Bleeding gums may be a sign of scurvy (lack of vitamin C).

f) Enlargement of the thyroid gland (goiter) may be caused by vitamin deficiency.

g) Rashes, itching, soreness, scaliness, and cracking of the skin may indicate a number of vitamin deficiencies.

h) Obesity often creates breathing difficulties.

i) Backache may result from obesity.

j) Too much food, especially fats and carbohydrates, leads to obesity. Too little wastes tissues and leads to starvation.

k) Obesity causes heart disease, anorexia nervosa, heart failure.

l) Soft bones may indicate rickets (lack of vitamin D).

m) Loss of motor function in the legs may be a sign of beriberi (lack of vitamin B1 or thiamine).

n) Lesions in the spinal cord may indicate lack of vitamin B12.

o) Many complaints of the stomach and digestive system result from diet; symptoms include diarrhea, nausea, pain, cramps, vomiting.

p) Kidney stones may form as a result of insufficient fluid intake.

q) Gallstones are associated with a fatty diet.

r) Too much alcohol may cause cirrhosis of the liver.

s) Insufficient iron can cause anemia.

t) Constipation can be caused by a lack of fiber in the diet.
u) Piles (hemorrhoids) may also be a result of a lack of fiber.
v) Painful feet may be a sign of vitamin B12 deficiency.
w) Numbness in toes may be caused by vitamin deficiency.
x) Gout is made worse by excessive rich food and alcohol.
The West offers the most varied, cleanest, and most readily available supply of food in the history of the world. But this brings its own problems, including obesity, diabetes (associated in some cases with excessive carbohydrate intake) and digestive diseases associated with lack of fiber. However, 75% of the world's population lives mainly on a diet of one food, usually a cereal such as rice. Deficiency diseases and lack of food because of crop failure are common in developing countries; yet in times of plenty, these diets often provide more nutrients than the average Western diet.

Food Additives

A food additive is any substance not normally consumed as food, which is added to food to preserve it or to enhance its flavor, color or texture. Most packed foods contain additives. About 3500 additives are currently in use worldwide. Some occur naturally, eg pectin, which is used to set jams and comes from plants. Others are made by food manufacturers, eg azodicarbonamide, which is added to flour to improve the consistency of bread dough.

Growing public concern has led governments in several countries to pass legislation obliging food manufacturers to list all the ingredients in their products. They are now listed in descending order of weight; additives usually have to be listed by type and chemical name or by number, or both.

Improved labeling helps people avoid additives that might provoke an allergic reaction; most people do not have an obvious reaction to additives, but a significant minority does. Symptoms of additive intolerance are wide ranging and include asthma, rashes, headaches and a general feeling of malaise. In children, such intolerance may also be an important contributory factor to behavioral problems. Research has pointed to the artificial azo dyes, such as Tartrazine, as a possible cause of hyperactivity.

8

Calorie Needs

A person's need for energy from food is measured in calories (or kilocalories, see pp.294-95). Needs vary from person to person, depending on a variety of different factors. Age, sex, size, physical activity and climate all affect the number of calories that are needed.

Calories are used to maintain body functions and to provide energy for exercise (see pp.312-13). An increase in weight results if a person takes in as food more calories than are needed (see pp.322-3). If calorie intake is below requirements, fat stored in the body is converted to energy and weight is lost.

Girls' and women's daily calorie requirements

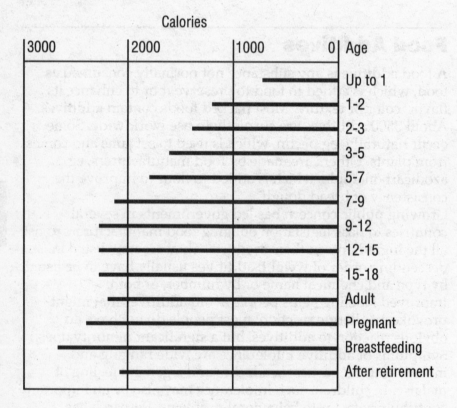

Calories

3000	2000	1000	0	Age
				Up to 1
				1-2
				2-3
				3-5
				5-7
				7-9
				9-12
				12-15
				15-18
				Adult
				Pregnant
				Breastfeeding
				After retirement

Calories in Childbearing

Women have higher daily calorie requirements during pregnancy and when breastfeeding. Estimates of these increased requirements vary, but the increases suggested below should be sufficient to meet the needs of most women today.

Pregnancy

During the second half of pregnancy, an increase to 2250 calories per day is suggested. This estimate assumes some reduction in the level of exercise toward the end of pregnancy.

Breastfeeding

A woman who is breastfeeding her child should allow 500 calories per day above her usual requirements.

Use of Calories

Calories are needed to supply energy for every activity. Approximately 1400 calories a day – about $2/3$ of her total daily requirement – are needed by a typical woman in order to maintain basic life processes such as heartbeat, breathing and digestion. A further 600 to 800 calories a day should probably be plenty to provide the energy needed for all her other activities at work and during recreation.

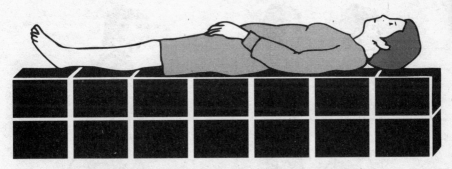

To maintain basic life processes: 1400 calories per day

Calories and Exercise

People use up calories every minute of the day. This is true even when they are asleep or lying doing 'nothing'. When a person is resting, most of this calorie expenditure is used to maintain body functions. A typical woman uses about 55 calories an hour when she is asleep. Estimating the rate of

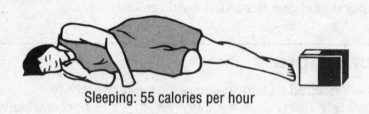

Sleeping: 55 calories per hour

Standing:
90 calories
per hour

Walking:
200 calories
per hour

Running:
400 calories
per hour

calorie expenditure during different activities is more difficult – some people are naturally more energetic than others, even when each is doing the same thing. For example, a person walking at 4mph obviously uses more calories than another walking at 2mph. The figures on this page are, however, of interest in that they provide an indication of likely rates of calorie expenditure during a variety of different activities.

Walking upstairs: 800 calories per hour

Sitting: 75 calories per hour

Knitting: 90 calories per hour

8

Nature and Nutrition

Carbohydrates, proteins, fats, minerals, vitamins and water are all ingredients of a healthy diet. Some aspects of diet planning require special attention, but generally speaking nature is an excellent nutritionist – letting us know what our bodies require. Moreover, in developed countries, where different nutrients are readily available, most people eat more than enough different types of food to prevent any serious nutritional deficiencies.

Fats and Diets

Fats are an essential part of a balanced diet. They provide energy in concentrated form; they enable the fat-soluble vitamins, A, D, E and K, to be absorbed from the intestines; and they stimulate the production of bile by the gall bladder, which aids digestion.

The body breaks down fats into glycerin and fatty acids. The body can synthesize some fatty acids from other foods, but three are made only from fats.

There are two basic types of fat: saturated fats and unsaturated fats. Saturated fats, which harden at room temperature, are in meat and dairy produce, solid shortening products, coconut oil, cocoa butter and palm oil (used in commercially prepared cookies and pastry). Research has shown a relationship between consumption of saturated fats and high levels of cholesterol (a type of fat) in the blood, and heart and artery disease. A high level of saturated fats in the diet is also associated with intestinal cancers.

Vegetable fats tend to be unsaturated. Polyunsaturated fats are found in vegetable oils, especially safflower, soybean and corn oil. There is good evidence that consuming polyunsaturated fats can counteract the effects of foods high in saturated fats.

Protein and Diet

Protein is vital to growth and cell repair – yet estimates of protein needs vary enormously. An average estimate for good nutrition is about $2^1/2$oz (70g) a day in adulthood (with protein supplying about 7% of calorie intake). But people have been found to adapt in a healthy way to intakes under half to more than twice this amount. All this is dependent, of course, on all essential amino acids being eaten, and in the right proportions. Lack of protein can be a problem in old people with little money, and in those following unusual diets.

Carbohydrate and Diet

Too much carbohydrate in the diet shows itself in unhealthy weight gain. It is not, however, only the quantity of carbohydrate intake that is important. The type of carbohydrate eaten is also significant.

Traditional cereal products, such as bread and potatoes, contain other nutrients as well as carbohydrates and so can make an important contribution to total diet planning. The current widespread replacement of traditional carbohydrate foods by highly refined and sweetened carbohydrate products has serious implications. Pastries, cakes, chocolate, ice cream, and alcohol all have high carbohydrate counts but contain little of nutritional value apart from their energy content. They provide little or no roughage. Most important, however, are the harmful effects of too much sugar in the diet. Some scientists believe:

a) that the rush of sugar into the bloodstream causes the body to overreact – withdrawing too much sugar from the blood and so leaving us feeling tired and irritable;

b) that eventually excessive sugar intake can cause diabetes in people who would not otherwise suffer from it; and

c) that sugar has a role in producing heart disease.

Certainly sugar promotes tooth decay and destroys the appetite for more nutritious foods.

Such criticisms apply not only to white sugar, but also to brown sugar, raw sugar, honey and molasses. But white sugar is the main culprit, simply because the amounts of sugar added in the cooking or processing of foods usually dwarf the amounts of sweetening added at mealtime.

8

Water Requirement

The normal requirement is the equivalent of about 6 or 7 glasses of fluid a day. Thirst usually provides a very accurate indication of need, but in very hot conditions may not keep up with the intake needed to replace perspiration loss.

Minerals and Diet

Most of the body's mineral requirements are met without special diet planning. Some care, however, is needed in the following cases.

a) Sodium intake is usually far higher than necessary, but may be insufficient for very heavy work in hot conditions.

b) Calcium intake depends on daily consumption of milk, cheese, and other foods rich in calcium (see p.300). However, sunlight is important for the absorption of calcium by the body (see p.220).

c) Iron is needed for the hemoglobin in red blood cells. It is found in meat and eggs, brewer's yeast, and wheat germ. But it is only absorbed in tiny quantities, and hardly at all if vitamin C in the body is low (see p.299). Women, with their regular menstrual blood loss, often develop an iron shortage (anemia), with resulting fatigue and breathlessness.

d) Iodine shortage occurs if the diet contains no seafood and only vegetables grown in iodine-free soil. A lack of iodine causes thyroid deficiencies and thyroid gland enlargement. This is less common with modern food transport and availability of iodized salt.

Vitamins and Diet

Vitamins B1 and C can be lost by overcooking, but there are abundant uncooked sources of both.

Vitamin A may be deficient if the diet contains no dairy produce, margarine, or green, yellow, orange or red vegetables.

Vitamin D is especially important in the diets of children, nursing mothers, and post-menopausal women (see p.220). Butter, margarine, and liver are good sources. Vitamin D deficiency has been found in children in poor urban areas – especially in children with pigmented skin, which impedes the formation of the vitamin by the body from sunlight. It is also likely to be found in housebound people. Regularly sitting or walking in sunshine and bright daylight helps to prevent vitamin D deficiency.

Excess and Deficiency

Enough is enough

In diet, enough is enough; more is not better. It is well known that too many calories result in obesity in many people, which can in turn result in heart and other disorders (see pp.326-7). Taking certain minerals and vitamins in excess can result in deficiencies in others, by upsetting their absorption or storage. Too much vitamin B1, for example, can cause deficiencies in other B vitamins. Excessive intake in certain vitamins can result in illness (see p.298). Vitamin A and D, for example, are not soluble in water, so excessive quantities cannot be excreted; they remain in the body, causing poisoning.

Interaction of nutrients

Nutrients do not act totally independently of one another. The body is too complex for that. A deficiency of one nutrient can lead to a deficiency of another by affecting the body's ability to make use of the second nutrient, even if it is present in the diet. For example, vitamin A deficiency can lead to vitamin C deficiency; vitamin C deficiency to iron deficiency. Interactions occur not only among vitamins, and between vitamins and minerals, but also between vitamins and proteins, vitamins and carbohydrates, vitamins and fats; and there are many multiple relationships as well.

Nutritional Medicine

8

Attention to diet has proved beneficial for all manner of ailments. Nutritional medicine, also called nutrition therapy, is in some ways related to naturopathic healing techniques. Naturopathy aims to help the body assert its own powers of healing in the face of stress or disease; nutritional medicine emphasizes the role of healthy eating habits as an essential part of this process. Many of the dietary principles propounded by naturopaths agree with traditional medical thinking: both agree on the harmfulness of eating large amounts of fats and refined carbohydrates. However, nutritional therapists think that many ailments are provoked by poisonous or allergy-producing substances in a normal diet; they may recommend supplements of vitamins, minerals, and other substances, calculated on individual requirements. Treatment with supplements should always be under the guidance of a trained practitioner.

A Healthy Diet

There is no one ideal diet. First, needs differ (and so does the impact of availability, cost, taste, habit and cooking facilities and skills). But, more important, there are a million different ways of satisfying those needs in healthy eating. It is possible to live healthily on a diet of milk, wholewheat bread and green vegetables. It would not be very interesting, though. Variety is the spice of food.

Processing and Cooking

It is hard to generalize, but the more processed a food is, the less desirable it is likely to be as a regular part of a healthy diet. Canned and precooked foods, mass-produced breakfast cereals, cookies, pastries, and ready-made meals all tend to be open to criticism. Defects include:
a) lower nutritional value;
b) added sugar and saturated fats;
c) added preservative chemicals and, often, untested colorings and flavorings; and sometimes
d) unhygienic production.
In general, the 'wholefood' movement is a sensible one (though, incidentally, there is no agreed evidence that 'organic' vegetables have higher food value than chemically fertilized ones – even though they may taste better and contain fewer pollutants). However, nutrients can be lost in home cooking as well as in processing, and undesirable ones added. 'Boiling' of vegetables should always be done by steaming in a very shallow amount of water, if vitamin C is to be preserved. (Salt should only be added at the last moment.) 'Frying' should be in a tiny amount of unsaturated oil, not hard fat. Grilling is better, where applicable.)

Daily Food Guide

Included here is a daily food guide devised by a dietitian to provide a balanced diet. (Those suffering from certain illnesses, eg diabetes, may need a more carefully planned diet, about which a physician should be consulted.) The guide divides foods into four groups, and recommended daily servings per person are given for each group. Carbohydrates (groups B and D) should provide 50–55% of dietary energy, fat 30%, and protein 15%.

Notes

1) Group A uses 1 cup whole or skimmed milk as the basic measure. Alternatives are: 1 cup buttermilk; $^1/_2$ cup evaporated milk; $^1/_4$ cup nonfat milk powder; 1oz cheddar cheese; $1^1/_2$ cups cottage cheese.

2) If amounts in group A are doubled in the course of the day, not more than one serving of group C is needed.

3) Whole milk (not skimmed) and butter or margarine should be used during childhood, pregnancy, and lactation.

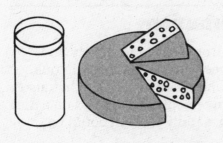

A: MILK AND CHEESE
Age 0-9 years: 2-3 cups
9-12 years: 3 or more cups
13-19 years: 4 or more cups
Adult: 2 or more cups
Pregnancy: 3 or more cups
Lactation: 4 or more cups

B: FRUIT AND VEGETABLES
Four or more servings.
Serving size examples:
a $^1/_2$ cup dark-green or deep-yellow vegetable (served at least every other day);
b $^1/_2$ cup or 1 medium-sized raw fruit or vegetable rich in vitamin C;
c 1 medium potato.

C: MEAT AND PULSES
Two or more servings.
Serving size examples:
a 2-3oz cooked meat, poultry, or fish (excluding bone and fat)
b 2 eggs;
c 1 cup beans, peas, or lentils.

D: BREAD AND CEREALS
Four or more servings.
Serving size examples:
a 1 slice bread;
b 1 cup ready-to-eat cereal;
c $^1/_2$ to $^3/_4$ cup cooked cereal, macaroni, spaghetti, rice, noodles, or bulgur.

8

Vegetarianism

A vegetarian is a person who does not eat the meat of any mammal, bird or fish. There are two main types of vegetarian:
a) vegans, who eat nothing at all of animal origins, and
b) lacto-ovo-vegetarians, who do allow themselves animal products such as milk, cheese, eggs and honey.
There are also people who call themselves vegetarians but do eat fish.

Reasons for Vegetarianism

Reasons for vegetarianism vary from society to society and individual to individual. It has been advocated for religious, philosophical, moral, economic and health reasons. It has also been adopted as a necessity. Many peoples have lived on a diet of fruit, nuts and berries, with meat only when it could be obtained.
Perhaps the most powerful arguments for vegetarianism in modern society are:
a) the inefficiency of the animal food production chain (see pp.290-1) in a largely underfed world;
b) the relative cheapness of the ingredients of vegetarian diet; and
c) the possible unhealthiness of eating meat that contains crop pesticides and antibiotics and hormones given to the animals, and that has been processed in many ways that are not necessarily hygienic or beneficial.
Also, many people feel that the slaughter of animals is cruel and debasing, and that vegetarianism is part of a more peaceful and harmonious way of life.

Vegetarian Diet

Despite the claims of some vegetarians, there is no established evidence that eating meat is unhealthy in itself. But it is certainly as possible for a vegetarian to be healthy, strong and long-lived as it is for a meat-eater.
A person who chooses to give up meat must be careful that her diet still provides enough of the right nutrients.
There are no problems with:
a) healthy carbohydrates (grains, cereal products, potatoes, fruits);

b) fats (vegetable oils, dairy products, nuts, margarine); and
c) minerals and most vitamins (vegetables and fruits).
Obtaining an adequate supply of protein and certain vitamins
can, however, be more problematic for vegetarians than for
meat-eaters (see below).

Diet Planning

Vegetarians must take particular care that their diet provides
them with adequate supplies of the following nutrients.
Protein is readily available from eggs and dairy produce,
nuts, soybeans, raisins, grains and pulses. But a vegetarian
should be sure to get a good selection of essential amino acids
at each meal.
This is not difficult where eggs or dairy produce are eaten:
cereal and milk, bread and milk, and bread and eggs are all
good amino acid combinations. But vegans must depend on
soybeans, or on carefully planned vegetable combinations.
These include: lentil soup and hard wholewheat bread; and
beans and rice.
Vitamins requiring particular attention in a vegetarian diet
are:
a) cobalamin (vitamin B12) – available from dairy produce and
yeast and, particularly useful for vegans, in synthetic form;
b) vitamin D – also needed in synthetic form by vegans where
sunlight is insufficient.
Iron and calcium are also worth mentioning, as they are
sometimes lacking even in the diets of meat-eaters. In fact,
there are many excellent vegetarian sources.
Iron is found in raisins, lentils, wheat germ, prunes, spinach
and other leafy vegetables, and in bread, eggs, and yeast.
Calcium occurs in dairy produce, dried fruit, soybeans, sesame
seeds, and in leafy vegetables.

8

1½ cups beans + 4 cups rice = protein equivalent of 12oz
(340g) steak

Are You Overweight?

It is not always easy to say whether a person is overweight. But there is no doubt that weight problems are on the increase in modern industrial society.

One way of learning whether you are among the overweight is to check your weight against a desirable-weight table – such as the one given on p.324. (Note that 'desirable' weight tables give lower figures than 'average' weight tables – in a society

Why People Put on Weight

Overweight is always caused by taking in more food energy than the body uses up. The bulk of food energy is taken in in the form of carbohydrates and fats. Both these supply calories (the measure of energy); and both are converted to fat deposits if the calories they supply are more than the body uses. The diagram shows what happens to the food energy input.

a) Most of it is used to supply body energy needs – to maintain basic life processes and for all physical activity (see pp.311-13).
b) It is still the subject of scientific controversy, but it does seem that some people get rid of surplus input because their

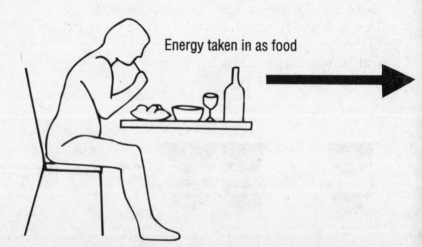

Energy taken in as food

where more people are overweight than underweight, the average will be higher than is healthy.)

Even without weighing yourself, it is possible to do a quick check for overweight. Start by asking yourself the following questions. Do you have any telltale bulges? Do you look much fatter than you used to? Have your measurements increased appreciably? If you pinch your upper arm, thigh, or midriff, is there more than 1in (2.5cm) of flesh between your thumb and forefinger?

---

bodies automatically speed up their metabolism and burn up the surplus rather than store it. This burning up process is called 'thermogenesis'. Also, there is a rise in the body's metabolism after every meal. So two people may eat exactly the same food, but one will burn up more than the other if the food is taken in several small meals rather than two or three large ones.

c) Food energy that is neither needed nor burned up is stored by the body in the form of fat. In overweight people the store far exceeds any normal future demand.

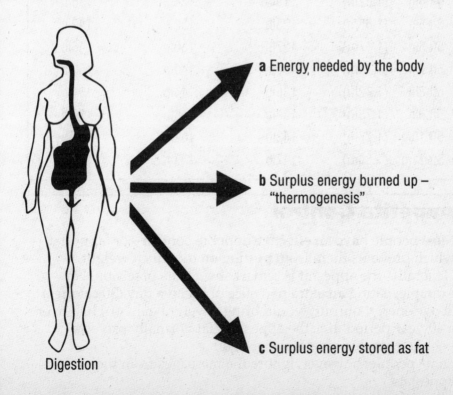

a Energy needed by the body

8

b Surplus energy burned up – "thermogenesis"

c Surplus energy stored as fat

Digestion

Desirable Weights

Desirable-weight tables are based on statistics, usually collected by insurance companies, showing the correlation between different weights and health standards. The table included here shows desirable weights, according to height and body size, for women aged 25. Older women can expect to exceed these weights, but at age 45, for example, probably should not be much more than 12 to 18lb (5.4-8.16kg) over the weights given for age 25.

Height		Small frame	Medium frame	Large frame
4ft 9in	(1.45m)	98lb	104lb	114lb
4ft 10in	(1.47m)	100lb	107lb	117lb
4ft 11in	(1.49m)	103lb	110lb	120lb
5ft 0in	(1.52m)	106lb	113lb	123lb
5ft 1in	(1.54m)	109lb	116lb	126lb
5ft 2in	(1.57m)	112lb	120lb	130lb
5ft 3in	(1.60m)	115lb	124lb	134lb
5ft 4in	(1.62m)	119lb	128lb	138lb
5ft 5in	(1.65m)	123lb	132lb	142lb
5ft 6in	(1.67m)	127lb	136lb	146lb
5ft 7in	(1.70m)	131lb	140lb	150lb
5ft 8in	(1.72m)	135lb	144lb	154lb
5ft 9in	(1.75m)	139lb	148lb	159lb
5ft 10in	(1.77m)	143lb	152lb	164lb
5ft 11in	(1.80m)	147lb	157lb	169lb

Appetite Control

Most people have an effective appetite control – or 'appestat' – which prevents them from putting on too much weight. Generally, the appestat is remarkable for its precision. For example, eating an extra half slice of bread a day (30 calories) above energy output, would bring a weight gain of 110lb over a 40-year period. It is the appestat that normally protects people from this type of weight gain.

Some people, however, ignore the messages from their appestats.

Typical reasons are:
a) social habit or custom;
b) excessive love of food in general or of certain foods in particular;
c) habits of overeating acquired during childhood;
d) lack of exercise (see pp.348-9); and
e) eating for psychological support, whether as a general addiction or as a response to shock or stress (for psychological aspects, see pp.383-4).

Appetite and Exercise

Some people put on weight because their appestat (see opposite) is put out of action by an excessively sedentary existence. When physical activity falls below moderate levels, research has shown that appetite may actually increase – even though the body has no need for the extra food. Increasing the amount of exercise in such cases not only increases calorie output, but also appears to put the appestat back into good working order. Of course, exercise above moderate levels will increase the appetite.

When People Put on Weight

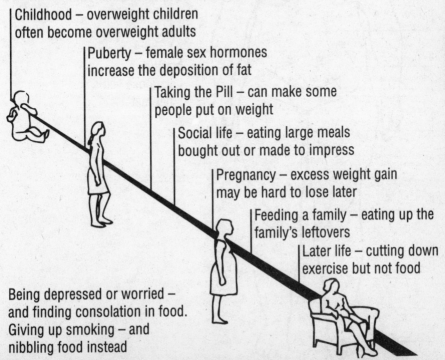

Childhood – overweight children often become overweight adults

Puberty – female sex hormones increase the deposition of fat

Taking the Pill – can make some people put on weight

Social life – eating large meals bought out or made to impress

Pregnancy – excess weight gain may be hard to lose later

Feeding a family – eating up the family's leftovers

Later life – cutting down exercise but not food

Being depressed or worried – and finding consolation in food. Giving up smoking – and nibbling food instead

8

Effects of Being Overweight

Overweight people are not just more tired, short of breath, and physically lethargic, with aching joints and poor digestion; if obese (more than 20 percent above the maximum desirable weight) they are also more likely to suffer from high blood pressure, heart disease, diabetes, kidney disorders, cirrhosis of the liver, pneumonia, inflammation of the gall bladder, arthritis, hernias and varicose veins. They have more accidents, are more likely to die during operations, and have higher rates of mortality in general (including three times the mortality from heart and circulatory disease).

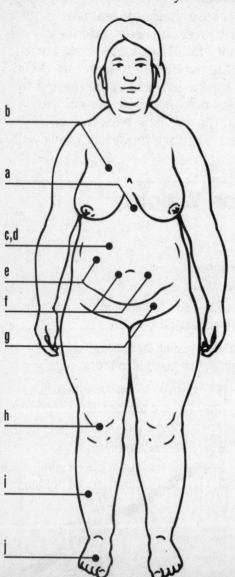

Problems of being obese
Obese people are more likely to suffer from the following:

a heart disease and high blood pressure
b pneumonia
c cirrhosis of the liver
d diabetes
e inflammation of the gall bladder
f kidney disorders
g hernias
h arthritis
i varicose veins
j flat feet

Some of these effects arise from mechanical causes: the burden of extra weight and its particular location as fat deposits. Others arise chemically, from the need to supply more body tissue than normal. For example, the spread of hormones over increased body tissue is sometimes a cause of infertility. It can also cause serious problems in pregnancy (eg toxemia, see p.129). In many cases, reduction to desirable weight removes all the symptoms of disorder and results in increased life expectancy.

Excuses for Being Overweight

Many overweight people like to blame something outside their control – their heavy bones, heavy family, hormones, even their body water level. But:
a) variations in bone density cannot account for more than about 7lb weight difference;
b) though overweight does 'run in families', it may be due more to acquired eating habits than genetic factors;
c) hormonal malfunctions can cause obesity, in very rare cases, but these show themselves clearly in other bodily symptoms; and
d) the body water level is very well regulated except in very hot weather and in some illnesses.

Losing Weight

Losing weight is not easy. It demands controlled eating habits, discipline, patience and a change of attitudes. Before you start:
a) do not be tempted by any promise of easy weight loss – there are no miracles;
b) adopt a definite diet plan and stick to it:
c) if you need advice, get it from your doctor. It is best to aim to lose weight steadily over a long period. Constant yo-yo weight changes are as bad for you as being overweight. Once weight is lost keep a constant check, and deal with small gains as they occur.

8

Choosing a Diet Plan

All genuine diets restrict calorie intake. If a person's intake of food does not contain sufficient calories to meet energy requirements, the body makes up the deficiency by burning up its stores of fat. Three basic types of diet plan are popular at the present time. Each of them can work if you are sufficiently determined.

a) Low-calorie plans set a numerical limit to daily calorie intake (usually 1000 to 1500 calories). Calorie tables make it easy to calculate the energy content of a meal.

b) No-count plans, simplified versions of the low-calorie system, divide food into three categories: high-calorie food that must be avoided; medium-calorie food that can be eaten in moderation; and unrestricted foods.

c) Liquid diets have been developed that provide approximately 330 calories per day. As calorie intake is under 1000 calories per day, these diets should only be followed for brief or intermittent periods, and under medical supervision. Maintenance programs can be followed after the weight has been lost.

Slimming Aids

A considerable variety of slimming aids is widely available – but not all of them are effective or recommended.

a) Substitute meals (wafers, chocolate bars, packaged foods, etc) have a stated calorie content and sometimes contain cellulose to give a fuller feeling in the stomach. Some slimmers find them useful, but they do nothing to encourage the eating habits needed to stay slim.

b) Low-calorie substitute foods and drinks (eg skim milk, slimmers, bread, crispbread) can help slimmers reduce total calorie intake.

c) Prescribed drugs may reduce appetite and do not seem to be addictive, but do nothing to encourage good eating habits.

d) Proprietary slimming pills usually contain cellulose and are meant to suppress appetite. Amounts are so small that their effectiveness is probably more psychological than real.

e) Saunas, Turkish baths and reducing garments cause loss of body water through sweating. This can reduce measurements and weight, but the effect is rapidly canceled out by the drinking needed to replace the fluid loss.

f) Vibrator belts and other massagers are meant to break down fat deposits. There appears to be little evidence to support claims made for them.

g) Machines using electric impulses to relax and contract muscles are recommended by some slimmers.

h) Liposuction is an option; many plastic surgeons now practice this technique of removing unwanted body fat.

i) Exercise will not on its own make much difference to your weight. It would, for example, take 12 hours of tennis to lose 1lb of fat. Exercise does, however, increase the sense of well-being that dieting brings (see also pp.348-9).

j) Attending a support group such as Overeaters' Anonymous can be an effective, though expensive, way of getting slim, and can give an invaluable psychological boost.

8

SELF HELP

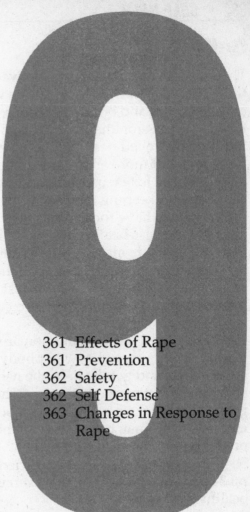

9

Self Help

The self-help movement is a relatively recent development in the history of health care. For years women remained ignorant of their bodies and bodily functions, and unfortunately the medical profession did little to discourage this. Women have traditionally relied heavily on doctors for both diagnosis and treatment, but more and more women are now taking responsibility for their bodies and playing an increasingly active part in keeping themselves healthy. As a result of this, many women have formed self-help groups where they can meet and discuss health care, sexuality and other matters.

Many women are also anxious about overdependence on drug-based treatments which deal with the symptoms but do not always tackle the cause, and interest in branches of alternative medicine such as acupuncture is continuing to grow (see pp.346-7).

Health care and self-examination are not just for eccentrics; if a woman really gets to know her body, she can spot any changes as they arise and get the help she needs to check up on them. She is not rejecting medicine care: she is simply playing a greater part in the care of her own body. There are many measures a woman can take to establish a personal health-care program.

She can ensure that she gets sufficient rest and exercise (see pp.348-9 for details of suitable exercises) and that her diet is healthy.

Above all, a woman can start to familiarize herself with her body and how it works. The simple anatomical diagrams on the following pages will help, and the techniques of self-examination, described on pp.338-9, will do much to increase a woman's confidence in her ability to take care of herself.

SKELETON

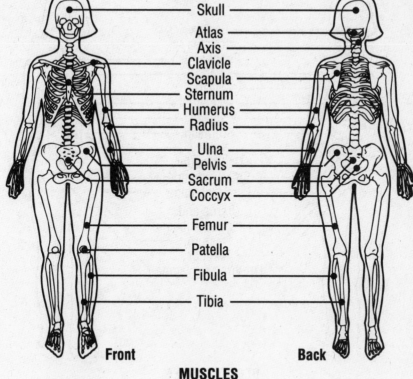

Skull
Atlas
Axis
Clavicle
Scapula
Sternum
Humerus
Radius
Ulna
Pelvis
Sacrum
Coccyx

Femur

Patella

Fibula

Tibia

Front   **Back**

MUSCLES

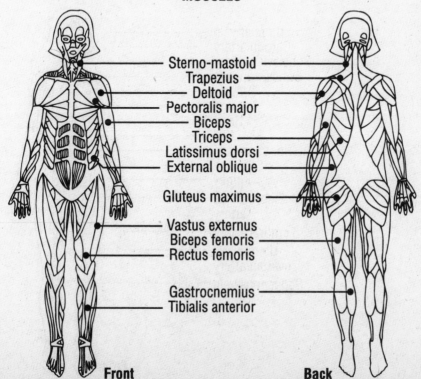

Sterno-mastoid
Trapezius
Deltoid
Pectoralis major
Biceps
Triceps
Latissimus dorsi
External oblique

Gluteus maximus

Vastus externus
Biceps femoris
Rectus femoris

Gastrocnemius
Tibialis anterior

Front   **Back**

9

INTERNAL ORGANS

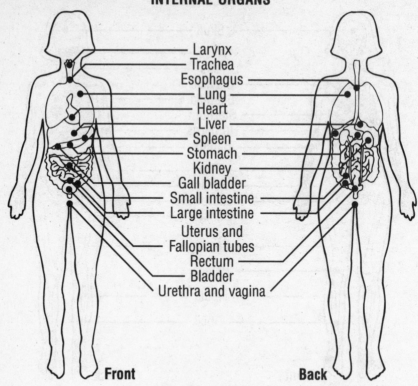

Larynx
Trachea
Esophagus
Lung
Heart
Liver
Spleen
Stomach
Kidney
Gall bladder
Small intestine
Large intestine

Uterus and
Fallopian tubes
Rectum
Bladder
Urethra and vagina

Front　　　　　　　**Back**

BLOOD SYSTEM

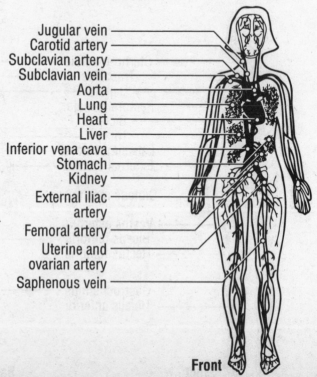

Jugular vein
Carotid artery
Subclavian artery
Subclavian vein
Aorta
Lung
Heart
Liver
Inferior vena cava
Stomach
Kidney
External iliac
artery
Femoral artery
Uterine and
ovarian artery
Saphenous vein

Front

HORMONAL SYSTEM

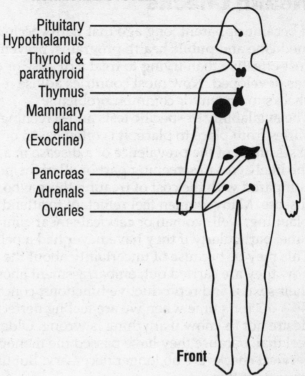

Pituitary
Hypothalamus
Thyroid &
parathyroid
Thymus
Mammary
gland
(Exocrine)

Pancreas
Adrenals
Ovaries

Front

LYMPHATIC SYSTEM

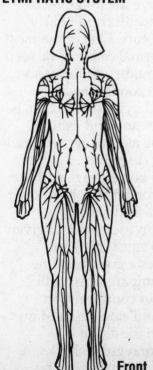

Front

NERVOUS SYSTEM

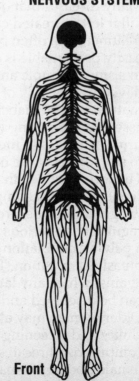

Front

9

Health Checks

It became apparent long ago that with vaccination, nutritional medicine and public health programs, prevention is far more cost-effective than trying to treat a disease or condition once it has developed. Now most countries advise regular health checks to screen for common problems.

The availability of specific tests and screening techniques varies from place to place. It is often based on an economic assessment of the prevalence of a disease in a community and the likely cost in screening part or all of the population, compared with the cost of treating those who would get the disease. Many women feel reluctant to attend a family-planning, well-woman or cervical-smear clinic for the first time, particularly if they have never had a pelvic examination. This may be because of uncertainty about the procedures and how they are carried out; embarrassment about our bodies and their sexual and reproductive functions; concern about taking up a doctor's time when we are feeling perfectly well; or a desire not to know if anything is wrong. Older women may feel that, because they have passed the menopause, breast and cervical checks are no longer necessary. But they are even more important then.

Many diseases that develop slowly but have the potential to kill if left untreated can be detected by a health check. Early treatment can often bring about complete cure. One of the most easily preventable is cervical cancer: abnormal cells can be seen in a smear sample and treatment carried out before the cancer develops. The risk of developing common conditions like maturity-onset diabetes, osteoarthritis and hypertension can be assessed measuring weight and blood pressure and testing urine. Changes in lifestyle and diet may be all that are required to stop or delay the onset of a debilitating disease.

The form that health checks take depends on your age and the scope of the screening program. Young women may have their weight and blood pressure measured, be asked about regularity of periods and any contraception used, and be given a pelvic examination (including a cervical smear test) and breast examination. This examination gives a good baseline against which any later changes can be compared. Anxieties can be discussed and decisions made about contraception. Older women may also be offered urine and stool tests. Many clinics and screening systems are run with the aid of computerized recall systems, which ensure regular checks. A female doctor is usually available, or a female nurse can be present. A urine sample may be requested. Try to collect early-

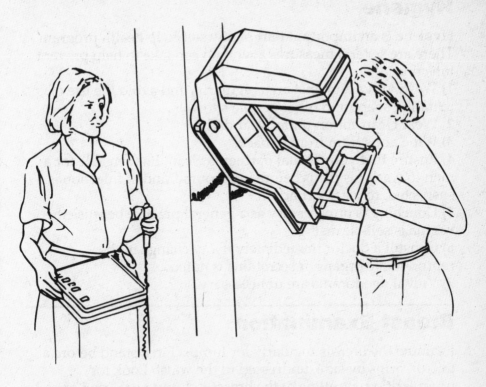

Mammography is a painless breast-screening technique using low-dosage X-rays. It is important to relax during the test.

morning urine in a clean bottle. Don't wash or douche rigorously before an examination as this can eliminate signs of a discharge. Young women are advised to have their first cervical smear as soon as they become sexually active, and a second a year later. Women at high risk (eg those with genital warts) should be tested annually or more often.

Mammography is a low-dose breast X-ray that screens women for breast abnormalities. The American Cancer Society recommends a baseline mammogram for all women at age 35-40; a mammogram at 1- to 2-year intervals for women between 40 and 49; and annual mammograms for those aged 50 and over. Annual screens may be recommended for women at particularly high risk of breast cancer (those with a history of breast cancer, those with a mother or sister who has had bilateral or premenopausal breast cancer, and those with abnormalities on breast biopsy).

When choosing a doctor, enquire about facilities like a well-woman clinic. Monthly breast self-examination is also vital.

9

Hygiene

Hygiene is an important part of any self-help health program. There are several measures a woman can take to help prevent infection.

1) Wash vulva and anal area regularly, and avoid the use of irritating soaps and other people's towels.

2) Wear clean cotton underwear daily.

3) Wipe anus from front to back.

4) Ensure that your sexual partner is clean. It is sensible for a man to wash his penis before intercourse, and, if infection is suspected, to wear a condom.

5) Douching is unnecessary as a general practice because the vagina is self-cleansing.

6) Consult a doctor immediately if any change in the reproductive organs or secretions is noted.

7) Vulval deodorants are unnecessary.

Breast Examination

Examine the breasts regularly for lumps. First, stand before a mirror, arms by side, undressed to the waist. Look for irregularities in outline of the breasts, or any puckering or dimpling of the skin. Then check nipples for discharge or bleeding (see p.432).

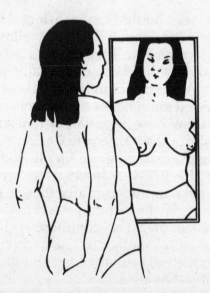

The next part of the examination is performed on 5 separate areas in turn – each quarter of the breast, and lastly the armpit.

1 Lie on bed, folded towel under right shoulder, right arm behind head. With flat of fingers, feel upper, inner quarter of right breast.
2 Repeat on lower, inner quarter.
3 Bring right arm to side, and examine lower, outer quarter.
4 Repeat on upper, outer quarter and area between breasts and armpit.
5 Examine armpit.
Then move towel under left shoulder and repeat the examination on the left breast.

Alternative & Complementary Treatments

Although the medical profession often questions the validity of therapies unproven by clinical trials, the attraction of complementary and alternative medicine might in fact lie in its fundamentally different approach. At least 40% of clients seeking orthodox help have been shown by studies to have no apparent physical ailments. Practitioners of alternative and complementary medicine take invisible complaints seriously as a warning of future illness. Alternative systems are based on theories of disease and its treatment that are incompatible with orthodox medical beliefs and practice in a community. Complementary systems are those used by orthodox doctors in circumstances in which they appear to work, though the reasons may not be clear. Among the most established and accepted alternative and complementary systems are the following:

Homeopathy operates on the principle that 'like cures like'. Samuel Christian Hahnemann (1745-1843) discovered that, while large doses of certain plant or mineral extracts were lethal, smaller doses could inhibit disease; minimal doses were often curative. He said they replicate on a cellular level the correct pattern of response to disease. First, there must be a detailed case history. Each remedy matches a symptom, even temperament and physical appearance. Over 2000 remedies have been formulated, to treat a wide range of disorders, but you should consult a homeopathic doctor before buying remedies from a pharmacy.

Osteopathy, founded by Dr. Andrew Taylor Still (b.1912), proposes that, to be well, the structure of the body, especially the spine, must be sound. Illnesses such as headaches, nervous conditions, and skin complaints are caused by the vertebrae being out of alignment. Disease is treated by massage and manipulating the bones. Osteopathy is popular in some areas of the United States; as many as half the licensed health-care providers are osteopaths. Currently, however, most practice conventional medicine, using osteopathy mainly to treat back problems.

Chiropractic, similar to osteopathy, also involves manipulation, but it has greater concern with the direction of the manipulation and tends to use X-rays more often. It is currently experiencing a tremendous increase in popularity and acceptance. Some physicians provide regular referrals to chiropractors, most commonly for back problems.

Herbalism, using plants as cures, is one of the foundations of Western medicine. Much of the pharmacopea of orthodox medicine is based on ancient plant remedies: eg atrophine is extracted from deadly nightshade (belladonna).

Naturopathy is mainly a self-help therapy: the patient is ultimately responsible for the correct functioning of her body. Health is a vital state, not merely the absence of disease; cure is thought to be brought about by the body's own healing power which is undermined by three basic causes: biochemical (eg inappropriate food), structural (eg bad alignment of bone and muscle), and mental and emotional factors. It is particularly effective in relieving recurrent complaints, eg allergies, bronchitis, and some digestive and gynecological conditions.

Massage

Massage – the manipulation of muscles or other parts of the body – has long been used to treat various joint injuries. Apart from its purely medical aspect, massage is also successful as a means of relieving body tension and aiding relaxation.

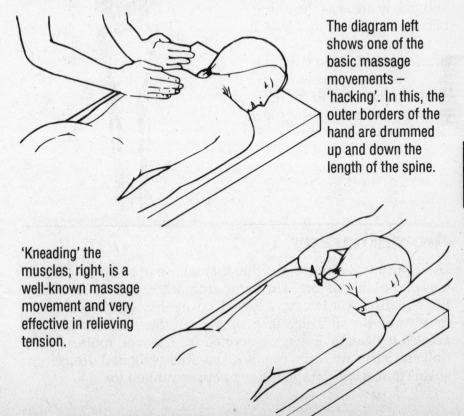

The diagram left shows one of the basic massage movements – 'hacking'. In this, the outer borders of the hand are drummed up and down the length of the spine.

9

'Kneading' the muscles, right, is a well-known massage movement and very effective in relieving tension.

The Alexander Technique

This is a postural reeducation system founded by Frederick Matthias Alexander, a former actor born in 1869. He noticed that the natural grace and poise of children disintegrate as they mature into adults, sometimes causing physical malfunction. Bad posture is usually caused by laziness and misuse of the body through tension. Alexander evolved a technique to free the musculoskeletal system from negative habits. Alexander saw his therapy as having effects beyond the physical, declaring that we translate everything – physical, mental, and spiritual – into muscular tension.

Realigning the body is thought to be effective on a mental/emotional level, imparting a feeling of well-being, exhilaration and a greater sense of effectiveness. Lessons by trained Alexander teachers emphasize the relationship among the head, neck, trunk and pelvic areas as the link between the spine and legs. It is a method of self-improvement, not a cure. It is very effective in general stress reduction and for relief of some conditions, eg migraine, asthma and back pain.

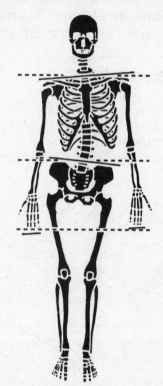

Aromatherapy

Until early this century, the therapeutic use of essential oils was part of herbal lore. The name aromatherapy was coined by Rene-Maurice Gattefosse, a French cosmetic chemist who discovered the antibacterial properties of the oils, which accelerate healing. Essences, derived from leaves, roots, flowers, bark and resin, can be taken orally (about 3 drops in sugar) for certain complaints, eg peppermint oil for indigestion. Three types of eucalyptus oil may have antiviral properties. The volatility of the oils makes them easy for the body to absorb and effective on mental and emotional levels. In the 1950s, Mme Marguerite Maury developed aromatherapy massage. Essential oils can also be used in the home as mood enhancers (take care with self-dosage: some oils are acutely toxic or cause allergic reactions). Drops may also be sprinkled in hot water and inhaled – eg ylang ylang for relaxation.

Color Therapy

The psychological effect of color has been used in therapy since ancient times. Rudolph Steiner was the founder of modern color therapy. It is based on the concept of the aura, an invisible field linked to seven energy centers or chakras, which interpenetrate the physical body. White light is absorbed by the aura and split into component color energies to revitalize different parts of the body. One explanation of SAD (Seasonal Affective Disorder) links winter 'blues' to lack of ultraviolet light.
Color therapy is a subtle art, employing several different techniques. A therapist can see the auric colors directly through a Kilner screen, which penetrates the UV spectrum. Illness manifests as a dark or discolored patch over the affected area. All or part of the client's body may be bathed in colored light; color filters may be combined with rhythm and pattern.

Reflexology

Reflexology is based on the zone therapy system, developed by Dr. W. Fitzgerald in the 1920s, which divides the body longitudinally into ten zones. Organs in the same zone are said to be connected: eg an untreated kidney malfunction could affect sight, since both are located in zone 3; they can be treated by massaging any area in the zone. His zone therapy was extended by his assistant, Eunice Ingham, into reflexology. Treatment is confined to the extremely sensitive feet and, to a lesser extent, hands. Various reflex maps of the feet and schemes of massage evolved.
Diagnosis is made by questioning the patient and examining the condition of the feet both visually and by palpitation. As with acupuncture, though very different, a soreness will register on the skin where there is a dysfunction: eg the ankle

9

Reflex map of the feet

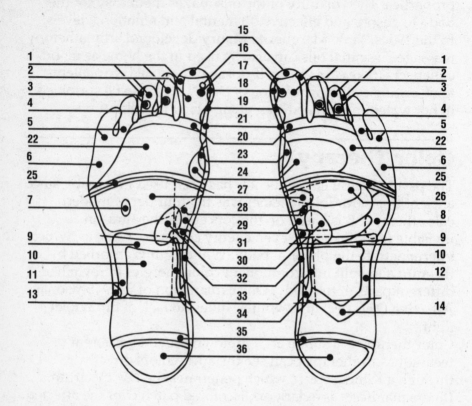

1 Side of the neck	**19** Throat
2 Sinuses	**20** Neck/thyroid
3 Ear	**21** 7th cervical
4 Eye	**22** Lungs
5 Shoulders	**23** Thymus
6 Axilla	**24** Heart
7 Gall bladder	**25** Diaphragm
8 Spleen	**26** Solar plexus
9 Transverse colon	**27** Liver
10 Small intestine	**28** Adrenal gland
11 Ascending colon	**29** Stomach
12 Descending colon	**30** Kidneys
13 Ileocecal valve/appendix	**31** Pancreas
14 Sigmoid colon	**32** Spine
15 Brain	**33** Ureter tubes
16 Hypothalamus	**34** Bladder/rectum
17 Pituitary	**35** Sciatic nerve
18 Nose	**36** Pelvis

area is often tender at particular points in the monthly cycle. The big toe is the reflex for the head, and the inside edge of the foot represents the spine. Thumb massage and manipulation are employed over the total area of both feet, thereby treating the whole body system. For foot injury, the hand is used. Patients receive several treatments lasting about 45 minutes until the condition is cleared. Symptoms often worsen initially, but this is believed to indicate that the healing process is under way.

Metamorphic technique, also known as prenatal therapy, takes a more metaphysical approach. Focusing on the spinal reflex, practitioners aim to clear psychological blocks which may have rooted themselves in the spine during the gestation period.

Psychic and Spiritual Health

It is mainly philosophy that distinguishes the psychic from the spiritual healer. Spiritual healers believe that healing power comes from God. The psychic healer claims that personal powers activate the body's own healing processes. Both require the cooperation of the patient to bring about cure. Diagnosis tends to be either clairvoyant or by the use of the hands, often an inch or so from the body, to sense areas of heat and cold, indicating areas of energy imbalance. Treatment can often be sensed as heat, tingling and surges of energy along the limbs or up the spine.

Though a high rate of cure is claimed, failure, it is said, can be due to incompatibility. Several visits may be required and prescriptions (which may involve diet or imaging techniques) must be followed.

9

Acupuncture

Acupuncture is an ancient Chinese system of healing. It is based on the theory that good health depends on the correct balance between the two energy forces within the body – Yin and Yang. These energies are thought to flow through the body along 'meridians' (see right). The practice of acupuncture involves inserting acupuncture needles into the skin at particular points on the meridians in order to relieve pain, or swelling, in a particular organ.

Auriculotherapy is a branch of acupuncture based on the similarity in appearance of the human ear and an upside-down fetus. Diseased organs in the body are treated by puncturing the ear at points which would correspond to the positions of these organs in a fetus.

Acupuncture should only be practiced by a trained specialist.

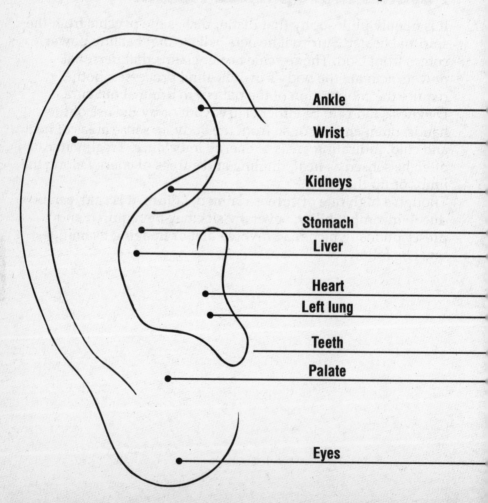

Ankle
Wrist
Kidneys
Stomach
Liver
Heart
Left lung
Teeth
Palate
Eyes

Acupuncture lines of energy

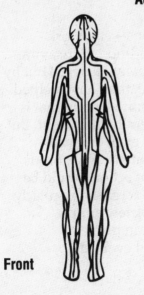

Front

Back

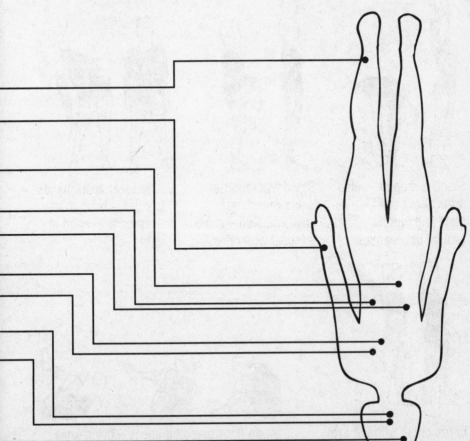

9

Keeping Fit

A daily exercise program – even a gentle one – can work wonders for almost everyone. Automobiles and labor-saving equipment have made our lives easier in many respects, but by reducing general levels of physical exercise, they have helped produce a population that is chronically unfit. A body that is short of exercise is stale, sluggish and generally inefficient. But the situation can be remedied – easily, and even enjoyably. There is no need to embark at once on an intensely vigorous exercise program – indeed, such a course of action would be positively unwise for most people today. Exercising regularly is the real key to improving fitness levels. A few simple exercises – such as those described here – can prove dramatically effective if they are carried out every day.

Stand feet apart – raise arms above head – bend and touch ground between feet.

Stand feet together – grasp raised leg by knee and shin – stand – repeat with other leg.

Stand feet apart, hands to sides – bend to left – repeat with bend to right.

Large circle with left arm, forward then back – repeat using right arm.

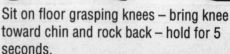

Sit on floor grasping knees – bring knee toward chin and rock back – hold for 5 seconds.

Lie face down, arms by side,
legs together – raise upper
body and legs into position shown.

Lie on back, knees bent, feet on
floor, arms back – swing arms
forward to sit and touch toes.

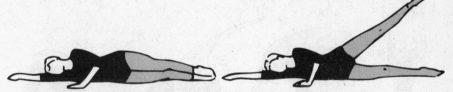

Lie on side in position shown –
raise one leg – legs together – roll
onto other side and repeat.

Lie face down with hands under
shoulders – push body off floor,
keeping knees on the floor.

9

Lie on back, legs together, arms by
sides, palms down – raise leg –
lower leg – repeat with other leg.

Yoga

Many thousands of women are now discovering the physical and mental benefits to be gained from the pursuit of yoga. This ancient discipline, developed in the East over thousands of years ago, has in recent decades won many enthusiastic followers in North America and Europe. Illustrated on these two pages are representative examples of popular yoga postures. Combined with breathing control, the attainment of such postures acts to produce deep levels of relaxation in both body and mind. Because of the precise nature of yoga postures, potential students are strongly recommended to attend classes to ensure that all postures are correctly learned. Hard work and dedication are essential for the serious yoga student, but the results will prove well worth the effort

Examples of standing yoga postures

1 Stand erect, feet together, with weight on both feet. **2** Feet apart, legs straight, arms stretched, side bent to clasp ankle. **3** Similar to 2 but with one arm above head and one knee bent. **4** Feet apart, legs straight, hands behind back, head touching leg.

5 Arms above head, one leg bent forward, other leg stretched behind. **6** Similar to 5 but with body turned to side and arms outstretched. **7** Feet together, legs straight, body bent, head touching legs, hands on floor behind feet. **8** Stand on one leg, other leg bent to side, hands together.

Examples of sitting and resting yoga postures

1 Basic sitting posture. **2** Sitting posture, legs raised straight and together, hands at back of head. **3** Sitting, legs to side, back twisted, one hand behind back. **4** Shoulder stand, back straight.

5 Lying posture, arms straight by sides, hands palms down, feet touching floor beyond head. **6** Lying posture, arms straight behind head, hands palms up, feet touching floor beyond head. **7** Resting posture, whole body relaxed – used with breathing exercises to end each session.

A combination of yoga postures forming a short sequence

1 Stand, hands and feet together. **2** Inhale, adopt posture shown. **3** Exhale, adopt posture shown. **4** Inhale, adopt posture shown. **5** Exhale, adopt posture shown. **6** Inhale, adopt posture shown. **7** Exhale, return to first posture.

9

The Facts about Rape

Rape is a violent, aggressive, hostile crime, usually committed by men against women. However, children and men are also raped, and this makes the act hard to define. The US National Women's Study defines 'forcible rape' as 'an event that occurred without the woman's consent, involved the use of force or threat of force, and involved sexual penetration of the victim's vagina, mouth or rectum'. Attacks not involving force, threat of force, or penetration, and assaults against men and boys are termed sexual assault.

Attitudes

The reasons for rape, and the treatment of rapist and raped, reflect society's attitude to sex and to women. Women are still generally regarded as passive sex objects, and prevailing attitudes still say that if they do not 'belong' to a man, they secretly desire or invite rape, and either get what they want or deserve what they get. The attitudes of the police and the courts, as well as people in general, have been formed more by myths than by facts.

Rape in America

In 1990, the United States was the world leader in the rate and number of reported rapes. Adult American women were 8 times more likely to be raped than European women. An official study in 1990, 'Rape in America' (RIA), estimated that as many as 683,000 women over 18 are raped every year, and that 12.1 million (1 in 8) have been forcibly raped at some time in their lives. The FBI Uniform Crime Report for 1991 records 106,600 reported rapes, and the US Department of Justice Bureau of Justice Statistics estimates that there were 130,000 rapes in 1990. It is estimated that 1 in 5 women are likely to be raped in their lifetimes.

Even so, rape still makes up a relatively small portion (about 6%) of the reported amount of violent crime perpetrated against women in the United States.

Increase in Reported Rape

Despite their widely differing statistics, the four reports mentioned above record a large increase in the rate of rape.

1988	1989	1990
1.5%	2.2%	6.5%

Under-reported Rape

In spite of the increase in the rate of rape shown opposite, new studies have shown that there is far more rape than is reported. The Judiciary Committee Majority Staff Report 1990 estimated that only 7% of rape is reported; the RIA study estimated that about 16% of rape victims report the crime. Both estimates are significantly lower than the figures for other violent crimes: about 50% of robberies, burglaries, and assaults are reported. In addition, many rape crisis centers are informed about rapes that are not reported to the police, so they record greater increases and higher rates of rape than do law enforcement agencies.

Failure to Report

Of the total number of rapes committed, RIA found that 84% of victims do not report the incident. Of the 16% who do report the crime, one-fourth do so more than 24 hours after the rape. Rape survivors are suspicious of reporting to the police. The Senate Judiciary Committee contacted rape crisis centers in more than half the states. Two-thirds of those surveyed showed dramatically higher totals than the police. For example, the police in Louisiana reported a 0.3% increase in the number of rapes, while the central rape crisis center reported a 39% increase. In Michigan the police reported a 4.7% increase and the central rape crisis center at least 36%. Women are more likely to report a rape:
a) if the rapist is a stranger;
b) if a weapon is brandished;
c) if there is additional physical abuse; and
d) if the victim is injured.

Reasons for failing to report

The need to ensure confidentiality is the main reason why rape survivors do not report attacks. In a survey of rape crisis agencies, RIA found that 96% of victims were less likely to report rape to the police if they thought their identity would be disclosed to the media.

Knowing the rapist The Department of Justice's Sourcebook of Criminal Justice Statistics noted in 1990 that one-third of women did not report rape if they knew the offender, even if they had suffered serious physical injuries.

9

Other reasons given are:
a) not wanting the family to know (71%);
b) fear of being blamed for the attack (69%);
c) lack of proof, or could not see how to find the rapist;
d) the police would be inefficient, ineffective, or insensitive, or would not think it important enough;
e) the victim reported it to someone else;
f) the incident was not important enough;
g) it was inconvenient or too time consuming;
h) did not realize at the time that it was a crime.

Should rape be reported?

All rapes should be reported to the police. In 1987, Dr. Gene Abel and others studied 561 sex offenders, of whom 126 admitted to raping. The 126 rapists had committed a total 907 rapes involving 882 different victims. The average number of different victims per rapist was seven. The number of unreported rapes is increasing faster than the number of reported rapes. The stigma of rape is not diminishing.

Here are some good reasons for reporting rape, given by rape survivors:
a) to help to stop it from happening again;
b) to punish the offender;
c) to get help after the assault;
d) because it is a crime;
e) because the survivor has evidence;
f) to recover property;
g) to collect on insurance;
h) because it is the survivor's duty.

Myths about Rape

Many people still think of rape only as a sexual act forced on a seductive adult woman by a complete stranger in a dark alley. Over the past 20 years, society has been educated by human rights groups and women's organizations that this is a misleading stereotype, one of several myths about rape that have been used to try to excuse rapists' behavior and to lay the blame for rape on women. Below are some of the most common myths, followed by the facts that frequently show a different picture. Figures are based on reported rapes, both attempted and completed:

'Rape happens in dark, empty streets at night.'

In 1990, 35% of rapes took place at or in the victim's own

home; 20% on the street; 15% at or near a friend's home; and 22% in various other places (eg offices, schools).

As to time of day, 65% of rapes took place at night, 31% in the daytime, 4% at dawn.

Home would seem to be the least safe place (especially with increasing recognition of marital rape). Commercial offices, public transportation, schools and parks are almost as great a threat by day as the streets are at night.

'Women are raped by black, rough-looking strangers.'

In 29% of rape cases the rapist was a non-relative the victim knew well, such as friends or neighbors; 22% were someone the victim had never seen before or did not know well; 11% were fathers or stepfathers; 16% were other relatives; 10% were boyfriends or ex-boyfriends; 9% were husbands or ex-husbands.

In 93% of the rape cases in one study, rapist and victim were of the same ethnic background.

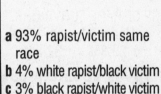

a 93% rapist/victim same race
b 4% white rapist/black victim
c 3% black rapist/white victim

'Men's uncontrollable sexual urges cause them to rape.'

In a study of 225 offenses analysed at the Boston City Hospital, three elements were constant: power, anger and sexuality. Power and anger were always present; sexuality always played a secondary role. The study concluded that in rape, sex is simply a way of expressing power and anger, and that rape itself is not an expression of sexual desire.

'Women provoke rape.'

Time and again women are accused of leading men on and provoking rape by their appearance or behavior. Again, past studies show this to be be wrong. One showed that only 4.4% of rapes are sparked off by a victim's behavior – a lower rate than for homicide or robbery.

9

'Women create dangerous situations.'

The stereotype that women put themselves in danger of rape by walking home alone, hitchhiking, or going to singles bars is contradicted by the estimate that two-thirds of rape victims are women who never leave home unless accompanied by someone they know.

 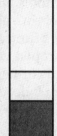

a 47.8% Rape by 'trustable' people

b 15.7% Rape by stangers encountered at home

c 36.5% All other rapes

'Rape victims are young and highly desirable.'

Victims are usually singled out for their vulnerability. One of the most disturbing revelations that recent studies have brought to light has been the youth of many rape victims. The National Women's Study found that 6 out of 10 victims are raped before they are 18:

AGE OF RAPE SURVIVORS

Under 11	11-17	18-24	25-29	29+	Not known
29.3%	32.3%	22.2%	7.1%	6.1%	3%

'Rape is spontaneous.'

Statistics indicate that some 70% of all rapes are premeditated.

 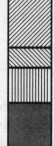

ALL RAPES

a 33% Planned single rapes

b 13% Planned pair rapes

c 24% Planned group rapes

d 30% Spontaneous rapes

High-risk Groups

a) Black women are nearly twice as likely as white women to be victims of rape.

b) Women and girls from poor backgrounds and with lower social status are at much greater risk of rape than women and

girls from affluent backgrounds.
c) Unemployed women are $3^1/2$ times more likely to be raped as women who are employed.
d) Women who rent their homes are more than 4 times as likely to be raped as home owners.
e) Women who live in the inner cities are twice as likely to be raped as women who live in the suburbs or rural areas.
f) Women who live alone are more likely to be raped than women who live with other people.

Teenage Rape

The 1990 Department of Justice Sourcebook reports that teenagers are twice as likely as adults to be victims of crimes of violence, and that the women most at risk of rape are in the 16-19 and 20-24 age groups. Rape in America reported that of 13% of women who said they had been victims of one completed rape in their lifetimes, most were raped when they were young. More than 6 out of 10 of all rape cases occurred before the victim was 18.

Teenage victims are most likely to be raped in the street, on school property, and in school, in that order. Among teenagers, the 16-19-year-olds are least likely to report rape. Fewer than 5% of college rape victims report to the police; half tell no one about what has happened to them.

Date Rape and Sexual Harassment

An encouraging indication of a change in attitude toward rape has been the publicity given in the 1990s to trials in which 'date rape' (the coercing of an unwilling woman to have sex on a date) has figured prominently. Although the women in the cases were not all treated sympathetically, the fact that such cases were brought to court and attracted media attention indicates a tendency among women not to be intimidated into silence by the stigma of rape.

Sexual harassment

This is the forcing of unwanted sexual attention on another person and includes verbal innuendo, body language, touching, and attempts at direct sexual contact. Women are voicing their unwillingness to put up with sexual harassment in the workplace to the extent that complaints procedures have been introduced in many commercial companies and colleges.

Marital Rape

One survey found that in the US 1 in 7 wives had been raped by their husbands. This indicates that rape within marriage is more common than any other type. It is also a crime that is frequently repeated. Rape crisis agencies believe that statistics do not reflect the true level of rape by husbands and ex-husbands.

Rape in marriage is illegal in many countries, including much of Australia, Canada, and the UK. In the US, the crime has only recently been recognized by the law, which varies from state to state. However, the laws that have been passed are proving highly effective. For example, of 56 cases that had been brought by 1983, 43 ended in conviction. This made a conviction rate of 75%.

Domestic violence

Women are beaten by sons or brothers, but most often it is by male partners. This type of battering, which often includes rape, is seriously under-reported, and the law has been slow to recognize it. The violence is closely linked to the oppression of women and male views of women as possessions. It may continue for years. To a woman demoralized by ill-treatment, the prospect of leaving home with young children and no money may seem too terrifying to face. Any woman in this position should seek help at a refuge or women's center. A sympathetic lawyer, evidence from doctors or social workers, and, if possible, support from family and friends – especially other women with similar experiences – can help a battered woman become independent.

Rape Using Weapons

According to Violent Crime in the US, firearms were used in 6% of all rapes. Using a small sample of rape cases in 1989, it is estimated in the Department of Justice Sourcebook that of the 28,740 weapons used, over one-fourth were handguns.

RAPE USING WEAPONS (based on 10 or fewer sample cases)

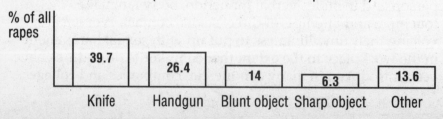

% of all rapes

Knife	Handgun	Blunt object	Sharp object	Other
39.7	26.4	14	6.3	13.6

Legal Definition

Rape is typically defined as intercourse occurring forcibly and against the victim's will. (Statutory rape applies to any sexual intercourse where the victim is judged incapable of consenting – eg being underage or mentally subnormal.) 'Force' includes duress or intimidation, not necessarily physical violence. But the courts may require actual resistance by the victim to be proved – not just a refusal to consent.

Medical Examination

A woman who has been raped should: stay in the same clothes; not wash away evidence of rape; call the police as early as possible; go directly to a hospital or doctor whether prosecuting or not, however distressing this may be, both for her own protection (to be examined for internal injuries and, if possible, to minimize the danger of sexually transmitted disease, pregnancy, etc) and to provide medical evidence. She may request a female doctor.

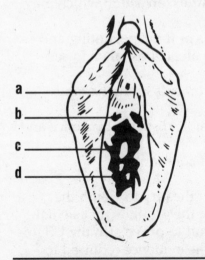

Possible physical signs of rape
a Scratches
b Bruises
c Tears
d Seminal fluid

9

Rape and the Courts

In court, a rape survivor often receives harsher treatment than the suspect. The reasons are complex. They include the rules of evidence and their interaction with society's attitudes to women and to sex. Attitudes to rape are contradictory. At one extreme are the penalties – many US states provide very severe penalties – while at the other is the attitude that assumes rape to be the woman's fault.

Issues

The main issues in a rape case are:

a) to prove that the defendant is the rapist;

b) to prove lack of consent by the person raped;

c) to prove resistance by the person raped.

Resistance

Different degrees of resistance are expected by the courts of different states for rape to be established. Some expect only slight resistance or just a demonstration of unwillingness. Some expect the person raped to have resisted unless resistance was futile or the person was terrified. Some expect the victim to have resisted until overcome, or for as long as possible. A women's group and an attorney will advise on the specific expectations of the court in the state where the case will be heard.

For the above reasons it is important for someone who is raped to try to write down as early as possible after the event (however distressing it may be) any action she took, however small, apparently futile, or successful, to fight off the rapist.

Deciding to bring charges

A woman who decides to bring charges (an action which may protect others) should:

a) write down and memorize details of the rape, noting and stressing lack of consent and listing all actions taken in self-defense;

b) get advice and support from a women's group or rape center;

c) prepare with an attorney for possible disbelief by police and courts;

d) emphasize force used and lack of consent.

Evidence required

In a rape case the judge will instruct the jury to weigh the victim's testimony very carefully on the grounds that sexual charges are 'easy to make but difficult to prove'. (In the US this guidance applies to all sex cases.) The evidence required to prove rape varies from state to state. In some the raped person's testimony only is sufficient; in others, corroboration is needed either as a matter of course or whenever the rape survivor's testimony is not considered credible. A women's group or an attorney will advise on the situation in the state where the case is to be heard. Corroboration is generally medical – signs of sexual intercourse, physical injury, etc.

Rules of procedure

In a rape case, as in all criminal cases, 'the defendant is innocent until proven guilty'. Burden of proof falls on the prosecution for whom the rape victim is the complaining witness. Because of its nature, there are rarely any witnesses to rape and the outcome may well depend on who is the more credible –alleged rapist or victim.

Nothing can be said in court about any prior arrest of the defendant for similar offenses or about his sex life. The victim, however, can have her credibility attacked in any way. Defense tactics rely largely on the perception that rape is a woman's fault. In effect, a woman has her character and personal life put on trial to such an extent that she may well begin to doubt or blame herself.

Sentencing

In 1988, prison sentences were imposed in 87% of rape convictions. The average sentence (ie not the typical – very few life sentences were imposed) was 15 years 3 months and expected time served 5 years 11 months.

A BJS Special Report on state prison inmates in 1986 found that of the offenders in state prisons in 1986, an estimated 55% had been convicted of a violent offense, 4% of rape. Violent prisoners reported more than 40,000 young victims, 71% of whom had been raped or sexually assaulted.

Effects of Rape

Rape is physically and emotionally damaging. In addition to physical injuries, some of which may be permanent or long lasting, 1 in 3 rape survivors suffers Rape Trauma Syndrome, which includes depression, loss of self-respect, flashbacks, nightmares and suicidal tendencies. Rape victims are 13 times more likely than victims of other crimes to have made a suicide attempt. But women who talk out the experience with others tend to recover more quickly; counseling is an important aspect of healing. A growing number of rape crisis agencies around the country offer such counseling.

9

Prevention

Reducing the incidence of rape in society will require large-scale changes in prevailing attitudes toward women. It may be, for example, that the accessibility of pornography contributes to rape, although studies show conflicting findings on this. Changes on a large scale, however, are slow. In the meantime, there are measures – such as self-defense training and increased self-awareness – that women can take to reduce the risk of rape and/or to improve their chances of fending off an attacker. These measures, however, are not intended to transfer responsibility to the woman or her behavior. It is never a woman's fault if she is raped; blame and responsibility always rest with the rapist.

Safety

At home Secure your home as well as you can and to the level with which you feel comfortable. A woman living alone should consider using her initials rather than full name in the telephone directory and on the mailbox.

While out Women do not 'provoke' rape by their dress or behavior. It is important, however, to avoid areas where you feel unsafe or isolated. Especially at night, walking 'with a purpose' keeps you from appearing vulnerable.

If threatened, avoid panic. Loud yells – 'fire', not 'help' – might bring people, or at least scare off the attacker.

Self-defense

It has been estimated that one reported rape takes place every 1.8 minutes in the US. In the face of such daunting statistics, awareness training and self-defense are important for women. Even if such skills cannot guarantee that a woman could escape from or fend off an attacker, they are likely to improve self-confidence, which is important to prevent a woman from appearing to be vulnerable and a 'soft target'.

Assertiveness training

Being able to insist on what you want and what you don't want is important protection. There is increasing recognition that many rapes happen in social and workplace situations, and that many rapists are known to their victims as friends, dates, colleagues or acquaintances. Pressure, especially from someone trusted by the woman, can play a large part in such rapes, and the notion of whether or not the woman gave her consent to a sexual act becomes blurred. Many organizations and colleges offer assertiveness training courses specifically for women who want to overcome fear or nervousness about resisting such pressure.

Evasive action

Other important protective mechanisms involve getting yourself out of a situation that puts you at risk. This can involve physically removing yourself – by, for example, running away from a potential rapist or moving into an area crowded with people. It can also involve talking to the potential rapist in an attempt to defuse the situation.

Weapons

Weapons can be a dangerous self-defense tactic; more often than not they are used against the person being attacked. Some articles – often items that would not normally be considered weapons – can be carried safely and, if used quickly, can at least provide time for escape.

a Pepper shaker
b Artificial lemon juice container full of vinegar
c Hairspray or personal alarm

Courses in self-defense

Women's short self-defense courses are a good introduction, and they will make you feel – and look – more confident, which is part of self-defense. There is a limit to how effective they will make you, however. The best way is to learn a martial art – eg judo, karate, and the arts of the stick. In studies, 51% of victims threatened with a knife and 72% by an unarmed man managed to fight off the attack (58% fought off attackers armed with guns, but note that the FBI does not advise tackling an attacker with a gun unless you are certain he will kill you).

Changes in Response to Rape

9

Large-scale changes to greatly reduce the incidence of rape will require changes in societal attitudes as well as in the law and police procedures. Yet small changes are taking place – these can be seen in greater sensitivity in the treatment of rape survivors by police and courts; more discussion of aspects of rape, especially controversial ones such as marital and date rape; recognition of Rape Trauma Syndrome; and increased support for rape survivors. Some police departments have set up comfortable rape units, specially staffed 24 hours. There are many rape crisis and support organizations advocating change and increasing public awareness that rape is a crime and not the survivor's fault.

MIND AND BODY

10

Stress Situations

Stress is nervous tension caused by external factors. A person may or may not be aware of it. It is either environmental or psychological: a person may be reacting to a physical or a mental threat. It may be acute or chronic, depending on whether the threat is an event or a continuing situation. Whatever the cause, stress is a person's reaction.

Most women's lives are dotted with potential stress points. Some of these are related to a woman's changing body – puberty, motherhood, and the menopause, for example. Others may relate to work, to family, or to the struggle to balance many roles. Still others involve the decisions a woman makes about her own life, and society's response to those decisions.

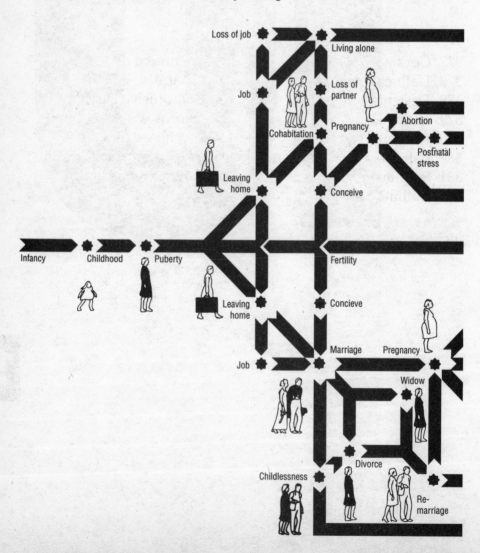

Reactions to stress

Modern life is stressful for everyone. Most people manage to get along without letting stress overwhelm them, but others react by seeking refuge in a form of dependence, or addiction. Food or a drug often becomes a false center around which their lives revolve. This is often particularly true of women. The traditional female roles encourage dependence which can cause conflict in women and in their relationships with their partners and children. Today, women are redefining these roles in terms of self-fulfillment.

The diagram below illustrates some of the many stress points a woman might face in her lifetime.

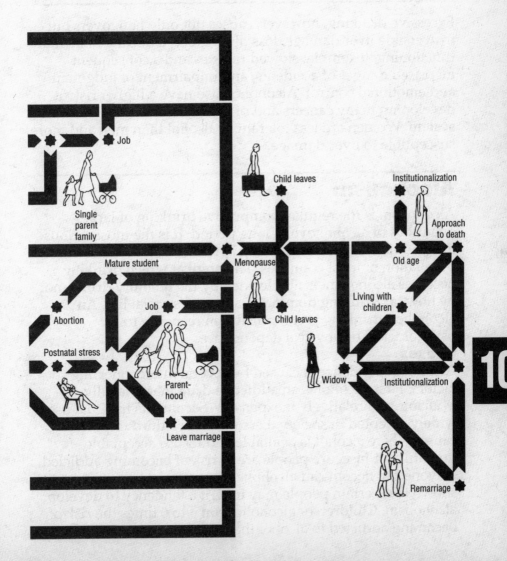

Effects of Alcohol

Moderate drinking of alcohol is not harmful to health. Statistics show that very moderate drinking can have a beneficial effect on the heart, and appears to prolong life.

Safe drinking limits for women
2 units per day

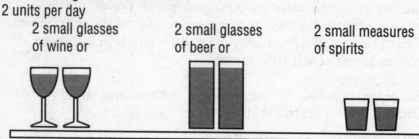

2 small glasses of wine or

2 small glasses of beer or

2 small measures of spirits

Excessive drinking, however, causes not only hangovers but irreversible liver damage, loss of memory, a decline in mental functioning, insomnia, slowed reflexes and a consequent increased danger of accidents, and impairment of judgment and emotional control. Alcoholics also have a higher risk of developing many cancers and of malfunctions in the immune system. Women are less tolerant of alcohol than men and more susceptible to liver damage.

Alcoholism

Alcoholism is the regular, compulsive drinking of large quantities of alcohol over a long period. It is the most serious drug addiction today, involving between 1% and 5% of the population of most countries. The point at which drinking becomes alcoholism is not decided by the quantity drunk, nor by how far drinking dominates a person's social life. An alcoholic's drinking is compulsive, in response to psychological or physical dependence.

Causes

Alcohol dependence is caused by several interconnecting factors. First, alcohol is an addictive drug that is legally available and relatively inexpensive. Second, its habitual use is widely accepted in society. Personality is a third important cause. Where alcohol is available and its use acceptable, immature or insecure people are at risk of becoming addicted. Anyone can become an alcoholic. However, studies have shown that certain people may inherit a tendency to develop alcoholism. Children of alcoholics run 4 to 6 times the risk of becoming addicted to alcohol than children of nonalcoholics.

Women and alcoholism

Approximately one-third of alcoholics seen in clinical medical practice are women. Most begin by symptomatic drinking – turning to alcohol in response to stress. Among the reasons women alcoholics give are physical troubles, such as PMS, infertility, miscarriage, and emotional troubles, such as frigidity and divorce. But case studies show that alcoholism is often part of a general picture of depressive illness. Many alcoholics have emotional problems stemming from disturbed childhoods, often typified by the loss, absence or inadequacy of one or both parents.

Stages in Alcoholism

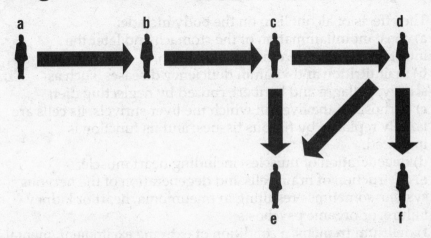

a) Social drinking can lead to alcoholism if a drinker begins to turn to alcohol for relief from stress ('symptomatic drinking') or because her social drinking is so heavy that the beginnings of dependence are not noticed ('inveterate drinking').

b) Early alcoholism is marked by the beginning of memory blackouts. Surreptitious drinking and the urgency of first drinks indicates increasing dependence. The drinker feels guilty, but cannot discuss the problem.

c) Basic alcoholism is indicated when the drinker can no longer stop unless forced by intoxication. She bolsters herself with excuses and grandiose behavior, but her promises and resolutions fail. She starts avoiding family and friends, and neglects food, interests, work and money. Physical deterioration sets in. Finally, tolerance for alcohol decreases.

d) Chronic alcoholism is marked by further deterioration in lifestyle, irrational thought, vague fears, fantasies and

10

psychotic behavior. Physical damage continues. The drinker has no alibis left, and can no longer take any step to recovery for herself. Reaching this point may have taken from 5 to 25 years.

e) Recovery usually depends on the alcoholic undergoing a treatment program (see below). Psychologically, the patient regains the desire to be helped and thinks more rationally as a result. Ideally, she also develops hope, moral commitment, outside interests, self-respect and contentment in abstinence.

f) Terminal alcoholism is the result if the alcoholic refuses treatment or relapses during or after treatment. Irreversible mental and physical deterioration usually ends in death.

Physiological Effects

The effects of alcoholism on the body include:

a) constant inflammation of the stomach and later the intestines, with severe risk of ulceration;

b) malnutrition and vitamin deficiency diseases, such as scurvy, pellagra and beriberi, caused by neglecting diet;

c) cirrhosis of the liver, in which the liver shrivels, its cells are largely replaced by fibrous tissues, and its function is impaired;

d) degeneration of muscles, including heart muscle;

e) destruction of brain cells and degeneration of the nervous system, sometimes resulting in pneumonia, heart or kidney failure, or organic psychosis;

f) delirium tremens, a condition of extreme excitement, mental confusion, anxiety, fever, trembling, rapid and irregular pulse and hallucinations, which often occurs when a bout of heavy drinking is followed by a few days' abstention.

Treatments for Drug Addiction

Treatments for all types of addiction are similar. They are long term and depend on the individual's desire to be cured.

Detoxification

This first stage of treatment takes place in a clinic or hospital. The patient is deprived of alcohol or other addictive drug. This results in severe withdrawal symptoms: sweating, vomiting, body aches, running nose and eyes, convulsions and hallucinations. Sedatives give relief, but must be withdrawn before new addictions are formed. Any physical problems are treated and the alcoholic is encouraged to eat a balanced diet.

Therapies

While supporting the patient's motivation, self-confidence and trust, health-care workers try to identify the psychological reasons for addiction and treat them. The most common treatments are:

Aversion therapy, based on creating conditioned reflexes of sickness and aversion to the addictive drug. Techniques include electric shock therapy and sensitizing drugs that produce unpleasant symptoms when the drug is used.

Psychotherapy, aimed at bringing the reasons for addiction to light and helping the patient to accept and face up to them.

Group therapy, aimed at giving the patient objective outside views of herself and helping her come to terms with them; and helping her overcome her isolation by developing personal relationships by contact with others.

Support organizations, such as Alcoholics Anonymous, run by former addicts, which provide group therapy and guidance outside the hospital situation in regular meetings. These provide essential support for continued abstention and rehabilitation.

Tranquilizers

Barbiturates

Drugs made from barbituric acid (nicknamed 'barbs', 'candy', or 'goof balls') are depressants. They reduce the impulses reaching the brain and so are prescribed to relieve anxiety and tension and to induce sleep. Some have been used as anesthetics. Barbiturates vary in the immediacy and duration of their effect according to the rate at which they are metabolized and eliminated; eg Seconal is short acting, Phenobarbital long lasting. Long-term use of barbiturates can cause physical dependence.

Symptoms of barbiturate abuse include drowsiness, restlessness, irritability, belligerence, irrational behavior, mental confusion, and impaired coordination and reflexes with staggering and slurred speech. The pupils constrict and sweating increases. The user experiences euphoria at first, then depression.

Withdrawal symptoms can be more severe than those of alcohol or heroin, and include irritability, restlessness, anxiety, insomnia, abdominal cramp, nausea and vomiting, tremors, hallucinations, severe convulsions and sometimes death.

10

An 'overdose' or excessive amount depresses the nervous system so much that unconsciousness results, followed in extreme cases by death from respiratory failure.

Types of abuse

Addicts are attracted by:

a) the possibility of escaping from emotional stress through sedation;

b) the feelings of euphoria on initial ingestion, when large amounts of the drug are tolerated;

c) the ability of barbiturates to counteract the effects of stimulants. This cyclical use of 'uppers' and 'downers' can lead to dependence on both. The common prescription of barbiturates to induce relaxation and sleep has resulted in the largest group of dependent people being the middle aged, especially housewives. The same ready availability also makes the drug a common suicide weapon, while the combination of barbiturates' depressive effects with those of alcohol has brought many accidental deaths through taking barbiturates after heavy drinking.

Benzodiazepines

Because of their addictive effects, barbiturates have been largely replaced by benzodiazepine drugs, such as Valium (Diazepam) and Librium for the treatment of anxiety, tension and insomnia. They cause drowsiness, dizziness and confusion, but an overdose is rarely fatal. They are habit-forming and should not be taken regularly for more than two weeks. Withdrawal should be gradual to avoid symptoms that may include extreme anxiety, sweating and sometimes seizures.

Tranquilizer Nicknames

Drug (Nickname)	Description	Drug (Nickname)	Description
Amobarbital (Blues, blue devils)	Green blue	**Thorazine**	Orange
Pentobarbital (Yellows, nembies)	Yellow	**Miltown**	White
Secobarbital (Reds, red devils, red bird)	Red	**Librium**	Green white
Tuinal (Rainbows, tooeys)	Red blue	**Valium** (Goofers)	Various

(Note that nicknames change frequently and that descriptions vary with dose and source.)

Opiates

The opiates are known in drug-taking circles as 'the hard stuff'. Opium and its derivative heroin are the archetypal drugs of addiction. Codeine and morphine, which are also derived from opium, are better known for their medical uses.

All depressants inhibit the central nervous system, impairing coordination, reflexes, etc. Opiates, particularly morphine, prevent pain signals being transmitted from sites called opiate receptors in the brain to the rest of the body. This action may cause initial excitement, as inhibitions are removed. In large doses, the opiates act on the pleasure centers of the hypothalamus, producing feelings of peace, contentment, safety and euphoria. General symptoms of opiate use include loss of appetite, constipation and constriction of the pupils. An overdose of an opiate is likely to cause convulsions, unconsciousness and death. All opiates create tolerance and physical dependence. The symptoms of withdrawal from abusive use begin with stomach cramps, followed by diarrhea, nausea and vomiting, running eyes and nose, sweating and trembling. These are accompanied by irritability, restlessness, insomnia, anxiety, panic, depression, confusion and an all-consuming desire for the drug.

Opium

Opium is the dried juice of the unripe seed capsules of the Indian poppy. The plant is cultivated in India, Iran, China and Turkey. Opium is prepared in either powder or liquid form. The poppy possesses its psychoactive powers only when grown in favorable conditions of climate and soil. Poppies produced in temperate climates have only a negligible effect. Opium is traditionally smoked, using pipes, but it can also be injected or taken orally.

Codeine

Codeine (methyl morphine) is the least effective of the opiates. It is white and crystalline in form, and is often used with aspirin for treating headaches. Because of the inhibiting effect on nervous reflexes it shares with all opiates, it is used in many cough medicines and sometimes in the treatment of diarrhea, since it reduces peristalsis (the automatic rhythmic contractions of the intestine). The risk of tolerance and abusive use are very small because of the large amounts necessary to produce pleasant effects.

10

Morphine

Morphine is the basis of all opiate action – it is opium's main active constituent. It was isolated from opium in 1805, and since then has been medically important as a painkiller. It is 10 times as strong as opium, and must be administered with great care to avoid tolerance and physical dependence.

Heroin

Heroin (diamorphine) was isolated in 1898. It is 3 times as strong as morphine and has a quicker and more intense effect, though a shorter duration. Among drug takers it is often known as 'H', 'horse', or 'smack'. Its production, possession, and use are all connected with drug abuse. A grayish-brown powder in its pure form, for retail purposes it is mixed with milk or baking powder. This results in a white coloring. The high cost of the drug, and its necessity to those dependent on it, account for the high crime rate associated with its users. The powder may be sniffed but is usually injected – normally into a muscle when use begins, but then into a major vein ('mainlining') as tolerance develops. Mainlining gives more immediate and powerful effects. Constant injection into the same vein causes hardening and scarring of the flesh tissue and eventual collapse of the vein. Unhygienic conditions and use of unsterilized needles can also cause infection, often resulting in sores, abscesses, hepatitis, jaundice and thrombosis. Almost immediately upon injection, intense feelings of euphoria and contentment envelop the user. The strength of these depends on the purity and strength of the heroin and the psychological state of the user – the higher the previous tension and anxiety, the more powerful the subsequent feelings of pleasure and peace. It is the force of the initial pleasure that makes heroin more popular than morphine. Physical dependence on heroin is reached if one grain (60mg) of heroin is used in a period of up to two weeks. Withdrawal effects will then begin four to six hours after the effect of the last shot has worn off. These include intense abdominal cramps, diarrhea, vomiting, shivering, insomnia and restlessness. Heroin addicts also suffer from malnutrition and weight loss due to inadequate diet, impotence, infections such as hepatitis B and HIV, transmitted via infected needles, and death from overdose.

Glue-sniffing

The fumes of adhesives, gasoline, nail varnish, lighter fuel and paint-thinners are used to get a 'high'. Effects are very much like drinking alcohol: slurred speech, confusion, dizziness, hallucinations, and afterwards, a headache. Sniffing glue is not illegal, but in several countries it is now an offense to sell solvents to anyone under 18 if the vendor believes they will be misused. School students are those most likely to abuse solvents 'for kicks' or out of boredom. Solvent abuse can cause direct permanent damage to several of the body systems. Inhaling similar fumes daily in a factory sometimes results in damage to the liver and kidneys. A very real danger is the occurrence of an accident during intoxication. Many children die from this cause each year.

Amphetamines

The amphetamines ('pep pills' or 'uppers') generally stimulate the sympathetic nervous system, which mobilizes the body for action with the 'fight or flight' syndrome, including increase in epinephrine production, heart rate, blood sugar and muscle tension.

Effects The user experiences a sense of well-being and, with strong doses, euphoria. Alertness, wakefulness and confidence are accompanied by feelings of mental and physical power. The user becomes talkative, excited, and hyperactive. Accompanying physical symptoms include sweating, trembling, dizziness, insomnia and reduced appetite. Mood effects are probably due to stimulation of the hypothalamus, and sudden shift to anxiety and panic can occur.

Dependence Amphetamines create tolerance, but are not considered physically addictive. However, psychic dependence is easily produced. The extra energy is 'borrowed' from the body's reserves: when the drug's action has worn off, the body has to pay for it in fatigue and depression. This creates the desire for more of the drug to counteract these effects.

Medical usage has become rarer since realization of the dangers. But amphetamines are still used for some purposes, eg to prevent sleep in people who have to be alert for long periods; to treat minor depression; to counteract depressants; and to suppress the appetite in a few cases of obesity.

Abuse of amphetamines is common because of the feelings of euphoria and alertness they give. The dangers include not only psychic dependence, but also: physical deterioration due to hyperactivity and lack of appetite; induced psychotic conditions of paranoia and schizophrenia, resulting from prolonged overdose; suicide due to mental depression following large doses; and death from overdose.

10

Amphetamine Nicknames

Drug (Nickname)	Description		Drug (Nickname)	Description	
Benzedrine (Bennies)	⬭	Red pink	**Methadrine** (Speed, meth, crystal)	○	White
	◖◗	pink	**Biphetamine** (White)	⬭	White
Dexadrine (Dexies)	⬭	Orange	**Edrial**	○	white
	◖◗	Orange	**Dexamyl** (Christmas tree)	◖◗	Green

(Note that nicknames change frequently and that descriptions vary with dose and source.)

Tobacco

Nicotine is a stimulant found in tobacco that acts on the central nervous system. It is a habit-forming drug that increases the amount of adrenaline released into the blood. Smoking has many ill-effects. It encourages the build-up of cholesterol inside blood vessels, which results in atherosclerosis and leads to heart disease and stroke. Inhaling tobacco smoke irritates the bronchial passages in the lungs, causing breathlessness, bronchitis, emphysema (destruction of the alveoli, the sacs in the lungs through which oxygen passes into the bloodstream), and lung cancer. Many of the 3000 or so chemicals in cigarette smoke are absorbed into the blood and can cause a range of disorders, including cancer in various parts of the body. Nonsmokers who inhale air containing tobacco smoke ('passive smoking') can also develop these illnesses. In pregnancy, carbon monoxide, a by-product of tobacco smoking, can cross the placenta into the bloodstream of the fetus, increasing the likelihood of miscarriage and stunting fetal development.

Giving up cigarettes

Breaking any habit is difficult and success depends on real determination and planning. Cravings take time to die down. Plan to stop by following these rules. Then join a self-help group to reinforce your resolve to quit.

a) Analyse your smoking habits. Keep a record.
b) Decide that you want to stop smoking. Think of the benefits.
c) Then stop. Change your habits. Avoid trigger situations.
d) Spoil yourself with a positive reward from money saved.

e) Give yourself time. It takes time to break a habit.
f) If necessary, use extra help: eg nicotine chewing gum, nicotine skin patches, acupuncture, and groups or clinics.

Caffeine

This stimulant of the central nervous system is present in or added to many foods and drinks, including coffee, tea, cocoa and cola drinks. It is a relatively mild drug, acting to relieve fatigue. It is also a diuretic, ie it increases the urine output of the kidneys. It is often included in headache pills to counteract the dulling effect of the painkilling ingredient. Abuse of this drug is rare because large quantities are needed, but it has recently been discovered that some people are especially sensitive to it. They, and people who drink large amounts of coffee, may experience shakiness, heart palpitations, nausea and indigestion. Feelings of tiredness are often experienced when the stimulation wears off.

Cocaine

Cocaine (often nicknamed 'coke' or 'snow') is a white powder obtained from the coca plant found in South America. Synthetic derivatives are also available.
Effects Cocaine stimulates the central nervous system, dispelling fatigue, increasing alertness, mental activity, and reflex speed. Local application has anesthetic effects. It is used as a local anesthetic in minor operations on the eye, ear, nose, and throat. Cocaine derivatives may be injected into the spinal fluid to anesthetize the lower limbs. Inhaled, it induces euphoria. After an initial 'rush', the effects steady. Accompanying physical symptoms include dilation of pupils, tremors, loss of appetite and insomnia.
Dependence Cocaine does not create physical dependence, but psychic dependence easily develops for the same reasons as with amphetamines.
Abuse is the main use found for cocaine. As a powder, it is inhaled, which eventually results in deterioration of the nasal linings and finally of the nasal septum separating the nostrils. Injection of a liquid form is an alternative, but using cocaine alone in this way is unpopular because of the violence of the sudden effects; instead heroin and cocaine are often injected together. Cocaine is a short-acting drug and must be taken repeatedly to maintain the effects.

10

Cocaine narrows the blood vessels and reduces the blood flow to the heart. Dangers of prolonged use include inflammation of the heart and disturbances in heart rhythm, and perforation of the thin partition between the air passages of the nose, plus insomnia, paranoia, hallucinations in the sense of touch, called 'the cocaine bugs', and weight loss and malnutrition through loss of appetite. An overdose causes convulsions, and a large dose can cause death by respiratory failure.

Crack

Crack is a purified form of cocaine sold as pellets, which are heated and smoked. Crack reaches the brain rapidly, producing a brief, intense 'rush', followed after about 10 minutes by an equally intense 'down'. Addiction deadens basic human emotions and can lead to psychosis. Children of mothers who used crack during pregnancy have birth defects and developmental problems.

Hallucinogens

The most common is LSD (lysergic acid diethylamide), which can produce all manner of effects, among them visual and other sensory distortions and out-of-body experiences. Other hallucinogens include mescaline and psilocybin. All are illegal in most parts of the world. Physical dependence is thought unlikely; there is little evidence to show long-term damage. Very disturbing reactions can occur, however. Serious accidents and fatalities have resulted from a 'bad trip'. Hallucinogens have strong effects on the brain: the limbic system, influencing mood and emotions; the reticular formation, making the user acutely aware of sensory input; visual centers, producing visions, from flashes of light to complex scenes; and memory centers and judgment, which are suppressed.

Designer Drugs

Chemical substances engineered to have similar effects to illegal drugs are not illegal at the time of manufacture, but are usually rapidly scheduled. Synthetic versions of heroin (eg MPPP and 'China White') are drugs of abuse; each illustrates the dangers inherent in the abuse of such 'designer drugs'.' With MPPP, a substance similar to meperidine (Demerol), a contaminant (MPTP) was frequently present, affecting nerve cells and linked to cases of Parkinson's disease. Powerful

'China White' has caused overdoses in heroin users. MDMA ('Adam' or 'Ecstasy') has features of both hallucinogens and amphetamines: hallucinations occur with high doses; there are feelings of greater empathy, sensuality, and euphoria; physical effects include tension of jaw muscles, nausea, dizziness, then fatigue and insomnia; negative effects include panic attacks during a 'high' and, with repeated use, psychological effects, dependence and nerve damage.

Eating Disorders

Societies vary hugely in their perception of what is beautiful and desirable in a woman's appearance. In various cultures, for social and esthetic reasons women have extended their necks, bound and mutilated their feet, and deformed their lips by inserting wooden plates into them and their earlobes by hanging heavy objects from them. Some cultures value obesity in a woman, but in most developed countries today the pinnacle of female glamour is considered to be a slender, small-boned, young woman. This 'ideal shape', widely promulgated by fashion, advertising, and other media as being the key to attractiveness to the opposite sex, can lead not only to dissatisfaction that one is not, or can never hope to be, that shape, but also to lack of confidence and self-esteem, particularly if there are other factors in a woman's life that reinforce those feelings.

Anorexia nervosa is probably the best-known eating disorder, but it constitutes the severest end of a wide spectrum of eating and food-related problems that many women suffer. Eating can be a comfort in the face of stress, and fondness for certain foods can become an 'addiction', leading to unhealthy obesity. At the other end of the spectrum, anxiety to limit food intake in order to maintain body shape can become an equally undesirable, even fatal, obsession. Women who are prone to eating disorders may eat compulsively in early adolescence, suffer later from prolonged or eccentric dieting, and eventually develop bulimia nervosa.

Treatments for eating disorders have varied from wiring up the jaws of obese women to forcing anorexic patients to stay in bed until they have put on weight. Amphetamines were prescribed as a slimming aid until the problem of addiction became apparent. Diet plans based on the efficacy of wonder substances and dependent for their success upon women's gullibility and desperation to lose weight, are still widely

10

advertised. After years of distress caused by such manipulation, many women are now finding more appropriate support in self-help groups, where they can discuss with other sufferers the emotional and social factors involved in their eating problems. In this way, some find the confidence to be satisfied with their bodies as they are.

Anorexia Nervosa

True anorexia nervosa has been described as the 'willful pursuit of thinness through self-starvation'. It is a serious disorder mainly affecting adolescent women. The onset of anorexia nervosa typically occurs during adolescence. The diagram shows the percentages of a sample group of anorexics who became ill at different ages.

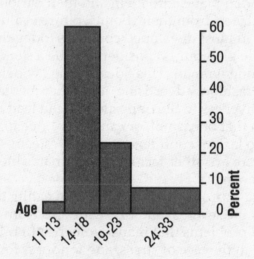

Symptoms and behavior
Dieting begins because the anorexic either is or believes herself to be overweight. It develops into a morbid fear of fatness and continues to the point of extreme emaciation (rarely recognized by the anorexic). Loss of weight can be accompanied by cessation of menstruation, constipation, discoloration of skin and the growth of fine body hair. Despite the extreme loss of weight, most anorexics are hyperactive. True loss of appetite is rare, and starvation may be interspersed with secret eating binges followed by self-induced purging.

Background and causes

Anorexia nervosa and its causes are highly complex. It is often associated with preexisting stresses, such as tensions within the family, academic pressures or sexual abuse in childhood. The anorexic may feel that she lacks control over anything except her body; she may be alarmed by her development of female characteristics; she may have some reason to be anxious about turning into a woman. Many anorexics suffer from an overwhelming sense of ineffectiveness. Continuous starvation and refusal of food represent a gesture of independence, possibly from an overdominant parent, while slimness is seen as desirable.

Pattern of Development

The development of a typical case of adolescent anorexia nervosa is described in the diagram below – from initial carbohydrate starvation until medical diagnosis. Response to treatment varies considerably. At the two extremes are obesity and starvation. More typically a patient responds to treatment and attains normal weight.

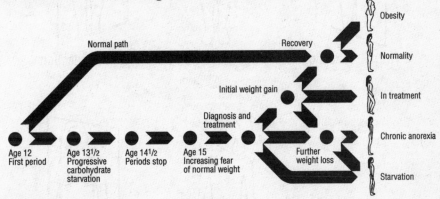

Self-Image

All people have a distorted view of their own body proportions, but whereas the normal person underestimates face, chest, and hip size, while slightly overestimating waist size, the anorexic grossly overestimates each of these sizes even when severely emaciated (see illustrations overleaf).

10

Degree of distortion in the perception of body size

	Normal (%)	Anorexic (%)
Face	94.7	157.6
Chest	95	134.2
Waist	100.2	146.6
Hips	96.6	128.8

(100% equals actual size)

 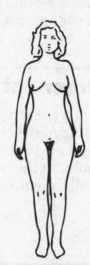 

Normal reflection   Average-sized woman   Anorexic reflection

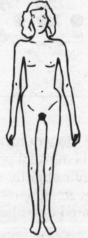 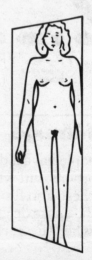

Chronic anorexic   Anorexic reflection

Bulimia Nervosa

This illness is characterized by bouts of grossly excessive eating ('bingeing'), usually of any food available, followed by self-induced purging through vomiting or laxatives. (In a related form, known as 'exercise bulimia', excessive exercise is used instead of purging to burn off calories.)
Bulimia may coexist with anorexia nervosa and can endanger long-term health, although it is not likely to be fatal. The root causes and treatment are similar for both bulimia and anorexia.

Treatment

Treatment for anorexia and bulimia has moved away from techniques such as enforced bedrest and drug therapy. Most treatments involve pressure to eat until a specific weight is reached, or strong encouragement to reach weight-gain targets, but these are accompanied by counseling or psychotherapy.

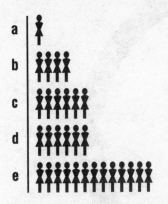

The diagram summarizes follow-up information on a group of anorexics. Follow-up material was available on 30 of the original sample of 45 patients.
a Obese (1)
b Dead (4)
c Anorexic (6)
d In treatment (6)
e Recovery (13)

Compulsive Eating

Compulsive eating is a common problem among women – and with the resulting obesity it can cause considerable distress. Many women indulge in occasional bouts of 'stuffing', but these are rarely significant. The compulsive eater, however, is addicted to food. She may use it to relieve feelings of stress, loneliness, isolation, frustration, dissatisfaction or boredom. She may use it to comfort herself if she feels guilty, depressed or unattractive. During adolescence girls sometimes overeat to stifle their emerging sexuality, and later in life they might use obesity to avoid contact with the opposite sex. Overeating – a

10

secret and solitary activity – needs handling with sensitivity and understanding. To help overcome the problem, a woman should avoid being alone for longer than necessary, ensure that only low-calorie snacks are kept in the house, and divert herself with physical activity when the craving for food starts. Severe cases often need clinical help. Reasons for compulsive eating vary, but the vicious circle illustrated here is common to many women. In self-help groups and 12-step groups such as Overeaters Anonymous, participants explore their self-image and attitudes to food and their bodies, and many find their own way to recovery. Compulsive eaters should keep a food diary to pinpoint when binges are likely to occur, so that avoidance measures can be taken.

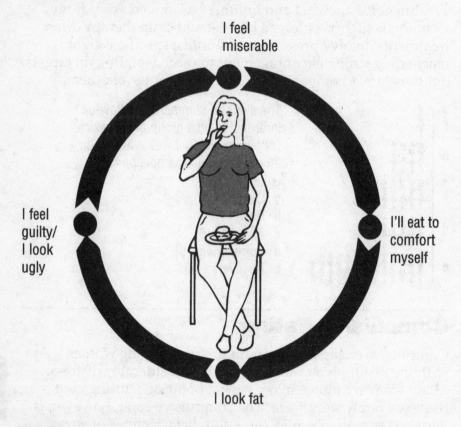

I feel
miserable

I feel
guilty/
I look
ugly

I'll eat to
comfort
myself

I look fat

Compulsive Dieting

Compulsive dieting, like anorexia and compulsive eating, is a disorder related to a woman's self-image. Often the image is distorted, as in anorexia. Sometimes the act of dieting itself becomes a crutch or a reaction to stress or disappointment. Although it is unlikely to be fatal, compulsive dieting can be harmful. Evidence is growing to show that prolonged or repeated low-calorie dieting merely alters the body's metabolism, slowing it down and making it more energy-efficient. When dieting stops, the body has a greater tendency to store fat than it did before. Worse, in a very calorie-restricted diet or fast, weight loss will consist largely of lean tissue such as muscle. Hunger pangs may lead to bingeing on fatty, unhealthy foods and to eating disorders.

Neuroses

The term 'neurosis' describes relatively mild forms of mental illness which, nonetheless, are very distressing to the sufferer and may result in an inability to lead a normal life. Neurosis generally represents a tendency to react excessively or abnormally to stress, and the level of anxiety felt appears inappropriate to the triggering factors; it may seem to constitute a part of the sufferer's personality. Neurosis may take any of several forms, indicating severe underlying anxiety expressed in a characteristic but inappropriate way. Each type of reaction is described here, but neurosis can manifest itself in a mixture of forms of unusual behavior.

Anxiety states

This is the most common form of neurosis. Physical symptoms include trembling, sweating, breathlessness and nausea. Panic attacks are also sometimes associated with a particular situation; they are, therefore, also known as situational anxiety states or phobias. For example, agoraphobia is commonly defined as 'fear of open spaces' and is usually characterized by the onset of symptoms when the sufferer attempts to leave her home, use public transportation, or enter crowded places such as department stores.

Hysterical or conversion reactions

Sometimes anxiety is 'converted' into physical symptoms: eg a person suffering from severe stress may become blind or lose the use of a limb, apparently without any physiological reason. The sufferer frequently appears relatively unconcerned by her disability, and symptoms disappear as the causes of anxiety are removed. Other types of hysterical behavior, in which the person shuts herself off from unbearable anxiety, include sleepwalking, amnesia, and (rarely) multiple personality.

10

Obsessional neuroses

Many people occasionally worry about seemingly trivial matters: eg 'Did I lock the door when I left the house?' It is not neurotic behavior to return quickly to make certain the door is locked if we are then able to reassure ourselves and abolish worry. Obsessive neurosis is characterized by continuing feelings of unassuageable anxiety. These surface in persistent intrusive thoughts or repetitive patterns of behavior which disrupt the person's life.

EFFECTS OF ANXIETY

An anxiety reaction may include any or all of the following physical symptoms:

a Tension migraine
b Sweating
c Dilated pupils
d Pallor
e Dry mouth
f Vomiting
g Breathlessness
h Irregular or rapid heartbeats
i Tremor
j Heightened muscle tone

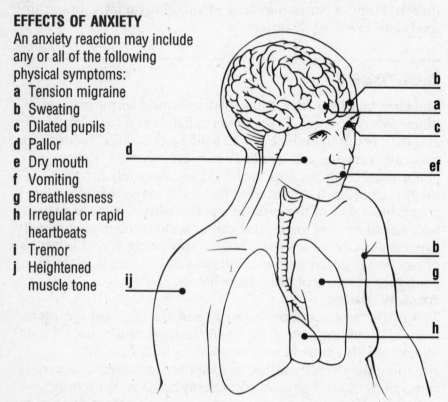

Treatment

Treatments vary widely according to practices prevailing within a particular country. If the behavior is very disturbed, specialist help will be needed. If the causes of anxiety are obvious, treatment will be aimed at removing those causes or decreasing their influence. In the United States and parts of Europe, psychotherapy is extensively used.

Deep-seated anxiety resulting from events in childhood may require lengthy psychoanalysis to help the patient recognize its causes and so come to terms with it. Behavior therapy, in which the patient is encouraged to gradually confront situations which cause anxiety, can be highly effective in dealing with anxiety states and phobias. Obsessive behavior may also respond to reeducative forms of treatment. If relationships within the family are thought to be the principal cause of anxiety, family counseling with a doctor or social worker may be most appropriate. Worries about health, money or work may also require practical advice in order to be alleviated.

Psychoses

More severe forms of mental illness than neuroses, psychoses manifest themselves mainly as loss of contact with reality. Psychotic illness is thought to result from a chemical imbalance within the brain or damage to a part of it. Drug treatment is often effective in controlling symptoms; the underlying illness, however, may be long lasting, perhaps permanent.

Schizophrenia

The cause or causes of schizophrenia have long been sought, and some factors have been identified. The tendency to develop it is at least partly inherited; pathological studies have failed to demonstrate any positive brain changes specific to schizophrenia. Not every person genetically at risk will develop it; factors like stress and family problems may be triggers. Faculties such as intelligence and memory are retained, but there are disturbances of emotional responsiveness and perception, resulting in apparent 'splitting' of the normally integrated processes of the mind. Some schizophrenics believe they are being persecuted; others may hear voices, telling them to behave in a certain way or suggesting false ideas. Sufferers may also become withdrawn or, if overstimulated, very excitable.

Drug treatment may help to 'damp down' symptoms sufficiently for psychological and social adjustment; response is variable. Schizophrenia is usually a long-term problem.

Manic-depressive psychosis

Everyone experiences fluctuations of mood. One day we wake up feeling full of energy and optimism, the next we are despondent and sluggish. Manic-depressive psychosis is an extreme disorder of mood swings: a phase of mania, characterized by feelings of elation, restlessness and self-confidence in one's abilities (often misplaced and sometimes

10

with disastrous consequences), alternates with deep depression during which suicide may be attempted. Imbalance of the brain chemistry which regulates mood is thought to be the main cause of the disorder, and closely monitored treatment with lithium carbonate is often effective in suppressing symptoms.

Brain scans

Scans of psychotic individuals have revealed abnormalities in the brain's glucose consumption. Scans of schizophrenics showed decreased glucose consumption in some areas; scans of manic-depressives showed increased glucose consumption during the manic phases.

 Glucose consumption

 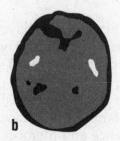 

a

b

c

a Scan showing normal glucose consumption **b** Scan showing glucose consumption of a schizophrenic **c** Scan showing glucose consumption of a manic-depressive

Psychosomatic Illness

Research into various disorders is increasingly implicating the role of mental stress in their development and progression. Some health problems – such as asthma, high blood pressure and stomach ulcers – may be initiated or worsened by factors such as anxiety and overwork, although they can have other causes and should always be medically investigated. In other important conditions, such as certain types of cancer and heart disease, the contribution of emotional factors is less easy to quantify and is controversial. Some doctors think prolonged stress caused by an accumulation of adverse life events, such as unemployment and family breakdowns, has the effect of lowering the body's resistance to illness. Statistics indicate that this may well be the case, but the direct physiological effects of stress are harder to determine. People who suffer financial hardship or depression might understandably be less motivated to restrict their diet or participate in regular physical exercise.

Antidepressants

In general, drugs are used to treat depression when the depression is long lasting and involves physical symptoms such as lethargy and loss of appetite. There are two main types of antidepressants. Tricyclics, also known as mood elevators, include amitriptyline, clomipramine, and trimipramine. Side effects include dry mouth, dizziness, headache, nausea and drowsiness. The other common antidepressants are known as monoamine oxidase inhibitors (MAOIs); they include isocarboxazid, phenelzine, and tranylcypromine. Dizziness, diarrhea, and increased heartbeat are among the side effects; in addition, when taken with certain foods or other medicines they can cause dangerous reactions. Lithium, another antidepressant, is more commonly prescribed for manic-depressive illness.

One antidepressant that has come into widespread use recently is Fluoxetine, better known as Prozac. It has also been used to treat bulimia nervosa and some obsessive-compulsive disorders. Its main advantage over many other drugs, and the reason for its popularity, is that it is virtually free of many of the side effects caused by other types of antidepressants. It should not be used by children nor by adults with certain other medical conditions, and it must always be prescribed by a doctor. The drug's mechanism of action is not really understood, but it is known to inhibit the uptake of serotonin by neurons. This causes an increase in the concentration of serotonin in the central nervous system, though why this has an antidepressant effect is not clear.

10

Although antidepressants are less dependence producing than, for example, barbiturates, they do have disadvantages. In addition to the discomfort of mild side effects, most also carry the risk of potentially serious side effects such as high blood pressure. They take some weeks to begin working; tricyclics generally take two to three weeks, and MAOIs as much as six weeks. Chemical approaches to treating depression alleviate only the symptoms, of course, and will not resolve any underlying problems that might be the cause of the depression.

ILLNESS

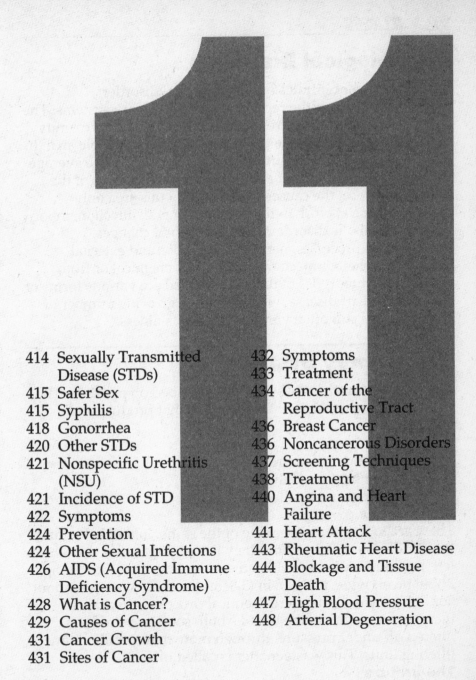

11

Physiological Disorders

This chapter concentrates on physiological disorders, particularly those of the reproductive and urinary systems. The complexity of the female reproductive tract and its proximity to the urinary outlet make this an especially vulnerable area. In spite of this, it has been difficult, until recently, for the average woman to educate herself about the special problems of the female body. Yet the causes of disorder in this area only illustrate those at work in the body in general: infection, inborn defects, metabolic disorders, developmental changes, degenerative processes, nervous conditions and external irritations (whether mechanical, thermal, chemical or from radiation). Other types of illness discussed are various forms of cancer and heart disease, which affects a growing number of women but is still often viewed as a man's illness.

The Urinary System

The female reproductive system is described on pp.34-37. The urinary system consists of those organs that produce and excrete urine:
a) a pair of kidneys;
b) a pair of tubes called ureters;
c) a muscular bag called the bladder;
d) another single tube called the urethra.

The kidneys

These are located on either side of the spine, in the region of the middle back. The right kidney lies slightly lower than the left. Each kidney is bean shaped and is about 4in (10cm) long, $2^1/2$in (6cm) wide, and $1^1/2$in (3.8cm) thick. Each weighs about 5oz (140g). The kidneys are chemical processing works. In them, waste matter in the blood – both solid and fluid – is filtered off under pressure, through more than 2 million tiny filtering units. This waste matter is called urine.

The ureters

These are muscular tubes, each one about 10in (25cm) long. One tube leads from each kidney, and down them the urine passes to the bladder, at the rate of a drop every 30 seconds.

The bladder

This is a balloonlike, muscular bag that acts as a reservoir for the urine. When full, it holds about 1 pint (.57 liters) of urine –

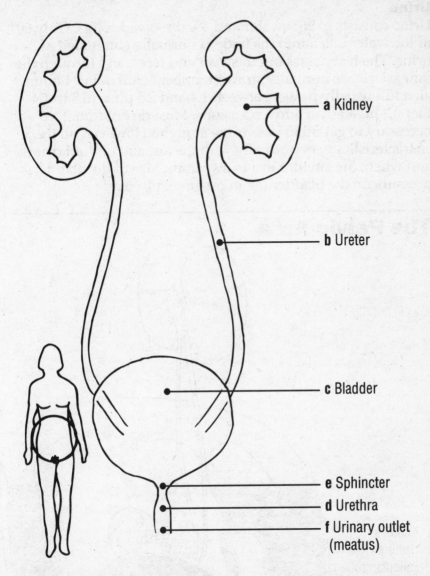

a Kidney

b Ureter

c Bladder

e Sphincter
d Urethra
f Urinary outlet
(meatus)

though the desire to urinate is usually felt when about half that amount is present. A muscular ring (sphincter) surrounds the exit from the bladder into the urethra. When this is contracted, it prevents leakage of urine out of the bladder. Upon urination the sphincter is relaxed, and the urine passes into the urethra.

The urethra
This is a muscular tube, about $1^1/2$in (3.8cm) long in a woman (compared with 8in – 20cm – in a man). It leads from the bladder to the exterior, and it is along this tube that urine leaves the body ('urination' also called 'micturition').

11

Urine

Urine consists of 96% water and 4% dissolved solids. Only 60% of the water taken into the body is normally eliminated as urine. The rest passes out in sweat and feces, and through the lungs. Urine is normally straw or amber colored. In 24 hours an adult usually passes between 1.4 and 2.5 pints (0.8 to 1.4 liters), spread over 4 to 6 occasions. Most do not find it necessary to get up to pass urine at night. However, all these characteristics vary normally with the amount of fluid drunk and when, the amount lost in sweat, the size of the bladder, pressure on the bladder (eg in pregnancy), etc.

The Pelvic Area

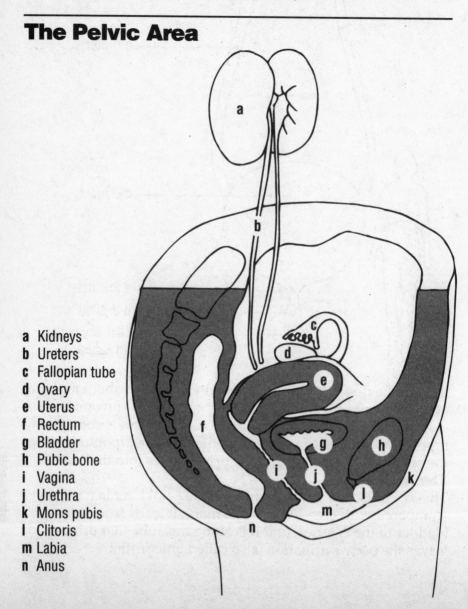

a Kidneys
b Ureters
c Fallopian tube
d Ovary
e Uterus
f Rectum
g Bladder
h Pubic bone
i Vagina
j Urethra
k Mons pubis
l Clitoris
m Labia
n Anus

Prolapse

Prolapse of the uterus is not an uncommon condition – the uterus sags down into the vagina, and may even protrude out between the legs. The symptoms include frequent and difficult urination; incontinence; vaginal discharge; low backache; and a feeling that something is coming out of the vagina; additionally, all the above symptoms immediately disappear on lying down. The condition is produced by weakening of muscles that support the uterus. The cause is usually damage done in childbirth; 99% of women with prolapsed uteruses have given birth. But aging and heavy physical activity also contribute, and the symptoms often appear only after the menopause, when the affected muscles may lose tone and ligaments atrophy. Mild cases require no treatment, but more serious or troublesome ones require a pessary inserted by a doctor, or sometimes surgery.

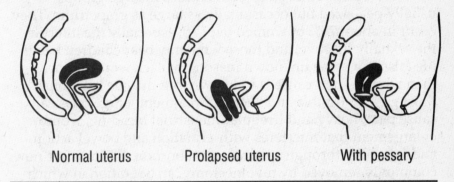

Normal uterus   Prolapsed uterus   With pessary

Retroversion

In most women, from puberty on, the upper end of the uterus is tilted forward in the body, and moves backward only as the bladder fills or when the woman lies on her back. But in about 10% of women the uterus is always retroverted (tilted backward). Once blamed for many ailments, in fact this may be troublesome only in pregnancy, when the enlarging uterus may fail to rise into the abdomen. Urine retention in the bladder results. A doctor can usually correct the situation. If it seems very troublesome, surgery is needed. Untreated, it could cause cystitis and even miscarriage. Retroversion can also start after childbirth. Doctors disagree whether this can cause backache, etc. Other causes of displacement can include pelvic tumors (such as ovarian cysts) and connective tissue joining to

11

other structures. Surgery can deal with these.

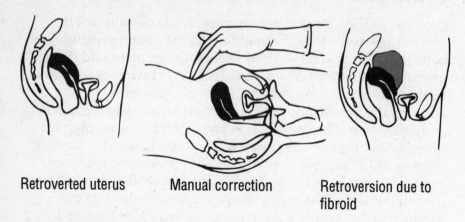

Retroverted uterus   Manual correction   Retroversion due to fibroid

Fibroids

These are lumps of fibrous tissue growing in the muscle wall of the uterus, sometimes singly, sometimes in large groups, usually pea-sized but occasionally as large as grapefruits. They occur in about 20% of women over 30, especially the infertile, the sexually inactive, and those who only bear children late in life (also, for some unknown reason, in black women more than white). Their cause is unknown, but may be hormonal. Most give no trouble and need no treatment. Large ones can cause pain, heavy and irregular menstrual bleeding, womb enlargement that interferes with urination and bowel action, and infertility through spontaneous abortion. Fibroids are now commonly removed by myomectomy, an operation in which the fibroids are removed by laparoscopy, leaving the uterus intact. (A laparoscope is a fiberoptic device fitted with surgical tools.) Hysterectomy is the most common treatment for severe cases of fibroids in women who have completed their families. An alternative is a drug that reduces the body's estrogen levels, which causes the fibroids to shrink. Polyps are another type of lump, also usually harmless, but developing from mucus tissue and forming dangling shapes.

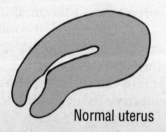

Normal uterus

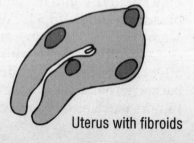

Uterus with fibroids

Cervical Erosion

The cells lining the cervical canal sometimes extend down until they show as a reddened area at the head of the vagina. This happens naturally in puberty and first pregnancy and requires no treatment unless it persists for more than 6 months after childbirth and causes much vaginal discharge. It then requires electric cauterization, which produces a heavy, discolored vaginal discharge for 4 to 6 weeks until healing is complete. It may also occur in women on the Pill or using IUDs. Again, it usually disappears without symptoms or treatment, but regular 'Pap' tests (see p.434) are advised to check for cancer.

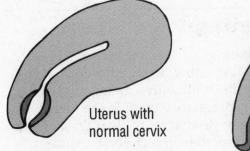
Uterus with normal cervix

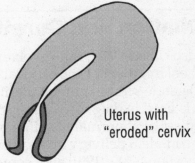
Uterus with "eroded" cervix

Incompetent Cervix

A weak cervix is often a cause of repeated miscarriages. It may be due to problems during a previous birth or to a previous termination of a pregnancy. Treatment is by means of a 'cervical stitch' to keep the cervix closed throughout the pregnancy; the stitch is removed prior to the birth.

Endometriosis

Endometrial cells (see p.41) can grow in the wrong place, forming cysts in the uterine muscle, the ovaries, or other parts of the pelvis (see illustration overleaf). This is most common in women in their thirties who have not had children or are infertile. On menstruation these cells bleed a little so the cyst swells, causing pain in the lower abdomen especially before or at the end of menstruation, and sometimes pain on intercourse. Where ovaries or Fallopian tubes are blocked, infertility results. Treatment involves hormones or surgery (eg removal of the cyst, or part of an organ, or in severe cases hysterectomy).

11

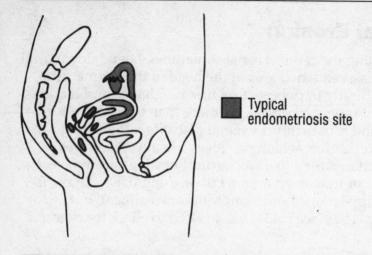

Typical
endometriosis site

Dilation and Curettage

Also called D&C, this involves:
a) enlargement of the cervical opening, using dilators;
b) gentle scraping of the uterine wall with a metal curette.
It is used to diagnose cancer, pregnancy outside the uterus, or
causes of abnormal bleeding or discharge; to clear waste from
incomplete delivery or abortion; to help fertility; to cause
abortion (see p.199); and, sometimes, as routine preparation for
gynecological surgery.
Anesthetic is needed. Recovery takes 6 hours to 2 days.

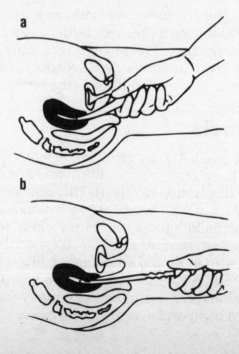

Hysterectomy

This is surgical removal of the uterus. It can be:
a) subtotal: removal of the uterus except for the cervix (rarely performed);
b) total: removal of uterus and cervix; or
c) radical: removal of uterus, surrounding tissue, and part of the vagina.
With any of these, ovaries and Fallopian tubes may also be removed (see p.402).
If the uterus is not enlarged by disease, removal can be via the vagina. Otherwise, an incision is necessary: a vertical one below the navel or a horizontal one just above the pubic region. (The scar left is almost invisible.) The operation takes less than 1 to 3 hours.

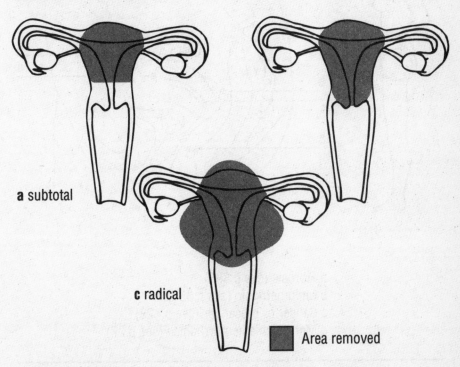

a subtotal

c radical

Area removed

Reasons for Hysterectomy

11

By the mid-1980s, hysterectomy had become the second most common major surgical operation in the US, performed on 35% of women under 60. As the population is gradually aging, this figure is likely to increase, despite progress made in the last year in reducing the number of 'routine' hysterectomies carried out, eg for cancer prevention or sterilization. It is estimated that in 2005, annually 854,000 procedures will be performed, as compared with approximately 670,000 per year today. Doctors are against 'unnecessary' hysterectomy because hysterectomy within 13 weeks of conception can endanger the mother's life.

The diagram below shows some valid reasons for the operation.

Possible reasons for hysterectomy

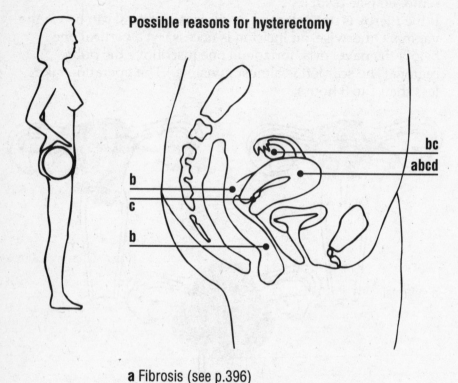

a Fibrosis (see p.396)
b Endometriosis (see p.397)
c Cancer or precancer (see p.429)
d Metropathia hemorrhagica (see p.27)

Physical After-effects

The diagram opposite shows how the immediate effects of the operation wear off. Other considerations are long term:

a) Menstruation ends immediately, and with it fertility and the need for contraception.

b) Hysterectomy usually has no effect on sexual performance. Some women claim loss of sexual pleasure after cervix removal. Some complain of shortened vaginas, but with careful surgery vaginal shortening should be minimal.

c) The ovaries are normally not removed with the uterus, so female hormone production continues. If both have been removed, the menopause occurs and hormone therapy must be given to prevent symptoms, such as hot flushes (see Chapter 6).

d) Obesity does not follow hysterectomy unless the patient eats too much and exercises too little after the operation. However, psychological factors may encourage this.

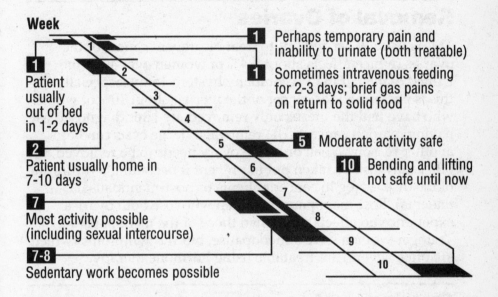

Week

1 Patient usually out of bed in 1-2 days

2 Patient usually home in 7-10 days

7 Most activity possible (including sexual intercourse)

7-8 Sedentary work becomes possible

1 Perhaps temporary pain and inability to urinate (both treatable)

1 Sometimes intravenous feeding for 2-3 days; brief gas pains on return to solid food

5 Moderate activity safe

10 Bending and lifting not safe until now

Psychological After-effects

Hysterectomy affects women differently. Some enjoy the relief given from heavy bleeding or threat of disease, feel more active and healthy, and are happy that they can no longer conceive accidentally. But younger women often resent the loss of fertility, and many become depressed. Research in the United States shows that hysterectomy patients:

a) grow more dissatisfied with the operation as time passes (4 years on, only 41% are satisfied);

b) are more likely to be dissatisfied if the ovaries are also removed (causing hot flashes, lethargy, obesity);

c) are four times more likely than other women to become depressed in the 3 years following surgery;

d) are likely to remain depressed for twice as long (2 years on average) as other women;

11

e) are especially liable to depression if under 40 when operated on;

f) are five times more likely to make a subsequent first visit to a psychiatrist than other women (peak period 2 years after surgery).

Such statistics probably reflect the fact that many hysterectomies are unnecessary. When the operation is genuinely necessary, psychological disturbance is much less likely.

Removal of Ovaries

This is usually carried out to treat or prevent cancer of the ovaries (which affects about 3-4% of women over 40 in the United States). It may accompany hysterectomy, especially if this is performed for cancer of the uterus (about 10% of women who have had the uterus only removed are later diagnosed as having ovarian cancer). The removal of large cysts can be another reason. When only one ovary needs to be removed, the other may also be taken out to prevent it becoming a future site of the disease (eg in cancer patients or post-menopausal patients). Post-menopausal women who lose both ovaries experience no effects other than those of the menopause. Younger women have a menopause, but the symptoms (which are often severe) are treatable using hormone therapy.

Ovarian cysts

Swelling of the abdomen, pain during intercourse, and irregular periods can all be symptomatic. A doctor may be able to feel a large ovarian cyst during a pelvic examination. Large cysts must be removed surgically to prevent further problems. Sometimes this can be done without affecting the ovary.

Toxic Shock Syndrome (TSS)

This is very rare, but it is a medical emergency. Micro-organisms in the vagina multiply and cause a sudden, severe illness with fever, shock, vomiting, diarrhea or rash. TSS usually arises during menstruation; links include the use of highly absorbent tampons, the diaphragm or sponges. All retain menstrual flow and may thus provide conditions under which bacteria can thrive.

Pelvic Inflammatory Disease (PID)

If harmful microorganisms enter the uterus and Fallopian tubes, they may result in infection causing any of the following: fever, abdominal pain or swelling, discharge, bleeding, nausea, menstrual pain, malaise and backache. Symptoms are persistent.

PID can lead to infertility and general abdominal pain. Frequent causes are gonorrhea and chlamydial infection. IUDs, childbirth and gynecological treatments may allow bacteria to pass through the cervix.

Vaginal Discharge

Apart from menstrual flow from the uterus (see p.24), normal vaginal discharge consists of:

a) a clear watery mucus from the cervix (especially midway between periods;

b) clear fluid that is "sweated" through the walls of the vagina (usually a small amount, but more in pregnancy or during emotional upset, and a great deal during sexual excitement);

c) dead cells from the vaginal wall;

d) a small amount from Bartholin's glands at the vaginal entrance during sexual excitement. This discharge is transparent or slightly milky, with little or no odor, slippery, and perhaps yellowish when dry. It keeps the vagina moist and clean. It is more noticeable at certain times in the monthly cycle.

Signs of disorder

Signs of abnormal discharge are irritation (itching, chafing, soreness, burning of vagina, vulva or thighs), unpleasant odor, or unusual color.

Causes

For abnormal menstrual discharge, see pp.26-27. Possible causes of other abnormal discharge are:

a) forgotten foreign bodies, eg tampons or diaphragm (thick odorous discharge);

b) chemical irritation, eg soap, disinfectants in bathing water, vaginal deodorants;

c) post-menopausal atrophy (see p.218);

d) 'cervical erosion' (see p.397);

e) infection, including candidiasis (pp.404-05), trichomoniasis (p.400), gonorrhea (pp.418-20), and NSU (p.421). Many bacteria live harmlessly in a healthy vagina. Some help to keep its surface a little acidic, restricting the development of harmful

11

organisms. Factors favoring infection include lowered resistance, cuts, abrasions, and excessive douching – potentially all factors that affect the acidity of the vaginal mucus.

Trichomoniasis

Trichomoniasis vaginalis is a one-celled animal parasite and the most common infectious cause of vaginal discharge. Perhaps 50% of women carry it at some time; about 15% develop symptoms at least once. The discharge is often greenish-yellow or grayish, thin, and foamy, but may be thicker and whiter if other infection is also present. Other symptoms are: itching and soreness of vagina and vulva; clusters of raised red spots on cervix and vaginal walls; and an unpleasant odor. If it spreads to the urinary tract, it can cause cystitis; if to the Fallopian tubes, infertility. Transmission can occur sexually (men carrying it generally have no symptoms), and also very occasionally via moist objects such as towels, washcloths and toilet seats (the parasite can live briefly outside the body). It cannot be passed on to a baby in childbirth. Qualified medical treatment is vital, especially as it often occurs in conjunction with gonorrhea (this should be checked for once the symptoms of trichomoniasis clear up). Both partners should be treated. But the usual treatment is with oral metronidazole (Flagyl) or tinidazole, both thought suspect drugs by some. (Prescribed vaginal suppositories or gels may be adequate alternatives, though infection may recur.) Especially avoid oral metronidazole if you are pregnant, have peptic ulcers or another infection, or have a history of blood or central nervous system disease. Also do not take alcohol with it. Avoid intercourse until tests show clear. (For measures to help prevent recurrence, see p.338.)

Candidiasis ('Thrush')

This is caused by a yeast organism (a type of fungus). It can be passed on sexually, men usually having no symptoms. But it often occurs in the vagina anyway, kept at bay by the acidic conditions and only thriving if these get milder. Itching and soreness of vagina and vulva then result, especially when the body is warm (eg in bed at night). There may also be a thick creamy discharge that smells of yeast and looks like cottage cheese. Self-treatment may help (eg one or two yogurt treatments; or vinegar douches twice a day for 3 days), but will not usually clear up an established infection. The usual treatment is a single dose of fluconazole, 150mg by mouth. Other tablets include econazole, miconazole and clotrimazole, all members of the same family of antifungal agents. Nystatin vaginal suppositories are also sometimes used – one a night for one or two weeks. Tampons cannot be worn, as they soak up medication; Nystatin gives a yellow stain, so a pad and old underpants are needed. Creams are still occasionally prescribed for direct application to the vagina, cervix, and vulva, but these destroy all vaginal bacteria; when treatment ends it is important to recreate acidic conditions in the vagina, to encourage normal bacterial growth. Persistent recurrence of infection suggests lack of hygiene by the partner (eg thrush can live under the male foreskin), incipient sugar diabetes, or the effects on the vaginal mucus of oral contraceptives or antibiotics. If a woman with thrush gives birth, the baby may have the infection in its digestive tract, and should be treated with Nystatin drops.

Other Infections

Hepatitis B can be spread through blood or semen and is a contagious disease that can last for several months. An infected individual may have no symptoms but can still pass on the infection, even through saliva.

Nonspecific vaginitis or Bacterial vaginosis is the name for any unidentified vaginal infection. In recent years, the search for the organism or organisms causing this complaint has resulted in the discovery of a single organism, variously called *Haemophilus vaginalis*, *Gardnerella vaginalis*, and *Mobilunccus*. Clinicians have now agreed to call the complaint *Bacterial vaginosis*.

In some areas it is more common than candidiasis (with similar symptoms), but it is often misdiagnosed. Cystitis-like symptoms may be the first sign of disorder, followed by a discharge that is often white, yellow, or green, creamy in consistency, and with an unpleasant odor. The vaginal walls may be puffy and coated with pus, and there may also be lower back pains, cramp, and swollen glands in the groin. The infection is usually diagnosed by looking for 'clue cells' on microscopic examination. These are vaginal epithelial cells whose walls are ragged due to white blood cell activity. The usual treatment is with metronidazole

11

(Flagyl), taken orally for about a week. This infection is often sexually transmitted, so both partners need treatment.

Vaginal Organisms

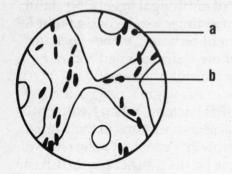

1 Normal vaginal organisms:
a dead mucus tissue cells
b lactobacillus bacteria

2 Trichomoniasis:
a one-celled animal parasites
b,c dead white defensive blood cells (pus)

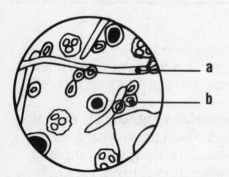

3 Candidiasis
a yeast masses
b yeast buds
with other abnormal organisms

Symptoms of Urinary Disorders

For a doctor, the urine and urination are among the most useful signs of disorder – relating sometimes not just to the urinary system, but to the general health of the body. Characteristics of urination that may interest a doctor include: changes in quantity and frequency (including rising at night); slow and weak or unusually forceful flow; stopping and starting, and dribbling; difficulty in beginning or continuing; inability to restrain (incontinence); sudden stopping; and, of course, pain or other unusual sensation on urinating or

inability to urinate at all. Characteristics of the urine that may
be of interest include unusual color, odor, cloudiness,
frothiness and content. Abnormal chemical content can include
albumen (which may indicate kidney disorder) or sugar
(diabetes). Chemical testing can be carried out very easily,
using a treated paper that changes color when moistened with
urine. Other abnormal contents can include bacteria, parasites,
kidney tube casts, bile pigment and especially blood or pus.
However, many unusual characteristics of the urine or
urination will more usually be due to insignificant causes than
to disorder. For example, having to get up from bed to urinate
is often due to drinking tea or coffee last thing at night.
Strikingly unusual colors can be produced by certain
medicines and foods.

Other symptoms

Other symptoms of disorder include: itching, redness or
stickiness at the urethral opening; any discharge of fluid from
the urethra; pain or swelling in the area of the kidneys; and
shivering, temperature or fever.

Types of Disorder

Infection

This can reach the urinary system in two ways: 'downward',
via the bloodstream and then the kidneys; or 'upward', via the
urethral opening in the genitals. An example of the first can be
tuberculosis. But the second is much more common in women
because:
a) in women the closeness of anus and genitals helps bacteria
pass between them;
b) the shortness of the female urethra allows bacteria to reach
the higher parts of the tract more easily. Most bacteria entering
the tract from outside are killed by the urine; but 5% of women
(both adults and children) have active bacteria in the bladder.
Often there are no symptoms.
If there are, frequency of urination and pain on urinating are
typical. Diagnosis is by bacteriological examination of a urine
sample. Treatment is with an antibiotic.

Inflammation

Inflammation of the tract is mostly caused by infection, but
also by: dietary irritation (eg alcohol, and perhaps food
allergy); use of chemicals (vaginal deodorants, contraceptive
foams, etc); and tissue damage during sexual activity,
childbirth or surgery. Even when inflammation is not caused

11

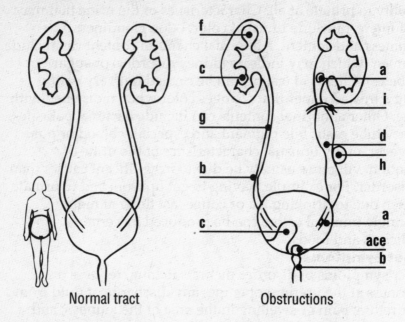

Normal tract   Obstructions

OBSTRUCTIONS include:
a stones
b strictures
c tumors
d blood clots
e foreign bodies
f TB fibrosis

Also external pressure from:
g pregnancy
h tumors
i congenitally displaced arteries

INFECTIONS include:
j TB
k kidney infections

Also especially bacteria:
l in the bladder
m in stagnant or obstructed urine
n in stones
o in foreign bodies
p in structural inflammations

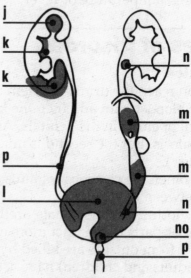

Sites of infection

by infection, an inflamed area is a favorable site for infection. Inflammation of the urethra is called 'urethritis', that of the bladder 'cystitis' (see pp.410-11). Symptoms include pain on urinating. Treatment depends on the cause, but drinking large quantities of fluid usually helps.

Flow abnormality

This includes obstruction of flow, complete or incomplete; also apparently normal flow that nevertheless leaves stagnant pools of urine in the tract. Causes include:

a) blockage by extraneous objects (eg stones, blood clots, etc);
b) malfunction of the tract itself (eg through congenital controlling malformation, tumors and other growths or tissue changes, and temporary spasm);
c) outside pressure on the tract (eg from fibroids, displaced uterus or pregnancy).

Stagnant urine is always a likely site for infection. When there is flow blockage as well, pressure builds up behind the obstruction, and that section of the tract may be stretched and dilated. Eventually the pressure and dilation may reach back up the ureters toward the kidneys. Kidney infection may result, and rapid surgical treatment is needed before the kidneys suffer permanent damage.

Incontinence

This is inability to control urination. For incontinence in the old, see p.457; but it also occurs in younger women. Causes include: psychological stress (eg severe fright); disorders of the bladder; congenital defects; tissue damage occurring in childbirth or surgery; and impairment of the nerves due to injury or disease. Two types are fairly common:

a) urgency incontinence, where there is a shortened time gap between the desire to urinate and uncontrollable urination – it occurs quite often in older women;
b) stress incontinence, typified by small amounts of urine escaping when the person strains, coughs or laughs – whether the bladder is full or virtually empty. This is usually only seen in post-menopausal women; special exercises, or sometimes surgery, are needed.

11

Kidney Disorders

These include: congenital defects; tumors; stones; damage through injury; inflammation without infection; and infection. **Infection** is especially common in women. It can arrive via the bloodstream or the urinary system. In acute attacks, bacterial infection via the urinary tract is typical. Symptoms are shivering and fever, acute pain in loin or under ribs at back, and frequent urination. Qualified medical attention is vital, as are prescribed antibiotics, bed rest and plenty of fluids. Long-term infection may follow acute infection or arise from urinary obstruction or blood-borne infection. (Stones are frequent sites.) Symptoms include dull back pain, painful and frequent urination, tiredness, headache, nausea, loss of appetite and fever. Treatment depends on causes. In neglected cases, kidney damage may result, with possible high blood pressure and blood poisoning.

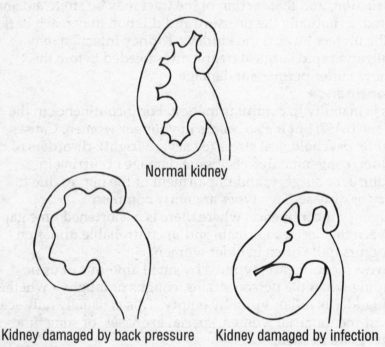

Normal kidney

Kidney damaged by back pressure   Kidney damaged by infection

Cystitis

Strictly, this means inflammation of the bladder. However, it is now generally used for a certain collection of symptoms, usually in women, which can arise in a variety of ways. The main symptoms of an attack (acute cystitis) are:

a) great frequency of urination (perhaps every few minutes);
b) pain on urination – often extreme; and
c) a recurrent or even continuous desire to urinate even when there is no urine to pass. As the attack continues, there may also be increasing incontinence, and often blood in the urine. Other associated symptoms can include: pain just above the pubic bone or in the loin; and a foul smell from, and perhaps debris in, the urine. Also, extreme pain may be felt if sexual intercourse is attempted. This syndrome is very common: perhaps 80% of women suffer from it at some time in their lives, and it is often recurrent (chronic cystitis) and hard to eradicate. In its extreme forms it can bring depression, disrupted career and home life, and even (since it can both derive from sexual intercourse and interfere with it) broken emotional and marital relationships.

Causes of Cystitis

There are two main alternative causes:
a) infection;
b) inflammation without infection (though infection may also set in later).
Infection
This is usually by Escherichia coli (E.coli) bacteria from the rectum finding their way into the urethral opening. E.coli are often found on the perineum (the skin between anus and genitals). Their progress toward the vulva is often helped mechanically by careless use of toilet paper or by sexual activity (petting, or just the movement of the penis).
Other sources of infection are:
a) similar cross-infection from the vagina (eg candidiasis, trichomoniasis or gonorrhea);
b) lack of male hygiene (eg when uncircumcised);
c) infections from the kidneys that pass downward (eg tuberculosis).
Infection may be aided by: stones; stagnant pools of urine due to retention (see p.409); lowered resistance, as in anemia; and (for bacteria preferring nonacidic urine) diabetes.
Inflammation
For general causes of this, see pp.407-9.
In cystitis, the normal cause (apart from infection) is bruising or skin cracking through sexual activity. Relevant here are: frequency of intercourse (hence 'honeymoon cystitis');

11

insufficient lubrication; use of certain positions (depending on the individuals); and overforceful petting. Other relevant causes are:

a) tissue irritation through use of vaginal deodorants, foam contraceptives, unsuitable lubricants, etc;
b) strain on the bladder due to prolapse of the uterus;
c) damage through childbirth or surgery;
d) allergic reaction of the urinary tract to certain foods.

Inflammation can, in turn, provide a breeding ground for infection (and an entry for infection into the bloodstream).

Chronic cystitis

This is usually a case of repeated attacks of acute cystitis, but there may be long-term tissue changes also involved, including changes in the urethra due to the menopause, and changes in the bladder lining from bacterial or other infection.
Occasionally there may be psychological factors.

Investigation

The sufferer should always see a doctor – and always try to get proper tests made to pinpoint the cause. First step should be laboratory testing of a urine sample for infection and (if present) responsiveness to drugs. The patient should drink before going to the doctor, so as to be ready to pass urine for this. A clean sample is important: the vulva should be swabbed, and only a small midstream sample (ie from halfway through urination) taken. During menstruation, a tube (catheter) inserted into the urethra should be used. The patient may also be able to give useful information, eg the amount of time between the attack and the last previous intercourse. (Cystitis due to inflammation alone will follow intercourse sooner than that due to infection, since bacteria need time to multiply. Unfortunately, estimates vary – from 'very soon after' for inflammation and 12-24 hours after for infection, to 24 hours after for inflammation and 36 for infection.)

If no infection is found, or if it fails to clear after a course of drugs, hospital investigations may be needed; such as:

a) physical examination by a specialist;
b) taking of bacteria samples from vagina and perineum;
c) early-morning urine samples;
d) blood samples;
e) X-rays of the urinary tract, often using injections of dye into

the bloodstream to show up obstructions, or introducing dye into the bladder to show its action;
f) cystoscopy, which is the surgical inspection of the inside of the urethra and bladder, using a 'periscope tube' inserted into the urethra under general anesthetic.

The diagrams show 'intravenous pyelograms' (IVPs): X-rays of the urinary tract taken after iodine dye has been injected into the bloodstream. The iodine passes out through the urinary system.

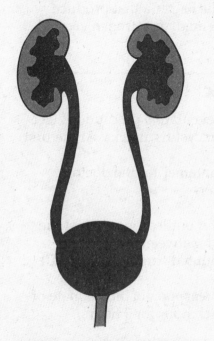
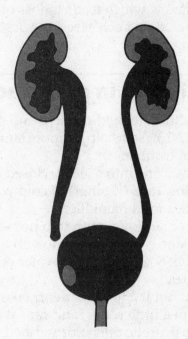

IVP showing normal functioning of the kidneys and urinary tract

IVP showing blockage in one ureter, distention above the blockage, and a growth in the bladder

Treatment

Depending on the cause of trouble, treatment may include:
a) antibiotics and similar drugs, to combat urinary and/or kidney infection;
b) increase of the patient's fluid intake (cranberry juice is especially efficacious);
c) drugs to relax the muscles of the bladder;
d) drugs to combat vaginal infection;

11

e) hormone therapy to restore mucus and tissue characteristics;
f) surgery for urinary blockages;
g) surgery to deal with other causes of inflammation, eg repair for a prolapsed uterus.

When on a course of drugs, the symptoms may vanish soon after starting the course, and there may be side effects, eg nausea or depression. But it is important to finish the course. Drinking a vitamin C source may help to bring urinal acidity into a range where the drug works best.

Sometimes cystitis results from post-menopausal estrogen deficiency, which leads to loss of the bacteria that produce lactic acid. In such cases, the best remedy is estrogen vaginal cream.

Self-Help in an Attack

In addition to medical help and preventative precautions (see pp.412-13), self-help is important in cystitis attacks. At the first hint of trouble:

a) pass urine into a clean, closed container for the doctor;
b) drink 16oz ($^1/_2$ liter) of cold water;
c) take a mild painkiller;
d) lie or sit down with two hot water bottles, one against the back, one (wrapped in a towel) high between the legs;
e) drink 8oz ($^1/_4$ liter) of water or diluted fruit juice every 20 minutes;
f) (but not if a heart patient) take a teaspoon of bicarbonate of soda in a little water, and repeat each hour for 3 hours;
g) use diuretic pills if prescribed;
h) after every urination, wash between anus and vulva and dab dry. After half an hour, the attack should begin to ease.

Sexually Transmitted Diseases (STDs)

The term 'sexually transmitted disease' (STD) is used to describe infections that are almost always passed on by sexual contact. They are also known as 'venereal diseases' (VD). They spread because:

a) the microorganisms that cause STDs usually live in the infected person's genitals or in some other place (such as mouth or anus) where they have been transmitted during sexual activity;
b) to infect another person, they usually have to enter the body

through an orifice (such as the genital opening, anus or mouth), and sexual activity gives them this chance.

The first symptoms of disorder appear on the part of the body that has been in contact with the infected part of the infected person. Otherwise, these disorders have little in common. Some are caused by bacteria, some by viruses, some by other microorganisms. Some are rare in our society, others epidemic. Some may be merely painful or troublesome; others, if untreated, may be crippling or fatal.

Safer Sex

'Safer sex' practices to prevent the spread of AIDS (see pp.422-3) will help protect you from other sexual infections as well. These practices include the following:

a) Your partner should wear a condom (for vaginal, anal and oral sex).

b) Reduce the number of sexual partners you have.

c) Before a sexual relationship begins, both partners should be checked for infection at a special clinic.

d) If you are infected with an STD, stop having sex until a doctor confirms that you are clear. If in doubt, ask your doctor.

Syphilis

Syphilis is sometimes nicknamed 'the pox' or 'scab'. Until the appearance of AIDS it was the most serious of sexual infections. Its prevalence varies. In the United States, it was common in the gay population but has shown a decrease since the 1980s – probably due to the adoption of safer sex practices. Otherwise, it is comparatively rare. Worldwide, there are about 3.5 million cases of infectious syphilis.

Causes

Syphilis is caused by tiny bacteria shaped like corkscrews: 'spirochetes'. These thrive in the warm, moist linings of the genital passages, rectum and mouth, and can live in concentrated sites (sores) on the skin surface, but die almost immediately outside the human body. So the infection always spreads by direct physical contact, and in practice almost always by sexual contact. Whether the probing organ is a penis, tongue or (occasionally) finger, and whether the receiving organ is mouth, genitals or rectum, a syphilitic site on either one can infect the other. Very occasionally syphilis

11

does occur from close nonsexual contact (and cases have occurred in doctors and dentists from their professional work); but it cannot be spread by physical objects such as lavatory seats, towels or cups. It can, however, be inherited from an infected mother, resulting sometimes in stillbirth or deformity, and in other cases in hidden infection that causes trouble later.

Incubation

There is an 'incubation period' between catching syphilis and showing the first signs – always between 9 days and 3 months, and usually 3 weeks or more. About ,000 germs are typically picked up on infection. After 3 weeks these have multiplied to 100 to 200 million. If the disorder is untreated, they can invade the whole body, eventually causing death. Syphilis has 4 stages. Each has typical symptoms, but these can vary or be absent.

Primary stage

The first symptom is in the part that has been in contact with the infected person: genitals, rectum or mouth. A spot appears and grows into a sore that oozes a colorless fluid (but no blood). The sore feels like a button: round or oval, firm, and just under $1/2$in (1.27cm) across. A week or so later, the glands in the groin may swell – but they do not usually become tender, so it may not be noticed. There is no feeling of illness, and the sore heals in a few weeks without treatment.

Primary sore

a The primary-stage syphilitic sore is hard with a clearly defined edge

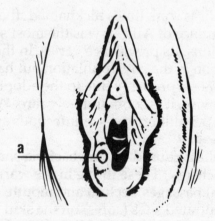

a

Secondary stage

This occurs when the bacteria have spread through the body. It can follow the primary stage immediately, but usually there is a gap of several weeks. The person feels generally unwell. There may be headaches, loss of appetite, general aches and pains, sickness and perhaps fever. Also there are breaks in the skin, and sometimes a dark red rash, lasting for weeks or even months. The rash appears on the back of the legs and the front of the arms, and often too on the body, face, hands and feet. It may be flat or raised, does not itch, is not infectious, and looks like many other skin complaints. Other symptoms can include: hair falling out in patches; sores in the mouth, nose, throat or genitals, or in soft folds of skin; and swollen glands throughout the body. The sores – like the original primary stage sore – are very infectious. All these symptoms eventually disappear without treatment, after anything from 3 weeks to 9 months.

Latent stage

This may last for anything from a few months to 50 years. There are no symptoms. After about 2 years, the person ceases to be infectious (though a woman can still sometimes give the disease to a baby she bears). But presence of syphilis can still be shown by blood tests.

Tertiary stage

This occurs in about $1/3$ of those who have not been treated earlier. The disease now shows itself in concentrated form and often causes permanent damage in one part of the body. Common are ulcers in the skin and lesions on ligaments, joints or on bones. These are painful, but tertiary syphilis is more serious if it attacks heart, blood vessels or nervous system. It can then kill, blind, paralyze, cripple or render insane.

Tests

Syphilis is not easy to diagnose. Its symptoms are often mild or indistinct. Testing sores for bacteria, or blood for antibodies, is necessary. Neither always works, so repeat tests are important.

Treatment

This involves antibiotics – usually penicillin. Given in primary or secondary stages, it completely cures most cases. Tests and examination often last more than 2 years afterward, to make sure the cure is complete. In the latent and even tertiary stages, syphilis can still be eradicated and further damage halted; but existing tertiary-stage damage often cannot be repaired.

11

Sites of syphilis symptoms

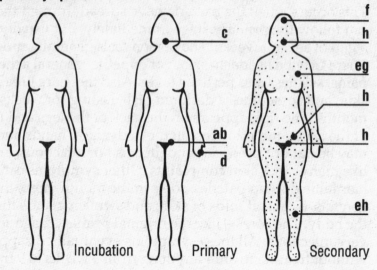

Incubation   Primary   Secondary

The primary sore may develop
in or on the:
a genitals,
b anus,
c mouth, or sometimes
d hands.

Secondary-stage symptoms include:
e skin rash,
f patches of loose hair,
g swollen lymph nodes, and
h secondary sores in the mouth,
   nose, throat, genitals or skin.

In the latent stage syphilis may be
present throughout the body, but
there are no symptoms.
Tertiary syphilis can attack almost
any part of the body.

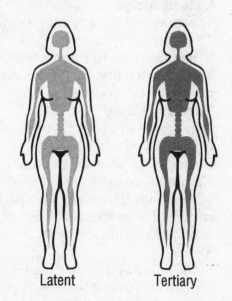

Latent   Tertiary

Gonorrhea

Gonorrhea (sometimes nicknamed 'the clap') has become
epidemic in recent years – partly because it is so easy for a
woman to have it without knowing it. There are now nearly a
million reported cases in the United States every year, and the
true figure is probably many times that. Several infections in a
person in a single year are not uncommon. Worldwide, there
are about 25 million cases.

Causes

Like syphilis, gonorrhea:

a) is caused by a bacterium that thrives in the warm moist lining of urethra, vagina, rectum or mouth;

b) is normally only passed on by sexual contact, but may be sometimes by close body contact or by inheritance from an infected mother; and

c) cannot be picked up from objects (though perhaps it can be carried by pubic lice, which can sometimes be picked up from objects such as lavatory seats).

Unlike syphilis, the form of sexual contact involved is normally only genital or anal intercourse. Oral contact does not often pass on gonorrhea; if it does, it is usually fellatio, rather than cunnilingus, that is responsible. (But some scientists allow the possibility of infection through kissing.)

Symptoms in men

These are considered first, as they are more noticeable. Incubation is usually under a week, but can be up to a month. It is followed by:

a) discomfort inside the penis;

b) thick discharge, usually yellow-green, from the penis tip; and

c) a burning feeling on urinating. Later there may be swollen glands, urethral abscess, and swollen infected testes (with danger of sterility).

Symptoms in women

In women, incubation is longer, and the eventual symptoms, if any, are much less severe or identifiable. There may be discomfort on urinating, more frequent urination and vaginal discharge. The discharge is distinctively yellow and unpleasant in smell – but this may be unnoticed due to the typically small quantities involved. Often there are no symptoms. So up to 90% of cases in women occur without the woman being aware of the disease. But she is still just as infectious – and just as much at risk. For if untreated, the infection may spread (see diagram overleaf) to:

a) glands around the vaginal entrance, making them swell, sometimes as large as a golf ball;

b) the rectum (because of the closeness of the two openings), causing inflammation and perhaps a discharge; and/or

c) the cervix, uterus, Fallopian tubes and pelvic interior. Fallopian infection can result in fever, abdominal pain, backaches, sickness, painful or excessive periods and pain during intercourse. If not treated quickly, sterility can result. It

11

can also kill mother and fetus, by causing any pregnancy to be ectopic (see p.105). Even where gonorrhea does not affect the Fallopian tubes, it can result in premature birth, umbilical cord inflammation, maternal fever and blindness in the child. Finally, gonorrhea can spread to the bloodstream and infect bone joints, causing arthritis. If oral contact results in infection, it is mainly as a throat disorder that is often not recognized as gonorrhea. It is also unlikely to infect others, because the lymph tissues where the bacteria can survive are deep in the tonsil area.

Test and treatment

Gonorrhea is diagnosed by laboratory analysis of any discharge or of a smear from an affected part. Treatment is with antibiotics – usually penicillin, though many forms of gonorrhea are becoming more resistant to it. Qualified medical surveillance is vital. Alcohol can interfere with the cure.

Spread of infection through the reproductive tract

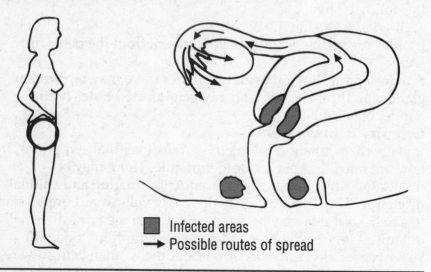

Infected areas
→ Possible routes of spread

Other STDs

Soft chancre (chancroid) is caused by a bacillus (a rod-shaped bacterium), and is contracted sexually (usually by intercourse). After 3 to 5 days' incubation, it generally produces an ulcer on the genitals and painful swollen glands (but either sex can carry the infection without symptoms). Treatment is with antibiotics and other drugs.

Chlamydia is a bacterial infection similar to gonorrhea, and is responsible for up to 25% of the cases of pelvic inflammatory disease each year in the United States. Symptoms may include an unusual yellowish discharge, pelvic pain, pain or bleeding during intercourse and/or fever. It can also cause burning urination. Treatment is generally with antibiotics. Your partner must also be treated.

Lymphogranuloma venereum is caused by a very small bacterium, and can be contracted from infected bedding and clothing as well as (more usually) from sexual intercourse. After 5 to 21 days' incubation, it produces a small genital blister or ulcer. Later there can be internal complications. Treatment is with antibiotics.

Granuloma inguinale is caused by a bacillus, and is contracted sexually (usually by intercourse). After 1 to 3 weeks' incubation, it produces bright red, painless genital sores. Treatment is with antibiotics.

Nonspecific Urethritis (NSU)

NSU is the most common of all sexual disorders in men, but in women the symptoms are often insignificant or hard to diagnose. Also, it is not a sexually transmitted disease in the strict sense, or even necessarily an infection, since it does not always seem to require intercourse with an infected person to develop. In fact, its cause is uncertain – as its name implies. It may be due to an unidentified microorganism, or possibly just to a reaction between the penis and the chemistry of the vagina. Certainly it can develop in two people who have never had intercourse with anyone else. It often seems linked with changes in sex habits. Symptoms in men resemble gonorrhea: discharge and discomfort when urinating. It can be very recurrent, and untreated it can spread to other parts of the body, sometimes even causing permanent damage to joints and eyes.

Incidence of STD

Statistics from state, county and municipal public health agencies show marked changes in the pattern of sexually transmitted disease in the US over the last few years. Increased public awareness of the dangers of STDs, resulting from publicity about AIDS, may account for some changes. For example, the trend for gonorrhea has been downward, and among the reasons cited for this have been improved public

11

awareness, increased use of condoms, and a decrease in promiscuity among American women – all due, it is believed, to higher awareness of AIDS. Gonorrhea is most prevalent in the south (with some of the poorest and least-educated populations) and the east (with large urban centers). The incidence of syphilis rose through the 1980s, with a downturn apparent only since the beginning of the 1990s. The rise has been national, but the heaviest concentration of cases is in the south – again, the population most affected has the least education, the poorest living conditions, and the lowest level of access to care. Accompanying the rise in primary and secondary syphilis has been a rise in congenital syphilis. This can be prevented, but requires good prenatal care and follow-up by health-care providers.

Reported cases of AIDS across the United States rose steadily through the 1980s to more than 45,000 in 1991. The pattern of known deaths from AIDS is different, showing a rise from a negligible number in 1981 to above 25,000 in 1988, and then a fall in 1991 to just over 15,000. The northern states show the lowest incidence; the highest is right across the southern half of the US. Initial awareness of HIV/AIDS brought a renewed willingness to use condoms and a decrease in promiscuity among women, but recent polls indicate that among teens and college-aged women, condom use and concern has not continued to increase with public awareness of AIDS.

Symptoms

The diagrams show possible signs of STD in women. All these symptoms usually have some other cause. But do not delay in getting proper medical advice. If symptoms disappear, it may just mean that the infection has progressed naturally to its next stage. You may still have a disease; and you may still be able to infect others.

Possible symptoms in the genital area include:

a a sore, rash or ulcer on, in or around the genitals;

b similarly, a sore, ras, or ulcer, on, in or around anus;

c unusual vaginal discharge;

d pain or a burning feeling on urinating;

e increased frequency of urinating;

f itching or soreness of vagina or vulva; and

g swollen glands in the groin.

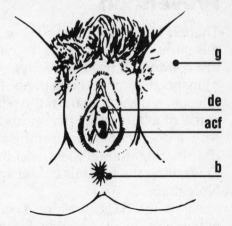

Possible symptoms in the head and body include:

h a sore, ulce, or rash on or in the mouth (or sometimes the nose);

i an eye infection;

j loss of patches of hair;

k persistent sore throat after fellatio;

l a rash on the body;

m sores in soft folds of skin;

n swollen glands in the armpits;

o a sore, ulcer or rash on the fingers or hand.

Possible symptoms if infection spreads up the reproductive tract include fever and:

p nausea;

q backache;

r abdominal pain;

s pain during intercourse;

t painful or excessive periods;

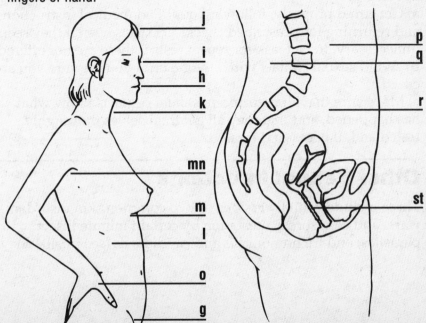

11

Prevention

There is no immunity to STD or vaccine against it. But various measures can help reduce the chances of infection:
a) a condom, if used correctly;
b) inspection of the male penis, for an ulcer or sore, or for infectious discharge from the penis tip;
c) use of a 'morning after' antibiotic dose, under prescription from a doctor or clinic (but this may be very difficult to obtain);
d) urinating immediately after intercourse; and possibly
e) washing the genitals before and after intercourse.
Note that:
a) As an anti-STD measure, a condom needs to be put on before any sex play begins. It then guards fairly effectively against STDs.
b) To wash out the vagina after intercourse, a low-pressure douche can be used. But no vaginal washing should be carried out if the contraceptive method used involves a foam, jelly, or cream, whether alone or with diaphragm or condom.
c) To check a penis for discharge, roll back the foreskin, if necessary, and squeeze the penis firmly – preferably before it becomes erect. One or two drops of thick white, gray or colored fluid appearing at the tip, may indicate infection. Clear liquid is usually just urine or semen.
Equally important is to stop infection spreading if you do develop it:
a) Get cured properly, following qualified medical instructions, and returning for prescribed checks and tests even if they seem unnecessary. In fact, ask for repeat tests if these are not offered.
b) Avoid sexual contact with anyone until you are sure you are cured.
c) Make sure that all your recent sexual contacts know what has happened, and that they all get themselves thoroughly tested and, if necessary, treated.

Other Sexual Infections

These include genital versions of two common skin disorders – warts and cold sores; infestation by certain minute insect parasites; and trichomoniasis and candidiasis (see pp.404-5).

Genital warts

These are fairly common and very contagious. They are spread by sexual contact, perhaps caused by a virus, and appear, after 1 to 6 months' incubation, on, in or around genitals or anus. They are usually cured by repeated use of a resin application. If this fails, they may have to be burned off with chemicals or electricity.

Genital herpes

Genital herpes, or cold sores, are contagious. The virus responsible is thought to lie dormant in the skin for long periods. When activated, it causes a genital or anal sore that weeps colorless fluid and forms a scab. There is no sure treatment (though bathing in salt solution may help), but the sore usually disappears after about 10 days.

Infestations

These are passed on by sexual or sometimes other close body contact, and are not especially common.

a) Scabies, or 'the itch', is caused by a tiny mite, which mainly lives on or around the genitals. The female mite burrows beneath the skin to lay her eggs. The symptoms – itchy lumps and tracks – become noticeable after 4 to 6 weeks' incubation. They can occur between the fingers, on buttocks and wrists, and in the armpits, as well as on the genitals. The itching is worse in warm conditions (eg in bed).

b) Pubic lice, or 'crabs', are genital versions of lice that can also occur in other hairy parts of the body. They feed on blood, and cause itching that can be severe. Treatment of both parasites involves painting the hair-bearing parts with appropriate chemicals.

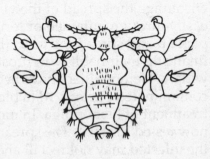

a Scabies mite, very highly magnified

b Pubic louse, highly magnified

11

AIDS (Acquired Immune Deficiency Syndrome)

The disease AIDS first came to public attention as a 'plague' afflicting San Francisco's homosexual community during the late 1970s. But the virus that causes AIDS, though only identified and named in 1983, may have existed as long ago as 1959. It will infect anyone, whatever their sexual orientation. The virus is present in the body fluids (blood, saliva, semen and vaginal secretions) of an infected person. It is transmitted by: sexual activity; by mother to baby during childbirth; by blood transfusion; and by the use of infected needles.

The human immunodeficiency virus (HIV) attacks the body's immune system, but AIDS does not develop immediately after initial infection. Some individuals who are HIV-positive do not show any symptoms for years and may never show any. They are, however, still capable of infecting others. There are several recognized stages. Stress or new infections may precipitate progression.

There is no vaccine or cure for AIDS yet. Drugs that slow down the growth rate of the virus are effective in dealing with some of the symptoms and may delay further progression.

Risk groups

There are well-defined, high-risk groups for infection with HIV. These include male homosexuals, drug users, prostitutes and hemophiliacs who may have received transfusions of infected blood. Once established, the virus can be passed on through heterosexual relationships to people who appear to be outside any high-risk group. Promiscuity and anal intercourse encourage the spread of the virus. The virus in semen passes easily through inflamed or torn membranes. Drug users may pick up and spread the virus through shared needles. Those financing their habit with prostitution spread infection more widely. Hemophiliacs have become infected because of contaminated Factor VIII (a blood derivative) used in the treatment of hemophilia. In most countries, donated blood is now tested for HIV. The spread of AIDS is hard to measure: the infected may not feel ill and may unwittingly continue passing the virus on. Anyone who participates in sexual activity and has more than one partner is at risk. The only absolute protection is celibacy. Condoms, used correctly, can prevent transmission of the virus.

HIV-positive

Blood tests to detect infection with HIV are available. By about 12 weeks after contact it is usually possible to say whether or not someone has contracted the virus. There may be flu-like symptoms lasting for up to 14 days, but there are frequently no symptoms.

Being diagnosed as HIV-positive can be a frightening experience; apart from worries about when AIDS will develop, patients are likely to suffer discrimination in employment and life insurance, and possible loss of social and economic status. It is therefore important for patients to seek counseling and for their families and friends to offer love and support. To be diagnosed as HIV-positive is not an immediate death sentence. In one survey, 75% of HIV-positive men were well and symptom-free two years after diagnosis.

Persistent generalized lymphadenopathy (PGL)

About 30% of people with HIV develop persistent swelling of the lymph glands. This is often accompanied by tiredness and malaise. Patients with PGL may be advised to avoid stress as much as possible and to keep to a healthy diet in order to prevent the condition from worsening.

AIDS-related complex (ARC)

A proportion of patients infected with HIV go on to develop definite symptoms of immune system damage: thrush, skin disorders, fever, diarrhea, weight loss and constant tiredness.

AIDS

The development of the disease is the last stage. The immune system is destroyed, making sufferers vulnerable to a variety of infections that are normally trivial but now potentially fatal. In about one-third of patients there are symptoms caused by infection of the brain. An otherwise rare tumor, Kaposi's sarcoma, is a common symptom of AIDS; it is sometimes the first symptom. Certain symptoms and infections can be treated, but the underlying damage to the immune system cannot be repaired. AIDS is a terminal illness.

Pregnancy and AIDS

Pregnancy in a woman with HIV can be a two-fold tragedy: the baby may be born infected, and the mother runs an increased risk of developing ARC or AIDS. Many of the babies born to HIV-positive mothers are infected at birth; the virus might also be transmitted in breast milk. Babies reach the late stages more rapidly than adults because their immune systems are immature.

11

What is Cancer?

Cancer is one of several disorders which can result when the process of cell division in a person's body gets out of control. Such disorders produce tissue growths called 'tumors'. A cancer is a certain kind of tumor.

Cancer attacks one in every five people.

Normal cell division

The body is constantly producing new cells for the purposes of growth and repair – about 500,000 million daily. It does this by cell division: one parent cell divides to form two new cells. When this process is going correctly, the new cells show the same characteristics as the tissue from which they originate. They are capable of carrying out the functions that the body requires that tissue to perform. They do not migrate to parts of the body where they do not belong; and if they were placed in such a part artificially they might not survive.

Tumors

In a tumor, the process of cell division has gone wrong. Cells multiply in an uncoordinated way, independent of the normal control mechanisms. They produce a new growth in the body that does not fulfill a useful function. This is a tumor, or 'neoplasm'. A tumor is often felt as a hard lump, because its cells are more closely packed than normal.

Tumors may be 'benign' or 'malignant'. A cancer is a malignant tumor. That is, it may go on growing until it threatens the continued existence of the body.

Benign tumors

In a benign tumor:

a) the cells reproduce in a way that is still fairly orderly;

b) they are only slightly different from the cells of the surrounding tissue;

c) their growth is slow and may stop spontaneously;

d) the tumor is surrounded by a capsule of fibrous tissue, and does not invade the normal tissue; and

e) its cells do not spread through the body.

A wart is a benign tumor. Benign tumors are not fatal unless the space they take up exerts pressure on nearby organs which proves fatal. This usually only happens with some benign tumors in the skull.

Malignant tumors

In a malignant tumor, the cells reproduce in a completely

disorderly fashion. Characteristics include:

a) the cells differ considerably from those of the surrounding tissue (generally, they show less specialization);

b) the tumor's growth is rapid, compared with the surrounding tissue;

c) the tumor has no surrounding capsule, and can therefore invade and destroy adjacent tissue; and

d) the original tumor is able to spread to other parts of the body by metastasis (see p.431) and produce secondary growth there. A malignant tumor is usually fatal if untreated, because of its destructive action on normal tissue.

Biopsy

A biopsy is the most certain way of distinguishing between benign and malignant tumors. A piece of the tumor is surgically removed and then studied under a microscope.

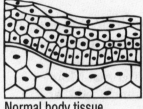 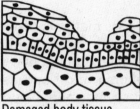 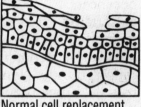

Normal body tissue　　Damaged body tissue　　Normal cell replacement

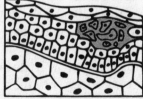 

Abnormal malignant growth　Loss of basement membrane integrity

Causes of Cancer

Chromosome damage

In cancerous cells, the characteristics of malignant growth are passed on from one generation to another. This means that the genetic code must have been damaged. This, in fact, is seen if the chromosomes of cancerous cells are examined. Normal cells have 46 chromosomes arranged in 23 pairs. Almost all cancer cells are abnormal in the number and/or structure of these chromosomes.

11

Normal deviance

Cells with genetic defects appear in the body every day; so many millions of cells are being made that some mistakes are inevitable. But most die almost immediately because they are too faulty to survive or because they are recognized as abnormal and eaten by white blood corpuscles. Others are only slightly defective, and not malignant. Only very rarely do malignant cells survive and reproduce successfully.

Appearance of cancer in a person may simply be due to this unlucky chance. Alternatively, it may be that the body has 'immunity' to such malignant cells, and that this sometimes breaks down. This would explain why cancer can sometimes remain 'dormant' in a person for many years.

Special factors

A few factors have been recognized that make cancerous damage in cells more likely. But they only explain a proportion of cancers.

a) Certain viruses can pass malignant tumors from one animal to another, and the same may occur in humans. Viruses have been implicated in the development of cervical and liver cancer, Burkitt's lymphoma, and Kaposi's sarcoma. More usually, human cancer seems not to be virus induced – and therefore not infectious.

b) Without protection, X-rays can cause skin cancer, and the resulting radiation may cause leukemia. Ultraviolet rays (as in prolonged exposure to intense sunlight) can also cause skin cancer.

c) Some experts believe that continued physical irritation of the skin or mucous membranes can cause cancer (not just accelerate it).

d) Smoking is an established cause of lung, bladder and other cancers.

e) Many industrial chemicals are known to cause cancer.

f) Certain fungi, such as *aspergillus* – found in old buildings or decaying plant matter – carry cancer-producing toxins.

Correlative factors

Some individuals are more likely to develop cancer than others. Factors include:

a) Heredity. Actual cancerous growths are not inherited, but a predisposition for cancer can be passed on. It may be that some inherited characteristics make a person's cells more likely to become malignant.

b) Age. Most cancers occur in the 50 to 60 age group. However, children and adolescents are susceptible to leukemia, brain tumors, and sarcomas of the bone.

c) Gender. In almost all countries, cancer occurs more frequently in men than in women.

d) Geographical location – for some unknown reason, gastric cancer is most frequent in coastal countries with cold climates.

e) Cultural habits – cancer of the penis is much less common in societies where circumcision is usual.

Cancer Growth

Cell division

Generally, cancerous cells cannot divide faster than normal cells. But normal cell division reaches its maximum rate only in times of injury and repair. Cancerous growths are continually producing cells at this maximum rate without check. They are less successful than normal tissue could be, because many of the faulty cancerous cells die. Nevertheless, the result is that cancerous growths grow faster than normal tissue.

Metastasis

Metastasis is the process by which cancerous cells travel from the original (primary) cancer site to other parts of the body. It occurs when cancerous cells get caught up in the flow of blood or lymph. The cells are carried along in the vessels, until they lodge in another part of the body. If they succeed in establishing themselves there, this becomes a new (secondary) cancer site. If a secondary site gets large enough, it can also metastasize in turn. Cancer that has metastasized along the lymph vessels normally sets up its secondary sites in the glands. Cancer that has metastasized in the bloodstream sets up secondary sites in the bones, lungs, and liver. Cancers in the brain do not metastasize but cancers elsewhere can metastasize to the brain. Some sites are more receptive than others. The most common locations for secondary growths are the bones, brain, lungs, kidneys and adrenal glands. Others are much rarer. A cancer can also spread through the body simply by the process of growth.

Sites of Cancer

11

Cancers can grow almost anywhere in the body, but the most common sites are shown in the diagram. Cancers are classified by the kind of tissue in which the primary growth occurred. Tumors originating in the 'epithdial' cells (eg skin, mucous membrane and glands) are called carcinomas; those in connective tissue (eg muscle and bone), sarcomas. Secondary tumors are classified by the kind of primary tumor that they came from. This is possible because metastasized growths still show some of the characteristics of the tissue from which they originated. Cancer has become vastly more prevalent in the present century: in 1900 it was the seventh main cause of death in the United States; today it is the second. (Some experts believe this is simply because people are living longer – likelihood of cancerous growths increases with age.) Nevertheless, some types of cancer have shown a dramatic fall in recent years. The decrease in stomach cancer, for example, may be linked with changes in techniques of food preservation.

Most common cancers
(approximate percentages)

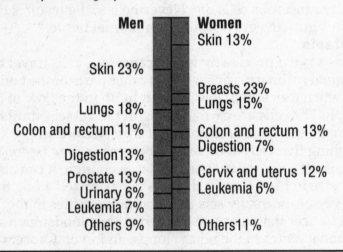

Men	Women
	Skin 13%
Skin 23%	
	Breasts 23%
Lungs 18%	Lungs 15%
Colon and rectum 11%	Colon and rectum 13%
Digestion13%	Digestion 7%
Prostate 13%	Cervix and uterus 12%
Urinary 6%	Leukemia 6%
Leukemia 7%	
Others 9%	Others11%

Symptoms

Symptoms of cancer include:
a) any unusual bleeding or discharge from mouth, genitals or anus (including, in women, bleeding from the breast and menstrual bleeding between periods);
b) any lump or thickening or swelling on the body surface, or any swelling of one limb;
c) any increase in size or change in color or appearance in a mole or wart;
d) a sore that will not heal normally;
e) persistent constipation, diarrhea or indigestion that is unusual for the person;

f) hoarseness or dry cough that lasts more than three weeks;
g) difficulty in swallowing or urinating; and
h) sudden unexplained weight loss or persistent pain.
If you notice any of these symptoms, or believe you may be at risk, see your doctor. The cause of any symptoms may well be something else, but if it is cancer, quick diagnosis is essential.

Treatment

Treatments for cancer have a good chance of success only if the tumor is still localized. Early diagnosis is vital. Once a tumor has metastasized, successful treatment is almost impossible.

Surgery
Surgical removal of localized malignant tumors at an early stage is the only completely successful form of treatment known at present. In later stages, surgery may be attempted in conjunction with other techniques.

Radiotherapy
Cancer cells are killed by radiation more easily than normal cells. Radiotherapy seeks to destroy cancerous tissue by focusing a stream of radiation on it. This can be done only if the cancer is still localized and can be destroyed without causing radiation damage to the rest of the body. The rays used are either X-rays or those of radioactive materials such as radium or cobalt.

Chemotherapy
This is treatment by the administration of chemicals. Again, the major difficulty is finding drugs that will destroy cancer cells without harming normal cells. Three main types of chemicals are used: those that interfere with the cancer cells' reproductive processes; those that interfere with the cells' metabolic processes; those that increase the natural resistance of the body to the tumor cells. These chemicals can affect the whole of the body, specific regions, or the tumors themselves, depending on how they are applied.

Hormone therapy
This is used mainly for tumors of the endocrine glands and related organs. It is also useful in the treatment of metastases originating from these areas (eg in women, against disseminated breast cancer). Success depends on whether the cancerous cells still have the specialized relationship with the hormone that the original tissue had. In women, hormone therapy may include removal of the ovaries.

11

Cancer of the Reproductive Tract

Cervix

Cervical cancer is on the decline. Nevertheless, about 2 women in 100 get it, and one of these dies from it. It can occur at any age, but 45-50 is most common. A possible symptom is unusual vaginal bleeding, eg between periods, after intercourse, or more than 6 months after the menopause. But analysis of the cervical tissue is the only sure evidence. The well-known 'Pap' smear test involves the painless gathering of a few sample cells on the end of a wooden spatula (the physician may well do a pelvic examination to check the uterus and ovaries at the same time). The sample is sent to a specialist laboratory, fixed in alcohol, stained in solution, and examined for abnormal cells. In 1,000 smears, 20 might show some abnormality, and perhaps 3 the early signs of cancer. (The other abnormalities will include signs of vaginal infection, etc.) A woman should have such a test within 6 months of first having sexual intercourse. Then the smear test should be repeated every 1-3 years. (Rarely, cancer appears after a negative smear.) Also, there is a link between cervical cancer and a sexually transmitted wart virus, Human Papilloma Virus (HPV). A condom reduces risk. If cell changes that might lead to cancer are found, a repeat smear may be taken, followed by a larger specimen using curettage or a tiny punch. If cancer is confirmed, alternatives include conization or hysterectomy. (In conization, cervical tissue is cut away and the cervix stitched; healing is rapid, with little pain and usually no after-effects.) Other treatments include laser treatment, diathermy (heat treatment) and cryosurgery (cold treatment), all of which may help to avoid extensive surgery. The type of treatment chosen depends on the type of tumor. Once malignant growth has begun to spread, a hysterectomy is carried out. This method has shown a high success rate in eliminating cancers that are diagnosed early enough. Very advanced cases may also need radiotherapy or further surgery.

Uterus

Cancer here usually only occurs in older women (typically 50-60). The diabetic and obese are susceptible, and it can run in a family. Tumor growth is slow; bleeding symptoms are significant. Diagnosis is by curettage of the uterus under anesthetic; treatment by hysterectomy and X-ray therapy. If treated early enough, 80% of patients survive more than 5 years.

Ovaries

This accounts for approximately 5% of cancers in women; it is more frequent after 40, especially after the menopause. Its slow growth is hard to detect; enlargement of the ovaries shows up on pelvic examination, though only 4% of enlargements are cancerous. Pelvic examinations every 5 years should catch them in time.

Vulva

Cancer of the vulva is rare. It usually occurs only in older women and is preceded by long-standing vulval itching or an ulcer. In 99% of cases these symptoms do not signify cancer.

Vagina

Rare, except in girls and women whose mothers were prescribed the drug diethylstilbestrol (DES) in pregnancy.

Cancer of the cervix and uterus

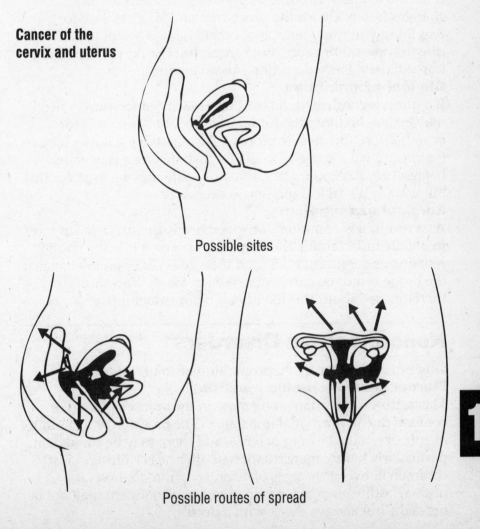

Possible sites

Possible routes of spread

11

Breast Cancer

Almost a quarter of cancer in women is breast cancer, and 5% of women contract it. If it is caught before metastasis, 9 out of 10 survive. But metastasis can occur within a month of the tumor appearing. Despite medical advance, the death rate from breast cancer has been steady for more than 40 years.

Who gets breast cancer?

The disease is most common in women aged 40 to 60. Heredity, diet and estrogen levels in the body are under investigation as possible significant factors. Research suggests that early first childbirth, and breastfeeding, might make breast cancer less likely in the mother.

Self-examination

It is vital to check the breasts once every month for any changes (see p.334 for the procedure and what to look for). Anything you find – lumps or other changes – will usually be due to some other cause, not cancer; but check with a doctor immediately. Early detection can save your life.

Clinical examination

If a lump is confirmed, it is not necessarily cancerous. A needle may be inserted into the lump, to draw out some cells for examination (fine needle biopsy). Alternatively a larger biopsy (see p.429) will be taken, to distinguish between cancer and a benign tumor. Again, sometimes a needle may be used for this, but usually a surgical incision is necessary.

Surgical examination

As a result, it is common, for speed of treatment, for a surgeon to obtain and examine the suspicious tissue while the patient remains under anesthetic – and then go on to operate at once if the tissue is judged cancerous (see pp.438-9). You should therefore see about this likelihood before any biopsy.

Noncancerous Disorders

Other disorders have symptoms similar to breast cancer.

Fibroadenosis (chronic mastitis)

This features a permanent increase in the breast's glandular content, due to hormonal imbalance. The breast may feel lumpy or rubbery, all over or in patches, and there may be some pain, particularly before menstruation or after heavy lifting. Most common between the ages of 40 and 55, fibroadenosis is a normal bodily change for many women. Treatment may not be needed – but always check with a doctor.

Cysts and benign tumors

Perhaps 75% of breast lumps are nonmalignant. Breast cysts are small sacs in the breast tissue, filled with liquid, and usually harmless. Most common in women aged 35 to 45, they do not always need treatment. Benign tumors may swell until pressure on nerves or neighboring tissues causes pain and requires their removal; but they cannot invade or destroy other tissue as cancer can.

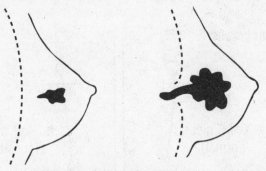

Growth of malignant tumor

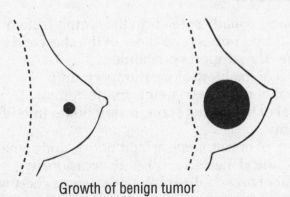

Growth of benign tumor

Screening Techniques

Mammography

This is a common diagnostic technique that is rapidly being introduced as a routine check for women over 50. It involves placing the breasts in direct contact with an X-ray plate. Usually, two views of each breast are taken. Malignancy shows up as an irregular opaque patch in the breast. Mammography alone is not considered sufficiently reliable for certain diagnosis, but in combination with clinical examination and biopsy, about 97% of lumps examined can be correctly diagnosed. The test takes only half an hour.

11

Thermography

This is another method helpful in the detection of breast cancer. In a normal person, 45% of the heat given off by the skin is infrared radiation. Thermography records in a photograph the way in which this heat is given off. A malignant growth emits more heat than the surrounding tissue, and so shows up as a light patch on the photograph. Thermography, however, is less successful than mammography and clinical examination.

Typical thermographs

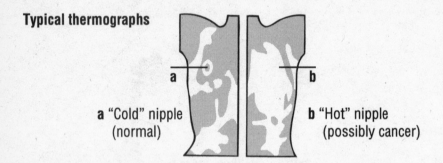

a "Cold" nipple (normal)   **b** "Hot" nipple (possibly cancer)

Treatment

Breast cancer usually spreads in the lymph system, beginning with the armpit nodes (also those of the chest and spine). This determines the surgical possibilities:

a) removal of the lump alone (lumpectomy);

b) removal of the breast (simple mastectomy);

c) removal of breast and some armpit nodes (modified radical mastectomy);

d) removal of breast, some armpit nodes, and some chest wall muscles (radical mastectomy); and, occasionally,

e) removal of breast, all armpit nodes, some chest wall muscles, and some chest nodes (superradical mastectomy).

Which surgery is chosen depends on:

a) the decision about which to minimize – deformity or the risk of recurrence;

b) surgical opinion: eg does simple mastectomy with radiotherapy give results just as good as a 'radical'; and, especially,

c) information about the tumor's size, type, position, and spread.

This last must mainly come from actual surgical observation;

and as a result a patient can go under anesthetic not knowing how much of her body she will lose. Preliminary diagnostic surgery, though, may be impossible to arrange and may take up vital life-saving time. Surgery may, as noted, be accompanied by drugs and/or radiotherapy (see p.433). But again there are difficult issues of effectiveness versus side effects, and of timing. The more extensive operations are followed by physiotherapy, to minimize the effects of muscle loss on arm movement and breathing abilities.

Following a mastectomy, some women choose to wear a breast prosthesis. There are several types available, and some are fitted so successfully that it is possible to wear a swimsuit without the prosthesis being noticeable. The art is matching the other breast, so that there is no obvious difference.

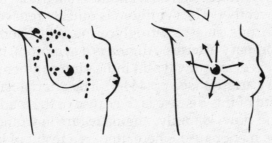

Lymph nodes near the breast, and likely routes of spread in breast cancer

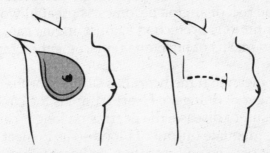

Simple mastectomy: area removed and stitching

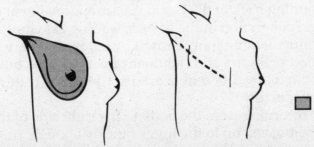

Radical mastectomy: area removed and stitching

11

Angina and Heart Failure

Angina pectoris

Angina is the Latin word for 'sore throat'. Although that meaning persists in the name Vincent's angina – a severe infective ulceration of the tonsils – nowadays the word is used almost exclusively to refer to the pain or gripping sensation felt in the center of the chest when more work is demanded of the heart muscle than its blood supply, through the coronary arteries, can support. Coronary artery blood carries oxygen and fuel (glucose) to the heart muscle, and if this is insufficient, pain-stimulating substances are produced by the muscle. The pain can vary in intensity and may be severe and frightening. It often spreads up the neck and down the left arm. It is brought on by physical exertion, emotional tension, a heavy meal or cold weather. The symptom is quickly relieved by resting or by drugs, such as nitroglycerine, which temporarily widens the coronary arteries. Angina is a symptom, not a disease, but it is nearly always an indication of atherosclerosis of the coronary arteries (see pp.444-5). The arterial narrowing that is a feature of this disease is the cause of the inadequacy of coronary blood flow. Happily, angina is rare in women up to the time of the menopause. Thereafter, as a result of loss of estrogen hormone, it becomes increasingly common. Eventually, the risk of angina becomes as great in women as it is in men. Continuous protection against angina can, however, be achieved by means of hormone replacement therapy.

Heart failure

This does not mean that the heart has stopped or that it is in imminent danger of doing so. Heart failure is the condition in which, as a result of disease, the heart is no longer capable of producing an adequate output of blood so as to meet the needs of the body for oxygen and nutrition. In heart failure the blood flow to the tissues and to the lungs is diminished and slowed. The damming back of the blood causes engorgement of the veins and congestion of the tissues, leading to symptoms. Heart failure is commonly caused by coronary artery disease, high blood pressure, and rheumatic heart disease, but may result from many different heart disorders. The features may vary considerably.

If blood returning from the body to the right side of the heart cannot be pushed on to the lungs quickly enough, this is called right heart failure. The result is blueness (cyanosis) of the skin and accumulation of fluid (edema) causing ankle swelling, enlargement of the liver, and, in severe cases, a considerable accumulation of fluid within the abdomen (ascites).

When the left side of the heart is unable to clear the blood from the lungs quickly enough, there is fluid accumulation in the lungs. This is called left heart failure. The main feature is breathlessness. This may occur on mild exertion or even when the affected person is at rest. There may be attacks of sudden breathlessness during the night. As the condition worsens, the tendency to breathlessness increases. Eventually, the degree of disability becomes extreme and in both right and left heart failure there is severely restricted activity.

Heart failure can usually be helped, especially if the underlying cause of the heart damage is remediable.

The drug digitalis is valuable in increasing the strength and effectiveness of the heartbeat (contraction), and its use often greatly improves the condition. Other stimulating drugs, such as norepinephrine, may also be used. Fluid in the lungs and the tissues can be removed by the use of diuretic drugs, which greatly increase the urinary output. Free fluid in the abdomen may sometimes be sucked out through a wide-bore needle.

Heart Attack

In women, the estrogen hormones protect against the principal obstructive arterial disease that causes heart attacks – atherosclerosis. This means that, before the menopause, heart attack is comparatively rare in women. Unfortunately, unless hormone replacement therapy is used, this protection is lost after the menopause. The incidence of heart attacks rises steeply in post-menopausal women until it equals that of men. The mortality from heart attack in post-menopausal women is more than four times that from breast cancer and uterine lining cancer combined.

A coronary thrombosis, or heart attack, is usually described by doctors as a myocardial infarction. This is the result of an obstruction to blood flow in one of the branches of the two coronary arteries through which the heart muscle is supplied with blood. Because it must beat (tighten or contract) continuously, the heart has a considerable oxygen and fuel (sugar) requirement. Any substantial diminution in this fuel supply to any part of the muscle interferes not only with its ability to function but even with its survival as a living tissue. Atherosclerosis is present, to some degree, in most adults in the western world and affects particularly the coronary

11

arteries. The disease increases in both sexes with age. This is why coronary thrombosis is responsible for about half of all deaths in western countries and is generally regarded in medical circles as the major problem in preventive medicine. Blockage of a main coronary artery branch (coronary thrombosis) occurs when blood is prompted to clot by a roughened plaque of fatty, degenerative cholesterol containing material called atheroma in the inner lining of the vessel. Prior to the thrombosis, these atherosclerotic plaques cause no symptoms, nor any other indication of their presence, until they narrow the artery so severely – to less than half its normal width – that the blood flow is insufficient to permit full exertion.

At rest, the person concerned may seem normal, but a fixed amount of exertion causes the heart pain of angina pectoris (see above).

When total blockage occurs, part of the heart muscle loses its blood supply and dies. Depending on the size of the artery blocked, this dead area may involve the full thickness of the heart wall, or only part. The heart cannot continue to function as a pump if more than a certain proportion of the muscle is destroyed. Blockage of a major branch, with destruction of about half of the muscle in the main, left, pumping chamber, is almost always immediately fatal. Previous smaller attacks make death more likely.

Coronary thrombosis usually causes a severe pain, or sense of pressure, in the center of the chest. The pain often spreads through to the back, up into the neck, or down either arm.

Areas where pain can occur during a heart attack

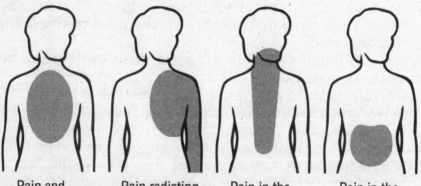

Pain and pressure in central chest area

Pain radiating down the left arm from the shoulder

Pain in the jaw and back

Pain in the upper abdomen

There is a horrifying sense that one is about to die, and often extreme restlessness. The pulse is weak, difficult to feel and often irregular. Sometimes it is very slow. Severe pain is not always a feature. In less major cases pain may be absent, and there is evidence that up to 20 percent of mild coronaries are not recognized as such by those affected. This means that there are millions of people who, because of previous unrecognized attacks, are much more vulnerable than average. Half of those who die from a particular attack do so from heart stoppage (cardiac arrest) within three or four hours of onset, so there is always great urgency to get a person with a coronary thrombosis to a hospital with minimum delay. Many who might have been saved have died because they did not recognize or believe that they had a life-threatening condition. Factors that increase the risk of coronary thrombosis are, or should be, well known. They are:

a) smoking;

b) lack of exercise;

c) overeating with resultant obesity;

d) a high-fat diet;

e) a lack of adequate levels of the antioxidant vitamins C and E; and

f) parents who died of arterial disease.

Only the last factor is beyond individual control, and there is now ample evidence that people able to benefit by advice are now reducing the likelihood of having a heart attack by behaving accordingly. Since these facts have been widely known, the incidence of coronary thrombosis has declined significantly among certain groups, although many individuals continue risky behavior such as cigarette smoking, overeating and lack of exercise.

Heart disease has long been considered a "man's disease" that affects few women. Today, however, there is growing recognition among medical practitioners that, in many parts of the West, the incidence of heart disease among women is rising dramatically. The rise may be attributable to the increase in smoking among women.

11

Rheumatic Heart Disease

In spite of the name, rheumatic fever does not seriously affect the joints; although arthritis does occur, this is fleeting and does not produce any permanent disability. Rheumatic fever is important because of the frequency with which it affects the heart and because of the severity and permanence of the resulting damage. Fortunately, rheumatic fever is quite rare in the United States and Europe. In the United States the Centers for Disease Control reported in 1989 that the incidence of rheumatic fever, nationwide, had dropped to only about 1.3 cases per million. In India, however, the incidence in children can be as high as 1 in 100. The cause of the disease is unknown, but rheumatic fever always follows a throat infection with a particular strain of streptococcus – the Group A hemolytic strep. It is not caused by the normal processes of infection and is generally believed to be some form of immune system disorder induced by streptococci. No positive proof of this has yet appeared. It can always be prevented by prompt treatment of the streptococcal throat infection with antibiotics. The avoidance of overcrowding and of other conditions promoting the spread of respiratory infection is also important in prevention. The heart involvement is often insidious, and there may be no symptoms until a late stage. The most common and most serious effect on the heart is a fibrous thickening and scarring of the valves, with narrowing or leakage. This may seriously interfere with the heart's action and cause severe secondary effects, even heart failure (see above), on the health of the affected person. Heart valve replacement may be necessary.

Children who have had rheumatic fever should be protected from further damage by long-term preventive penicillin, taken until they are about 20 years of age.

Blockage and Tissue Death

Thrombosis

This means clotting of blood within an artery or vein. This is always abnormal and often dangerous as it may restrict, or even totally cut off, the flow of blood. Thrombosis, when it affects vital arteries – such as the coronary arteries to cause a coronary thrombosis (heart attack) or the arteries supplying the brain with blood to cause a cerebral thrombosis (stroke) – is a major cause of serious illness and even death. Thrombosis of arteries supplying the limbs leads to pain, disability, and, if severe, even gangrene and loss of the limb. The arteries to the intestines sometimes suffer thrombosis, leading to gangrene of a segment of bowel, calling for emergency surgery.

Thrombosis seldom occurs in healthy arteries because the smooth inner lining prevents the starting of the sequence of

events that leads to blood coagulation. Injury to a vessel,
however, or any disease process affecting the smoothness of
the inner lining may initiate thrombosis. By far the most
common cause of thrombosis is the common artery disease
atherosclerosis (see pp.448-9). Even when arteries are normal, a
clotting tendency may, rarely, occur as a result of hormonal or
biochemical changes in the blood. The tendency to thrombosis
in arteries may be greater during pregnancy, in women using
oral contraceptives, in people with cancer which has affected
vessels, and in people whose blood is more viscous than
normal (polycythemia). Thrombosis in veins is encouraged by
local pressure, inflammation (thrombophlebitis), and
stagnation of blood flow, as occurs in varicose veins. In women
in particular, predisposing factors are pregnancy, oral
contraceptives, previous episodes of vein thrombosis, obesity
and undue immobility, especially after injury or surgical
operation.
The clot (thrombus) that forms in arteries is called a white
thrombus. It is securely fixed and tends to progress in layers
until the artery is blocked. Thrombi in deep veins are red, soft,
loose and easily detached, and may break loose to cause
embolism (see below). Thrombosis may be prevented by the
use of anticoagulant drugs, such as heparin and warfarin, and
the risk can be reduced, to some extent, by small daily doses of
aspirin. The use of enzymes to break down the thrombus
(fibrinolytic therapy), as soon as possible after its formation, is
an important factor in treatment. There is good evidence that
the combination of fibrinolytic drugs, such as streptokinase,
with aspirin can significantly reduce the death rate from
coronary thrombosis.

Embolism
This is the sudden blocking of an artery by solid, semisolid or
gaseous material brought to the site of the obstruction in the
bloodstream. The object, or material, causing the embolism is
called an embolus (plural: emboli). It is always abnormal for
any nonfluid material to be present in the circulation, and
because blood proceeding through arteries encounters ever
smaller branches, such material will inevitably impact and
cause blockage, thereby depriving a part of the body of its
essential blood supply.
Many different forms of emboli can occur. Embolism is
commonly caused by blood clot emboli, often arising in the
veins and passing through the right side of the heart to enter

11

the arteries carrying blood to the lungs. It may also be caused by:

a) crystals of cholesterol from plaques of atheroma in larger arteries;

b) clumps of infected material in severe injuries;

c) air or nitrogen in diving accidents;

d) bone marrow and fat in fractures of large bones; and

e) tumor cells and other substances.

The chief danger in deep-vein thrombosis is the formation of long, soft, snaky blood clots that may become very large before breaking loose into the bloodstream. Such clots pass quickly through the right side of the heart and impact in the main branches of the arteries to the lungs. This is called pulmonary

Thrombosis

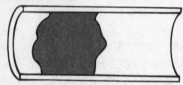

Embolism

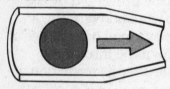

Three pulmonary embolisms and affected areas

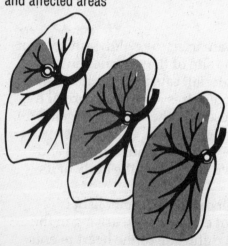

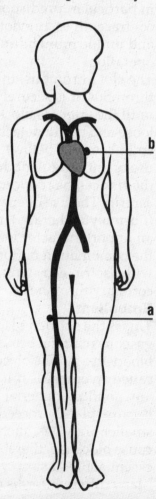

How a leg thrombosis at **a** may lead to an embolism at **b**

embolism and is a common cause of sudden, unexpected death. Similar, but smaller, emboli may form on the inner lining of the heart, often on the left side, after a coronary thrombosis. These can be carried upwards to cause embolism in vital brain arteries, leading to stroke. Small cholesterol emboli, arising from disease of the carotid arteries, commonly cause "mini-strokes" (transient ischemic attacks).

High Blood Pressure

Abnormally high blood pressure is called hypertension. The circulation is a closed system in which, under the influence of the tightening (contractions) of the chambers of the heart, the pressure varies constantly, rising to a peak (the systolic pressure) soon after the contraction, and falling to a lower level (the diastolic pressure) between heartbeats. Because of this dynamic situation, a person's blood pressure cannot be represented by a single figure, but is given as two numbers, the systolic first and then the diastolic, commonly thus: 120/80. These numbers indicate the pressure in terms of the distance in millimeters which a column of mercury would be forced up a glass tube by the pressure.

Blood pressure also varies constantly with the level of physical exertion, with anxiety, emotional stress, and other factors. So a single measurement is not significant, and the blood pressure should be checked repeatedly under resting conditions, at different times.

If the main arteries are healthily elastic, they will stretch a little with each heartbeat and the systolic pressure will not be particularly high. The recoil of the arteries will then drive the remainder of the additional blood onwards. If, however, the arteries are stiff and rigid, or abnormally narrowed from disease, the pressure with each heart contraction will rise to a high peak. In addition, the diastolic pressure will also be higher. Contrary to popular belief, raised blood pressure seldom causes symptoms until secondary complications develop in the arteries, kidneys, brain, eye, or elsewhere. Uncomplicated high blood pressure does not cause dizziness, headache, fatigue, nose bleeds or facial flushing. By the time symptoms occur, the affected person is in serious trouble. No one can afford to ignore raised blood pressure because its complications cause an enormous number of deaths and much severe disability. Sustained high pressures are very damaging

11

to the blood vessels, causing an acceleration of the aging processes. In particular, they promote the killer arterial disease atherosclerosis (see below). Coronary thrombosis and stroke are the major risks, but raised blood pressure can also severely damage the heart, kidneys and eyes. Hypertension has to be looked for, and every adult should have regular checks. It is estimated that 60 million Americans have high blood pressure, but that only a quarter of these are aware of it. Fortunately, proper and effective treatment can largely eliminate the additional risk of these serious complications. In many cases, maintaining a healthy lifestyle, with regular exercise, reduced food intake, no smoking, and perhaps a reduction in salt intake will be sufficient to get the blood pressure down to normal and keep it there. Regular attendance at the doctor for check-ups will give confidence and help to reduce stress levels. The three main classes of drugs used to treat hypertension are:
a) diuretics, which act on the kidneys to cause them to pass more water and salt in the urine and reduce the volume of the blood, so bringing down the pressure;
b) beta blockers, which interfere with hormones and nervous control of the heart, slowing it and causing it to beat less forcefully, so reducing the pressure; and
c) vasodilators, which act on the arteries to widen them. This group contains drugs acting in quite different ways. They include the alpha blockers, the calcium antagonists, and the ACE inhibitors.
In some cases the drug treatment of hypertension may actually cause the patient, for a time, to feel worse rather than better. Until readjustment to normal pressures has occurred, there may be weakness, lack of energy, depression and a tendency to dizziness or faintness on standing up.

Arterial Degeneration

Atheroma
Literally, this means 'a lump of porridge'. Atheroma is the degenerative, fatty material containing cholesterol and other fats, broken-down muscle cells, blood clot, blood-clotting elements (platelets) and fibrous tissue. Atheroma forms on the inner surface of arteries and eventually may lead to obstruction and serious blood deprivation.

Atherosclerosis
This form of arterial degeneration is the number-one killer in

Atheroma forming inside an artery

the western world. It is a disorder of arteries in which fatty plaques (atheroma) develop on the inner lining of arteries so that the normal flow of blood is impeded. Atherosclerosis affects almost everyone, the earliest signs being apparent in childhood, and the condition is, in general, steadily progressive with age. Although most arteries are affected, those in which the condition is most dangerous are the coronary arteries supplying the heart muscle with blood, and the carotid and vertebral arteries, and their branches, which supply the brain. Atherosclerosis of these two systems leads, respectively, to coronary thrombosis and stroke. Atherosclerosis is responsible for more deaths than any other single condition. It is important to prevent or delay its development, or to halt its progress once established. This can be achieved through several lifestyle-related measures, including:

a) eating little more than is required to maintain normal body weight;

b) avoiding saturated (dairy and meat) fats;

c) taking exercise to the point of breathlessness once a day;

d) not smoking cigarettes;

e) drinking alcohol only in moderation;

f) having regular blood pressure checks; and

g) ensuring an adequate intake of the antioxidant vitamins C and E.

Arteriosclerosis

This word, once widely used, has become so imprecise that it is now seldom heard in medical circles. Literally, it means 'hardening of the arteries'. It has been replaced by the term atherosclerosis (see above), which more accurately describes the common degenerative disease of arteries.

11

AGING

Aging Starts Young

Everyone grows old; though some people show – and feel – their age more than others. And as the illustration shows, the process of aging begins surprisingly early. Decline in a few capabilities is already occurring in adolescence; by the middle to late 20s the main process of aging has begun. However, the most obvious symptoms of aging only become apparent late in life. It is then that profound changes in the human body go on to influence an individual's abilities, appearance, behavior and status in society. Modern medicine can prolong the life span – but it cannot yet prolong youth. Many of the troubles of old age can be eased; but efforts to slow down the aging process itself are still simply guesswork.

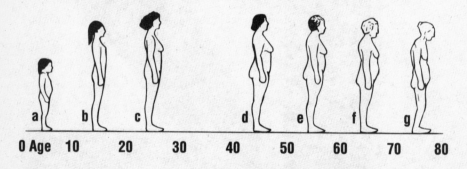

a   b   c   d   e   f   g

0 Age   10   20   30   40   50   60   70   80

a CHILDHOOD

b EARLY TEENS Peak of physical energy passed at 12. Eyes have begun to lose their ability to change focus.

c YOUNG ADULT Irreversible nerve cell loss starts in the brain and spinal cord. In childless women, the chances of conception begin to become less predictable.

d MIDDLE AGE Muscle strength and some mental capabilities already past their best. Female hormone production is likely to start to decline.

e AFTER THE MENOPAUSE Fertility has ceased. Body fat becomes redistributed.

f THE ONSET OF OLD AGE Weakened muscles cause the spine to droop. Hearing of high-frequency sounds reduces by up to 75%. Disorders of the joints may now appear. Body weight diminishes.

g OLD AGE Decline of body's efficiency continues. Muscular strength is half that of a 20-year-old. Intellectual efficiency may be reduced; character changes and organic brain disorders are possible.

Why Aging Occurs

The underlying causes of aging are not yet properly understood. However, there are two tentative theories.

Cell mutation

This is currently thought of as the main cause of aging. Most cells in the body reproduce to replace cells that have died. They do so by 'somatic division', ie by dividing into two. In this way the exact characteristics of the original cell are preserved. However, it is possible for mutation to occur in a cell. This is any form of damage affecting the chromosomes, which are the code system built into the cell that decides how it operates. Mutation can be caused by the gradual exposure over a lifetime to natural radiation (from the sun or from naturally occuring isotopes). Less normally, it may also be caused by disease, chemicals, or radiation from nuclear activity, exposure to X-rays, etc.

When mutation occurs, a cell may become inactive, or do its job badly, or be actively dangerous (as in the case of cancer). Moreover, because chromosomal damage is involved, the distortion is passed on whenever the original cell reproduces. Somatic division means that the number of mutated cells increases in geometric progression (1, 2, 4, 8, 16, 32, 64). In this way, areas of the body's activities become inefficient or disrupted.

Nerve cell loss

From the age of about 25, there is a continuous loss of nerve cells ('neurons') from the brain and spinal cord. These cells cannot be replaced once lost; and the rate of neuron loss is accelerated in age. The consequences of this are probably a major element in the aging process.

Other Factors

Some other factors have been seen to play a part in aging, but they are not 'causes' in the same sense as cell mutation and nerve cell loss are thought to be.

Stress

Psychological stress often has physical manifestations, and it has been noticed that stress of all sorts (physical danger, pain, mental strain, etc) can cause premature aging. However, the biological process whereby this happens is not known.

12

Metabolism

As people grow older, there is a drop in the basal metabolic rate: that is, the energy production of the body at its lowest waking level. For example, the body temperature of an old person is on average 2°F (1.1°C) less than that of a 25-year-old. Metabolic decline is a sign of the aging process, rather than a cause, but it has a wide impact on the body's functions and abilities.

Hormone production

During the menopause, the ovaries stop producing estrogen. In men, production of testosterone similarly declines after the middle years, though it never reaches zero level. It was therefore natural for gerontologists to consider using injections of the appropriate hormone to make up the body's failing supply (see pp.212-213) . However, although injections of these hormones can reduce some physical signs of aging (smooth out wrinkled skin, for example), they do not seem to prevent the basic physiological process of aging.

In general, hormonal decline seems to be one of the ways in which aging expresses itself, but it is not a basic cause.

Changes Inside the Body

As a person ages, there is a general decrease in body efficiency. However, in the absence of disease, the natural changes that bring these about only occur very gradually and do not necessarily cause discomfort.

a) From about the age of 25, there is a continuous loss of nerve cells (neurons) from the brain and spinal cord. These cannot be replaced by the body.

b) With age, the skeleton, especially in women, becomes thinner and more brittle, as calcium is lost from the bones.

c) This calcium tends to be deposited in other areas, especially the walls of the arteries and the cartilage of the ribs, causing loss of elasticity. One effect can be a restriction of lung capacity.

d) Hardening and narrowing of the arteries (arteriosclerosis) is also likely. This is responsible for the rise in blood pressure (which goes up about 0.5mm Hg a year from the onset of aging). The speed of blood flow also rises – though not excessively.

e) When arteriosclerosis is combined with atheroma (fatty deposits on the arteries' inner lining), the condition is known as atherosclerosis.

f) These disorders of the vascular system speed up tissue decay, through inadequate blood and oxygen supply. This especially affects the heart and brain.

g) As aging proceeds, most internal organs – such as liver, heart and kidneys – become reduced in size and function. This is reflected in a reduction in the basal metabolic rate (that is, the energy production of the body at its lowest waking level); eg as noted, the energy production of an elderly person is on average 2°F (1.1°C) lower than that of a 25-year-old.

h) Deterioration of the vertebral disks causes a slight reduction in the length of the spine.

i) Hormonal changes during the menopause (see pp.204-5) mean that it is no longer possible for a woman to bear children, and in the subsequent years her uterus shrinks to approximately one third of its former size.

j) Muscles lose much of their strength, shape and size. Joints become worn and lose some of their ease of articulation. Combined with the degeneration of the nervous system, ease and often confidence of movement are lost.

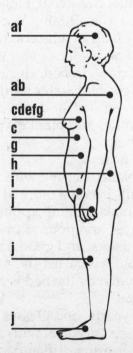

af
ab
cdefg
c
g
h
i
j

j

j

12

Body Care

Exercise

Lack of exercise will speed physical decline, just when maintaining the ability to get out and about is vital for self-esteem. Any exercise chosen should be started gradually, without strain, and kept up regularly. Gardening, walking and golf are ideal. Keep-fit programs can be followed, but only after expert medical advice.

Sleep

Recent evidence suggests that sleep needs do not decline with age. Still, during old age, sleep at night is often fitful and shallow. Daytime naps, illness, anxiety, loneliness and discomforts such as stiffness of the limbs can all contribute. An aging person may well try to accept the changed pattern of her sleep, and try to use waking hours whenever they occur. But a little exercise each day, avoidance of afternoon naps, a warm bedroom, a warm and comfortable bed, and a hot milky drink can all help in achieving a sound night's sleep. If lack of sleep causes anxiety or depression, a doctor should be consulted.

Warmth

Adequate home heating is essential. Central heating is ideal. Open gas or electric bar heaters, or freestanding stoves, can be fire risks, while solid-fuel fires (coal, etc) can be both dangerous and difficult to maintain. Also, diminished awareness of pain may lead to self-scorching through sitting too near. With gas and oil heaters, good ventilation and regular safety checks are important. In bed, electric overblankets are safer than underblankets. Hot water bottles should always be cloth covered, never overfilled, and never used with electric blankets. Hot water bottles and blankets can also be a tremendous daytime help.

Moving around the house

Reaction speed and balance decline with age, and bones and muscles weaken, so falls become more of a problem. Highly polished floors, loose mats, trailing appliance wires, frayed carpet or linoleum edges, and poor or uneven lighting are all dangerous. Strong banisters, and good bath and toilet hand supports, are important. Awkward steps can be outlined in white paint. A light switch by the bed is also important.

Tests and check-ups

Eyes should be tested yearly, and glasses changed if necessary: increasing farsightedness is typical with age. A doctor should be consulted over any hearing difficulties. The ears can be checked for wax, and the help of a hearing aid should not be ruled out. Elderly people who still have their own teeth should brush them regularly and visit a dentist every 6 months. Denture wearers should have a checkup every 5 years, or if the dentures cause discomfort or difficulty in eating or speaking.

Feet

Shoes should be fitted with care; low heels are safest. Stockings should not be too tight. A chiropodist will help with problems caused by corns, calluses, bunions or toenails too thick to cut.

Illness

A doctor should always be told of any symptoms appearing, such as poor appetite, loss of weight, blood in urine, etc; also of any discomfort, for in an old person even a bone fracture may feel no more than troublesome. Medicines should be clearly labeled. Sleeping pills should not be kept by the bedside, in case of mistakes.

Bladder and bowel control

The causes of incontinence are often temporary, and control is regained naturally. Otherwise, medical treatment can often help. Pads, special sheets, and mattress covers can be used. If suitable help is available, it is usually best for the sufferer to remain at home.

Diet

Nutritional needs

The main change is simply in quantity. With age, decreasing physical activity and falling metabolic rate lower food energy needs; calorific intake should be gradually reduced (see p.306). Otherwise, the kind of food needed stays basically the same at any age, though in old age there is reduced need for protein, fat, thiamin, glucose, and calcium (but see Osteoporosis, p.218). However, more foods may cause digestive problems, because of slower and therefore incomplete digestion and absorption.

Daily diet

Ideally, two portions of meat, fish, cheese, or eggs should be taken each day, and some milk as well. Vegetables and fruit, wholemeal bread, and butter or margarine are also important as sources of vitamins, minerals, and roughage. Several small meals during the day may be better than one or two large ones; breakfast should never be missed. Large meals late at night are best avoided, since they can interfere with sleep. Liquid intake should be at least 2.5 pints (1.4 liters) daily. Also, when catering for an old person, variety and attractiveness of food count as much as good nutritional balance.

12

Poor nutrition

Many old people eat badly. The lonely, impoverished and neglected may do so through apathy, poverty, lack of facilities, lack of judgment or general physical or mental disability. Others, unrestricted economically and practically, may overeat such foods as pastries and cakes, with a resulting weight gain that impairs health. Finally, unhealthy teeth and badly fitting dentures can encourage the old to choose comfortable rather than nutritious foods.

Disorders of Aging

There is no escaping from the fact that the atrophy of age reduces the body's efficiency, increasing the likelihood of malfunction. The body is susceptible to all the disorders of young people, but its maintenance, defense and repair processes are weaker. Respiratory and heart disorders are more common in old people than in the young; bone fractures heal with greater difficulty. Nevertheless, most people know a healthy and happy old person, and it can be valuable to bear in mind that although there are many disorders of old age, you will not necessarily suffer from all of them, or even the most serious. Also, the younger you begin taking preventive measures by following the healthiest possible lifestyle, the less likely you are to be ill when you are old.

Preventing Illness

Regular exercise and a good diet are the best measures you can take at any age to prevent illness. Both are part of the treatment of the most feared disorders of old age, such as incontinence, Parkinsonism (trembling due to degeneration of the nerve cells in one part of the brain) and arthritis. The best way to exercise is to continue enjoying sports or other physical activities you have been enjoying since you were young. If you have led a sedentary life, it is very important not to suddenly begin some energetic sport or other exercise. Begin by simply going for regular walks, and consult your doctor about taking up more strenuous activities.

Exercise is effective in keeping at bay one of the most debilitating disorders that affects women in particular. This is osteoporosis, the thinning of the bones due to the amount of calcium they contain. It is osteoporosis that makes some old women look small and frail, often with a pronounced – and painful – curvature of the spine. It is caused by the fall in estrogen levels after the menopause.

Luckily, for more than a decade now, hormone replacement therapy (HRT) has been available to women reaching the menopause. It has been found that starting HRT shortly after the menopause prevents osteoporosis. HRT is proving to be highly effective in preventing other diseases of aging, such as heart disease and circulatory disorders. Osteoporosis and HRT are explained on pp.212-13 and 218-19.

The Joints

It is the constant wear and tear the joints receive throughout life that causes degeneration. Injuries may accentuate and accelerate any disorders. Nevertheless, it is essential to exercise to keep the joints moving. Osteoarthritis occurs to some degree in 80 to 90% of people over 60. It originates from loss of elasticity in the cartilage of the joints. Fragments of cartilage may loosen, be deposited in the joint, then grow and become calcified, causing great discomfort.

Women are more prone than men to rheumatoid arthritis, which is an immune disorder causing joint deformation and disability. It usually affects the fingers and wrists, but other joints can also be affected. The condition can also cause weight loss, lethargy, muscle pain, loss of appetite and anemia.

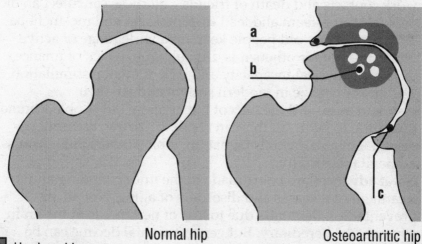

Normal hip   Osteoarthritic hip

▨ Hardened bone
a Spur
b Cyst
c Reduced joint space

Treatment consists of painkilling and anti-inflammatory drugs, physiotherapy and rest.

Replacement of worn-out hip joints is a commonplace operation these days, bringing much relief to sufferers from arthritis. Some artificial hip joints have a chromium head attached to a titanium shaft, lined with acrylic plastic. It is designed to replace the ball part of the ball-and-socket joint, which allows the leg its great mobility. Contractures are deformities of the joints due to shortening (contraction) of the surrounding muscles and ligaments. If untreated they become permanent and cause severe disability. Treatment is with muscle-relaxing drugs and physical manipulation. They can be caused by arthritic or neurological disorders – or simply by prolonged inactivity.

Self-image

Changes in temperament and behavior in old people may be accepted as inevitable. But how far they are really due to neurological and mental deterioration is often hard to judge. The changes may rather be a psychic reaction to the person's social, psychological and physical situation. Old age often brings with it a dramatic change in a person's experience of life. Declining physical ability and efficiency, perhaps involving being looked after by others; the end of the working life; and isolation, due to family mobility, disappearance of work contacts and death of friends – all these can affect an old person's self esteem and lead to depression and melancholia. Of course, many old people keep up a wide range of active interests – but for others it is difficult, due to lack of finance, isolation, physical incapacity and lack of mental stimulation. The rate of change in modern society adds to their disorientation; and the way of life in many old people's homes does little to help. All this can result in apathy, listlessness, resentment and mental stagnation, which others then dismiss as inevitable senility.

Great advances are being made in the understanding and treatment of diseases and disorders of aging. Not all are preventable – dementia due to loss of nerve cells in the brain may well be hereditary. But general mental decline can be prevented, like physical decline, by exercise. Constantly learning, developing new interests, meeting new people, keeping in touch with the world – all keep the mind active.

Age and Society

Life expectancy has risen steadily in industrialized countries in this century. So, with declining birth rates, the populations of these countries are increasingly older ones. In the United States, more than 12% of the population are 65 or over: almost 30 million people. Of these, about 60% are women. It is important to realize the variety and naturalness of old age. For a working person, post-retirement can be up to a third of the life span, and the majority of old people are not lonely, poor, incapacitated, neglected or ignored.

Nevertheless, they can count it as individual good fortune or good planning if they are not. Our society does not have a good record for its treatment of the old. There is insufficient provision for their physical welfare; there is little or none for their self-esteem. After a lifetime of work, elderly people too often find they have no role to fulfill and no social label but that of 'old person'. Physical and financial difficulties can reinforce this. Society's subtle message can often seem to be: you are no longer really useful, and though you are enjoying the deserved fruits of your labor, your difficulties and incapabilities are something of a problem for us. Because they live longer, there are more retired women than men – and more living alone. Still, elderly women often keep their self-respect better than men. A man's identity faces a severe crisis when he retires from work. For many women, a crisis of identity comes earlier – with the menopause or the departure of children – when mental resources are stronger, so retirement may be less of a shock.

12

INDEX

INDEX